LANGUAGE, MAN and SOCIETY
Foundations of the Behavioral Sciences

INTRODUCTION TO THE STUDY OF THE HISTORY

OF LANGUAGE

by

HERBERT H. STRONG

With a New Introduction by

Keith Percival

AMS PRESS, INC.
NEW YORK
1973

LANGUAGE, MAN and SOCIETY
Foundations of the Behavioral Sciences

This reprint series makes available some of the most important works upon which the modern behavioral sciences were founded. Each book has been chosen for its relevance to the general theme of communication and, more specifically, to the various relationships between language, the individual, and society. The areas of discipline covered include psychology, anthropology, sociology, linguistics, and communication disorders.

Each book in the series contains an introduction or preface written by an expert in the field, thus supplying the reader with the orientation needed to place the data in its historic context. It is our hope that the reprinting of these works, with their added critical apparatus, will encourage further research into the history of the behavioral sciences.

We would like to express our thanks to the members of our editorial advisory board for their valuable assistance in preparing this series.

R. W. Rieber
John Jay College, City University of New York
General Editor

ADVISORY BOARD

INTRODUCTION TO THE STUDY

OF THE

HISTORY OF LANGUAGE

WITHDRAWN

BY

HERBERT A. STRONG, M.A., L.L.D.

PROFESSOR OF LATIN IN UNIVERSITY COLLEGE, LIVERPOOL
SOMETIME PROFESSOR OF CLASSICS AT MELBOURNE UNIVERSITY

WILLEM S. LOGEMAN, L.H.C. (Utrecht Univ.)

HEAD MASTER OF NEWTON SCHOOL, ROCK FERRY, CHESHIRE

AND

BENJAMIN IDE WHEELER

PROFESSOR OF GREEK IN CORNELL UNIVERSITY, U.S.A.

LONDON
LONGMANS, GREEN, & CO.
NEW YORK: 15 EAST 16th STREET
1891

WITTENSTEIN

Library of Congress Cataloging in Publication Data

Strong, Herbert Augustus, 1841-1918.
 Introduction to the study of the history of language.

 (Language, man, and society: foundations of the
behavioral sciences)
 An English adaptation of the 2d ed. (1886) of H.
Paul's Prinzipien der Sprachgeschichte.
 Reprint of the 1891 ed. published by Longmans, Green,
London.
 Includes bibliographical references.
 1. Grammar, Comparative and general. I. Logeman,
Willem Sijbrand, joint author. II. Wheeler, Benjamin
Ide, 1854-1927, joint author. III. Paul, Hermann,
1846-1921. Prinzipien der Sprachgeschichte. IV. Title.

P201.S75 1973   415   74-147995
ISBN 0-404-08238-6

BURGESS
P
201
.S75
1973
c.1

Language, Man and Society. General Editor, R.W. Rieber,
John Jay College, New York, N.Y.

Methodological Principles

An Introduction to the New Edition of

THE STUDY OF THE HISTORY
OF LANGUAGE

W. Keith Percival
University of Kansas
Lawrence, Kansas

The work reprinted here was, as its three authors point out in their preface, an English adaptation of Hermann Paul's *Prinzipien der Sprachgeschichte*. The purpose of the present introduction is to acquaint the modern reader with the basic issues discussed by linguists in the second half of the nineteenth century, in order that he may have a keener appreciation of the specific contribution made by Paul's book and so derive more benefit from reading the English adaptation.

But first it may be useful to discuss the exact relation between the two books. The edition of Paul's *Prinzipien* which is most familiar to readers at the present time is the fifth (1920). The first edition, a considerably smaller work, appeared in 1880. However, the book underwent its most extensive revisions for the second edition of 1886, and it is this edition which the authors of the present book adapted into English. Fortunately, it is organized in the same way as the final edition: it has the same number of chapters, and each chapter contains in all essentials the same material. Therefore the reader who has access to the standard edition of the *Prinzipien* can profitably compare it with the English adaptation.

There are two main differences between the two books. First, the adaptation lacks anything corresponding to Paul's introductory chapter, and second, the authors of the adaptation recast Paul's presentation of the subject into a form which they considered would be easier for the average English-speaking reader to understand. To this end, they replaced Paul's German examples with English ones wherever possible and made a practice of introducing theoretical issues only after a prior discussion of concrete data. Their purpose, therefore, was to present the substance of Paul's book in as accessible a fashion as possible. In this they may be considered to have been successful, and the present work can still be used today to gain ready access to the linguistic theories of Hermann Paul and his contemporaries.

The subject matter of the *Prinzipien* seems straightforward enough: the general methodological principles to be observed in any historical study of language. However, its author also wrote with an underlying polemical intent which is perhaps not too easy for the modern reader to appreciate. Paul's criticisms were directed mainly at the theory and operating practice of his immediate predecessors, and they reflected the views of a group of scholars, all born in the 1840s, who were jocularly referred to as *Junggrammatiker*, a term which is generally rendered in English (rather inadequately) by the word *neogrammarians.* The most famous members of this group were August Leskien (1840-1916), Berthold Delbrück (1842-1922), Hermann Osthoff (1846-1909), Karl Brugmann (1848-1919), and Paul himself (1846-1921).

What these men stood for can best be approached indirectly by looking first at the theories they disapproved of most strongly, namely, the ideas of the immediately preceding generation of scholars as epitomized, for example, in the monumental *Compendium der vergleichenden Grammatik* [Compendium of comparative grammar] by August Schleicher (1821-1868). Comparative grammar, as understood by Schleicher, consisted in reconstructing the grammatical system of the putative parent language of the Indo-European languages by means of a detailed comparison of their respective grammars. Basic to this enterprise was the belief that the only way to show that languages are related, that is to say, are divergent continuations of one and the same parent language, is to demonstrate that they share the same basic grammatical system. In the early part of the nineteenth century Franz Bopp (1791-1867) had demonstrated in this way that Latin, Greek, Gothic (the oldest attested Germanic language), the Slavonic and Baltic languages, Persian, and Sanskrit (the ancient liturgical language of the Hindus) were related languages in this sense, and had founded the new discipline of comparative philology.

The grammatical systems of such a group of related languages were not in fact identical, but scholars believed that they were sufficiently similar to make it possible to reconstruct the grammatical system of the parent language. By the mid-nineteenth century these reconstructions had become so precise that Schleicher introduced the practice of citing the reconstructed forms of the parent language alongside attested forms from the historically recorded languages. It was possible in this way to make perfectly clear in every case what specific inferences were being made about the phonetic shape of a particular word, root, or suffix in the parent language. For example, alongside Greek *hippos* 'horse', Latin *equus*, Sanskrit *aśvas*, Schleicher cited *akvas* as the reconstructed form in the parent language. This was to be understood as a claim to the effect that, for instance, Greek *i* and Latin *e* were modifications of the earlier vowel *a* in words of that type, that Greek *pp*, Latin *qu*, Sanskrit *śv* had developed from an original sequence *kv*, and so on. Schleicher did not, however, insist that his reconstructed forms had necessarily existed; they were what would nowadays be called theoretical constructs.

But the linguists of that period were not content to establish the phonetic shapes of particular words in the reconstructed parent language. What they were more specifically interested in was reconstructing the whole morphological system of that language. What was meant by morphological system was the set of suffixes (or endings) which occur in both nouns and verbs, with the general purpose of indicating abstract semantic relations. For example, in all the older Indo-European languages verbs contain suffixes which indicate such notions as person, number, and tense. Thus in Latin *amā-verō* means 'I shall have loved', whereas *amā-bunt* means 'they will love', and so forth.

What the linguists of the first half of the nineteenth century wanted to do was to establish the origin of these suffixes. They observed that the ending of the first person singular in Greek and Sanskrit is often *-mi*, which is strongly reminiscent of the shape of the first person singular pronoun: Latin *mē*, *mihi*, Greek *eme*, Sanskrit *mā-m*. Accordingly they hypothesized that *all* the personal endings of the verb were atrophied personal pronouns. Some idea of the kind of speculations scholars in that period thought were justifiable may be obtained from the accompanying figure, which lists the forms of the present indicative of the verb 'to be' in Greek, Latin, and Sanskrit, along with Schleicher's reconstructions for the Indo-European parent language.

	Attested forms in historically recorded languages			Schleicher's reconstructions	
	Greek*	Latin	Sanskrit	Proto-Indo-European forms	Shape of suffix in earlier root-stage
I am	eimi (emmi)	sum	asmi	as-mi	ma
you are	ei (essi)	es	asi	as-si	sa (earlier tva)
he is	esti	est	asti	as-ti	ta
we are	esmen	sumus	smas	as-masi	ma+sa
you are	estis	estis	stha	as-tasi	ta+sa
they are	eisi (enti)	sunt	santi	as-anti	an+ta

*Forms in parentheses from dialects other than Attic

What Schleicher assumed was that in the parent language each of the above words consisted of a verbal root and an inflectional suffix, but that the inflectional suffixes had at a still earlier period been pronominal roots. He claimed therefore that the suffix of the second person singular -si, a phonetically weakened form of the fuller -sa, had originally been identical with the second person singular pronoun (cf. Sanskrit tva-m, Latin tū, Gothic thu), and the suffix of the third person singular -ti (weakened from -ta) had been a demonstrative pronoun. Moreover, he assumed that each of the plural suffixes had originally been compounded of two such pronominal roots: -masi 'we' from ma 'I' and sa 'you', -tasi 'you' (plural) from ta 'that one' and sa 'you' (singular), and -anti 'they' from ta preceded by an, another demonstrative pronoun. Finally, Schleicher suggested rather tentatively that these pronominal roots were originally on a par semantically with regular roots. For example, he hypothesized that the ma which eventually yielded the first person singular suffix -mi had once been a root with the meaning 'human being, think, measure' (cf. Sanskrit ma-nu 'human being', mā-mi 'I measure', Greek metron 'an instrument of measuring'). As Schleicher put the matter himself: "What could 'I' originally have been but 'human being'? We clearly cannot ascribe the abstract notion of 'I' to the parent language."

Thus Schleicher divided the prehistoric development of the Indo-European language into two periods. In the first period the parent language consisted of nothing but unanalyzable roots, each of them expressing a concrete concept. In the second period, the period of grammatical formation, some of these roots lost their independence and came to express accessory concepts, giving rise in this way to inflectional and derivational suffixes. By the end of this second period the grammatical structure of Indo-European, as reconstructed by comparative linguists, had taken final shape. In the historical period the parent language split up into a number of related languages, and there occurred a gradual decay of the Indo-European grammatical system. The decaying process had many manifestations, the most important of which was sound change, or phonetic decay, as it was often called. Phonetic change was considered a degenerative process in that it rendered unanalyzable what had previously been analyzable into a root *as* 'be' and an inflectional suffix *-si* 'you', but Greek *ei* is not so analyzable, except with reference to the earlier form, *as-si*.

Although Schleicher assumed that linguistic change was a gradual and continuous process, he considered the progressive stages of linguistic development to be *qualitatively* different from one another, in much the same way as, for example, the larva, chrysalis, and butterfly can be considered to be qualitatively different stages in the life cycle of a particular organism. Indeed, like many of his contemporaries and immediate predecessors in the study of language, Schleicher laid great emphasis on the extent to which the history of language is not like the history of human contrivances such as art, literature, and religion, but rather like the evolution of species or the changes characteristic of the phenomena studied by geologists. Linguistics, he claimed, was a natural science, not one of the old historical disciplines like classical philology; it was, so to speak, an archeological rather than a chronological kind of enterprise. Its main purpose was to elucidate the grammatical forms of the historically recorded languages by restoring them to the phonetic shapes they had when they were clearly analyzable. Etymological reconstruction was the principal goal of the comparative linguists of the mid-nineteenth century.

If we move now to the linguistics of the latter part of the century, we notice a number of rather radical shifts of emphasis. First and foremost, linguists began to look upon linguistics as one of the social sciences (*Kulturwissenschaften*) rather than as one of the natural sciences (*Naturwissenschaften*). The opening sentence of Paul's *Prinzipien der Sprachgeschichte* is highly symptomatic: "Like any product of human culture language is an object of historical investigation. . . ." Accordingly, language was now regarded not as a physical organism but as a form of human behavior, namely, overt speech activity and the accompanying covert psychological events. The roots and suffixes that comparative linguists had been manipulating hitherto lost their reality and came to be regarded as no more than convenient abstractions; in their place linguists began to speak of the relations obtaining among the actual observable linguistic elements (words, sentences) which a speaker uses to make himself understood. Moreover, the development of language from one period to the next was seen as nothing but a shifting among these myriad relations. How was such a complicated set of phenomena amenable to scientific study? What was needed was a general theory to provide an understanding of language and linguistic change.

As for the nature of language itself, Hermann Paul was insistent on a psychological approach, and in particular an approach based on the psychological theories of Johann Friedrich Herbart (1776-1841). He considered that, although the speech act itself is a psychological and acoustic phenomenon, it is the set of underlying psychological processes which makes it what it is, i.e., more than a mere physical event. He then analyzed these processes in terms of three kinds of elements, namely, sounds, words, and sentences — in other words, the units of traditional grammar. He regarded a speech sound as the pairing of a motor sensation (*Bewegungsgefühl*) with an acoustic impression (*Tonempfindung*). Words, he claimed, are stored in the unconscious in groups of which there are two types: first, material groups (*stoffliche Gruppen*), which involve likeness in meaning, e.g., *go, goes, going, gone, goes, went;* and second, formal groups (*formale Grup-*

pen), whose members have the same grammatical function, e.g., *cats, tables, children, men*. The two types of groups intersect, that is to say, the same words figure in both formal and material groups. For instance, *house* belongs in the same material group as *houses* and in the same formal group as *box*.

The speaker stores all the words he has ever heard or spoken in his unconscious, arranged in the groups to which they belong. When he utters a sentence, it is not necessary that he reproduce each word from memory since the systematic character of the unconscious arrays of forms permits him to generate any form afresh on the basis of the regular analogies which obtain among them. Thus a speaker about to utter the word *boxes* may either reproduce the form from memory or create it on the analogy *house : houses = box : boxes*, where the last form is supplied by 'solving the proportion.' In this instance the process of analogical creation produces a form which is already in ordinary use. But sometimes this same process produces novel forms, like the child's *foots* for the customary *feet* on the analogy of *roots;* or neologisms such *peacenik*. However, since native speakers of a language have substantially the same internalized set of analogies, they can understand such novel forms just as easily as they can produce them.

In the case of sentences, very few are reproduced *in toto* from memory. Most sentences are created anew when the relevant occasion arises, on the basis of the analogies abstracted from previously experienced sentences. Syntax therefore, in contrast to morphology, is the area in which speech behavior is predominantly creative. Paul emphasized, however, that one should not underestimate the extent to which new lexical items and new grammatical features are constantly being created. This attitude toward linguistic creativity contrasts markedly with that held by linguists of the mid-century who tended to believe that after the original creative stage of linguistic development nothing new was added in language, and that everything which does not deviate from previous usage is simply reproduced from memory. In this regard Paul claimed to be doing no more than following to its logical conclusion the familiar principle, which had been enunciated earlier in the century by Wilhelm von Humboldt, that speech is a continuous process of creation.

Languages change because each speaker forms his own set of formal and material groups individually, on the basis of the particular sentences he hears and produces, and at no time in his life is a state of complete equilibrium in the various groupings reached. Since the speech of a single individual is in a constant state of spontaneous development, the speech of a whole community, which is nothing but a vast network of interacting individuals, gradually changes as these individual variations accumulate in any consistent direction. The conventional grammatical description of a language as it is spoken at a particular time is nothing more than a set of more or less crude generalizations about the average state of the groupings in the minds of the speakers at that time. If another description is made of the language some generations later, these generalizations will look different, as the changes which have taken place will be reflected in the new description. However, it would be a mistake, in Paul's view, to imagine that a mere compilation of the differences between the two descriptions would adequately account for the changes which had taken place in the intervening period. The study of the history of language involves more than cataloguing the differences between grammars of successive chronological periods. The historian of language, unlike the comparative linguist of the previous generation, is first and foremost concerned with the nature of the changes taking place in language. But the grammarian's description of a language does not get at the underlying psychological groupings which are operative in everyday speech behavior; it merely collects generalizations about usage and thus falls short of being completely scientific. As soon as the investigator injects an explanatory element into the study of language he inevitably becomes historically oriented. Hence, according to Paul, linguistics must be historical in approach if it is to be psychologically valid.

At the same time, however, this interest in the processes of historical development led to a rejection of the more speculative facets of comparative work, and an emphasis on the living languages and their recorded history. The linguists of the new generation did not by any means cease to be interested in the reconstruction of proto-languages; Karl

Brugmann, for example, produced a monumental summing-up of what was known at the end of the century about proto-Indo-European, modestly entitled *Grundriss der vergleichenden Grammatik der indogermanischen Sprachen* [Outline of the comparative grammar of the Indo-European languages], and Berthold Delbrück founded the study of comparative syntax in a series of brilliant monographs. But more typical of the future development of linguistics were such scholars as August Leskien, who worked in the Slavic and Baltic languages, Eduard Sievers, who worked in general phonetics and in Germanic, and Hermann Paul himself, who devoted most of his life to his historical grammar of Modern German. It is also worth pointing out in this connection that the two founders of modern descriptive linguistics, the Swiss Ferdinand de Saussure and the Pole Baudouin de Courtenay, both received an important part of their training in Germany in the sixties and seventies among scholars of the new generation.

The two most important motive forces which mold the development of language, according to the new view, are phonetic change and analogical new formation. The neogrammarians insisted that sound change is regular; they laid down as a general principle that phonetic change affects a particular sound-type in a clearly defined set of phonetic contexts, and that every token of that sound-type so situated undergoes the change with iron necessity. Where there are apparent exceptions to the operation of sound changes these are the result of *subsequent* interfering factors of certain well defined varieties. This means, for example, that it is not possible for a sound change to be blocked in certain words because the affected sound was felt to be too significant to undergo alteration, as some of the linguists of the older generation claimed. Nor is it possible for a sound change to worm its way gradually through the vocabulary, as Hugo Schuchardt, a contemporary critic of the neogrammarians, suggested.

However, in defending the principle of the regularity of sound change Paul and Brugmann frankly admitted that it could not be demonstrated to be true on *empirical* grounds. Their arguments were theoretical and methodological. They reasoned on theoretical grounds, for example, that there is no way for a sound change to be selective in its operation since it is an unconscious psychological process. The physiological production of sounds, they believed, has a certain random quality; it is in some sense a hit-or-miss operation. The summation of such random variations in a consistent direction leads to a shift in the associated motor sensations and acoustic impressions, and a sound change is nothing but such a shift. The members of a speech community keep in step while a change is taking place because the overall acoustic impression which a speaker associates with a sound is largely a product of the way he hears the sound pronounced by his fellow speakers. Consistency is guaranteed therefore by the mere fact of constant interaction. On methodological grounds the neogrammarians argued that to postulate a sound change that was less than completely regular would be tantamount to admitting that language is not subject to the laws of causality, and hence not amenable to scientific study.

The second major type of linguistic change recognized by Paul and the other neogrammarians was analogical new formation, the creation of new grammatical forms on the basis of already existing analogies. When in English the plural of *cow* changed from *kine* to *cows* this was not due to any sound change but simply to the fact that a new plural was formed on the regular analogy. Analogical change is therefore one of the factors responsible for apparent exceptions to sound changes. The older generation of linguists especially resented the way in which the neogrammarians seemed to invoke the principle of analogy whenever they needed to explain away an exception which might conceivably be used as a counterexample to disprove the principle of regular sound change. It also scandalized the older scholars to be told that such degenerate processes as analogical changes, which they disparagingly referred to as *false* analogies, occurred in such venerable languages as Greek and Sanskrit, which they had always assumed were spoken at a time when human beings had a more highly developed 'sense of language' (*Sprachsinn*) than people have had in more recent centuries, and never committed such linguistic indiscretions!

It should be borne in mind, however, that although Paul considered sound change and analogical new formation to be the two most important developmental factors in the history of language, a considerable part of his book, and likewise of the English adaptation, is devoted to other topics, e.g., semantic change (chapter 4), syntactic theory (chapter 6), syntactic change (chapter 7), word-coinage and onomatopoeia (chapter 9), changes in the membership of material and formal groups (chapters 10, 11 and 13), grammatical categories and their relation to psychological categories (chapter 15), word-classes (chapter 20), the problem of the origin of inflection and word-formation (chapter 19), and so forth. In many of these areas, too, Paul adopted theoretical positions which involved him in controversy both with scholars of the older generation and with contemporaries. For example, his notions of syntactic theory and semantic change came in for very rough treatment at the hands of Wilhelm Wundt, the founder of experimental psychology in Germany. Wundt's theories of syntax and semantic change were naturally enough based on his own psychological doctrine rather than on the Herbartian principles to which Paul subscribed. Moreover, his emphasis on the extent to which word-creation was still going on in modern languages set him at loggerheads with the comparative linguists of the previous generation, one of whom had on one occasion stated categorically that no new root had ever been invented since the end of the root-stage of linguistic development and that therefore "we may be said to handle the very words which issued from the mouth of the son of God, when he gave names to 'all cattle, and to the fowl of the air, and to every beast of the field'."

The essential property of Paul's system, then, is a firm belief that the processes at work in both speech behavior and linguistic change have always been and still are due to causes and forces which operate continuously and with absolute uniformity. Such a belief is obviously incompatible with the notion that languages pass through a series of developmental stages of the kind hypothesized by the linguists of the early and middle nineteenth century. Moreover, much of the attractiveness which morphological reconstruction had was precisely that it enabled the investigator to penetrate to a stage of linguistic development significantly different from the one accessible to normal observation. When the parent language was declared to be a language like any spoken at the present time, the whole research strategy of historical linguistics underwent a gradual shift away from the concentration on origins and in the direction of a painstaking study of the ubiquitous phenomenon of linguistic change.

It is interesting to note that no linguists of Hermann Paul's generation actually attempted to justify this uniformitarianism on empirical grounds. But it may be doubted that such a demonstration is feasible. Be that as it may, this belief has been basic to all subsequent work in linguistics up to the present day. In a very real sense the general view of language and linguistic change which underlies Paul's book and its English adaptation is as topical now as it was ninety years ago.

Notes

Hermann Paul's *Prinzipien der Sprachgeschichte* was published by the Max Niemeyer Verlag in Halle in 1880. Subsequent editions appeared in the same place and with the same publisher in 1886, 1898, 1909, and 1920. Herbert A. Strong, one of the authors of the English adaptation, published an English translation of the second edition: *Principles of the history of language*, London: Sonnenschein, 1888. Benjamin Ide Wheeler, another collaborator on the English adaptation, wrote *Analogy and the scope of its application in language*, n.p., John Wilson and Son, University Press, 1887.

A general history of nineteenth-century linguistics can be found in Berthold Delbrück's *Einleitung in das Studium der indogermanischen Sprachen* which first appeared in 1880 (Leipzig: Breitkopf & Härtel) and went through six editions, the final one appearing in 1919. An English translation of the first edition made by Eva Channing was entitled *Introduction to the study of language* (Leipzig: Breitkopf & Härtel, London: Trübner, 1882). See also Otto Jesperson, *Language: its nature, development and origin* (London: George Allen & Unwin, 1922), pp. 32-99; and Antoine Meillet, *Introduction à l'étude comparative des langues indo-européennes* (Paris: Hachette), 1937, pp. 453-483.

My account of August Schleicher's theories is based on his *Compendium der vergleichenden Grammatik der indoger-*

manischen Sprachen which first appeared in two volumes in 1861-62 (Weimar: Hermann Böhlau). The third (1871) edition was translated into English by Herbert Bendall as *A compendium of the comparative grammar of the Indo-European, Sanskrit, Greek and Latin languages* (2 parts, London: Trübner, 1874-77). I have used the fourth German edition (Weimar: Germann Böhlau, 1876), and my quotation above (p. 00) is from § 265, p. 626 of that edition.

For other contemporary expositions of the linguistic theory of the mid-nineteenth century the reader may consult Max Müller's *Lectures on the science of language* (2 vols., London: Longman, 1861-64, and many subsequent editions). I quote above (p. 00) from vol. 1, lecture 1 (last paragraph but one). See also William Dwight Whitney's *Language and the study of language* (New York: Scribner, 1867, and later editions) and the same author's *The life and growth of language* (New York: Appleton, 1875, and later editions).

The theory that all inflectional suffixes were originally independent words was shared by most linguists of the first half of the century, and in particular by Schleicher's most influential predecessors Franz Bopp and August Friedrich Pott (1802-87). Bopp's ideas can be found in his *Vergleichende Grammatik* (first edition, Berlin: F. Dümmler, 1833-52), third and final edition, Berlin: F. Dümmler, 1868-71). This work was translated into English by E. B. Eastwick (*A comparative grammar, etc.*, London: Madder, 1845-53, 3 volumes in 4, and three subsequent editions). For Pott's theories see his *Etymologische Forschungen auf dem Gebiete der Indo-Germanischen Sprachen* (2 vols., Lemgo: Meyersche Hofbuchhandlung, 1833-36, second edition, 1859-76).

The neogrammarian position was clearly stated by Hermann Osthoff and Karl Brugmann in their preface to the first volume of *Morphologische Untersuchungen auf dem Gebiete der indogermanischen Sprachen* (Leipzig: S. Hirzel, 1878). In the ensuing controversy the theories of the older generation were defended by George Curtius (1820-85) in his *Zur Kritik der neuesten Sprachforschung* (Leipzig: S. Hirzel, 1885). Curtius's criticisms were answered by Berthold Delbrück in *Die neueste Sprachforschung* (Leipzig: Breitkopf & Härtel, 1885), and by Brugmann in *Zum heutigen Stand der Sprachwissenschaft* (Strassburg: Trübner, 1885).

The issue of the regularity of sound change was hotly debated. The neogrammarian view was stated by August Leskien in his monograph *Die Declination im Slavisch-Litauischen und Germanischen* (Leipzig: S. Hirzel, 1876). The opposing position was defended by Hugo Schuchardt (1842-1927) in *Uber die Lautgesetze: gegen die Junggrammatiker* (Berlin: Oppenheim, 1885), reprinted in Leo Spitzer (ed.), *Hugo Schuchardt-Brevier: ein Vademecum der allgemeinen Sprachwissenschaft* (Halle: Max Niemeyer, 1928), pp. 51-87. The American linguist Leonard Bloomfield (1887-1949) was a spokesman for the neogrammarian theory of sound change; see his *Language* (New York: Holt, 1933), pp. 346-368.

Wilhelm Wundt's syntactic theories can be found in his *Logik: eine Untersuchung der Prinzipien der Erkenntniss und der Methoden wissenschaftlicher Forschung*, vol. 1: *Erkenntnisslehre* (Stuttgart: F. Enke, 1880), pp. 50-58, and subsequent editions, and also in his *Völkerpsychologie: eine Untersuchung der Entwicklungsgesetze von Sprache, Mythus und Sitte*, vol. 1: *Die Sprache*, part 2 (Leipzig: W. Engelmann, 1900), chapter 7, and subsequent editions.

For Herbart's psychological theories see his *Lehrbuch zur Psychologie*, 3rd edition, edited by G. Hartenstein (Hamburg & Leipzig: Leopold Voss, 1887). An English translation of this work by Margaret K. Smith is entitled *A textbook in psychology: an attempt to found the science of psychology on experience, metaphysics, and mathematics* (New York: Appleton, 1891). Herbart's influence entered linguistics by way of the works of Chajim Steinthal (1823-99), in particular his *Abriss der Sprachwissenschaft*, which was the first part of his *Einleitung in die Psychologie und Sprachwissenschaft* (Berlin: Harrwitz & Gossmann, 1871).

Paul's allusion to Humboldt's linguistic theory is on p. 110 of the fifth edition of the *Prinzipien*. For Humboldt's general views on language see his treatise *Uber die Verschiedenheit des menschlichen Sprachbaues und ihren Einfluss auf die geistige Entwicklung des Menschengeschlechts* (Berlin: F. Dümmler, 1836), reprinted in *Wilhelm von Humboldts gesammelte Schriften*, herausgegeben von der k. preussischen Akademie der Wissenschaften (Berlin: B. Behr, 1903-4), vol. 7, pp. 1-344. The notion of creativity is discussed ibid., vol.

7, § 12, pp. 45-47. For an English translation of parts of this treatise see Marianne Cowan, *Humanist without portfolio: an anthology of the writings of Wilhelm von Humboldt* (Detroit: Wayne State University Press, 1963), pp. 251-298. The passage which discusses the notion of creativity is translated on p. 280.

PREFACE

In the following pages an attempt has been made to enable students to grasp the main points of the contents of one of the most important philological works which have been published during the last ten or twenty years—Paul's 'Principien der Sprachgeschichte.'

With this object in view, that work has been here, with more or less freedom, as the subject seemed to demand, rewritten. Though a translation of Professor Paul's book has been published by one of the authors, it has been felt that the existence of that translation did not render a work like the present superfluous, nor should a student whose interest has been awakened by the reading of these pages consider he can dispense with studying what Paul has written in his great work.

It may be best to state in how far this and Professor Paul's book are alike, as well as in what points they differ.

We have closely followed Paul in his division of the subject. Our chapters correspond in number, order, and subject with those of Paul. The views set forth in our pages are in the main those of Paul; the arguments are mostly his, even in the very few cases (such as the question of the consistency and nature of the laws of sound-change) where the authors might feel inclined to differ from Paul's views. Also the order in which the various points in each chapter are discussed has been generally preserved.

On the other hand, we have altered much, as we hope, in the interest of our readers. Professor Paul wrote for Germans in the first place, and secondly for such students as were able to read books like his in the original, *i.e.* for those who not only knew German enough to feel all the weight and import of his German examples, but who also, like most German students, could be assumed to possess a sufficiently intelligent interest in the history of the German language to appreciate quotations of its older forms (a point which Englishmen have unfortunately too much neglected), and who, thirdly, might be expected to be sufficiently familiar with at least some of the other languages from which he drew his quotations.

Now though, in deference to a generally expressed opinion, a second edition of the translation of Paul's work is now in the press, in which all these examples have been translated, this Englishing of the illustrations will, we think, be found to be of use in but few cases.[1] It is, in fact, almost invariably not so much the mere word or sentence chosen as an illustration,

---

[1] And this opinion was the cause of the omission in the First Edition.

as the peculiar form, its peculiar connotation, its peculiar construction, which is of importance. All these almost invariably disappear or differ in the translation, unless such translation be accompanied by such discussion and explanation as will bring out the meaning *as an illustration of the point in question.* It is self-evident that such additions in a translation could not be thought of.

Moreover, Professor Paul very frequently follows the German manner of exposition : first giving us the statement of abstract principle, and then illustrative examples. Though the authors are very far from wishing to say that no English student could or would follow this style of reasoning, they believe that it is generally preferable to lead English students from the concrete to the abstract.

All these considerations have led to the following deviations from Professor Paul's work.

Everything has been illustrated from English wherever possible, and much also from French ; examples from other foreign languages have, as a rule, been admitted only when they illustrated something new, and even then an attempt has generally been made to add such translations (literal and idiomatic) as would enable the reader to appreciate the force of the illustration, even without further knowledge of the language from which it was taken.

The order of the argument has sometimes been inverted.

Where what was said seemed sufficient to explain the nature and bearings of the subject of a chapter, some minor points have sometimes been omitted. They have not been omitted because they were thought unimportant, but generally because they could not be so well illustrated from English, and it was felt desirable to economise space for a full discussion of everything of which English *does* furnish illustrations. It will consequently be found that some of our chapters differ much more than others from the corresponding ones in Professor Paul's book. But even where, from the nature of the case, we had to follow Paul closely, we have always aimed at supplying further English examples or at explaining fully the illustrations from other tongues.

A word should, perhaps, be said as to the joint authorship. In all cases what the one wrote has been read by the other, and Mr. Logeman wishes more especially to acknowledge in this matter his obligations to Professor Strong for many a correction of sentences where his style might have betrayed the foreigner. Professor Benjamin Ide Wheeler has perused the greater part of the work, and supplied many apt illustrations. Several important passages are from his pen. The authors at the same time have to acknowledge their gratitude to Mr. R. H. Case, B.A., who has patiently read the whole work. It was of immense advantage to them to have the benefit of the observations of a highly cultured mind, well versed in English and its literature, but new to a subject like this, such as Mr. Case brought to the work. Many improvements were thus made in various places where he could show the need of fuller explanation or of a different way of expressing the matter.

It may perhaps cause some surprise that we have omitted the introduction, and, unless a word in explanation of this fact were added, this omission might seem to imply but slight courtesy to Professor Paul, or respect for his emphatic statement that he considers this introduction by no means useless, nay, an integral and important part of his book.

We do not at all share the opinion of some critics of Professor Paul's work, to whom he almost indignantly refers as having said that this introduction has no bearing upon the chapters which follow. But we do consider that the book in this our present form can be profitably studied without it, and especially that his introduction is of so general a nature that there would be no advantage whatever in recasting it; and that it can be equally well studied, and should be studied, either in the original or in the translation of Paul's own book—a work of such importance that, as we would once more insist, we do not wish our book to supersede it, but rather that our pages should cause the reader to 'ask for more' and peruse the original work.

The authors feel, of course, quite certain that their work is not final: they are but too keenly aware that they may have overlooked important illustrations which might be drawn from English, and are quite prepared to discover that here and there they may have added sins of commission to such errors of omission. They will heartily welcome all criticism and all indications of such imperfections, and if ever the demands for the work may necessitate a second edition, they hope that it will be found that they—in the words of a well-known author of a well-known book—have spent their time since the publication of the First Edition in trying to find out those things which they ought to have put in and did not put in, and those things which they did put in and ought not to have put in.

H. A. S.
W. S. L.
B. I. W.

September 1, 1890.

CONTENTS

ERRATA.

Page 57, line 1, *add* 'a gulf or bay.'
,, 176, line 7, *for* 'ƌoances' *read* 'ƌances.'

CHAPTER I.

IT is the province of the Science of Language to explain, as far as possible, the processes of the development of Language from its earliest to its latest stage. The observations made on these processes would naturally be registered in different *historical grammars* of different definite languages; these grammars would follow the different steps in the development of each single language from its earliest traditional origin to its most recent phase. Wider and more general observations on the processes of this development would naturally be expressed in a *comparative grammar*, whose task would be to examine and compare the relations between cognate families of speech, the common origin of which is lost: but it would in this case be necessary to insist that the comparisons instituted should only be between languages in the same stage of development; or that the same stage of development, in each of the languages selected for comparison, should be taken for the purpose.

It is the task of *Descriptive Grammar* to ascertain and record the grammatical forms and the conditions generally of a given linguistic community at a given time; to register, in fact, all the utterances of any

B

individual belonging to such community which might
fall from him without exposing him to the suspicion
of being a foreigner. It will naturally register its
observations in abstractions, such as paradigms and
rules. Now, if we compare the abstractions made at
any given period of a language with those made at
another time, we find that the results are different, and
we say that the language has *changed* in certain
respects : nay, we may even be able to detect a certain
regularity in these changes ; as, for instance, if we note
that in English every *th* in the third person singular
present indicative of a verb is now replaced by *s :* but
we gather by such comparisons no information as to
the true nature and origin of these changes. Cause
and effect do not and cannot exist between mere
abstractions : they exist only between real objects and
facts. It is only when we begin to take account of the
psychical and bodily organisms on which language
depends, and to seek for relations of cause and effect
in connection with these, that we are on safe ground.

The true object of the Science of Language, as
distinguished from Descriptive and Comparative
Grammar, is the entirety of the utterances of all individuals that speak ; and the relations of these utterances
to each other. A full history of the development
of language would demand an exact knowledge of
all the groups of sound ever uttered or heard, and
of all the ideas awakened by such sound-groups and
symbolised by them. The impossibility of attaining
to any such knowledge is obvious ; it is, however, possible for us to get a general idea of the play of the
forces at work in the vast and complex series of processes involved in the development of language. A
part only of these operating forces is cognisable by our
senses. Speaking and hearing are two of the pro-

cesses which can be apprehended; and, again, the ideas, or pictures, called up by language, and those which, though unspoken, pass through our consciousness, are to some extent capable of cognition. But one of the greatest triumphs of modern psychology is the proof, due to its agency, of the unconscious activity of the human mind. All that has once been present to our consciousness remains as a working factor in unconsciousness. Power consciously acquired by exercise in consciousness may be translated into power operating and manifesting itself unconsciously. The mind forms from the groups of ideas with which it is stored, psychological groups, such as sound-groups, sequences of sounds, sequences of ideas, and syntactical combinations. Strong and weak verbs, derivatives from the same root, words fulfilling identical functions, such as the different parts of speech, associate themselves into groups; and again the plurals of nouns, their different cases, their different inflections, and even entire clauses of similar construction or similar cadence, group themselves in the same way. These groups arise naturally, automatically, and unconsciously, and must not be confused with the categories consciously drawn up by grammarians; though the two, of course, must frequently coincide.

These groups must obviously be in a constant state of change, some growing weaker from the fact that they are strengthened by no fresh impulse, and some being strengthened and, it may be, changed by the accession of new ideas which ally themselves therewith. It must not be overlooked also that, as each person's mind is differently constituted, the groups of his linguistic ideas will take a development peculiar to himself; even though the sources whence the groups take their rise should be identical, yet the elements

which go to form the groups will be introduced differently and with different intensity in the case of each
individual.

The action of our physical organs, unaided, would
be unable to bring about the development of language.
The word, when once spoken, disappears and leaves
no traces ; psychological activity, and this alone, connects the pictures of the past with the present. It
must, therefore, be the task of the historian of language
to give as complete an account as possible of the
psychical organisms on which the production of language depends; and the psychical organism of language
in each individual is the aggregate of more or less
conscious recollections of words, nay, even of entire
phrases, and of their connections with certain ideas,
which is lodged in his mind. It is the business of the
historian of language to watch and examine these
organisms as closely as possible : to describe the elements of which they are composed, and their connection with each other. A state or condition of a
language at a particular period could only be described
by one possessed of a full knowledge of the psychical
conditions at a particular time of all the members of
any linguistic community. The more fully such observations as those referred to above are carried out, and
the greater the number of individuals thus examined,
the more nearly shall we be in a condition to give an
accurate description of a state of language. Without
a rigidly scrupulous examination such as we have
described, it would be impossible to say how much in
the language of any individual is common to all or
most individuals speaking the same language, and how
much is to be set down to individual peculiarity. In
every case it will be found that the standard of the
language governs to some extent the language of every

individual; but in the case of each individual there are likewise elements which do not conform to the standard or normal language, and which are, in fact, individual peculiarities.

In any case, the observation of a psychical organism of language is difficult. It cannot, like the physical side of language, *i.e.* the sounds actually produced and even the mode of their production, be directly observed; for it lies unseen in the mind, and is only known by its effects.

Of the physical phenomena of linguistic activity, the acoustic are those which lend themselves most readily to our observation. We can make the same individual repeat sounds practically identical as often as we please; and we can note these with more or less accuracy in proportion as our own sense of hearing is exact and developed. But as the transitions between the different sounds are so infinitely small, it follows that it must be a matter of extreme difficulty for the listener to decide whether the sounds are indeed precisely the same in colour, pitch, etc.; while, again, if it be desired to reproduce any sound, the process has to be carried out by orally repeating it and striving to reproduce it by an appeal to another's sense of hearing.

We register the sounds of a language by mastering and registering the movements of the organs of speech that produce them. Alphabetical symbols are at best but very imperfect pictures of sound-groups: they are used inconsistently in most cases: and in any case even the most perfect phonetic alphabet cannot give a true and exact picture of the countless sounds in speech— sounds which require to be constantly denoted anew in every language. We can only succeed at all in registering such sounds, when we are able to closely observe the sounds uttered by living individuals. But when we cannot do this, we must always think of the sounds which the writing is intended to represent; and the power so to do demands some acquaintance with phonetics, and with the relation between writing and language. Thus a certain special training is necessary before we can hope to be able to gain any real knowledge of even the physical manifestations of linguistic activity.

The psychical factors in linguistic activity lie, like everything else psychical, unseen in the mind, and can therefore only be scrutinised by means of examinations made upon our own minds. In the process of watching other individuals we can never perceive any other than physical results, and thus it happens that in order to acquaint ourselves with the psychical organisms of language in others, we have to watch as closely as possible the processes in our own minds, and then to classify the phenomena which we observe in the case of others by the analogy of what we observe in our own. As we both think and speak in the mother-tongue, our classifications by analogy will be easier when we have to deal with fellow-countrymen; so too, for obvious reasons, with the living subject rather than with what has been committed to writing in the past.

It will, then, be plain that the observation of any given state of language is no easy matter, owing to the manifold and complex way in which groups of ideas associate themselves in the human mind, and owing to the incessant progress of hardly perceptible sound-change. It may easily be gathered that even the most full and perfect of ordinary grammars are quite unable to portray the manner in which different ideas and groups of ideas range and classify themselves. Our grammatical system can give but the most imperfect picture of the relationships existing between different ideas. Certain categories, for instance, are drawn up, and under one or other of these are ranged words under the name of certain parts of speech. As a matter of fact, a large proportion of words is capable of being used to fulfil the function of several parts of speech, and in no language is this more obvious than in English. Again, we are accustomed in grammar to meet—even in the case of the Indo-European group of languages—with the same grammatical term employed to express quite different functions, as when we speak of the Latin *future*, and call the English future in " *I shall* " or " *I will* " do by the same name. Again, we are accustomed, in the case of a language which has passed from the synthetic to the analytic stage, to employ the same categories, regardless of the fact that, in the analytical form of the language, new shades of meaning have found expression as they have also come into being. Again, we often define the meaning of words by their etymology, even though the ordinary speaker may have no knowledge whatever of that etymology, and a new and very different meaning may have attached itself to the word.

The comparison of different epochs in the life of any language will enable us to draw some inferences as to its condition in the past. Of course, in proportion as the foreign factors that have made their influence felt in the regular course of the language are fewer, the simpler and more satisfactory will be the comparison. It would be impossible to reconstruct the sounds of Anglo-Saxon, for instance, from Middle English only ; as it would be necessary to remember that Norman, Danish, Celtic, and other influences had been busy with the language between its earlier and later stages.

We now proceed to ask what are the causes of

change in language? And how do these causes
operate? In the first place, they operate in most
instances without the consciousness of the individual.
There are, indeed, a few cases in which we may say
that conscious intention on the part of the individual
is operative, as where a botanist coins a name for
some new variety, and forces it upon all the scientific
men of his circle. But it must be repeated that
changes are for the most part involuntary and unconscious. It is of the essence of the life of language
to unconsciously select the forms and sounds which
may best serve for conveying the meaning present in
the speaker's mind. The material existing and forming the actual stock in trade of any language may very
aptly be looked upon as the survival of the fittest; in
this case, of the *material* fittest to survive. If we now
proceed to consider the causes of change in language,
we must remember that there is always in language
a certain amount of freedom left to the individual,
which is quite independent of ordinary linguistic development. As each speaker must have certain
psychical peculiarities, so must he express himself
differently from every other speaker; and if the
sound-producing organs of any given speaker have
any peculiarities, he will exhibit corresponding peculiarities in the sounds which he utters by their agency.
Again, there are circumstances which must not be
overlooked, like the natural tendency to imitation; and the further circumstance that all attempts
at imitation must necessarily be imperfect. Again,
each individual is prone to modify the sounds which
he utters, through carelessness and economy of effort
or laziness. Besides all this, we must reckon the
effects produced by such factors as climate, which,
however gradual in their operation, must still ulti-

mately leave some effects if only time enough is allowed. The result of these displacements, if only the tendency to displacement lasts long enough and operates in one direction, is a *displacement of usage.* The new usage starts from the individual, and, under favourable circumstances, succeeds in becoming permanent. There are, however, numerous other tendencies to displacement likewise constantly occurring which do not become permanent, because they are not consistent, and because they do not all run in the same direction.

It must, then, be the task of the historian of language to endeavour to settle the relationship between linguistic usage on the one hand, and individual linguistic activity on the other ; and in order to arrive at any satisfactory conclusions on this point, it is necessary to classify, as far as we can, the different changes of usage which occur in the growth and development of language. It is, then, his business to trace the relationship between the different classes which he has formed, and to remember that his province is to trace connections where ordinary grammar draws lines of demarcation, bearing in mind that the steps which lead from class to class are very gradual, and that the processes leading up to the smallest variation of usage are in very few cases due to a single cause, but are generally very complicated. The gradual development in the life of language in general may be best studied in individual languages, as when we compare the English of Chaucer's day with that of our own ; and, again, in the relations of individual languages to each other, as when we compare Spanish, for instance, with Italian, and note the different paths taken by these sister-tongues in their development from Latin.

Sound-changes come about in the individual partly from the tendencies of his own organs of speech, as when [*ii*] becomes [*ai*[1]] and when one sound is habitually substituted for another, as in the case of the Russian *F*eodor for *Th*eodore, or the similar substitution, frequent among children, in *f*ing for *th*ing. They partly, too, depend upon the influences which each individual receives from others, as when an endeavour is made to substitute a significant for an unmeaning whole, in cases of popular etymology and the like. To this must be added the possibility of imperfect audition, and consequently of imperfect reproduction of sounds. These influences are mostly operative and easiest of observation at the time that language is being learnt, *i.e.* most commonly during the time of infancy. To watch such processes as a particular language is being learnt must always be very instructive for the explanation of variations in the usages of language in general.

These changes in usage may of course be classified in various ways, but there is one important point which should be noted: the processes may either consist in the creation of what is new or in the disappearance of what is old; or, lastly, in the replacement of the old by the new in a single act, which is the process seen in sound-change. In the case of word-significations, the processes of change consist either in the disappearance of the old or in the appearance of the new. But these processes are in truth very gradual. A word may be perfectly intelligible with a certain meaning in one generation, and in another generation may be obsolete and not understood: but there will none the less have been an intervening generation, some members of which under-

---

[1] See Sweet, History of English Sounds, p. 17.

stood the meaning attached to the word or phrase by the former generation, while some only imperfectly understood it.

Again, we may classify changes in usage according to whether sounds or significations are affected. The sounds change without the signification being altered, as in the numerous words in Chaucer which as yet clearly retained their French pronunciation. Again, the signification is affected without any change affecting the sound, as in the case of metaphorical uses of a word, such as *a crane*, used alike for the bird and the lifting machine; etc. Thus it is that we arrive at the two classes of change : sound-change and change in signification ; not that the two kinds are mutually exclusive—they may both occur together, as in our *owe*, from A.S. *âgan*, to possess. But the two kinds of change are independent in their origin and their development; neither is caused by the other.

There is, however, an important class of cases in which Sound and Meaning develop simultaneously ; these are the original creations of language ; and we must suppose the entire development of language to rest upon this primitive combination. We must conceive the original utterances in language to have been the imitation of various natural cries and sounds, aided and interpreted by gesticulation. Then comes a stage in which the sound-groups already existing in language develop on the basis of this original creation. They develop in this way mainly by the influence of analogy, which is itself an imitative faculty and plays a larger part where sound and signification are united than in the department of pure sound. The principles of which we have spoken must be held applicable to all languages at all stages of their development. When once language had originated, it must have developed solely in the way we have indicated. The differences between early and later stages of language are merely differences of degree and not of kind.

It must also be noticed that we must not sharply separate the grammatical and the logical relations of language, as if they were in no way connected. Grammatical rules are simply convenient descriptions of the most ordinary and striking ways in which a language expresses itself at a particular time. But the groups of ideas in the mind of a speaker are constantly forming themselves anew, and finding expression in forms which do not tally with actual and received linguistic expression, and, as they change, give rise to so-called irregularities of grammar. The philologist must therefore discard neither the linguistic processes which are described and registered by grammar, nor the psychical ones which manifest themselves in speaking and hearing, but are not represented in linguistic expression, and yet are always operative in the direction of change in Language.

CHAPTER II.

THE most elementary study of Comparative Philology teaches us that from a language which, in all essentials, may be considered one uniform tongue, there have frequently sprung several others; and that these, in their turn, have parted into new dialects or distinct languages. This process has been usually compared to that which we see operative in the growth and development of organic nature; and the relationship between various languages has often been expressed by the terms applicable to the human family. Latin, for instance, is called the *parent* of French, Spanish, Portuguese, and the other Romance dialects; English and Dutch are called *sister*-tongues, while the last-named pair may be called *cousins* of German.

The comparison implied by such use of these terms is in the main correct; but it would be more exact to illustrate the relationship between languages from the language of Botany: we might consider the language of each individual speaker as the parallel of the individual plant, and compare the various dialects, languages, and families of languages, to the varieties, species, and classes of the vegetable kingdom. Even then our simile is but partially applicable, and a careful consideration of how far it holds good, and where and

when it becomes misleading, will be found instructive
to a student of language.

It is now an admitted truth in Zoology as well as in
Botany that nothing but the individual plant or animal
has any real existence, and that all our species or
classes are merely convenient and useful, but always
arbitrary, abstractions.   The difference between two
primroses is not as great as that between a primrose
and, *e.g.*, a daisy, it is true ; but the differences between
these pairs are merely differences in degree, and not
in kind.   When we classify or arrange in groups, we
select some characteristic and thereby give it a certain
pre-eminence over others.   All individuals that possess
this characteristic are accordingly ranged upon one
side, and all that do not possess it are ranged upon
the other.   If the characteristic has been well chosen,
our classification will be rational, but will none the less
remain arbitrary ; and very often—nay, nearly always
—the choice of any other quality or characteristic as
the principle of classification will be found to involve a
different grouping.

It is the same with language.   Strictly speaking,
there exist as many distinct languages as there are
individual speakers.   These millions of languages,
however, fall naturally into groups, whose component
individual parts differ but very little from one another,
though no two of them are exactly alike.   Now, in
order to decide whether the language of any one
individual belongs to some particular group, we must
select one or more particular characteristics, by which
to test its claim ; and, our selection made, we shall often
find ourselves excluding some language whose inclusion
would have resulted from any other test than the one
selected.   The difficulty is much increased when we
come to range our groups into dialects, or to classify

the latter among or around languages (using that term again in its conventional sense) ; and, again, to arrange languages into families.

At no single moment do we find all the individuals of any nation, community, or group of human beings, speaking the same language in the strict sense of the expression ; and thus, if we say that a language has broken up or separated into several dialects or into various new languages, we give a very inadequate description of what has really happened. It would be truer to state that amongst any given group of individual languages, the difference, once slight, between its various members has grown to such an extent that we can no longer conveniently class these members together.

In the next place, our comparison will also hold good in the following point. The nature and development of the individual animal depends upon two things —descent and environment. Animals, the offspring of similar parents, resemble one another in all essentials: they are, however, not absolutely alike, and their individual peculiarities and development depend largely on surroundings, such as climate, food, etc., —influences which, as might be expected, make themselves felt most strongly in infancy.

Again, it is the same in language. Speech is acquired by imitation, and those who speak to the child may be considered its linguistic parents. The special bodily and mental idiosyncrasies of the child take the place of the accidental surroundings to which reference has already been made. No two children hear precisely the same words spoken by the very same persons and exactly the same number of times ; no two parents and no two children are, in mind and body, exactly alike. From the beginning there is a difference, small though it may be, between the linguistic surroundings of any two individuals; and the development depends upon personal peculiarities, which, from a linguistic point of view, may be called accidental.

It appears, then, that our attention is engaged at the very outset of our linguistic inquiry, not merely by the fact that differences arise in the language of individuals, but more especially by the question why these differences are not even greater and more rapid in their development than they prove to be. We must seek an explanation not merely of the nature of the forces tending to differentiate the individual languages, but also of those which counteract such forces, and whose influence is exerted towards uniformity and the conservation of such unity as exists.

Yet if our comparison be sufficiently correct in two such important points, we must not forget that in one point at least there is an essential difference between the origin of species in the animal world and the differentiation of languages.

We saw that with descent in the animal world we must compare *linguistic* descent, which latter term implies that a child's language is acquired by imitation from the speakers surrounding him. The language of the community in which the child grows up is the parent of his speech. Now, it is evident that in the animal world the influence of descent, powerful factor though it be, is still limited, inasmuch as the *direct* effect of the parent's influence ceases at a fixed point. In language, on the other hand, the influence of the *linguistic* parent is permanently at work: strongest during infancy, it diminishes in force indeed, but never entirely ceases to make itself felt. Again, the animal owes its birth to a single pair only, while in language an indefinite number of speakers co-operate to produce the new individual. Moreover, as soon as a child acquires any speech at all, it becomes in its turn a member of the community and affects the language of others. Its speech is consciously or unconsciously imitated by those from whom it learned and is still learning; and thus, in language, parents may be said to become the children of their own offspring.

Differentiation of language is, of course, impossible unless usage alters; but it would be incorrect to conclude that differentiation must necessarily be greater as the variation in usage is more violent. There is no *à priori* reason why a large group of individuals, who at any given moment speak what may be considered to be *one and the same* language, should not alter their usage all in the same manner. Yet, if we remember that each individual has his own peculiarities, and that, while each acquires his speech by imitating others, such imitation is never perfect, we shall readily understand that language must change from generation to generation, even were other causes not present to promote such changes; and, in fact, that differences will and must arise. Alteration and differentiation are unavoidable; and it is intercourse between the members of a community or a nation which can alone keep these within bounds. The alterative forces are more free to exert their influence in proportion as such intercourse is restricted.

If we could imagine a large country where the intercourse between the inhabitants was of perfectly equal intensity throughout, we might expect to find the language of each individual differing but imperceptibly from the respective languages of his neighbours; and, though the tongues spoken at opposite extremities might show a wide divergence, it would be impossible to arrange the individual varieties into dialectical groups; for the speech of each man would be some intermediate stage between the individual tongues on either side. But such equal intensity of intercourse exists nowhere over any considerable area. Geographical, political, commercial influences, separately or combined, erect barriers or overcome them; and peculiarities of speech which, arising at one place, spread over others, are yet confined within certain limits. These peculiarities, then, will clearly distinguish those dialects of individuals which partake of them from such as do not; and consequently we shall have distinct limits for grouping the dialects spoken by separate individuals into those spoken by separate districts—that is to say, into what is most commonly understood when we speak of 'dialects.'

All would now be simple and easy if lines of demarcation thus arrived at were found to coincide with whatever peculiarities or characteristics we happened to choose for our criteria. But the fact is that groups which would be classed together in view of some special points of resemblance will fall asunder when other points are considered as essential characteristics; for the spread of characteristics derived from intercourse with one district must frequently be checked and thwarted by intercourse with another district that does not share the same tendency.

Thus, if we make use of the letter a to indicate a group of individuals speaking a tongue essentially identical, employing b for another such group, c for a third, and so on, then a and b may very possibly correspond in usage or pronunciation in some point, x, in which both may differ from c, while a and c, but not b, will be found to agree in y. In yet a third point, z, in which they both differ from a, etc., b and c may agree; whilst a, b, c and other groups may very well have points, w, t, etc., in common with one another

and with *d* or *e*, and in these same points will differ
from *f.* On the other hand, *f* may agree in some other
points with *a*, in some with *b*, in some with *c*, etc.

It is unnecessary to dwell further on this. We
see plainly that as different alterations have a different
extent and different lines of demarcation, the crossings
of groups and resemblances may be expected to become of infinite complexity.

But if, further, we suppose the differentiation between *a*, *b*, and *c* to be already so great that we may
regard these as separate dialects, yet it is by no means
impossible that a tendency to some alteration should
make itself felt in each of them, or that, having arisen
in one, the peculiarity should spread over all. It
follows from this consideration that any peculiarity
shared by all or many dialects of a language is not
necessarily older than one which characterises only a
few, though, of course, that such will be the case is
the natural assumption.

Nor are the most strongly marked characteristics,
by whose means we now distinguish existing dialects,
and according to which we range them into groups,
necessarily older than those which we overlook in
deciding these mutual relationships. To instance this,
we may refer to the various Teutonic dialects, which
undoubtedly had many marked differences long before
the process of sound-shifting began. It was some
time in or near the seventh century A.D. when some
of these dialects commenced to substitute *p* for *b*, *t* for
d, *k* for *g ; t* became *ts* (*z*), *k* became *h*, *p* became *f* or
pf, and in some cases *b* and *g* were substituted for
the sonant fricatives *v* and *g*.[1] This change or sound-
shifting was in progress during something like two

---

[1] As pronounced, *e.g.*, in Dutch *gaan.* This sound does not
now exist in English.

centuries, and it is according to the extent of their participation in this that we classify the various dialects as High German, Middle German, and Low German, respectively. We consequently class as Low German three dialects which otherwise present very strongly marked differences : the Frisian, the Saxon, and in part the Franconian, the case of which last is especially instructive.

The Franconian dialect did not as a whole participate in the changes to which we have alluded above. Only the more southern part of the Franconian tribe adopted the sound-shifting, in common with other southern tribes which spoke distinctly different dialects. Consequently, adhering to our above-mentioned principle of classification, we must class the so-called *Low* Franconian in a group totally distinct from that in which the *High* Franconian must be placed, notwithstanding the fact that in other respects these dialects have preserved many important resemblances.

It would also be incorrect to regard dialects which have become more strongly differentiated than others as having necessarily become so at an earlier date. The widest divergence is not necessarily the oldest, for circumstances may arise to facilitate the widening of a recent breach, as they may, on the other hand, arise to prevent a slight divergence of long standing from becoming a gap of importance. If two groups, *a* and *b*, are differentiated, and yet keep up sufficient intercourse, they may very well remain similar, though not equal, during a very long period ; while a subdivision of *a*, which circumstances only affecting a minority in that group have separated later, may develop a rapidly increasing divergence between its small community on the one hand, and the remaining members of *a* together with the whole of *b* on the other.

One more lesson resulting from the foregoing consideration is the following. It is too often assumed as a matter of course that the speech of districts lying between others that possess strongly differentiated languages is the result of the contact and commixture of the two latter. Such possibility is indeed not denied ; it, in fact, often occurs ; but the alternative supposition that the mixture is a survival of some intermediate dialect is equally possible, and must not be forgotten.

It is clear that what we now call languages are merely further developments of dialects ; but here once more we may easily err by assuming too much. If we find two distinct languages, it does not necessarily follow that they have passed through a stage in which they were two dialects, distinct indeed, but differing to a less extent than at present. Indicating dialects by a and b, and languages by A and B, we must not conclude, on meeting with the two latter, that A must have inevitably originated from a, and B from b. It is quite possible that both A and B may have arisen from (say) a alone ; and of this possibility Anglo-Saxon and its descendant Modern English furnish a clear instance.

The dialect spoken by the invaders differed, if at all, in a very slight degree from the Frisian (a), which followed a regular course of development in its ancestral home. But the language of the invaders (which, in view of its identity or close resemblance with the Frisian, we may also call a) had in the British Islands a different history and a different development. It was rapidly differentiated, and one of its dialects became a literary language, distinct in every point from its sister-tongue. Thus the modern representative of Frisian (A), and our present literary

English (*B*) are found to have sprung from one source
(*a*) alone.

The consideration of this case leads us to our next
point.   In all the foregoing cases we presupposed
that the speakers of the individual language or of the
group-languages were on the whole stationary.   We
need not here indicate at length the effect upon a
community of its migration into regions where other
languages are prevalent.   The result is commonly a
mixed language: and the subject of so-called mixed
languages we reserve for another chapter: here we
need only remind the student that by such migrations
the connection of the language of the emigrants with
that of other communities of similar speech is loosened,
and the action of differentiating forces, which thus
acquire free and unrestricted play, must necessarily be
augmented.

The criterion for distinction of dialects among a
community of individual languages is, and must be,
their phonetic character.   Vocabulary and syntax are
easily and generally maintained, or, if anything new
arises, it may possibly spread over wide areas; but
differences of pronunciation and peculiarities of
utterance do not necessarily result from the borrowing
of new terms.

For instance : a community which pronounces *a* of
father as *aw* (*i.e.* like *a* in *all*) will do so even when
borrowing a word from some dialect in which the pure
a is usual.

In conclusion, we must not omit to combat an error
too often repeated in books on language which enjoy
a reputation otherwise well-deserved.   It is a common notion that the tendency to differentiation is, as
civilisation advances, replaced by one towards unification ; in proof of which we are reminded of the one

uniform literary language which, among the educated members of a nation, replaces the various provincial dialects. But this literary language is by no means a regular and natural development of the pre-existing dialects.

One of these, favoured by circumstances political or literary, obtains a supremacy which causes its adoption by those who would otherwise ignore it and continue to speak the dialects of their own provinces, counties, or districts. Hence it is in a certain sense a foreign tongue to them, and though in course of time it may come to replace the indigenous dialect of any district, so that scarcely a trace of the latter remains, it would be misleading to say that this dialect has developed into a language before which it has in reality disappeared.

CHAPTER III.

LANGUAGE is in a constant state of change ; and the changes to which it is subject fall under two very different heads. In the first place, new words find their way into a language, whilst existing words become obsolete and drop out of existence: and, secondly, existing words remain, but gradually alter their pronunciation. It is the second of these phenomena which we have to study in this chapter ; and a clear idea of its nature, origin, and progress is indispensable to any real knowledge of philology.

To gain this idea we must carefully consider the processes which occur when we speak. We have to take note of no less than five elements, all of which are present each time that we utter a sound, and these should be carefully distinguished.

In the first place, whether we break silence and begin to speak, or proceed in the course of speaking to any particular sound, our vocal organs must move towards a certain position, in which they must remain during the time of the utterance of the sound. This is equally true whether they are set in motion after a period of rest, or after a position rendered necessary by their utterance of some other sound. Let us take, for instance, the sound which in the word *father* we represent by the letter *a*. In pronouncing this WORD we BEGIN by putting our lips, tongue, vocal chords, etc., all in such a position that, on the breath passing through them or coming into contact with them, the sound represented by *f* is produced; and as long as the vocal organs remain in that position, nothing but *f* can be pronounced. In order, then, to pronounce the *a* sound, we must alter the position of our vocal organs : our vocal chords must be approximated, our lips relaxed, our mouth opened wider, until the *a* position is attained. It is clear that the course which we take to reach our goal depends not merely upon the position of that goal, but likewise upon the point whence we start to reach it. Hence the course whereby we reach this *a* position will vary constantly and considerably, seeing that in our utterance of the *a* sound we can and do cause many other sounds to precede it. But all these movements agree in one respect, that they terminate in a certain position, which we maintain as long as the *a* sound lasts.

Secondly, we must notice that this position is maintained only by a certain balance of the tension in the various muscles of our tongue, throat, lips, etc. ; and this tension, though we may not indeed be conscious of it, *we feel.*

Thirdly, *we hear*, more or less exactly, the sound which we produce.

Fourthly, this feeling and this sound, like every physical occurrence in which we actively or passively participate, leave behind them in our mind a certain impression. This impression, though it may indeed disappear and sink beneath the level of consciousness, remains nevertheless existent, is strengthened by repetition, and can, under certain conditions, be again recalled to consciousness. We consequently come gradually to acquire a permanent mental impression of both feeling and sound. There is formed in our mind what we may call the memory-picture of the *position;* and

Fifthly, there is likewise formed 'a memory-picture' of the *sound.*

It will be readily seen that of these five 'elements' only the last two are permanent, and that they, and they only, are psychical. In every individual case of sound-utterance, all that is *physical* is momentary and transitory. We abandon the position; the corresponding tensions make way for others; the sound dies away: but the memory-pictures alike of position and sound remain in our mind. There is no physical connection between our utterances of the 'same' sound, or word, or phrase; there is only a psychical connection: and this reposes upon the two elements which we have already called the memory-pictures of sound and position respectively.

A word must be added on the nature of the association existing between these two. This association, however intimate it may be, is *external* only; there is no necessary *psychical* connection between any sensation of vibration in our organs of hearing and any other sensation of tension in the muscles of our vocal organs. If we gained the first-named sensation again and again from hearing others speak, yet we should still be unable to imitate them at once, even though, for whatever reason, we had set our vocal organs repeatedly in the same position. But the fact that when we ourselves utter a sound we also hear it, associates the physical sensations of sound with those of position, and this invariably; and it thus happens that the respective memory-pictures of the two are left closely associated in our mind.

When we speak of these movement- and sound-pictures as lingering or as existing in our memories, it is not implied that we are necessarily conscious of their existence. On the contrary, the speaker, under ordinary circumstances, is wholly unconscious of them : nor has he anything like a clear notion of the various elements of sound which together make up the spoken word, or it may be the sentence, which he utters. It would seem as though the art of writing and spelling, which presupposes some analysis of the sound of words, proved that the speaker, if capable of spelling and writing, must have at least some notion of those elements. But very little consideration will suffice to prove the contrary. In the first place, strictly speaking, it is absolutely impossible to denote in writing all the various elements of sound which combine to form any word or sentence. A word, however correctly and grammatically spelt, does not consist merely of those sounds which we symbolise in our writing. In reality it consists—or at least the syllable consists—of an *unbroken* series of successive sounds or articulations, and of this series, even if we spell 'phonetically,' our letters represent at best no more than the most clearly distinguished points ; whereas, between these sounds so symbolised by our letters, there lie an indefinite number of transition sounds, of which no writer or speller takes any notice.

The above is true in the case of languages like Spanish, Portuguese, Italian, and German, where the spelling is more or less consistent : much more is it true in the case of English or French, with their irrational and puzzling inconsistencies. A child which learns that it must represent the sound of the word *but* by letters to be called respectively bee-you-tea, or the word *though* by letters nick-named tea-aitch-o-you-

gee-aitch, does not receive a lesson in separating the
sound-group represented by the letters *but* into its
three, or the sound-group represented by *though* into
its two (or three) elements.

Even in the more correctly spelt languages, there
are numerous discrepancies between the spoken and
written word, which, until they are pointed out to him,
escape the attention of the native speaker or writer.
In English, some instances may be here considered.
Not a few English people are quite surprised when
they are informed that they have two distinct ways of
pronouncing *th*, or of pronouncing *x :* the *th* 'hard,'
as in *thin*, and 'soft,' as in *then ;* the *x* like *ks*, as in
execution (eksekyushion), and like *gz*, as in *executive*
(egzekyutiv), *exact* (egzakt), *example* (egzampl).   And
there are fewer still who have ever noticed that in
income many pronounce no *n* at all, but the same
guttural and nasal sound as terminates *king*.

Can is frequently pronounced *c^han*, with a distinct
h sound after the *c*, without the speaker being aware of
it ; and the same holds good of similar words.   Again,
none but the trained observer knows that the *k* in *keen*
is pronounced differently (more to the front of the
mouth) from the *k* (represented by *c*) in *cool ;* but the
fact that perhaps more than all excites incredulous
wonder is that the sound *i* is no vowel, but a diphthong,
as may be proved by dwelling on it.   The speakers to
whom these facts are new may nevertheless all be
perfectly correct speakers : no doubt they pronounce
the elements of the word ; but they have probably
never paid any attention to the nature of these elements,
or at least have not begun to do so till long after the
utterance became habitual and natural.

If, then, we speak without consciousness of the
separate *sounds*, much more are we completely uncon-

scious of the *movements* of our vocal organs. It is only very recently that these movements have been carefully investigated, and the results of the science of phonetics are in very many respects as yet *sub judice*, while even the most superficial knowledge of the subject can only be attained by a conscious and careful effort of attention, and by the exercise of much patience in the observation of our precise actions when speaking. It is only the trained observer who can at all follow these movements as he makes them, and even *he* does not so follow them generally, but thinks of the sense of his words as he speaks, and not of the way in which they are produced.

Moreover, even assuming that the speaker enjoyed a far higher degree of consciousness, both of phonetic elements and of phonetic movement while he is *acquiring* the faculty of speech, it would none the less remain true that in the ordinary course of word-utterance these facts remain outside the speaker's consciousness. A precisely parallel instance can be observed in the case of a pupil learning to play the piano or violin. At first every movement he makes is the result of a separate and conscious act of volition ; but soon practice, the repetition of conscious action, so much facilitates the playing of scales, arpeggios, etc., that the rapidity of their execution quite precludes all possibility of the bestowal of separate thought, even of the shortest duration, upon each individual note in succession. It is necessary at the outset to insist on this fact of the speaker's unconsciousness, both of the elements of sound which make up the word, and of the movements of his vocal organs ; for, once fully grasped, it will guard against an error which is too prevalent, viz. that sound-change is the result of conscious volition in those who speak.

But though the movements necessary for production of sounds are performed unconsciously, they are by no means beyond control; to illustrate which fact we may once more recur to the parallel instance of the piano-player. Like him, the speaker controls his work by listening to its result: but the player strikes either the right note or the wrong, and, unlike him, the speaker may vary his utterance in one direction or another without serious error ; he is not considered to make a MISTAKE unless the difference between his present utterance and that which is usual exceeds a certain limit. In this respect, the violin-player resembles the speaker more closely. They both appeal to their sense of hearing in order to decide on the correctness or otherwise of the sound produced, and the control they can exercise over that sound is exactly proportional to their delicacy of ear. Up to certain limits, the variations are too small to be perceived by the ear, but beyond these control becomes possible. The slight differences in pronunciation or sound do not yet, however, necessarily expose the speaker (or player) to the charge of incorrect utterance (or performance), and consequently, though he perceives the change, he pays little or no attention to it. He only then corrects himself or guards against repeating the 'mistake,' when the change in sound passes those limits which cannot be transgressed without detriment to what in music we term 'harmony,' or what in language we term 'correctness of utterance.' It commonly happens that these limits are wider than the limits of perception referred to above, more especially in the case of the speaker. A wider licence is accorded to the term 'correctness' in speech than is accorded to it in harmony.

While, then, control is theoretically and practically limited, the possibility of variation is unlimited. Take,

for instance, the case of the vowels. All the possible
sounds and variations from *u* (pronounced as *oo* in *cool*)
to *i* (= *ee* in *feel*) may be said to form one uninterrupted
series. In this series we distinguish only some of the
most important varieties. When we pronounce *u*, the
lips are rounded, and the tongue is drawn back and
raised at the back of the mouth : if we pass from *u* to
i, the lips are unrounded, and assume the shape of
a narrow and much elongated ellipse, while the tongue
is pushed forward with its back depressed and the fore-
part (the blade) raised. While this change is going
on, the mouth *never* assumes a position with which we
could not produce some vowel or other, but the difference in acoustic quality between any two 'neighbouring' vowels would not always be such that we should
regard them as distinct or different sounds. On our
way from *u* to *i*, we pass through the positions for the
o (*oa*) in *coal*, the *ŏ* in *god*, the *a* in *father*, the *ĕ*
in *net*, the *e* (*a*) in *hare*, the *ĭ* in *pit* ; but between
these there lie an indefinite number of possible shades
of sound, and every one knows how differently various
speakers of the same community pronounce what we
call the same vowel. So, too, we need but little attention to notice distinct occasional variations, at different
moments, in the same speaker. If, then, one and the
same speaker often *perceptibly* (though unintentionally)
varies his pronunciation, we may be perfectly sure that
his mode of utterance will vary at different times within
those limits where the divergence—though existing
—is not noticed. As with the vowels, so it is, though
not so completely, with many consonants and series of
consonants. The student who is unacquainted with
phonetics should pronounce *cool* and *keen* one after the
other, or better still *coo* and *kee*, getting rid of the final
consonants. He will have no difficulty in noticing the

difference between the two *k* sounds, the first of which requires a much more backward position than the second for its pronunciation. After a little practice, he will be able to pronounce the first (back) *k* with the *ee* vowel, and the second (forward, palatal) *k* with *oo*. Now, between these two sounds of *k* there is a whole series of intermediate ones, and, if this series be followed in the direction of the palatal *k* and then continued beyond it, we soon reach the articulation of the palatals proper, and pass, without any appreciable gap, to the linguo-dentals : first to the *t* which, in words like the French *métier*, sounds so much like *q* in the form *méquier* (as the French Canadians actually pronounce it) ; and next to our own *t*, and to the usual French *t*, which is pronounced more to the front with the tip of the tongue against the roots of the teeth.

Similarly, because perfect though slight closure is not remote from extreme narrowing, we can pass in a practically unbroken series from energetic *p* to laxly uttered *f*, from *k* to the guttural fricative of German *ach*—a sound which English, in its modern form, no longer possesses,—etc.

As we noticed in the instance of *k*, and as every one more easily perceives in the case of the vowels, two sounds essentially different in articulation and in acoustic character are often, in daily speech, accepted as identical, more especially where the difference is not great enough, or is not of a nature to cause ambiguity of meaning. If, for instance, there existed words in the English language alike in all respects but that the one began with the *k* of *cool* and the other with the *k* of *keen*, and if these words had different meanings, every Englishman would be aware of the existence of two sounds, which he would most likely indicate by two different letter-signs. As it is, the difference between the two remains unnoticed, and the choice between them depends upon the vowel which follows.   If, then, in the ordinary course of speaking, a 'back' *k* is pronounced a little more forward, or a palatal *k* more to the back, no notice will be taken of it, unless the variation oversteps a certain limit and, as a consequence, the unusual articulation sounds strange. Similarly, for the formation of *t,* the position of the tongue may be varied to a very great extent, and yet, though something unusual in the sound MAY be apprehended, the result will always be perceived as a *t.*

We must now once more emphasise the fact that the memory-picture of the sound, and the (unconscious) memory-picture of the movement and position, and these two alone, connect the various utterances of any sound or sound-group, and decide its character, and the appreciation of speaker and hearer to its correctness.

These memory-pictures and their nature and growth are therefore of the highest importance.   They are the results of *all* preceding cases of utterance, *of which, however, the last always has the greatest influence.* Every variation in pronunciation entails a variation in the memory-picture ; and this, small as may be the change, is cumulative and permanent, unless the different deviations happen to balance one another exactly.   Now, in the main this will be the case when the speaker finds himself amid his usual surroundings, and where no external causes co-operate to impel his deviations into one direction rather than into another : but let us suppose him transferred to another community, and brought in contact with a certain pronunciation habitual there and novel to him.   His memory-picture of the SOUND is made up of his own pronunciation *and* of what he hears from others.   At

first the new pronunciation strikes him as new, and
two pictures stand side by side in his mind. If, however, the difference be not too great, these soon blend,
and, the former one fading while the other constantly
gains in force, his pronunciation becomes influenced
without his own knowledge; he pronounces more and
more like the surrounding speakers, and every time he
does so his memory-picture of POSITION gets slightly
altered (always in the same direction) until nothing but
conscious effort of memory or renewed intercourse
with former surroundings can recall the one thus lost.

The same thing happens essentially and effectually,
though the change is slower and less violent, where
external causes favour deviation in any special direction
amongst an entire community. As far as the nature
of the effect goes, it can make no difference whether
we consider the case of a man entering a new community to find there a pronunciation which differs from
his own, or that of an entire community which alters
its existing pronunciation. But the process will go on
much more slowly in the latter case, since it has to
operate in a number of individuals, and the steps by
which each of them proceeds are in ordinary cases
imperceptibly small.

Of all causes which may tend to alter our pronunciation in any special direction, facility of utterance
is the most conspicuous and the most easily understood.
There are, in all probability indeed, several others :
climate, habits of diet, etc., all *seem* to have some
effect, but no one has as yet been able to explain how
they operate. Even ease of pronunciation is not yet
thoroughly understood in all its bearings. We must
not forget that ease is something essentially subjective,
and that the memory-pictures of movement and sound
and the attempt at correct reproduction of the usual

movement and sound are the main factors, while the
striving after facility of utterance is a very subordinate
one.

Yet there is no doubt whatever that in a number
of instances the new pronunciation is easier than its
predecessor: we now say *last* instead of *latst*, examples
of which earlier form may be found in the Ormulum, for
instance. Similarly, *best* is easier than *betst, impossible*
than *inpossible;* and we may refer also to the numerous words still written with a *gh* which is no longer
pronounced. In the word *knight*, the *k* was formerly
sounded before the *n*, and the *gh* represents a sound
which may still be heard in the German word *knecht;*
and, in fact, all spellings like *know, gnat, night, though,*
etc., with their numerous mute letters, represent older
and undoubtedly more laborious pronunciations. That
all these sounds have been dropped has unquestionably
facilitated the utterance of the words, and there is a
similar gain of ease in all the well-known instances of
complete or partial assimilation in all languages. So in
Italian *otto* for Latin *octo*, Latin *accendo* for *adcendo*,
etc. When, however, we come to estimate the comparative facility of separate single sounds, or even
many combinations, we find ourselves as yet without
any certainty of result or fixed standard. Much that
has been advanced is individual and subjective: all
depends on practice; and this practice we acquire at
an age when we are as yet wholly unable to form or
pronounce an opinion on any question. In fact, most
of our facility of speech comes to us in infancy.

But whatever the cause, we now understand that
the memory-picture of movement and position is shifting and unstable in its very nature. Unless the
majority of pronunciations around us all alter in the
same direction, the *sound*-picture does not alter, and it

exerts a retarding control upon the rapidity with which our *position*-picture, and therewith our own pronunciation, might otherwise do so.   Here, however, we must draw attention to the fact that we spoke of the majority of *pronunciations* around us and not of speakers.   For our sound-picture the number of persons from whom we hear a word is immaterial; it is the number of times we hear it pronounced that is alone of importance.

All that we have hitherto said has had reference to changes of pronunciation in *the same speaker*, and in this case alone can we speak of alteration or change in the strict sense of the word.   But when we say that 'a language has altered,' we use the term in a wider sense, and include the case when one generation is found to use a new pronunciation in place of one current at a former time ; when, in fact, it would be strictly correct to say that an old pronunciation has died out, and that the new one—created instead—differs more or less from that which was its model.

A child, in learning to speak, attempts to imitate the sound it hears ; and, as long as the resulting imitation *sounds* sufficiently correct, any small peculiarity of pronunciation is generally overlooked.   In such a case, therefore, the child acquires a movement or position-picture which at once materially differs from that of the former generation.   We all know by experience that sounds are difficult to 'catch,' and we must remember that the vocal organs may undergo certain variations in position without producing a correspondingly large difference in acoustic effect ;[1]

---

[1] This factor in the change of language (which has only recently received investigation) cannot here be dwelt upon, as readers who have not studied phonetics would be unable to follow the argument. Such should at once endeavour to obtain at least a mastery of the

and further, that any sound produced by a particular position of the vocal organs has a tendency to change in a different direction and at a different rate from the course which would seem natural to the same sound if it had been produced by a different position of the vocal organs.

If, then, we speak a word to a child, and if the child utters it (*a*) with a slightly altered pronunciation, and (*b*) with an articulation which differs from that which WE should naturally employ to produce the pronunciation which the child gives to the word, then two comparatively important steps upon the path of change have already been taken. And thus it is clear that, though changes in language are constantly and imperceptibly occurring throughout the whole life of the individual speaker, yet their rise is most likely and their progress is most rapid at the time when language is transferred from one generation to another.

The above, however, will not explain all the changes which words have undergone. There are some which have hitherto resisted any other explanation than this: they appear as the results of repeated errors of utterance, which errors, owing to particular circumstances attending each case, must have been committed by several or by most of the speakers of the same linguistic community. Such are—(1) Metathesis, *i.e.* where two sounds in the same word reciprocally change their positions, whether they are (*a*) contiguous or (*b*) separated by other sounds. Of the

elements of phonetics, without which they cannot possibly understand many of the problems with which we have here to deal, and all should then read the very interesting article on *Phonetic Compensations*, by C. W. Grandgent and G. S. Sheldon of Harvard University, in Modern Language Notes, June, 1888, No. 6, pp. 177–187.

first kind we have instances in the Anglo-Saxon forms
ascian and *axian*, both of which occur in extant docu-
ments, and also survive in the verb *ask* and the
provincial equivalent *aks*. Cf. also the form *brid*,
found in Chaucer, for *bird* (*e.g.* 'Ne sey I neuer er
now no *brid* ne best.'—Squire's Tale, 460), and, vice
versâ, *birde* for *bride* (*e.g.* Piers Plowman, 3, 14 : 'ᵭe
Justices somme Busked hem to ᵭe boure ᵭere ᵭe *birde*
dwelled'). Again, we may compare the English *bourn*,
Scotch *burn*, with Dutch *bron*, German *brunnen*; A.S.
irnan and *rinnan*, both meaning to *run*, and *irn*, as
pronounced by a west-countryman, with *run*.[1]

Of the second kind of Metathesis (*b*) we find traces
in O.H.G. *erila*, by the side of *elira* = N.H.G. *erle* and
eller; A.S. *weleras*, the lips, as against Gothic *wairilos;*
O.H.G. *ezzih*, which must have had the sound of *etik*
before the sound-shifting process began, = Lat. *acetum ;*
the Italian word, as dialectically pronounced, *grolioso*=
glorioso; and, again, *crompare* = *comprare;* M.H.G.
kokodrille = Lat. *crocodilus*. We may also refer to such
cases of mispronunciation as *indefakitable* for *inde-
fatigable*. These are evanescent, because they meet
with speedy correction.

Besides Metathesis, we must class here (2) the
assimilation of two sounds not standing contiguous in
the word (as Lat. *quinque* from *pinque; original
German *finf* (five)=*finhwi, etc.), and (3) dissimila-
tions, as in O.H.G. *turtiltûba*, from the Lat. *tur-
tur;* Eng. *marble*, from Fr. *marbre*, Lat. *marmor;*
M.H.G. *martel* with *marter*, from *martyrium; priol*
with *prior;* and conversely, M.H.G. *pheller* with
phellel, from Lat. *palliolum ;* O.H.G. *fluobra*, 'consolation,' as against O.S. *frôfra* and A.S. *frôfor;* M.H.G.

---

[1] For further instances, see Skeat, Principles of English
Etymology, p. 376.

kaladrius with *karadrius*; Middle Lat. *pelegrinus*, from *peregrinus*.

We must now conclude this chapter with a few words on the question, Are the laws of sound-change, like physical laws, absolute and unchanging? do they admit of no exceptions? In thus stating the question, we challenge a comparison between physical laws and the laws of sound-change, but we must never forget the essential difference existing between them. Physical laws lay down what must invariably and always happen under certain given conditions; the laws of sound-change state the regularity observed in any particular group of historic phenomena.

We must, in dealing with this question, further distinguish between two closely allied but not identical kinds of phenomena, *i.e.* between those which come under the law of sound-change in the strict sense of the word, and those which are rather to be considered as instances of sound-correspondence or sound-interchange. When, for instance, some sound happened to be, at any particular stage of some language, identical in the various forms of the same word; and if this sound, owing to difference in its position, or of its accent, or from some other cause, has changed into a different sound in some forms of the word, while in other forms of the same word it has remained unchanged; and if many similar cases are remarked in the same language,—we summarise them in our grammars in a form which, though convenient, is not strictly correct. There are in French, for instance, many adjectives which form their masculine termination in *f* and their feminine in *ve*. It is scarcely necessary to point out that in these words the feminine form, derived as it is from the Latin feminine, cannot correctly be described as *derived*

from the masculine in its contemporaneous form : nor
yet does the individual speaker, in using the two
genders, derive the one from the other ; he reproduces
both from memory, or, possibly by a process to be
discussed in Chapter V., he produces one by analogy
with other similar forms.

We nevertheless lay it down in our grammars, that
adjectives in *f* form their feminine by 'changing' *f*
into *ve*. The correspondence of sounds which we
thus register, though it is a consequence of phonetic
development, does not, strictly speaking, express a
law of sound-change ; we might call it 'a law of
sound-correspondence' or 'sound-interchange.' The
'law of sound-interchange' states in a convenient form
the aggregate results of events which have occurred in
accordance with some 'law of sound-change.' Our
question, then, refers to the 'laws of sound-change'
proper, and not to those of 'sound-interchange ;' and
if we say that a law of sound-change admits of no
exceptions, we can only mean that, within the limits
of some definite language or dialect, all cases which
fulfil the same phonetic conditions have had the same
fate : *i.e.* the same sound must there have changed
into the same other sound throughout the language,
or, where various sounds are seen to replace one and
the same other sound of the older language, the cause
for this difference must be sought in the difference of
phonetic conditions, such as accent, contact with or
proximity to other sounds, etc.

It must be clear, after all that has been said in this
chapter, that laws of sound-change, in the correct
meaning of this term, must be consistent and
absolutely regular. As regards the case of the
individual speaker, we have seen that the utterance
of each sound depends on the memory-picture of

motion and position, and that these pictures exert their influence without the speaker being conscious of it. It will then naturally follow that if these pictures alter gradually in the case of any one sound in any one word, they will do so for the same sound in all other cases where it occurs under like conditions.

It is indeed often stated that the sense of etymo-logical connection of a particular word with others which retain a certain sound unaltered may prevent that sound from taking the same course in that word as it does in other words not so influenced; but the existence and efficacy of some counteracting influence does not disprove the existence of the force against which it operates, and which it overcomes or neutralizes. Nor, again, could the inter-communica-tion between the individual speakers cause occasional suspension of the law of sound-change.

We have seen that the association which arises between memory-pictures of the sound, and of the motion of our vocal organs, etc., for its utterance, is—though but external—nevertheless very close, and that it soon becomes indissoluble. The slight and gradual changes in the utterance of the surrounding speakers alter the memory-pictures of the sound, and the corresponding memory-picture of motion and position follows in the same way. It is, then, only in case of mixture of dialect, *i.e.* when a considerable group of speakers of one dialect becomes mixed and scattered among speakers of another, that the following genera-tion *may* adopt one sound from the one dialect and another from the second; thus apparently exhibiting the differentiation of the same sound, under the same phonetic circumstances, into two, of which the one appears as the rule, the other as the exception. But then, again, such a case—though when it has happened we may not always be aware of it, and consequently may not always be able to assign the phenomenon to its true cause—does not prove that the law of sound-change admitted of exception. We merely have the results of two such laws mixed and confused.

CHAPTER IV.

CHANGE IN WORD-SIGNIFICATION.

SOUND-change is brought about by the repeated substitution of a sound or sounds almost imperceptibly differing from the original. The A.S. *hláfmesse* is now represented by the English *Lammas* : though the *mm* sound is clearly easier to pronounce than the combination represented by *fm*, generations passed away before the word as we have it in English became the recognised form. In the case of sound-change, we must notice that the rise of the new sound is simultaneous with the disappearance of the old one. In the case of change of signification, it is possible for the old meaning to be maintained by the side of the new one ; as when we speak of 'the House,' meaning the House of Parliament, we do not exclude the original and proper meaning of the word, but we merely narrow and define its signification. Indeed, change in signification consists invariably in a widening or narrowing of the extent of the signification, corresponding to which we find an impoverishment or an enrichment of the contents. As we saw that the employment of 'House' to denote the House of Parliament implied a narrowing or specialising of the extent of the signification of the ordinary meaning of *house*, so we may take a word like *moon*, properly and originally applied only to the earth's satellite, and apply it to a whole class, which we regard in some way as resembling it, as when we speak of *Jupiter's moons.* In this case we *widen* the application of the word by *narrowing* its contents, but even when thus *widened* the meaning still includes its original denotation. Frequently such a widened application becomes once more narrowed, by the widening of the contents: an instance of this double process we have, *e.g.*, in the word *crane.*[1] Originally only meaning the bird of that name, it was, by a metaphor, applied to a class of objects similar in some respects to the bird. A process of narrowing this application led to the use of the word as a specific name for a certain machine. The word, in this sense, no longer includes its original meaning, and is transferred. It is only by such a succession of widening and narrowing that a word can assume a signification absolutely different from its original meaning. This transference may be more or less *occasional*, or become *usual.* Thus in the case of *green* for *unripe* (*cf.* blackberries are red when they are green) the meaning is in a certain sense an 'occasional' one, the real and original meaning being still clearly felt. This original meaning is, however, quite lost sight of when we use *grain* in *to dye in the grain,* for 'to dye of a fast colour' by means of cochineal, etc., *grain* here being the name given to fibre of wood, etc.[2]

Change in signification, however, has this in

---

[1] A similar transference is observable in γέρανος, γρῦς, and in words in modern languages expressive of the same idea ; cf. also *corvus,* which means a raven, a grapnel, a battering-ram, a surgical instrument, and a sea-fish.

[2] See Marsh, English Language, in Students' Series, lect. iii., pp. 55–62, with note on p. 64.

common with sound-change, that it is effected by individual usage which departs from the common usage;
and that this departure passes only gradually into
common usage. Change in signification is a law of
language; it is a necessity: and change is rendered
possible by the fact that the signification attaching to
a word each time it is employed need not be identical
with that which usage attaches to it. As we shall
have to consider this discrepancy, we shall employ the
expressions 'usual' and 'occasional' signification: and
by the 'usual' we shall understand the ordinary or
general signification; by the 'occasional' we shall
understand that which the individual attaches to it at
the particular moment when he uses the word. The
'usual' signification means, as we employ it, the entire
contents of any word as it presents itself to a member
of any linguistic community: the 'occasional' signification means the contents of the conception which the
speaker, as he utters the word, connects therewith, and
expects the listener to connect with it likewise. The
word *shade*, used by itself and without any interpretation from the context or the situation, would suggest
to a hearer its USUAL signification of 'interruption of
light;' but the individual who employs the word may
have in mind, as he may easily disclose, the shade of
a tree or a lamp-shade.

The 'occasional' signification is commonly richer
than the 'usual' one in content and narrower in extent.
For instance, the word in its occasional sense may
denote something concrete: while, in its usual sense,
it denotes something abstract only; *i.e.* some general
conception under which different concrete conceptions
may be ranged. By a 'concrete' conception is here
meant something presupposed as actually existing,
subject to definite limits of time and space; by an

'abstract' one is here meant a general conception, the contents of a mere idea and nothing more, freed from all trammels of time and place. *The House of Commons* is concrete: *a house* is abstract. This division has nothing to do with the ordinary division of substantives into abstract and concrete. The substantives which in ordinary grammar we call 'concrete' often denote a conception as general as the so-called abstract nouns; as in *England's battles:* and, conversely, the latter are occasionally used as what we here call 'concretes' when they are used to express a single quality or activity defined by limits of space and time; as, *The days of thy youth.* In the phrase 'My horse has run well to-day,' *horse* is concrete in the sense which we attach to the term: but in the phrase 'A horse has four legs,' it is what we call 'abstract;' because the statement does not refer to any one definite concrete horse, but to horses generally, and the predicate therefore is associated with the abstract idea of *horse.*

The greater number of words can be employed in occasional use in either abstract or concrete significations. There are some words, indeed, essentially concrete, such as *thou, thine, he, there, to-day, yesterday;*—which, however, need individual application to render them immediately and definitely concrete. Words like *I, here, there,* serve to define some one's position in the concrete world; but it requires the aid of other words, or of the circumstances in which they are uttered, to render them thus definite. Even our demonstrative pronouns, and the word *the*, may be employed to denote abstract conceptions; as, *The whale is a mammal; it has warm blood. Pity the widow and the orphan.* Even proper names, which we might be inclined at first to take as the type of

concrete words, as denoting a single object or person,
may be used either 'usually' as concrete, or 'occasionally' as abstract, since the same name may be borne
by various people and various localities, as *Newton*,
Brighton: and, indeed, may be applied to objects
named after localities; as *Stilton, Champagne*, etc.
Then there is a small class of words which express
an object conceived of as existing once and once only,
such as *God, devil, world, universe, earth, sun.* These
nouns are concrete both in their 'usual' and in almost
all their 'occasional' meanings; but even they may be
regarded as abstract if regarded from a definite point
of view. Indeed, a proper name is essentially concrete; if it becomes abstract, this can only be because
it has become a generic name, *i.e.* because it has
become a common noun, a common noun being such
in virtue of its standing as the name of each individual
of a class or group of things. On the other hand,
there are some words which from their very nature
are abstract; such are the pronouns *ever, any;* the
Latin *quisquam, ullus, unquam, uspiam;* but the
abstract character even of words like these suffers
certain limitations in occasional usage; cf. *Did he
ever (i.e.* on any particular occasion) *act so*, and *Should
he ever really do it.* In these cases *ever* is in the first
instance limited to the past, and in the second to the
future.

A more important and deeper-lying distinction
between 'usual' and 'occasional' signification is that
a word may have various 'usual' significations, but
can only bear a single 'occasional' one; *i.e.* in each
case of 'occasional' use the meaning is one and definite:[1] except, indeed, when the word is of set purpose

[1] See the discussions of the examples below. The 'various'
meanings of these words there given are mostly 'usual' ones. When-

used ambiguously, either to deceive, or to point a witticism; as in 'If you get the best of port, port will get the best of you.' It happens in all languages that there occur words identically pronounced which may be understood in different significations : and, for practical purposes, we must regard these as the same word, since whoever hears the sounds of which the word is composed spoken cannot, without the aid of the connection, possibly tell which of the senses is intended by the speaker to be attached to the word. Under this head must be ranged, in the first place, words which accidentally happen to correspond in sound, though they differ in meaning. The English language is particularly full of such words, owing, in some degree, to the coincidence of many words coming from Norman French with words coming from a Teutonic source. Such are *mean*, intend ; *mean*, common ; *mean*, moyen : *match*, a contest ; *match*, mèche : *sound*, son and ge-sund. We have, in these and similar cases, instances of words which usually receive several significations. But besides these we have numerous words in English, as in other languages, which are etymologically identical and which yet have several significations. Such is the word *box* in English : it means in the first and most common case, 'a chest to put things in ;' then, 'a tree,' 'a small seated compartment in the auditorium of a theatre,' 'the driver's seat on a carriage,' 'a present given at Christmas' in the combination 'a Christmas box ;' besides the meaning of a 'box on the ear,' which comes from a different source. Such, too, are : *post* = (1) 'A stake in the ground,' (2)

---

ever a speaker utters any of these words in the body of his discourse, the word has only one of the various 'usual' senses. The use of the word 'body' in this very note may serve as illustration of an 'occasional' signification of a word with sundry 'usual' meanings.

'a professional situation,' (3) 'the system of delivering the mails;' *broom*, the shrub, and *broom*, 'a besom;' *bull*, 'a papal edict' and 'a blunder in language;' *canon*, 'a rule' and 'a church dignitary;' to *bait a horse* and to *bait a hook;* a *coach* in the sense of 'a teacher' and of 'a carriage;' *board*, 'a plank' or 'food supplied at lodging-houses:' so in French, *un radical*, 'a root in language,' 'a root in algebra,' 'a radical in chemistry,' or 'a radical politician;' *plume*, 'a feather,' and *plume*, 'a pen;' Lat. *examen*, 'swarm,' 'tongue of a balance,' and 'examination.' It is true that the derived meanings in these words spring from a primary one, but it is equally true that it is impossible, without some knowledge of the history of the word, to recognise the original connection between the various significations; and these bear the same relations to each other as if the identity in sound were purely accidental. This is especially true in cases where the primary meaning has entirely disappeared, as in the case of *villain*, used now only in the uncomplimentary sense which circumstances have affixed to the word, save, indeed, in historical treatises; though even in its early sense it is no longer 'the man who lives and works on the *villa.*' It is the same with *pagan*, and *recreant*. Another good illustration is afforded by the word *impertinent*, which signifies (1) not pertinent (obsolete); (2) having no special pertinency, trifling; (3) rude. Etymology, working by comparison, often serves to detect such disappearances: thus N.H.G. *klein*, small, has lost its original meaning, that still appears in Eng. *clean*.

But in many cases, too, where we can still recognise the relationship of the derived to the primary signification, we must nevertheless acknowledge the independence of the derived meaning; especially where,

E

as in the case of 'post,' it has become the usual one. The test, in these cases, of the independence of the word is whether a word 'occasionally' used in the derivative sense can be understood without any necessity arising for the primary meaning to force itself on the consciousness of the speaker or hearer. There are, further, two negative tests whereby we may judge that a word has not a simple, but a complex signification. The first of these is if no simple definition can be framed, including the whole of its meaning, and neither more nor less; and the second, if the word cannot, if employed 'occasionally,' be used in the whole extent of its signification. It is easy to apply these tests to the examples cited above. No simple definition of the word *post* would be possible; a whole series would be necessary to explain the meaning of the word to a foreigner. Again, any definition of the word *post* used in the 'occasional' sense of 'a situation' would leave the other meanings quite unexplained.

Even in cases where the 'usual' signification may be regarded as simple, the individual meaning may vary from this and yet may not become concrete, as it may develop on the lines of one of the special meanings included in the general conception. Thus the simple word *pin* may, in single cases, be understood as *lynch-pin*, *hair-pin*, etc.; so *bye-law* is now always used as if it were a secondary law.[1]

All understanding between individuals depends upon the correspondence in their psychical attitude. In order that a word may be understood in its 'usual' meaning, no more perfect mental correspondence is imperative than such as naturally exists between the members of a single linguistic community who have mastered their own language; should, however, the

[1] Vid. Murray, p. 1257.

signification of a word be specialised in 'occasional' use, as when we speak of 'the House,' and understand thereby 'the House of Parliament,' a closer understanding must be supposed to exist among the speakers. The same words may be intelligible or otherwise, or, again, may be misunderstood, according to the state of mind of the person who is addressed ; or, again, according to the chance surroundings, whose presence or absence may act as an aid or a drawback to the enforcement of the signification. And it seems well in this place to emphasise the fact that the body of ideas which may at any time be called up by a word is *never the same* in the case of any two speakers. The ideas will resemble each other less as the speakers are members of social communities more widely separated from each other, or more in proportion as the persons using the words possess similar degrees of cultivation or life-experience. For instance, we may understand all the words of a philosophic discussion, and still it may remain a mere jargon to us. This truth holds good even for the simplest language in its simplest stage. Hence it is that no perfect translation of a literary masterpiece is possible ; especially if such be written in the idiom of a civilisation far removed from that of the translator, alike in the circuit of ideas, and in the way in which these ideas present themselves. Every expression is in fact accompanied by a store of associative suggestion, which *must* suffer loss to a greater or less extent in the attempt to insert an equivalent expression from a stranger tongue. It thus results that the interpreter of the language of a past civilisation must undertake by laborious study to reconstruct and attach to each expression the body of associations which should be its native environment. The aids necessary for understanding words in their 'occasional' meaning do not require to be of a linguistic nature at all; although they may, on the other hand, be so. We have seen before that abstract words may be rendered concrete by connecting them with such words as essentially express the concrete, and that the article is one of the chief of these words. *Horse* is abstract, but *the horse* is generally, as we have seen, concrete. But even this rule is not absolute, and consequently this aid is not absolutely sufficient; for we have seen that in expressions like *The horse is a quadruped*, the article has come to express the general conception. Again, there are languages, like Latin and Russian, which have developed no article; and these employ abstract words, with no special mark of denotation, for the concrete.

In any case, whether the reference to the 'concrete' is expressly denoted or not, other methods may be adopted to define it more closely. The first of these depends upon the common environment of the speaker and hearer, and upon the perception common to both. The hearer cannot fail to understand the speaker if, in referring to a tree or tower, he means the definite single tree or tower which they both have before their eyes. The speaker may point to the object in question, or may indicate its position by his gaze. Nay, such signs may serve to indicate objects not directly cognisable by the senses, provided that the direction in which these objects lie is known.

Another method whereby the word is made to refer to something definite and concrete is found in the recalling by the hearer of the past utterances of the speaker, or, it may be, in a special explanation which the speaker has given. If the hearer understands that a word is once intended to bear a concrete sense, then this same sense may continue to attach to the word throughout the rest of the conversation. If 'the Church' have once been spoken of in the sense of 'the body of adherents to the Church of England,' it will be understood that this is the sense in which the word 'Church' is to be apprehended for the rest of the conversation. The recollection of the previous utterance will take the place of immediate perception. Again, this reference to the past can be emphasised by words like demonstrative pronouns and adverbs. If, after using 'the Church' in a definite sense, I employ a phrase like 'that Church' or 'that Church of which I spoke,' it is clear that this word 'that,' whose function was originally merely to express a perception, serves in its new function to call attention to the individualisation of the signification and to render it intelligible to the hearer.

In the third place, anything is capable of being represented and understood as concrete, when the speaker and the hearer are so similarly circumstanced that the same thoughts naturally rise into the consciousness of both at once. Such agreement or correspondence depends upon such circumstances as common residence, common age, common tastes, business, or surroundings of the speakers. An instance of this is seen in the rhetorical usage commonly known as κατ᾽ ἐξοχήν. If two people live near together in the country in the neighbourhood of a large town, they would both certainly understand by 'going *to town*' the town nearest to where they happen to live. If, on the other hand, they both had their business in London, they would certainly both understand 'London' by 'town.' Again, words like *the town-hall, the square, the market* are understood by the inhabitants of a particular town to refer to the town-hall or market of that particular town. Again, such words as *the kitchen, the larder*, when spoken of by members of a family, refer to the rooms in their particular house, which they know by these names. Thus, again, in speaking of *Sunday*, we mean the nearest Sunday to the day on which we are speaking; and, in fact, the Sunday can be fixed with *perfect* precision by merely affixing to the word *Sunday* a word expressing past or future; as, *next Sunday*, *last Sunday*. Words expressing relationship between persons are naturally and without effort transferred to persons who bear such relationship to hearer and speaker alike: and what is more, no doubt can arise from the use of the singular, as long as there is only one person who could naturally bear the description. Thus, if the children of a family speak to each other of 'father' or 'mother,' this concrete reference is just as intelligible to them as that of 'the Queen' or 'the President' to the British or the Americans respectively. Nay, even though the relationship exists only upon one side, whether of the speaker or the hearer, the reference may still be equally unmistakable, assuming that circumstances aid in pointing to the person named. If one man says to another 'The wife is better,' the hearer would at once understand that the speaker's *own wife* was referred to, assuming that her illness had been previously discussed between the two.

In the fourth place, a speaker may employ some more closely defining word, as an epithet, in order to render his meaning more definite and concrete. Thus he might say, *That is the old king's palace*, *That is the royal castle*. But even such defining epithets as these fail to give a perfect definition unless some other aid, like the memory aid of which we have spoken, or the aid of the situation, supports the definition. If the speakers have been conversing about 'the old king,'

both *palace* and *castle* would receive a concrete significance from what had been said before. Thus, the
phrase 'the king's castle' comes to mean a single
object only, when it is known that the king has only
one castle, or if the hearer be referred to a single place,
where he must know the castle to lie.

Finally, a concrete word may affect other words
connected with it, and may give them a concrete sense
as well. In sentences like *John never moved a finger;
I never laid hand upon him ; I took him by the arm; You
hit me on the shoulder*, the words *finger* and *hand* get
their concrete meaning from the subject, and *arm* and
shoulder from the object.[1] In French, in the sentence,
Il sauta dans l'eau, la tête la première, 'la tête' acquires
its concrete sense from the subject.

Just as general names receive a definite concrete
reference, so proper names applicable to different
persons come to denote but a single one. It may be
sufficient merely to speak of a man as 'Charles' in
order to sufficiently identify him; and indeed such
reference would suffice if he were before us, or had
recently been mentioned. Again, even without this,
the name 'Charles' would sufficiently identify any
person within his own family, or within any other
circle where no other 'Charles' was known. Under
other circumstances, we must naturally define him
more closely; as, 'Charles the Sixth of France,'
'Charles the First of England.' Just so, there are
many places bearing the same name; but a single
name is sufficient to define the place for the neighbourhood, and even for the world at large when the place
happens to be the most important of the places called

---

[1] A more definite and unmistakable instance of a word acquiring
a concrete sense would be, ' He raised his arm, and, with outstretched
hand, exclaimed, etc.'

by the name : cf. *Melbourne, Brisbane, London, Strass-burg:* otherwise a nearer definition has to be employed, as *Stony Stratford, Newton-le-Willows.*

Words are *specialised* in meaning in the same way as they are defined and rendered concrete, and by the same factors. When we hear a word, we naturally think of the most obvious and common of its various meanings, or else of its primary meaning. In the case of 'train,' we think of the means of locomotion : in the case of 'crane' we probably think of the bird. Sometimes the two tendencies work together. Should several meanings tolerably common stand side by side, the primary meaning will commonly present itself to the mind of the hearer before the others; as in the case of the word *head* used in so many metaphorical senses. But this general rule is liable again to be altered by the surroundings amid which the word is uttered. The situation awakens certain groups of ideas in the mind of the hearer before the word is uttered, and itself aids powerfully in fixing the meaning. We affix a different meaning to the word *sheet* according as we hear it in a haberdasher's shop, or on a yacht, or at a book-binder's : as we do to the words 'to bind,' according as we hear them in a book-binder's or in a harvest field. Different trades and professions use the same word and affix their own meaning to it, and no ambiguity arises in their own circle : take such words as 'a goose' in the mouth of a tailor ; 'a form' among hatters. Then, again, the connection in which a word occurs does much to fix its meaning. Observe how the meaning is affected by the connection in such utterances as *a good point, a point of view, a point of honour; the bar of a river, the bar of a hotel, the bar of justice; the foot of a mountain, the foot of a table; the tongue of a woman, a tongue of land, the tongue of a balance;*

a crowded ball, a round ball; a bay and a roan; the cock crows, the cock is turned on; ere the king's crown go down there are crowns to be broke; the train is starting, a train of thought; a bitter draught, a bitter reputation; clean linen, a clean heart; a donkey-engine, John is a donkey; the money goes, the mill goes; to stand still, to stand upon ceremony, to stand at ease.

Cases may, however, occur in which the '*occasional*' meaning may not include all the elements of the '*usual*' meaning, while it may contain something beyond and above this. Take, for instance, the words expressive of colour, such as *blue, red, yellow, white, black.* These words may be used to denote colours which, according to their simple meaning, they are inadequate to denote. Each colour may be mixed with another colour, and there must arise a succession of transition stages for which language has no name. For instance, the northern word *blae* varies in meaning from the purple colour of the blaeberry to the dull grey of unbleached cottons;[1] while the same word in old Spanish takes the form *blavo*, and is found to mean *yellowish grey*. Three centuries ago, *auburn* meant 'whitish,' and *drab* meant 'no colour at all' (= Fr. *drap*, 'undyed cloth ').

But the widest field for such inadequate application as that which we have been instancing is given by words whose signification consists of a complex assembly of ideas, as is the case, for instance, in metaphorical expressions. Metaphorical expressions are nothing else than comparisons instituted between groups of ideas *with respect to what they possess in common.* We compare in these only certain characteristics, and we leave the rest out of account. If we say of a man *He is a fox*, we mean merely that some of

[1] Murray, p. 898.

the qualities which go to make up the conception of a fox are found in the man as well. We may, indeed, express the point of comparison between the two, as by saying *He is as crafty as a fox*. On the other hand, we might say more simply *He is foxy*, in which case the adjective merely denotes such a selection of the qualities of a fox as may be necessary to characterise the man sufficiently : and, finally, we may say *He is a fox*, whereby we merely mean that he is in several respects like a fox. In this case, then, the words *foxy* and *fox* have passed beyond the limits of their proper signification. They have come to denote a single quality only, instead of a group of qualities, and this signification has come to be usual.

A word may, again, pass beyond the limits of its strict signification by the operation of what rhetoricians call *synecdoche*, or naming a thing by some prominent or characteristic part of it ; as, 'A fleet of twenty *sail ;* ' 'All *hands* to the pumps ;' 'They sought his *blood*.' In this case, something connected spatially, or temporally, or causally with the usual meaning is understood with the word when it is spoken.

When a word passes beyond the limits of its usual signification, it is liable to be misunderstood, unless, indeed, some impulse be present to serve as a sign-post to the sense in which it is intended to be used. We are naturally inclined to use a word in its ordinary meaning and in no other, unless, indeed, we are reminded by something that its ordinary sense is impossible. In simple cases, such as the proverb, *Speech is silvern, but silence is golden*, we think of the predicates as used metaphorically, simply because it is impossible to think of them as used in any other sense. But when Shakespeare talks about *the majesty of buried Denmark*, each principal word in the combination serves as a sign-post to the sense in which each other word is to be used, and we are enabled to guess the sense which we are to attach to each word.

Repeated departures from the usual meaning—in other words, the repeated employment of the occasional meanings of words—end in a true change of signification.   The more regularly these departures occur, the more, of course, do individual peculiarities approximate to common use.   The test of the transition from an 'occasional' to a 'usual' meaning is whether the employment of the 'occasional' meaning brings into the mind of the speaker or hearer a previous usage with which he was familiar, and in which he will naturally understand the word.   When such recollection naturally presents itself to the mind, and when the word is employed, as well as understood, with no reference to the original signification of the word, then the word may fairly be deemed to have accomplished its transition of meaning.   But it is clear that there may be many gradations between the two usages.   If I speak of *sweet* memories or of a *bright* future, there may or may not be any recollection on the part of the speaker or hearer that these expressions are metaphors from the use of the word *sweet* and *bright* in a physical sense.

It must further be remarked that it is difficult for the *occasional* meaning of a word to pass into the *usual* by the aid of an individual, unless those to whom he speaks reciprocate the influence which he has exerted upon them.   Milton, for instance, uses such words as *expatiate* and *extravagant* in their Latin sense, and *hear* in the sense of 'to be called;' thus, again, Chaucer and others use *copy* (copia) in the sense of *plenty:* but these words were not taken up by a sufficiently large number of persons to enable their 'occasional' use to become 'usual,' even though introduced by such authorities as these.[1]

Words have a strong tendency to change their meaning when they pass into the mouth of a new generation. A child fixes the meaning of a word by hasty and imperfect generalisations ; and not by means of descriptive or exhaustive definitions. The simple and unreflecting mind of childhood identifies objects on very imperfect grounds, and stays not to consider whether there be any basis for such identification or not.[2] And thus it is that, from the very first steps in the process of acquiring language, the child employs the same word to define several objects, and these not objects which *really resemble each other, but which have the appearance in any degree of doing so*. Of course this whole proceeding implies that no clear conception can exist of the contents and extent of the usual meaning. A child conceives of a word as covering an extent sometimes too narrow, sometimes too wide ; more commonly, however, too wide than too narrow, and the more so as the extent of his words is the more limited. He will include *a sofa* under the name of *a chair; an umbrella* under that of *a stick; a cap* under that of *a hat;* and this repeatedly. Another cause of inexact appreciation of meaning is the fact that the speaker, when indicating to a child certain objects, connects them in his own mind with certain other objects ; the child may fail to understand the limitations of meaning to be placed upon the word when it is parted from the idea as a whole. Take, for instance, such a word as *congregation.* In the mouth of a clergyman, this word might be used as an inseparable

---

[1] Shakespeare could not gain currency for his *forgetive*, nor Bishop Wilkins for his '*unwalkative* cripple.'

[2] Cf. Whitney's Life and Growth of Language, pp. 27, 28.

adjunct of a church, but he will still speak of the *congregation* as distinguished from the church, and as forming a distinct though necessary connection with the idea of 'Church.' The child, generalising faultily, may apply the word *congregation* to a collection of politicians, or of traders, or of animals; and it may be long before he is in a position to correct his wrong conception. The adult, again, constantly has to encounter the same difficulties as the child, when he meets with words of rare occurrence or denoting technical or complex ideas; and, supposing that he learns such words by their occasional application only, he is exposed to the same errors as the child. Thus the word *insect* has come to be so commonly used to mark the distinction between insects and other animals, that we read on labels, *This powder is harmless to animal life, but kills all insects.*

These inaccuracies in the case of the apprehension of the usual meaning are, taken singly, of little account, and are commonly corrected by the standard or ordinary usage which the speaker will naturally hear from the mouths of the greater part of the community. At the same time, in cases where a large number of individuals unite in a partial misapprehension or in investing simultaneously a word with an 'occasional' meaning, it will happen that this, though only partially corresponding with the meaning which was usual amongst an older generation, will be substituted.

Such, among others, are the significations attaching to certain terms, expressive of qualities ennobled by Christianity, such as *humility, faith, spiritual, ghostly,* etc.

Commonly speaking, the older generation gives the main impulse to change of meaning, controlling, as it does, the whole usage of language. But the younger generation has great power in aiding the process of change, from the fact that the very first time that a word has presented itself to one of its members, the word may have been used in an 'occasional' sense, which would by him have been taken to be its regular use. Thus, a child might often hear a horse spoken of as *a bay*, or a dolt as *an ass*. In such cases he understands the secondary meaning only ; nor does he even mentally connect this meaning with any other.

The change in 'usual' signification, then, takes its rise from modification in the 'occasional' application of the word. The most common case of change in signification owing to such modification, is where the meaning of the word is specialised by the narrowing of its comprehension and the enrichment of its contents. In the English word *stamp* we have a good instance of the difference between 'occasional' and 'usual' specialisation. The word may be employed of any object used as a particular mark. It may be used for a *receipt stamp* or for a *bill stamp*, or, again, metaphorically, as the *stamp of nobility*. These are instances of 'occasional' specialisation. But, while it requires some definite situation to make us think of *stamp* in its other significations, it immediately occurs to us to think of it as a *postage stamp*, and we then think little, if at all, of the general idea of stamping, but rather of an object of definite shape and construction and used for the definite purpose of franking letters. We must thus admit that this meaning has parted from the more general meanings, and stands independently as a special meaning; in fact, that it is specialised and 'usual.' Other examples are the use of *frumentum* for 'corn' in Latin ; *fruit* for the produce of certain trees as distinguished from 'the fruits of the earth ;' *pig*, originally the young of animals ;—in Danish,

pige, a young girl.   *Corn*, in English, is restricted to
'wheat,' and, in America, to *maize*, or Indian corn;
while, in German, *korn* denotes any species of grain:
fowl, in English, means specially 'a barn-door fowl;' *a
bird* means, in the language of sportsmen, 'a partridge;'
a fish, 'a salmon:' ὄρνις, in the conventional language of
Athens, as disclosed by the Comic poets, means 'a
barn-door fowl:'[1] and a special usage of this kind is
seen in the names of materials themselves employed
to denote the products of materials; as, *glass, horn,
gold, silver, paper, copper*,—as when we talk of paper
in the sense of *paper money*, etc.

Proper names owe their origin to the change of the
'occasional' concrete meanings of certain words into
'usual' meanings.   All names of persons and places
took their origin from names of species; and the usage
κατ᾽ ἐξοχήν was the starting-point for this process.   We
are able to observe it distinctly in numerous instances
of names both of persons and of places.   Such ordinary
names as the following are very instructive for our
purpose: *Field, Hill, Bridges, Townsend, Hedges,
Church, Stone, Meadows, Newton, Villeneuve, New-
castle, Neuchâtel, Neuburg, Milltown*, etc.   Such names
as these served in the first instance merely to indicate
to neighbours a certain person or town: and they were
sufficient to distinguish such person or town from
others in the neighbourhood.   They passed into
regular proper names as soon as they were apprehended in this concrete sense by neighbours too far
removed to judge of the reasons why they received
their special name: cf. names like *Pont newydd:* and
names like *Bevan, Pritchard*, from *ab* (*son*) *Evan* and
ap Richard.   There are, no doubt, beside these, many

---

[1] Other examples are *fera, thier, deer;* γυνή, *queen, quean;* and
the modern Greek ἄλογο(ν) (the unreasoning animal), for 'a horse.'

place-names which began by resembling real proper names, in so far as they are derived from names of persons : such are *Kingston, St. Helens.*

There is also one kind of specialising process which begins to operate as soon as ever a word comes into use. Instances of this may be seen in the case of words which may be derived at will, according to the ordinary laws of any language, from other words in common use, but which are not employed till a special need calls them into play. Such words as these are sometimes found, in the first stage of their descent from the root-word, to bear a more special meaning than the derivative, as such, would naturally bear. Thus the substantive formations in -*er* (A.S. -*er*, -*e*)[1] denote properly a person who stands in some relation to the idea of the root-word—commonly speaking, expressing the agent : but in the case of single words thus terminated the most varied instances of specialisation are found.[2] *The 'pauser' reason* (Macbeth, II. iii. 117) would naturally mean reason that pauses or halts ; but Shakespeare uses it as the 'reason that makes us pause ;'—similarly, there is no reason why the word *scholar* (M.E. *scolere*), an imitation of Lat. *scholaris,* should not signify 'he who schools or teaches ;' but, as a matter of fact, it always seems to have borne its present sense. In English, indeed, it bears the special sense of 'a student enjoying the benefit of a foundation.' A *poulterer* is one who vends poultry : a *fisher* is one who tries to catch fish ; a *burgher*, one who dwells in a burgh ; a *falconer*, one who trains falcons, or one who hawks for sport : while a *pensioner* is one

---

[1] Skeat, English Etymology, p. 257.

[2] In some cases the termination comes from the French -*eur ;* and in this case, too, the same remarks apply. Cf. also the words *butler* = *bottler ; usher, ostiarius,* etc.

who receives a pension. Take, again, the case of verbs derived from substantives, like *to butter, to head, to top, to badger, to earwig, to dust, to water, to pickle, to bone* (*a fowl,*) *to skin, to clothe, to book* (*a debt*). In many of these cases, the meaning of the verb is derived from a metaphorical sense of the substantive. In this case, too, the usage can only be formed gradually, and according to the general fundamental conditions of language.

When language demands the expression of a conception hitherto undenoted, one of the most obvious expedients is to choose a word expressive of the most prominent characteristics of the conception, as to name the horse 'the swift animal' (Sans. *açvas*), or the wolf the 'grey animal' or 'the tearer.' Many substantives have arisen in this way (cf. the old terms 'a grey' and 'a brock'[1] for a badger), but we must not therefore conclude that there was any general rule for such formation; such as, for instance, that all substantives proceeded from verbs.

The second principal kind of change in signification is the converse of the kind already spoken of. It is where the application of the term is limited to one part only of its original content, though such reduction on one side is commonly accompanied by amplification on another.

The great number of phenomena occurring under this head renders it hard to classify them: but certain ones of marked peculiarity may be mentioned. In some cases we name the object from its appearance to our sight: as in the case of the *eye* of a potato, the *head* or *heart* of a cabbage, the *arm* of a river, the *cup*

---

[1] So termed from the white streaked face of the animal. Gael. *broc*, O. Celtic *broccos*. Cf. Murray, Dictionary, i.v.

of a flower, the *bed* of a river.   A statue or a picture
is named after what it represents ; as, *an Apollo, a
Laocoon, the Adoration of the Magi :* or, again, a work
of art is named after its executor ; as, *a Phidias, a
Praxiteles.*   In all such cases the original signification
has been limited in one direction and amplified in
another.   For instance, in the case of 'the *bed* of a
river,' we exclude from consideration other beds, such
as beds for sleeping on ; but, on the other hand, the
word may be applied in its novel sense to as many
rivers as flow and have *beds.*   We call a part of one
object after the part of another object which corresponds to it in position ; we talk of the *neck* or *belly*
of a bottle, of the *shoulder* of a mountain, the *foot* of a
ladder, the *tail* of a kite.   The different uses of *caput*
are mostly reproduced in our own use of *head ;* as, *caput
urbis; capitolium ; caput fontis,* fountain head ; *caput
montis,* κορυφή ; *caput conspirationis ;* Ital. *capo ; caput
arboris ; caput libri,* chapter, κεφάλαιον ; *caput pecuniæ,*
capital ; cape.   We call a measure by the name of some
object which in some way resembles it in dimensions ;
as, *a cubit, an ell, a foot, a barley-corn.*   A *pen* or *feather*
writes : and so 'a pen' and 'une plume' may mean
a steel pen.   We transfer words expressive of conceptions of time to conceptions of place, and *vice versâ*, as
in *long* and *short ; before, after ; behind, before :* and
thus in the case of many other adverbs and prepositions.   We transfer the impressions made on one
sense to those made on another, as in the cases of
sweet ; beautiful ; loud (originally applicable to hearing alone), in the phrase 'loud colours ;' and the
Fr. *voyant,* in such a phrase as *une couleur voyante,*
originally applicable to the sense of sight alone.
Words which in their proper sense denote sensual and
corporeal ideas only, are transferred to the denotation

of ideas spiritual and intellectual : as in the cases of *apprehension, comprehension, reflection, spirit, inclination, penchant, appetite, penser* (lit. *peser* = to weigh, etc.). Consider, again, the various applications of such words as *to feel, to see ; bitter, lovely, fair, mean, dirty, great, small, lofty, low, warm ; taste, fire, passion ; to sting, to thrill*, etc. Words which properly denote one species only are given a wider extension ; as, *cat, crab, apple, rose, moon* (as in Jupiter's moons), *fishery* (as in whale-fishery, lobster-fishery, after the analogy of the herring-fishery, etc.), *le sanglier* (l'animal solitaire, *singularis*), *le fromage* (lac formaticum, *milk made into shape*), *le baudet* (O.Fr. bald, baud, *the spirited animal*,—originally *the male ass*). We make proper names pass into class names, as when we speak of *a Cicero, a Nelson, a Cato ; an Academy*, from Plato's gymnasium near Athens, called 'Ακαδημία; *Palace*, from Palatium, the seat of Augustus' Palace. Thus, again, we actually talk of a wooden house as being dilapidated. And we have such further development as *a martinet ; a cannibal ; a vandal ; Tom, Dick*, and *Harry ; John Doe* and *Richard Roe*. Such adjectives as *romantic, Gothic, pre-adamite*, may also serve as illustrations of the development, which is also manifest in the case of *sehr*, 'very,' formerly meaning 'painful,' of Eng. *sore*, with the like use in '*sore* afraid.' So compare *schlecht* (schlechterdings, schlichten) with *slight*, primitive signification 'plain ;' *silly* with *selig*, etc. The transference in the case of verbs is seen in such cases as ' I was sorry to *find* you out when I called;' 'He *enjoys* poor health,' etc. This development is similar to that illustrated above by *apprehension, reflection*, etc., to which we may add *understand, verstehen,* ἐπίστασθαι, *transpire*.

The third principal division of change in meaning

is the transference of the idea to what is connected with the fundamental conception of the word by some relation of place, or time, or cause.

The simplest sub-division of this is when a part is substituted for the whole—the figure called by rhetoricians *synecdoche*, and referred to before on p. 58. The part is, in such cases, always a prominent characteristic ; it suggests, as a rule, that aspect of the whole which it is desired to bring into prominence for rhetorical effect. Thus, 'all *hands* to the pumps ;' 'they sought his *blood ;*' 'the *blade*,' for 'the *sword ;*' 'a maid of twelve *summers*.' The German word *Bein* (leg) = Eng. *bone*, has been thus used by synecdoche : it retains its older value in *Gebeine, Elfenbein*. Persons and animals are named after characteristic features in the body or the mind ; as, *grey-beard, curly-head, thick-head, red-breast, fire-tail; a good soul, a bright spirit :* in French *blanc-bec, grosse-tête, rouge-gorge, rouge-queue, pied-plat, gorge-blanche, mille-pieds : esprit fort, bel esprit*. Names, again, are given to objects from some prominent feature with which they are commonly connected : such are those taken from garments ; as, *blue-stocking, green-domino, a red-coat, a blue-jacket;* cf. the use of *un cuirassier*. Other names are transferred from one object to another included in it : such as *the town*, for 'the talk of the town ;' *the smiling year*, for 'the spring ;' *the cabinet, the church, the court*, etc. Conversely, we find the idea transferred from the object to its surroundings, as in *the Round Table, the Porch, the Mountain, the Throne, the Altar*, etc. Sometimes the name of a quality is transferred to the person or thing possessing the quality, as in the case of *age, youth, plenty :*—

> ' The people's prayer, the glad diviner's theme,
> The young man's vision and the old man's dream,'

as Dryden calls the Duke of Monmouth:[1] cf. also *desert, bitters.* Other examples of this are—*his worship, the Godhead, your highness, his majesty, his excellence, his holiness,* etc. It will thus be seen that collective names take their rise in this way as well as the names for single persons or things; we can speak of *their worships,* meaning the magistrates. But these words do not always form substantives.

Nouns of action suffer the same transference as names of qualities. By nouns of action we mean names denoting activities generally, and conditions which are derived from verbs, such as *overflow, train, income, government, providence, gilding, warning, influence.* In the instances given, the name of the action has been transferred to its subject: but it is equally capable of being transferred to its object, if 'object' be taken in the widest sense. Thus, it may be transferred to a consequence or result of the verbal activity: such as *rift, spring, growth, a rise, assembly, union, education:* or to an object affected by the activity, such as *seed, speech, doings, lamentations, bewailings, resort, excuse, dwelling.* Writings are denoted by the name of their author; as, 'Have you read Shakespeare?' A person is named after some favourite word of his own; as, *Heinrich jasomir Gott: 'Cedo alteram'* (Tacitus, Annals, book iii.):[2] animals are named from their utterances, in nursery language, as a *bow-wow;* or from those used to appeal to them, as a *gee-gee:* besides these, we may add the names of such plants as *puzzle-monkey, noli me tangere, forget-me-not,* etc.

The different kinds of change in meaning may follow each other, and thus unite. Thus the word *rosary* has on one side gained in comprehension, since

---

[1] Bain's 'English Composition,' p. 23.

[2] Similar instances are *Capability* Brown, *Satan* Montgomery.

it is now used of a necklace composed of beads employed for a sacred pupose ; but, on the other, it has lost all connection with roses.   A *horn* is a wind instrument which may be, but is not commonly made of horn : the name may equally apply to an instrument made of other materials.

It frequently happens that some idea foreign to the essence of a word, and connected with it merely by accident, becomes absorbed into its signification as a mere accessory : and this is then thought of as the proper meaning, the primary meaning being forgotten : thus names of relations of time and place gradually pass into causal words ; as, *consequence, purpose, end* (to the end that), *means, way.*

Seeing that the unit of language is the sentence, and not the word—in other words, that we think in sentences,—it is natural that the change in meaning should affect, not merely the separate words, but also entire sentences.   These sentences may receive a meaning which is at the outset merely 'occasional,' but which by repetition may become 'usual'—a meaning not implied by the combination of words as we hear it for the first time.   Take, for instance, such phrases as *A plot is on foot; The business has come to a head; He has come to the front; I have a man in my eye ;* and such combinations as the following, in which the word *hand* plays a great part : *well in hand, off hand, hands off, at hand,* etc.   We cannot say that in these cases special meanings of the word *hand* have developed : rather, these meanings have become obscured by the attention which we have come to pay to the phrase as a whole. English is full of such terms of expression.   In many of these the sense can only be derived from the meanings of the several words by the aid of an historical knowledge of the language in which such combinations occur.   Take such cases as, *to dine with Duke Hum-phrey; to tell a cock and bull story; all his geese are swans; to stuff one up; to give one the sack; to be half seas over:* in French—*il raisonne comme un tambour; sot comme un panier* (for *un panier percé*); *triste comme un bonnet de nuit; donner une savonnade; faire une jérémiade.*

Language is incessantly engaged in an endeavour to express the entire stock of ideas in the human mind.   But it is met by the difficulty, in the first place, that the ideas of each individual in any society differ widely from those of the other individuals in the society : in the next place, by the difficulty that the ideas of each individual are liable to a constant process of expansion or contraction.   The conse-quence is that the ideas which language is constantly endeavouring to express are necessarily coloured by individual peculiarities ; though it is equally true that these peculiarities are unimportant in ordinary defi-nitions of the meanings of single words or groups of words.   For instance, it is no doubt true that the word *horse* has the same meaning for everybody, in so far as everybody refers it to the same object : but, on the other hand, each man in his own particular line, a hunter, a coachman, a veterinary surgeon, or a zoologist will connect with the idea a larger quantity of conceptions than one who has nothing to do with horses.   A father would be differently defined by a lawyer and a physiologist : but the points which in the thoughts of these make up the essence of paternity are absolutely wanting to the consciousness of the infant who uses the name of 'father.'   The differ-ences in the judgments applied to feelings and ethics are very great, and for obvious reasons.   What dif-ferent individuals understand by *good* and *bad, virtue* and *vice*, is impossible to bring under one definition, indisputable and undisputed.

The sum of the words at the disposal of any individual connects itself with his ideas: and it thus follows that the entire store of words forming the stock of any community must adapt itself to the whole stock of ideas belonging to any community, and must change as these change. The meaning of the words, again, must adapt itself to the standard of culture attained from time to time by each nation. New words must be created for new objects and new relations and kindred, though novel meanings must become attached to the old words—as in the case of *steel pen*, properly, 'a steel feather.' And again, a quantity of unobserved changes are constantly passing on language which are hardly remarked as such, and are the immediate result of a change in the whole culture of a nation. Such are the words *humility*, *talent*, *faith*, *spirit*, and the numerous other words referred to before, to which Christianity has given a deeper and more spiritual significance. Then, again, progressive skill may have worked striking changes in objects essentially the same: we call a Roman trireme, a Chinese junk, and a British man-of-war by the same name, *ship;* but we must admit that the ideas attaching to it have changed considerably. And thus it is with all objects capable of improvement by skill, and again with purely mental or intellectual conceptions, which change according to the changing conditions of culture of the community which possesses them.

CHAPTER V.

ANALOGY.

ALL the ideas consciously or unconsciously present in the human mind are directly or indirectly connected with one another. No thought, no conception, is so independent of all others as not to suggest some other idea or ideas in some way cognate or related. Thus, for instance, if we think of the action of walking, it is physically impossible not to call to mind, with more or less distinctness, the idea of a person who walks. And again, the idea of walking is likely also to evoke the idea of some of the varieties of that action, which we commonly indicate by such words as (to) *go*, *run*, *step*, *stalk*, *stroll*, *stride*, etc.

Thus it is clear that our *ideas* associate themselves into groups ; and, as a natural result of this, the words which we employ to express these ideas come similarly to associate themselves in our minds.

Words, then, which express related ideas, form themselves into groups. Another source, though not equally prolific, of such association, is similarity in sound. Thus the word *book* may remind us of *brook*, as it in fact reminded Shakespeare ; the word *alarms*, of '*to arms !* ' the word *hag*, of *rag* or *tag ;* the word *blue* may remind us of *few*. Such groupings are, how-ever, but very loose and ineffectual, unless a more or less close association (based on reality or fancy) co-operates in order to make them strong and suggestive. This may be seen by taking as examples the associations existing between *brook* and *book, blue* and *few*, on the one hand, and those existing between *alarms* and '*to arms !*' and *hag, tag,* and *rag*, on the other. There is no similarity of meaning, no similarity of contents between the words *book* and *brook;* the association, therefore, in this case is a very loose one, looser than that existing between *foot* and *boot*, for instance. On the other hand, the connection between the ideas of *alarms* and '*to arms !*' is more obvious : a sudden surprise, as in the case of an attack by an unexpected enemy, might often be connected with the idea of a call '*to arms !*' Similarly, *hag* and *rag* are ideas which often present themselves to our mind in connection with one another, and consequently the association between these two words is stronger than that, for instance, existing between *hag* and *flag*.

Correlation in the ideas, coupled with correlation of their contents, especially if accompanied by similarity of sound, makes the association most inevitable ; and the closer the correlation, or the greater the similarity, the stronger will be the tie which binds the members of the group.

It is necessary to the more exact classification of these groups, that we should first obtain a clear conception of the difference between what we may call the *material* contents of a word, on the one hand, and the *formal* or *modal* contents, on the other.

For this purpose, let us look at the two words *father* (singular) and *fathers* (plural). Both these words indicate a person or persons who stand in a certain and well-defined blood-relationship to some other person or persons. This meaning, common to both, we call their *material* contents. But the one form is used to indicate *one* such individual ; the other, to indicate any number more than one. This, the *unity* or *singularity* of the one, the *plurality* of the other, makes up the *formal* or *modal* contents of each. This *modal* part of the contents, in most of the languages of the Indo-European stock, is left without separate expression in the singular : in the plural, however, it is generally expressed or indicated by some change in form ; this change being, in most cases, made by the addition of some termination—in the example we have chosen, by the addition of *s.*

Before passing to another example, it is well to point out that the *modal* contents of a so-called "singular-form" by no means invariably imply unity ; nor, again, is the plural always, as in the case cited, formed from the singular. In such a sentence as *A father loves his child,* the idea expressed relates, or may relate, to more than a single father ; in fact, it may be taken as a statement made correctly or incorrectly of all fathers universally ; and, with regard to the second point mentioned, Welsh, among other languages, has many words in which the plural is expressed by the shorter collective form, and the single individual is indicated by a derivative, e.g. *adar,* birds ; *aderyn,* a bird : *plant,* children ; *plentyn,* a child : *gwair,* hay ; *gweiryn,* a blade of hay, etc.[1]

We can now come back to our point, and fix our attention on two such words as (*I*) *speak* and *speech.*

Both these words evoke the thought of some well-known and familiar activity called into play by our

[1] Cf. Rowland's Grammar of the Welsh Language, 4th edition, (Wrexham, Hughes), p. 23, § 132, where more instances, and also some from Armorican, are cited.

vocal organs. This constitutes the *material* contents of both alike. The former, however, conveys the idea that the action is being performed at the time the word is uttered; the other is the name of the result or product of that action. This, the *modal* part of their contents, is left unexpressed; or, to speak more accurately, we cannot divide the words so as to be able to say that one part serves to express the *material* contents, and another the *modal*,—a division which we could make in the case of *fathers*, and which we might make in, e.g., *speak, speaking; speech, speeches; book, books, booklet;* etc.

It will now be clear that, among associations based on correlation or on similarity of IDEA, this similarity may exist between the *material* contents of the words grouped together, or between their *modal* contents. We therefore are now in a position to distinguish between MATTER-GROUPS and MODAL-GROUPS.

To sum up, there exist association-groups based on—

    1. Similarity in sound only.
    2.   ,,   ,, meaning only.
    3.   ,,   ,, both sound and meaning.

These two latter classes (nos. 2 and 3) are sub-divided, as to the part of the meaning in which they agree, into (*a*) *matter*-groups and (*b*) *modal*-groups.

Instances of all these are numerous, and will readily suggest themselves; a few may suffice to illustrate further what has already been said.

If we were to set down in a vertical column the complete conjugation of some verb—say, of *to walk*,—and, parallel to this, with equal completeness and in the same order, the conjugation of the verbs *to write, to go,* and *to be,* we should then have in our vertical

columns four *matter*-groups. Taken horizontally, the
separate tenses would form so many *modal*-groups,
each divisible into smaller groups of singulars as
against plurals, or of first persons as against second
and third persons, etc. We should then, at the same
time, have illustrated the fact that in many cases
similarity of contents is accompanied by, or perhaps
we should say expressed by, similarity in sound, and
that it often happens that *similar change of modal
contents is accompanied by similar change in form or in
termination.*

Now, this fact, though far from holding good in all
cases, is of the greatest possible importance for the
development of language.

In order to realise this, let us for a moment suppose
a language in which no such 'regularity' held good :
in which 'I love' was expressed by *amo;* 'thou
lovest' by *petit;* 'he loves' by *audivimus;* and that
thus for every thought, every shade of meaning, every
modal variation of *material* contents, there existed a
new word in no way related to the others which indicate associated ideas. The language would in this
case be more difficult of acquirement for those born in
the country where it was indigenous than Chinese
writing and reading is to the Chinese, and would
almost defy the efforts of a foreigner to master it.
Like the Chinese, the natives would only by dint of
long-continued study be in a position to collect a
scanty vocabulary, which, in the case of the foreigner,
would prove more scanty still. The picture here given
of such a language is, indeed, nowhere fully realised ;
but some languages of savage tribes, in certain of their
features, approximate to the condition we have sketched.
Thus, for instance, in Viti, the *number* AND *the object
numbered* are expressed together in a single word,

varying for each number in each word; thus, *buru* signifies ten cocoa-nuts, *koro* a hundred cocoa-nuts; whilst *sclavo* signifies a thousand cocoa-nuts.[1]

Strange and far-fetched as this method of forming language may seem to us, and indeed is, it is after all merely a much exaggerated example of what we find in all modern languages, and, *e.g.*, in English, which, side by side with the normal terminations to indicate gender, as in *lion, lioness*, preserves such pairs as *bull, cow; stag, hind; cock, hen;* etc.

Now, why should a language constructed on such principles be so difficult to master as we have assumed it to be? Or, to put the case differently, why should a 'regular' language be more easily acquired than an irregular one? To discuss this may seem superfluous; but just as, in Algebra, some of the most important theorems are deduced from a thorough discussion of the principles of simple addition, so it will aid us in language to have a clear grasp of this point, to possess a full comprehension of the meaning of Analogy and its influence.

In our hypothetical language, *every* word would have to be acquired by a new and unaided effort of memory. In actually existing languages, this is not the case. Whether by precept or by observation, consciously or unconsciously, whether in the process of acquiring our own language in childhood, or in our study of a foreign tongue, we associate not only *words* but also *parts of words* with one another and with parts of *material* or *modal* contents of our thoughts. A child that learns to call a single book *book*, and more than one, *books*, and to proceed similarly in a large number of cases, comes unconsciously to connect the *s*, written or spoken, with

---

[1] Raoul de la Passerie: De la Psychologie du Langage. Paris, 1889, pp. 22, 41.

the idea 'many of them.' The child attaches regularly this sound or its symbol *s* to any word whose plural it needs to express; and (perfectly correctly as far as the logic of its case is concerned) says *one foot* and *two foots*, after the model of *one boot, two boots*. The child does not know that the form *foots* is contrary to established usage, while the form *boots* is in harmony with it; a series of corrections on the part of those who know the established usages will gradually imprint on its memory the usual form; but until this correction has occurred sufficiently often, the form *foots* will recur in the child's vocabulary. The sound or symbol *s*, or rather the habit of adding such a sibilant to a word or words which state something about more than one object, in order to denote plurality, leads sometimes to its being used in cases where 'correct' grammar omits it. A child will form words by a simple process of analogy, which seem curious enough to us, but are really quite simple and natural formations. Thus, *e.g.* a little one spoke of *two-gas-lits*, on seeing two gas-jets lit one after another; and—to add a parallel instance of another frequent termination—another child, when urged to 'come on,' replied, 'I cannot come quickerly.'

Such formations have been represented as the result of a kind of problem in linguistic proportion, somewhat like this :—

Given the knowledge of the formation *soon, sooner; large, larger;* etc., what is the value of *x* in the equation :—

Soon : sooner : : quick : x ?

Answer, *quicker*.

Next, given the knowledge of *large, largely; nice, nicely;* etc., what then is the value of *x* which satisfies :—

Large : largely : : quick : x ?
Answer, *quickly*.

When combined, these two problems yield a compound proportion sum, thus :—

$$\left. \begin{array}{l} Large : larger \\ Large : largely \end{array} \right\} : : quick : x.$$

To this, the answer would be quickli-er or quick-er-ly, and logically either answer is perfectly correct; they only differ in the practically all-important, but logically totally indifferent accident that the one happens to be usual, while the other is opposed to the normal usage.

In order to fully realise how readily such forms, whether 'correct' or 'incorrect,' may be coined, we must likewise bear in mind that for the apprehension of a child our divisions of sentences into words do not exist at all. The sentences which a child learns to understand are, at all events in the first instance, to its conception one and undivided, nay, apparently indivisible aggregates of sound, conveying somehow or another a certain notion. The infant answers to such a catena of sounds as *go-to-papa*, or *don't-do-that*, and *run-away*, long before it has the faintest conception of the meaning of such sentences as, e.g., *go that way*. It is only the incessant variations of the surroundings of a *word*, while that combination of sounds itself remains unaltered, which, by a *very* gradual process, brings to our consciousness the fact that the whole sentence is made up of separate elements, and enables us to distinguish the *word* as an unit of expression. This process, however, of the discovery of such units comes about unconsciously and tentatively ; whilst by all children and many adult speakers the extent of meaning attached to such units is very vaguely appreciated.

There is, therefore, in the linguistic history of each

speaker, a period in which such a sound-group as, e.g.,
noisier, seems to consist as much or as little of *two*
words as the group *more noisy*, etc.　The question
then presents itself, why, at a later period, we distinguish two words in the latter group, while we continue
to regard the former group as one?　The answer to
this is found in the fact that *both* the sounds, *noisy*
and *more*, are found to occur frequently alone or amid
totally different surroundings; they occur, however,
consistently maintaining the same meaning; whilst
of *noisier*, the first part only is used alone, and the
sound represented by *er*—whilst employed with many
other words to express a similar variation of idea—can
never, like *more*, serve independently to indicate that
variation, unaccompanied by the sound which expresses
the thought which it is desired to vary.　And the
same remarks hold good for other cases.

It would, no doubt, be going too far to assert that
the usual division of words in our written language is
wholly fanciful and unnatural.　But it is nevertheless
true that the division is not made in speaking, nor is
it always equally present in our consciousness while
we are uttering our thoughts.　The less educated the
speaker—in other words, the less he has been taught
to bring reflection into play—the less active and operative is this consciousness.

If, then, we represent the formation of such a word
as *quicker* in the shape of a solution of a proportion
problem, the identity between the linguistic and alge-
braical processes must not be too closely insisted on.
Similarly, we must not exaggerate the idea of clearness and distinctness present to the consciousness of
the speaker who expresses the idea 'rapid in movement' by *quick*, and a higher degree of rapidity in the
movement by the addition of the word *more* before it,

G

or *er* after it. The fact is that no comparison is an absolute identity. Both our descriptions of the process by which many of our words arise in our minds, viz. the proportion, and the composition of the two elements, are inexact in some respects; and in some respects one, in other respects the other, will prove less faulty. If in a formation like *quick, quicker*, it is more likely that the two syllables in *quick-er* maintain a certain independence of signification, still no such explanation could possibly apply to such a form as *brang*, heard from a child or a foreigner, instead of *brought*. No simpler way of describing this process can be found than the equation—

Sing : *sang* :: *ring* : *rang* :: *bring* : *brang*.[1]

Moreover, this is doubtless the process adopted by our reasoning in acquiring a foreign language. We are taught that *To speak* is to be rendered by *parler; I speak*, by *Je parle; I was speaking*, by *Je parlais*, etc. ; and our teacher expects (and naturally) that, possessing this knowledge, we shall be able, when he proceeds to inform us that *porter* means 'to carry,' to find the as yet unknown and unheard forms *Je porte, Je portais*, etc. At a later period, when we have read and spoken the language frequently, we form many similar tenses and persons of many verbs never or rarely encountered previously ; and no speaker could certainly affirm whether he owes the utterance of the word to his memory recalling it into renewed consciousness, or to a process of automatic regulation by analogy after the model of other similar and more familiar forms.

From the above examples it may be seen that

---

[1] So again, 'brung' can often be heard from children, and in German, 'gebrungen' appears as a humorous form, probably in imitation of an original blunder.

analogy is productive, not merely of abnormal forms, but also, and even to a larger extent, of normal forms. The operation of Analogy, however, attracts most attention when its influence leads to the formation of unusual forms, and this fact has prevented due credit being given to its full power and importance. It was once usual to speak of all forms employed by any speaker in conformity with normal usage as 'correct;' and of others, formed on the model of other examples, but deviating from normal usage, as 'incorrect;' in other words, as *mistakes*, or as formed BY FALSE ANALOGY. From what we have said it will be clear that this last term is wrong and misleading, and can only be applied as expressing that the analogy followed by the speaker in a certain case ought, for some reason or another, not to have been accepted as the *norm*.

Analogy, then, in most cases acts as a *conservative* agent in language by securing that its propagation and its continuity shall be subject to some degree of regularity. On the other hand, this very tendency to promote regularity and uniformity often makes itself felt by the *destruction of existing words or flections* which deviate from a given goal; and it is mainly when its destructive powers are manifest that its effects are deserving of separate discussion.

So long as a speaker employs or a nation continues to use the 'correct' form,—gradually, regularly, and naturally developing it according to the regular laws of phonetic change and growth to which it is subject for the time being,—it is immaterial for the student of language whether, in any particular case of the employment of a word, this regularity is due to memory or to analogy. It is when analogy produces forms phonetically irregular that its operation becomes of importance; and it is from the study of such

'novelties' amongst its productions, that we can alone
derive full information about its nature.   As long as
we find that the A.S. *stánas* remained *stánas*, or even
that this form was gradually changed into *stones*, we
are not tempted to call in the aid of Analogy, nor are
we challenged to prove its operation.   Similarly, as
long as the plural of *eáge* remains *eágan*, or *eáge*
changes into *eye*, and forms its plural *eyen*, no temp-
tation presents itself to inquire into Analogy or its
operation.   Even in this case, however, we cannot
help remarking that Chaucer might conceivably have
formed his plural *eyen* by analogy with other plurals
in *en*.   But it is when the form *eyen* is replaced by
eyes, that we naturally inquire whence comes the *s*?
And since no phonetic development can change *n* into
s, we know that analogy with other substantive plurals
is and must be the reason of the appearance of this
otherwise inexplicable form.   Thus the French *mesure*
could and did become the English *measure ;* but the
French *plaisir* could not, according to the laws of
phonetics, develop into *pleasure*.   We can only explain
the latter form by assuming that it is founded on the
analogy of the older forms *measure, picture*, etc.[1]

We ascribe to Analogy those cases of change in
form of words, in syntactical arrangement, or in any
other phenomenon of language, such as gender, etc.,
where the existing condition has been replaced by

---

[1] Cf. Studies in Classical Philology, No. II., B. I. Wheeler :
Analogy, and the Scope of its Application in Language (Ithaca,
N.Y., 1887), p. 7.   Much of what follows is taken from this little work,
which contains an admirable discussion of analogy, besides a highly
useful bibliography of the subject.   See also Jespersen's article in
the Internationale Zeitschrift für Allgemeine Sprachwissenschaft,
Zur laut-gesetz-frage, (1886).   Professor Wheeler, however, ranges
under 'Analogy-formation' much that we should prefer to consider
separately under 'Contamination.'

something new modelled upon some pattern furnished by other more numerous groups. Thus, for instance, we find that the Latin feminine nouns in *-tas, -tatis,* have developed French derivatives in *-té,* all of the feminine gender. Why, then, is *été* masculine, though equally derived from a feminine Latin *æstatem?* The answer lies in the fact that *printemps, automne,* and *hiver,* being all masculine, the feeling set in that the ' names of the seasons' should be masculine: just as names of trees are feminine in Latin, and this possibly under the influence of *arbor.* Thus *été* followed the example of the others, and was classed with them. The affinity in signification here caused the difference in gender to be felt as an incongruity, and the less strong came to be assimilated to the stronger and more universal type. Similarly, such words as *valeur* seem to have become feminine after the analogy of Latin abstracts in *-ura, -tas,* etc. In the former of these particular instances we had to deal with a ' MATTER-GROUP' of four cognate ideas, viz. ' the seasons ;' in which group, as three of the terms agreed in another accidental peculiarity, viz. that of gender, this peculiarity was imposed likewise upon the fourth member, so as to produce a more complete uniformity in every respect.

In other cases we find, perhaps indeed more frequently, MODAL groups thus extending their domain. Thus the comparative forms, which nearly all end in *er,* create the feeling that if a word expresses a comparative degree it may be naturally expected to end in *er ;* and *more* from *mo, lesser* instead of *less*—nay, even *worser* for *worse* is the result. In the case of *more,* its very form led to the supposition that *mo* was a positive form.

Similarly, the existence of the plurals in *s* in Anglo-Saxon, aided no doubt by the frequency of *s* plurals in

French, has caused this way of expressing the plural to embrace almost all English nouns; or, at all events, to embrace their formation to such an extent that the older methods (such as vowel modification, *e.g.* *mouse, mice; foot, feet;* formations in *en—ox, oxen,* etc.) now appear as exceptions, themselves needing explanation; and, again, as in the case of *more,* when once the rule was formulated which laid down that if a word expresses the plural it must end in *s,* the conclusion was drawn that, if a word ending in *s* be used as a plural, this *s* is the termination, and must be omitted in the singular. It thus happens that to the analogy of *fathers* as against *father,* *trees* as against *tree,* etc., we owe the sets *Chinese* used as a plural noun with its newly coined singular *Chinee; Portuguese* with its singular *Portuguee; cherries* (Fr. *cérise*), *cherry; pease* (Lat. *pisum*), *pea.* Nay, it is not even always necessary that the *s* form be used in a plural signification to cause the *s* to be 'removed' in order to express the singular; *a raedels* was perfectly good Old English, but as *two riddles* was right, the conclusion was natural that *one riddles* was wrong. *Two chaise* would not give offence, but it seemed natural to write and say *one shay.*

The modal group, again, consisting of such formations as *despotism, nepotism, patriotism,* etc., created the feeling that *tism* was the correct ending instead of *ism,* and so has manifested a tendency to supplant it. Thus the correcter form *egoism* has made way for *egotism.* Thus it is to the *pianist, machinist, violinist,* that the *tobacconist* owes his *n,* to which he has no right; he ought, properly speaking, to appear as *tobaccoist.*

The most widely reaching result of the operations of analogy is where *modal* and *matter* groups, in their cross classifications, unite to cancel irregularities created in the first instance by phonetic development. Thus the Anglo-Saxon form *scæd* (neuter) exists side by side with another form, *sceadu* (feminine). The Gothic form *skadus* proves the latter to belong to the *u* declension. But even in Anglo-Saxon this declension was but sparingly represented, most words originally belonging to it being declined according to the far more common scheme of words, like *stán*, stone; *dóm*, doom, etc.; others varying in their declensions between the feminines whose stem ended in *wâ*, or like those in *â*. In both these declensions the nominative ended in *u;* an example of the *wâ* declension being—

Nom. *beadu*, Gen. *beadwe*,

and of the *â* declension—

Nom. *giefu*, Gen. *giefe*.

Our word *sceadu* long oscillated between these two paradigms, and we consequently meet with a Gen. sing. *sceade*, as well as an Acc. plur. *sceadwa*. This termination, where *w* was maintained, developed into our present termination *ow*, seen in *shadow;* whilst the form *shade* is, properly speaking, a nominative form. Analogy, however, depending upon other nouns in which all cases in the singular had become identical in form, caused the form *shadow* to be used in the nominative as well as in other cases, and extended the use of *shade* over those cases which were declined. Similarly, the two forms *mead* and *meadow* are due, the one to a nominative, the other to the inflected cases of the same word, the A.S. *mǽd*. In these cases both forms survived, and the meanings became slightly differentiated; it more frequently happens that one succumbs. Thus the A.S. Nom. plur. of the pronoun for the second person *gé* developed into *ye*, the inflected case *éow* into *you*. The latter has now almost completely ousted the once correct nominative *ye*, which survives only in dialects or in elevated language, where, in its turn, it frequently supplants the accusative and dative *you*.

The regular development of preterite and past participle in many verbs, together with the dropping of the prefix *ge*, which in several Teutonic languages has become specialised as a mark of that participle, caused both these forms to converge into one. This has in its turn been the cause why, in the case of many verbs, where regular phonetic development kept preterite and participle asunder, one of these forms was made to serve for both.

The A.S. verb *berstan* was, in its preterite, conjugated thus :—

Indic.	*Bærst*	Subj.	*burste*
,,	*burste*	,,	*burste*
,,	*bærst*	,,	*burste*
,,	*burston*	,,	*bursten*
,,	*burston*	,,	*bursten*
,,	*burston*	,,	*bursten*

and its past participle was *borsten*. Thus the *u* was present in four of the six forms in the indicative, and in six subjunctive forms. The first effect of the operation of Analogy was to abolish this useless and cumbersome irregularity, and the *u* supplanted the *æ*, not long after this *æ* had become *a* (*barst*). Then the process set in which we explained above, and the past part. *borst* (*en*) was replaced by *burst*.

It would be easy to multiply these instances *ad infinitum*. Enough has, however, been said to explain the working of Analogy and to show how wide its application is. The student who has mastered this sketch, should proceed to study carefully the corresponding chapter in Paul's 'Principles of Language,' and the pamphlet, cited above, by Professor Wheeler, where many illustrations will be found taken from English and many other languages. One of the main points which are clearly brought out in the latter work is that the phenomena of folk-etymology show that these groupings are effectual in modifying form only in so far as a supposed likeness of contents or idea is associated (erroneously) with the resemblance of form.

Before concluding our remarks, we must, however, add a few words on the operation of Analogy where it works neither as a conservative nor as a destructive agent, but simply as a CREATIVE one.

In the cases hitherto discussed, the forms called into being have survived to the prejudice of older material which perished for lack of vitality. In the struggle for existence it succumbed. A new form, in order to survive, had necessarily to replace some unusual and inconvenient older one, or it was a necessary condition that several speakers, for some other reason, should concur in creating the same novel form.[1] That 'irregular' forms should continue to exist in the case of some of the commonest verbs, and in the pronouns, is explicable by the fact that these words occur with sufficient frequency to gain enough strength to resist innovation. The frequency of their occurrence induces familiarity. Any new form which some innovating speaker might create on the basis of some analogy is, in those words, too strongly felt as a

[1] The personal influence, or 'magnetism,' of the speaker or speakers who engender the 'mistake' is also an important element in determining its propagation. We, parrot-like, imitate the speech, like the manners, of some more readily than of others.

novelty; the speaker too frequently hears or reads the 'correct' form to permit the survival of the new candidate for general usage. The novelty is a 'mistake,' remains a 'mistake,' and succumbs in the struggle for existence. Frequency of use in the case of any particular word *may* assist its phonetic development and increase its impulse in that particular line, and its rate of speed on the road to phonetic decay:—this is as yet, however, a point of dispute among philologists, and a question which claims attention from all students of language. But there can be no doubt that the more frequent the occurrence of any particular form in ordinary speech, the more capacity it must gain for resisting the levelling tendencies, the absorbing influence of other more numerous but less common groups. It is, however, not true that all the offspring of Analogy is thus exposed to the struggle for existence. Where new ideas are to be expressed, Analogy guides us in our choice of terms, and even where the idea is not strictly new, but no term for it exists in the vocabulary or in the memory of a community, or even in that of the majority of such community, the new form will be adopted with little reluctance; nay, often without being felt as a new creation at all. In this way the language is always being enriched by new forms created on the analogy of existing ones. Where many instances might be given, a few will suffice.[1] The termination *y* of *mighty*, *guilty*, etc., was added to

---

[1] Cf. C. Goeders, Zur Analogie-bildung im mittel-und neu-englischen. (Kiel, 1884.) Dr. Goeders has collected an enormous mass of illustrative material. Some of his examples, however, may not prove as new as he thinks. Our posterity will be able to decide this point if Dr. Murray's Dictionary has made greater progress than at present. This apprehension, however, does not detract from the value of Goeders' work, nor from the truth of the proposition which he illustrates.

the nouns *earth*, *wealth*, etc., to form *wealthy*, *earthy*,—
nay, even used to form such hybrids as *savoury*, *spicy*,
racy. After the model of *kingdom*, *heathendom*, etc.,
were formed *princedom*, *popedom*, etc. The group
winsome, *blithesome*, etc., gave birth to *venturesome*,
meddlesome, etc. ; and whilst *sorrowful*, *thankful*, *baleful*, *shameful*, are found in A.S., no such antiquity can
be claimed for *blissful*, *youthful*, *faithful*, *merciful*,
respectful, etc.

It has been well remarked[1] that a perfect grammar
would be one which admitted no irregularities or
exceptions; and if all the operations of Analogy in
forms and syntax could be thoroughly mastered and
reduced to rule, exceptions and irregularities would be
far less common than they are.

[1] Henry, Étude sur l'Analogie en général et sur les Formations
de la Langue Grecque.   Paris, Maisonneuve, 1883.

CHAPTER VI.

THE FUNDAMENTAL FACTS OF SYNTAX.

A SENTENCE must be looked upon as the first creation of language. The SENTENCE IS THE SYMBOL WHEREBY THE SPEAKER DENOTES THAT TWO OR MORE CONCEPTIONS HAVE COMBINED IN HIS MIND; and is, at the same time, the means of calling up the same combination in the mind of the hearer. Any group of words which accomplishes this is a sentence, and consequently A SENTENCE NEED NOT NECESSARILY CONTAIN A FINITE VERB, as is sometimes alleged. In Latin, and in the Slavonic languages, the word answering to *is* is very commonly suppressed; and in Latin epistolary language whole sentences appear in which no copula occurs. Such combinations as *Omnia præclara rara; Suum cuique;* are perfectly intelligible. In English we often employ sentences like *You here? I grateful to you! This to me! Your very good health! Long life to you! Three cheers for him! Why all this noise?*—and, again, such proverbs as *Oak, smoke; Boys, noise; Ash, splash:* and these are just as much sentences as *The man lives.*

Language possesses the following means of expressing and specialising such combinations of ideas :—

(1) The simple juxtaposition of the words corresponding to the ideas ; as, *All nonsense ! You coward ! Away, you rogue !*

(2) The order of the words; as, *There is John*, as contrasted with *John is there ; John beats James*, as against *James beats John*.

(3) The emphasis laid upon these words; as in 'Charles is *not* ill.'

(4) The modulation of the voice; as when *Charles is ill* is stated as a mere assertion, and 'Charles is *ill?*' in which case the same words are turned into an interrogative sentence by the mere change of pitch during the utterance of the last word.

(5) The time, which commonly corresponds with the emphasis and the pitch ; the words in the previous sentences which are emphasised or spoken in a higher pitch respectively, will be found to occupy a longer time in utterance than the words composing the rest of the sentence.

(6) Link-words, such as prepositions, conjunctions, and auxiliary verbs.

(7) The modification of words by inflection, in which (*a*) the inflectional forms may, without other aid, indicate the special kind of combination which it is desired to express, as in *patri librum dat ; his books ; father's hat :* or (*b*) the connection between the words may be denoted by formal agreement; as, *anima candida, la bonne femme.*

The method of combining ideas by means of link-words and inflections is one which could only have set in after a certain period of historical development, for inflections and link-words are themselves of comparatively recent appearance in language; the other methods, on the contrary, must have been at the disposal of speakers from the very first development of language. It should, however, be noticed that 2–5 inclusive are not always consistently employed to represent simply the natural ideas as they present themselves, but are capable of a traditional development and, consequently, conventional application. For instance, in the Scandinavian languages the method of intonation is a purely artificial one ;[1] and in Chinese, homonyms are distinguished by lowering or raising the voice.

In Chinese the tones are five : a monosyllable may be uttered with (1) an even high tone ; with (2) a rising tone, as when we utter a word interrogatively; with (3) a falling tone, as when we say, *Go !*—with (4) an abrupt tone, as of demand ; or with (5) an even low

[1] Professor Almkvest kindly informs us that there are rules about the grave accent in the Swedish, but that they are difficult to investigate. The grave accent, as it occurs in Swedish, is quite peculiar, and nothing similar exists in other languages.

For instance, the first syllable in *bräder* (pl. of *bräde* = board) and *sånger* (pl. of *sång* = song) has the accent, but is musically lower than the second syllable, which has a feeble secondary accent, and is musically higher. This is different—in contradiction to *breder* (pres. of *breda* = to spread), where the first syllable has the accent, and is musically higher than the second syllable, which is quite without accent.

It is the first-named pronunciation, *brädè, brädèr; góssè* (a boy), *góssàr*, which has nothing corresponding to it in other languages.

(*a*) Short treatises for practical use :—
Sweet: On Sounds and Forms of Spoken Swedish (1½ pp. about accent), in *Transactions of the Philological Society*, 1877–79.
Schwartz and Noreen: Swedish Grammar: Stockholm, 1881 (4 pp. about accent, mostly practical).
(*b*) Scientific works—
Lythkius and Wulff: About the Rules of Sounds and Signs in the Swedish Language, and about the Accent; Lund, 1885; 460 pp. (in Swedish).
Koch: Philological Researches about Swedish Accent; Lund, 1878; 211 pp.
Paul: Grundriss der German. Philol., vol. i., abschn. 5, pp. 417, etc. : Geschichte der Nordischen Sprachen, von Noreen (gives the historical cause for, and explains the growth of the grave accent).

tone. These are the tones of the Mandarin dialect, which is the language of the cultivated classes ; and, in their application, they are limited by euphonic laws, so that they cannot all be used with all syllables.[1]

The idea, or the nature of the combination intended to be expressed by the speaker, need not be completely represented by words in order to render fully intelligible the thought present in the mind of the speaker. Much less than a complete expression will often suffice.

If a sentence is the means of inducing a certain combination of at least two ideas in a hearer's mind, a complete sentence must necessarily consist of at least two parts. We shall later discuss those sentences in which only one of the two parts is expressed in words, and shall here confine our attention to the complete sentence. Grammar teaches us that a complete sentence consists of a subject and a predicate. Now, these grammatical categories are undoubtedly based upon a psychological distinction ; but we shall soon see that it does not necessarily follow that the grammatical and psychological subject, or the grammatical and psychological predicate are always identical. The PSYCHOLOGICAL SUBJECT expresses the *conception which the speaker wishes to bring into the mind of the hearer ;* the PSYCHOLOGICAL PREDICATE indicates *that which he wishes him to think about it.* This, and no more than this, is required to impart to any collection of words the nature of a sentence.

In grammar we commonly attach a much more restricted meaning to the terms 'subject,' 'predicate,' and 'sentence.' For instance, when the predicate is a noun, we demand that the normal sentence should express the comprehension of the subject in a wider class ; as, *John is a boy :* or that it should express

---

[1] Byrne, Principles of the Structure of Language, p. 475.

some quality of the subject; as, *John is good:* or, lastly, that the subject be identical with the predicate; as, *John is King of England.* But in reality we have, in many sentences, noun-predicates which show us relations of quite another kind, expressed by the mere collocation of subject and predicate, as in many proverbs and proverbial expressions; e.g., *One man, one vote; Much cry and little wool; First come, first served; A word to the wise; Like master, like man; Better aught than naught; Small pains, small gains.* This is the way in which children make themselves intelligible; as, *Papa hat,* for *Papa has a hat on:* and this is the way in which even adults endeavour to express their meaning to foreigners when the latter have not mastered more of the language than perhaps a few nouns, viz. by mentioning the objects which they wish to bring under the notice of their companions, and trusting to the situation to enable these to understand their meaning. We say, *Window open,* and we are understood by the foreigner to mean that the window is open, or that we wish it open, as the circumstances may show.

Originally, there was only one method of marking the difference between subject and predicate, viz. stress of tone; as, *e.g.,* in the instance which we just gave, of 'Window open.' If these words are pronounced with a great stress on 'window,' we at once perceive them to mean, The thing which is (or which I wish to be) open is the *window.* If, on the other hand, we exclaim, 'Window OPEN,' with stress on 'open,' we at once convey the sense, The window is (or must be) *open,* not closed. This shows that, in the case of such isolated instances, the psychological predicate has the stronger accent, as being the more important part of the sentence, and the part containing the new matter.   Again, the place held in the sentence by the subject and predicate respectively, may have afforded another means of distinction between the two.   Different views have been held as to the respective precedence of subject and predicate in the consciousness of the speaker.   The true view seems to be that the idea of the subject is the first to arise in the consciousness of the speaker ; but as soon as he begins to speak, the idea of the predicate, on which he wishes to lay stress, may present itself with such force as to gain priority of expression, the subject not being added till afterwards.   Take, for example, the opening of Keats' Hyperion—

> 'Deep in the shady sadness of a vale
> Far sunken from the healthy breath of morn,
> Far from the fiery noon, and eve's one star,
> Sat grey-haired Saturn, quiet as a stone.'

In this case, the superior emphasis gained by the position of the predicate in the first place causes the speaker to set it there, and is indicative of the superior importance which he attaches to it.[1]

Similarly, the subject is sometimes expressed first by a pronoun, whose relation only becomes clear to the listener when expressed more definitely at a later period ; as—

> 'She is coming, my dove, my dear.'
> > (Tennyson, Maud.)

> 'She dwelt among the untrodden ways
> Beside the springs of Dove,
> A maid whom there were none to praise
> And very few to love.'
> > (Wordsworth, The Lost Love.)

> 'She was a staid little woman, was Grace.'
> > (Dickens, Battle of Life.)

This construction is extremely common in French ;

---

[1] Cf. Spencer, Philosophy of Style.

as, 'Elle approche, cette mort inexorable;' 'Mais ce qu'elle ne disait point, cette pauvre bergère.'

The transposition, then, of subject and predicate may be considered an anomaly; but it is an anomaly of frequent occurrence, and is based on the importance which the predicate assumes in the mind of the speaker.

We have seen that single words may possess concrete and abstract significations,[1] and it is the same with sentences. A sentence is concrete when either the psychological subject or the psychological predicate is concrete; as, *This man is good.* But as far as the mere form goes, concrete and abstract sentences need not differ; for instance, an expression like *The horse is swift* (which, when it does not refer to any particular horse, is an 'abstract' sentence) is identical in form with the expression *The horse is worthless*, which obviously refers to some particular horse, and is therefore 'concrete.' It is the situation and circumstances alone which mark the different nature of the sentences. There are, however, sentences which, with a concrete subject, have a partially abstract meaning. If, for instance, on hearing a lady sing, one remarks, *She sings too slowly*, the sentence is entirely concrete; but the same words may be used to express that the singer is in the habit of singing too slowly, in which case the predicate becomes abstract. Such sentences may be called 'concrete abstract.'

It was stated that at least two members are necessary to make up a sentence. It seems, at first sight, a contradiction to this statement that we find sentences composed of merely a single word, or of a group of words forming a unit. The fact is that, in this case, one member of the sentence is assumed

---

[1] On the sense in which the words *concrete* and *abstract* are here used, see Chap. IV., p. 45.

and finds no expression in language.   Commonly this member is the logical subject.   This subject may, however, be completed from what precedes, or is sufficiently clearly indicated by the circumstances of the case; or, again, in conversation, it is often necessary to take it from the words of the other speaker. The answer is frequently a predicate alone; the subject may be contained in the question, or the whole question may be the logical subject.   If I say, *Who struck you?* and the answer is *John*, the subject is, in this case, contained in the question, and the answer is, 'The striker is John.'   If I say, *Was it you?* the whole question is the logical subject, and the answer, *Yes, No, Certainly, Surely, Of course*, etc., is the logical predicate, as if the reply had been, 'My being so is the case.'   Many other similar words may serve as the predicate to a sentence spoken by another, such as *Admittedly, All right, Very possibly, Strange enough, No wonder, Nonsense, Stuff, Balderdash*, etc.

In other cases, the surrounding circumstances, or what is called 'the situation,' forms the logical subject. If I say, 'Welcome!' and at the same time stretch out my hand to a new arrival, this is equivalent to saying, *You are welcome*, and *welcome* is the logical predicate.   In exclamations of sudden astonishment and alarm, such as *Fire! Thieves! Murder! Help!* it is the situation which is the logical subject.   Challenges are instances of the same kind, e.g. *Straight on or not? Right or left?   Back or forward?*   When the poet sings—

> 'A wet sheet and a flowing sea,
>   A wind that follows fast,
> And fills the white and rustling sail,
>   And bends the gallant mast,'

the situation, again, is the logical subject.

It should be noticed that, in the case of sentences expressed by a single member, the word which for the speaker is the psychological predicate becomes for the hearer the subject. A man, seeing a house on fire, cries '*Fire!*' for him *the situation* is the subject, and the idea of *fire* is the predicate. The man who hears '*Fire!*' cried before he himself sees it, conceives of *fire* as the subject, and of *the situation* as the predicate. Sentences may, however, occur in which both speaker and hearer apprehend what is uttered as the subject, and the situation as the predicate. Supposing, for instance, that two persons have agreed that the fire shall be extinguished before they go out, and one of them, observing the chimney smoking, cries out, ' The fire!' in this case the fire, the logical subject, is alone denoted, and the predicate is gathered by the person addressed from the situation, which is evident from the speaker's gestures. If, again, two friends are travelling, and one remarks that the other is without his umbrella, the mere exclamation, 'Your umbrella!' suffices to make the latter complete the predicate. The vocative, again, pronounced as such, and intended to warn or entreat, suggests a psychological predicate which it lacks in words. On the other hand, by the side of a verb in the second person without subject pronoun, the vocative may be apprehended as the subject to the verb. If I say, ' Come!' the vocative (the person addressed) may be apprehended as the subject to this verb ; if it be Charles, the meaning is, *Charles should come.*

It is a question much disputed, and not yet decided, whether impersonal verbs should be regarded as lacking a subject or not. If we regard the grammatical form alone, we cannot doubt that sentences like *It snows, It freezes, It is getting late,* have a subject.   But there is no reason for alleging that this subject (*it*) can be treated as a logical subject; a logical subject must admit of a definite interpretation, and it is difficult to give one in this case.   Again, in the case of impersonal verbs, like the Latin *pluit*, the Greek ὔει, the Sanscrit *varśati*, (it rains), and the Lithuanian *sninga* (it snows), the formal subject *may* be found in the 'personal' termination, which is supposed to be the remnant of a word signifying *he*, *she*, or *it*.   And it seems natural to recognise a formal subject in this case, but, at the same time, to notice that this formal subject stands apart from the psychological subject.   It seems probable that an older stage of language existed, in which the bare verbal stem was set down; just as in Hungarian at the present day, where the third person of the present singular has no suffix, the first and second terminating in -*ok* and -*s* respectively.   In Anglo-Saxon we find passive and other impersonal verbs used absolutely, without any subject expressed or understood; thus, þám ylcan dóme e þé démoð eów byð gedémed (= With the same judgment that ye judge, to you (it) shall be judged); *him hungrede* (=N.H.G. es hungerte ihn).[1]   The psychological subject is, then, as little expressed in the sentence *It is hot*, as in the sentence *Fire*. But although it is not expressed, it would be unsafe to assume its non-existence, for here, as well as everywhere else, we have two ideas conjoined, in the same way as when we exclaim, *Fire!*   In this case there is, on the one side, the perception of a concrete phenomenon; on the other, the abstract idea of burning or of fire: and just as that perception is brought by our exclamation under the general idea of burning, so in the statement *It rains*, the perception

---

[1] Mason's English Grammar, p. 149, note.

of what is going on is by our words ranged under the general notion of water falling in drops from the sky. Our conclusion, therefore, is this : sentences like *Fire !* as well as those like *It rains,* have both psychological subject and predicate; but in the former case no subject is expressed, whereas in the latter *a formal* subject is employed, which, however, does but imperfectly, if indeed at all, correspond to the psychological one. This holds good unless we conceive of the formal subject, *It,* as standing for that which we see or that which is happening now. In this case, the peculiar nature of the impersonal verbs would be restricted to the difficulty, but not the impossibility, of explaining their subject.

We have defined the sentence as the expression for the connection of two ideas. Negative sentences may seem, at first sight, to contradict this, since they denote a separation. But the ideas must have met in the consciousness of the speaker before judgment can be pronounced whether they agree or disagree. In fact, the negative sentence may be defined as the statement that the attempt to establish a connection between the ideas has failed. The negative sentence is, in any case, of later date than the positive, and though, in all known languages, negation now finds a special expression, it is possible to imagine that negative sentences might be found in some primitive stage of language, wherein the negative sense was indicated by the stress alone and the accompanying gestures. Cf. such sentences as '*I* do this ?' or 'Eine ego ut adverser?' (Ter., And., I. v. 28.)[1] At all events sentences of assertion and sentences of demand border on each other very closely, and can be expressed by the same forms of language. The different shades of meaning

[1] Cf. Zumpt, Lat. Gr., § 609.

attaching to the words can be recognised only by the different tones conveying the feeling meant to be indicated.

Wishes and demands, again, touch each other very closely ; and it is natural to suppose that, in an early state of linguistic consciousness, a wish would have been equivalent to a demand. A sentence like ' Heads up !' expresses a demand or wish, but it might equally convey an assertion. We can say perfectly well, ' *They entered, heads up*,' or ' *erect ;*' and we hear quite commonly, *Heads up !* meaning, ' Hold your heads up !' And indeed such sentences of demand, or imperative sentences, would naturally be the first to present themselves to primitive mankind, whose utterances, like those of children nowadays, would naturally take the shape of requests that their immediate needs might be satisfied. We employ many such sentences at the present day, such as *Eyes right ! Attention ! Hats off ! This way ! All aboard ! Joking apart ; An eye for an eye ; Peace to his ashes ! A health to all good lasses ! Away with him ! Out with him !* Then, again, there are sentences composed of a single linguistic member ; such as *Hush ! Quick ! Slow ! Forward ! Up ! Off ! To work !*

Two kinds of interrogatory sentences must be distinguished : (1) those that put in question *one only* of the members of which they are composed, and (2) such as contain nothing affirmative, but are *purely* interrogatory in their nature. No satisfactory names have as yet been given to these two classes, but a study of one or two examples will show that the difference is real, and will tend to illustrate it. Such a sentence as *Who has done this ?* or *Where did you get that ?* no doubt asks a question as to the name of the doer of a certain deed, or the place where a particular object was obtained, but, at the same time, certainly assumes that the interrogator takes for granted that a certain deed was done by some one, or a certain object obtained by the person addressed.   In fact, the form of the interrogation is to some extent affirmative. No such affirmation, however, is present in such questions as *Can you speak French? Will you come? Have you money?* etc.

Of these two classes of questions, the former are certainly of the more recent origin, for they demand the employment of an interrogative pronoun or adverb, with which the latter can dispense.   It is noteworthy that in I.E. languages these interrogative words are at the same time indefinite; and it is hard to decide which of the two meanings should be regarded as the original.   On the one hand, it is easy to conceive how a word bearing an interrogative meaning could assume an indefinite one.   If we are accustomed to employ the word *who* when we wish to know who a person is, but are uncertain, we may easily proceed to apply this word in a case where we are uncertain (or wish to appear so), though we do not ask for information.   *A who-person has done this*, is not and has never been an English method of expressing, 'Some one has done it.'[1]   But it is conceivable that, at some stage of the I.E. languages, our linguistic ancestors may have adopted a similar mode of expression.   On the other hand, it is as easy to imagine that a word expressive of uncertainty, or absence of knowledge or information, should be used to indicate the desire for it.   In fact, we actually do employ a method akin to this when we use the indefinite *any* to show that we desire to know; *e.g.*, if, upon entering a dark room, we ask, *Any one*

---

[1] But cf. *Quisnam hoc fecit?* in Latin, by the side of *Si quis hoc fecit.*

here ? This, of course, is not, and never has been, in English, equivalent to ' *Who* is here ? '—but still it is quite conceivable that at some early linguistic period this transition has actually been made. Could it be demonstrated that it ever actually was made, the transition from the questions in our second category, to those falling under our first, would be explained. For suppose the question *Is any (one) here ?* (an order of words to which we now are bound, but which, as we shall see, was not always the necessary order) to be put as *Any (one) is here?* the proximity of this sentence to *Who is here ?* is at once evident.

Questions with an interrogative pronoun stand nearer still to questions with an indefinite pronoun where a negative answer is expected, as appears when we set *What can I answer?* by the side of *Can I answer anything?—Who will do this?* by the side of *Will any one do this ?—Where is such a man ?* by the side of *Is there such a man ?* The question to which the simple answer ' yes ' or ' no ' is expected is in many languages expressed by a special particle. Thus *ne* in Latin serves to mark an interrogation, and the stress is laid upon the word to which the interrogative particle is affixed. At present, the Teutonic and Romance languages almost universally express interrogation by the order of the words ; but this inverted order by no means necessarily involves interrogation, and in former times was very frequently employed in affirmative clauses. Thus, for instance, in A.S.—

> ' Ne hýrde ic cymlícor ceól gegyrwan : '
> Not heard I comelier keel to have been prepared
> = I never heard . . .   (Beowulf, 38).

> ' Saegde se ðe cûðe ' (ibid., 90) :
> Said he that knew = He . . . said.

> ' Waes seó hwíl micel ' (ibid., 146) :
> Was the time great = The time was long.

Even now we have many interrogations in which the stress or tone alone marks their nature ; as, *Any one there ? All right ? Ready ? A glass of beer, sir ?* (spoken by a waiter). We can thus conceive it possible that, for a long time, sentences may have existed without any sign except the tone to indicate their interrogative nature.

Simple interrogative sentences hold in some ways a middle position between positive and negative sentences of assertion. They may, in fact, be thrown into a positive or a negative form at choice; the positive form naturally presenting itself as the simpler, while the function of the negative form is to modify the question pure and simple. Such modifications may, indeed, cause the interrogation to take something of the character of the sentence of assertion. We may, for instance, mention a fact and expect it to be confirmed by another. In this case, we may employ a negative interrogatory sentence; as, *Were you not there ? I thought I saw you !* Or we may employ a positive interrogatory form of sentence, showing by the tone of query alone the nature of the sentence ; as, *You were there, I think ? You are quite happy ?* We thus see, by examples taken from both the positive and negative side, how nearly the sentences of interrogation touch the sentences of assertion.

Another way in which sentences of interrogation and assertion approach one another is in the expression of admiration or surprise. To express such feelings we may employ either (1) the interrogative or (2) the assertive form of sentence, marking the latter, however, by a tone expressive of interrogation. Thus we may say, *Is Francis dead ?* or express the same idea by saying, *Francis is really dead ?* emphasising the word *really* and raising the voice at the last word.

Thus, too, we can ask the direct question, *Are you here again?* or employ the assertive form, *You are here again?*[1]

Sentences expressive of surprise without a verb, may be classed either with the interrogative form, or with the assertive form with the interrogatory tone. They occupy a neutral ground between the two. Thus, *You my long lost brother?* *What, that to me?* *What, here already?* *So soon?*[2] And infinitival clauses are similarly used; as, *I to herd with savage races!* etc. (Tennyson, Locksley Hall); *Mene incepto desistere victam?* (Vergil, Æneid, I. 37). This use is very common in French; cf. *Moi vous abandonner!* (Andrieux); *Et dire qu'à moi seul je vins à bout de toutes ces prévisions!* (Daudet). We find, also, expressions of surprise in which the psychological subject and predicate are connected by 'and:' *So young and so worn out?* *A maid and be so martial?* (Shakespeare, 1 Henry VI., II. i.).[3] The expression of surprise is sometimes weakened into a mere conventional formula for opening a conversation; as, *Always in good spirits?* *Busy as always?* *Busy yet?*

The primitive form of expression without any finite verb is especially common in the indignant repudiation of an assertion; as, *I a liar?* 'She ask *my* pardon?' *How! not know the friend that served you?* *Ego lanista?* *Io dir bugie?*

What is vaguely known as the rhetorical class of

---

[1] Thus, in French: *Ma fille l'aimerait?* (Duval); *Vous n'avez nul remords?* (Delavigne); *Ces messieurs viennent de Paris?* (Picard). Latin: *Clodius insidias fecit Miloni?* (Cicero, pro Mil., xxii.).

[2] Thus, in French: *Richard député, pourquoi pas?* (Dumas); *Rien de Monsieur le duc de Richelieu?* (Dumas).

[3] Similarly, in French: *Quoi tu connais l'amour et tu n'es pas humain!* (Ducis).

questions arises from a desire, on the part of the interrogator, to make the person addressed reflect upon and admit the truth of information indirectly contained in the interrogation. Such are the questions in some catechisms, and those in the 'Guide to Knowledge;' e.g., *Do not mulberry trees often bear two crops of leaves in a year? Must not every substance be prepared before it receives the colour?* This use of the interrogation and interrogative form is, of course, of much more recent date than the other common usages.

The foregoing consideration of the sentence in its simplest form, as consisting of simple subject and predicate only, will have prepared us for the study of the development of all other syntactical relations from this the only primitive one. For all other extensions of the sentence—with the single exception of the copulative union of two simple ones — arise from the repetition of the relation between subject and predicate.[1] The copulative extension is now commonly indicated by means of conjunctions or other particles; e.g., ' John wrote *and* Alfred was reading : ' but even now mere co-ordination is sufficient; as, *John wrote, Alfred read ; He came, he saw, he conquered ; One rises, the other falls ; Men die, books live ;* etc. It is therefore easy to imagine that, at one time, this mere juxtaposition, which seems to us an exceptional usage, may have been the regular one.

Among the other extensions, two main cases are to be distinguished, as either (1) two equivalent members combine in the same clause with another (*i.e.* two subjects with one predicate, or two predicates with a single subject); or[2] (2) a combination (*a*) of

---

[1] We must not forget that these terms are here used in the very widest sense, and not in the limited meaning of ordinary grammar.

[2] See pp. 119, fol.

subject and predicate becomes, as such, the *subject* or predicate of some other word or combination (*b*), which latter is then the *predicate* or subject to (*a*) the former.

It is not easy to illustrate these extensions by instances drawn from modern English : nay, it is impossible if we insist upon invariably framing sentences which the present state of our language would regard as admissible.   But we must remember that we are now attempting to trace the probable development of our syntactical relations, or rather of our method of expressing the various syntactical relations, as it proceeded during a very primitive stage of the history of language.   At this period the speakers were struggling to find intelligible utterance for their thoughts, which were themselves but primitive, con-fused, childish.   All the examples which we have given heretofore should be regarded therefore merely as illustrating processes common in very remote lin-guistic periods, and not as instances of what is usual at the present period.   We have found it necessary on previous occasions to illustrate our arguments by combining English words in a way which is not and has never been English,—the advantage of such illustration being that it aided us to understand, at least in a certain measure, the mode in which our linguistic ancestors of ages long past thought.   To this artifice we shall find it necessary to revert some-what largely, as the analytical character of modern English, with its necessarily fixed order of words, has effaced most traces of this primitive state of language.

We should have an instance of the first main case of extension mentioned if, after saying, e.g., *John reads*, we remembered that *Alfred* too was reading, and then merely added this second subject.   We have shown that we must not suppose that *originally* the order of the words was, as is now invariably the case in modern English, (1) subject, (2) verb: so that *John read* (without inflection, *read* being a mere name of the action) was just as correct as *read John*, but not more so. If we clearly grasp this, we can fully understand that such a combination as *John read Alfred* (or, indeed, *John, Alfred read*) might once have been intelligible for what we should now express by *John and Alfred are reading.*

Similarly, a little linguistic imagination will suffice to enable us to conceive of the production by those primitive language-makers of a sentence like *Sing*(ing) *John dance*(ing) to express *John sings and dances.* Such constructions of two equal parts in combination with a third might be symbolised. Thus we might put *s* for subject, *p* for predicate, then the symbolisation would run *sps*, *ssp*, *psp*, or *spp*, etc., or $a+b+a$.[1]

In the first fictitious example, the two subjects stood BOTH IN PRECISELY THE SAME RELATION to the predicate, and in the second the two predicates stood in exactly the same relation to the subject. In such cases, the facts may be described just as correctly and just as completely by a sentence consisting of two parts only, viz., a compound subject, consisting of the two joined by a copula, + the predicate (or subject +

---

[1] This symbol is somewhat different from the one employed by Professor Paul, which is $(a+(b)+c)$. Though we think the one we have chosen is rather more simple, the other is not difficult to understand, as symbolising the result of combining $(a+b)$ with $(b+c)$. If, instead of two similar sets of brackets, different ones were used, say $\{a+[b]+c]$, the meaning of what now appears as (b) might be clearer still. Professor Paul uses a, b, and c as indicating three different *parts;* we use three letters for three parts, but make two letters alike, because two of the three parts have the same *function.* Cf., later on, for our symbol of the second case, page 119.

compound predicate). Of these two modes of expression, closely allied as they are, the one appears to us strange and, indeed, impossible,—the other so familiar that we can hardly imagine a state of language in which both alike may have been regular. On the other hand, we have no difficulty in seeing how the two systems have become confused.

All traces, therefore, of the construction which we have now lost are interesting and worth studying. A sentence like Cicero's *Consules, prætores, tribuni plebis, senatus, Italia cuncta a vobis deprecata est* (= Consuls, prætors, tribunes of the plebs, the senate, all Italy implored of you) is constructed much upon the model of the method now obsolete. In this case, however, the construction seems to us less unnatural, because the subject last named in the sentence, viz., *Italia*, may be considered to include all the others and to stand alone in their stead : hence it is that we find the verb in the singular, and hence the feminine gender of *deprecata* (implored). In another passage Cicero says, *Speusippus et Xenocrates et Polemo et Cantor nihil ab Aristotele dissentit.* This would be a perfect instance of *ssp* were it not for the insertion of *et*, which (due, as it is, to confusion with the compound subject in the sentence consisting of two parts only) would lead us to expect that the verb would be placed in the plural. It is, however, precisely this fact that the verb stands in the singular which demonstrates that it belongs as predicate to each subject separately, and not to the group indicated by the enumerated subjects jointly. In M.H.G. we meet with such constructions, especially those where *one* part — as the subject, for instance—is placed *between* the two others ; as, *Dô spranc von dem gesidele her Hagene alsô sprach* = ' Then sprang from the seat hither Hagen thus spoke.'

In A.S., too, we find occasionally a somewhat similar construction, as in Beowulf, 90–92 : *Saegde se ðe cúðe . . . cwæð ðæt se Ælmihtiga* = 'Said he who knew . . . spoke that the Almighty.' If we change the order, and add *and*, we transform this sentence into one of two parts : SUBJECT, *he who knew ;* PREDICATE (compound), *said and spoke.* Even in modern language this construction is not wholly without parallels. Cf. *Another love succeeds, another race* (Pope, Essay on Man, iii., line 130) ; cf. also, *Dust thou art, to dust returnest* (Longfellow).

Or, again, we find sentences where the two equal parts both follow or both precede. *He ðæs frófre gebád, wéox under wolcnum, weorðmyndum ðáh* (He received consolation [compensation], grew up under the clouds [= on earth], increased in fame) (Beowulf, 7) ; *He weepeth, wayleth, maketh sory cheere* (Chaucer, Canterbury Tales, 3618) ; *Is Bushy, Green, and the Earl of Wiltshire dead?* (Shakespeare, Richard II., Act III., ii., 141) ; *Of ðære heortan cumað yfele geðancas, mannslyhtas, unriht-hæmedu, forligru, stale, léase gewitnyssa, tællíce word* (Matt. xv. 19).

But it is also quite conceivable that (REMEMBERING THE EXTENDED MEANING WHICH, FOR THE PRIMITIVE STAGE OF LANGUAGE, WE MUST ATTACH TO THESE TERMS) two subjects should come into the consciousness as related to the same predicate, even though that RELATION is OF a very DIFFERENT NATURE in the case of the one from that in the other. To illustrate this, let us remember that the noun must once have been uninflected, or, at least, no definite system of inflection had been evolved ; the verb had a much vaguer and less definite meaning than at present ; the order of words had not yet begun to be significant ; that *John strike,* as well as *strike John,* or words equivalent in meaning, could stand for *John strikes*, or *John has been striking;* nay, even, if only accompanied by appropriate gestures, for *John was struck*, or *John is being struck.*

Even at present, in the case of a verb like *to smell*, the relation between the subject and predicate differs essentially when we say, *I smell the flower;* or, *The flower smells.* An effort on the part of our linguistic imagination is again needed, but the effort need not be very difficult, in order to enable us to realise that in a sentence like *John smell flower*, or *John strike Alfred*, BOTH nouns may once have been felt as standing in the subject relation to the predicate ; so that, again, in the latter sentence, gestures or circumstances were needed in order to make it clear who was the acting subject and who the suffering subject, whereas, in the former sentence, no such confusion could arise.

If we take a sentence like ' Give him a book,' we feel both the person and the thing as *objects* of the action ; and observation of this fact will enable us further to understand still more clearly that, at an older period of language, two subjects may have stood in the same sentence with the same predicate, though the relation between them and that predicate was not the same. It may further aid us to understand how, when once one of these subjects had developed into the grammatical category of OBJECT, the possible relations of such objects were so varied that the differentiation into various grammatical categories of accusative, dative, etc., becomes intelligible and natural.

The object, when once developed, may and often does become, by the nature of its relation to the predicate, a mere limitation or definition of such predicate, instead of remaining a member of the sentence equivalent in importance and weight with the subject, as it is, *e.g.*, in such sentence as *John strikes Alfred:* whilst in a sentence like *John runs a mile*, the object is a mere attribute to the predicate, and the sentence can no longer be looked upon as tripartite, but must be regarded as consisting of two parts, *i.e.* (1) the subject, and (2) the predicate with its extension. These two cases, however, are not separated by any clear line of demarcation.

And just as the predicate may receive such a defining word, so may the subject and the object developed from it. These now commonly occur in the shape of attributes,. whether substantival or adjectival, and genitives of substantives; as, *The cattle are the farmer's best; The cattle are beautifully fat.* This could not be expressed at all in languages which have as yet developed no inflections: these could merely employ the defining word in juxtaposition to the word defined; as, in Chinese, *T'su sin heu sin t'u ye*, literally meaning 'Origin Sin prince Sin spring *final part*,' *i.e.* 'Originally the prince of Sin sprang from Sin,' *i.e.* 'was born of a woman of the Kingdom of Sin.' The fact that the determinant attached to the subject is not a predicate can then only be discovered by the presence of a third word which is detached from the two words that together make up the subject by a greater stress or, it may be, by a slight pause. Thus, if we say, *liber pulcher*, it is impossible to say whether *pulcher* is a predicate or merely the attribute to *liber*, unless we add some verb like *est* or *habetur*, or unless the custom of the language leads us to apprehend *pulcher*, from its position, as a predicate.

In truth the determinant, in this case 'pulcher,' is nothing but a degraded predicate, uttered not so much for *its own* sake, *i.e.* for the information it conveys, as in order to assign to this group of subject and deter-

minant a further predicate, which predicate then conveys the real information ; as, *Liber pulcher nobis gaudio
est: Hæc res agetur nobis, vobis fabula* (Plautus,
Captivi, Prologue.)

We have stated that the determinant is merely a
degenerate or degraded predicate.   The meaning of
this statement may be most easily apprehended from
cases in which the finite verb is affected by this
degeneration, so that of the two predicates one might
be logically replaced by a relative sentence ; as, *There
is a devil haunts thee* (Henry IV., Pt. I., Act II., iv.) ;
I have a mind presages me (Merchant of Venice, I. i.) ;
He groneth as our bore lith in our stie (Chaucer, Canterbury Tales, 7411) ; *And was war of a pistel stood
under a wal* (Tale of Gamelyn) ; *I'll have none shall
touch what I shall eat* (Massinger, City Madam, I. i.) ;
I can tell you news will comfort you (ibid., III. i.) ;
The price is high shall buy thy vengeance (Middleton,
Spanish Gipsy, V. i. 443).

A similar construction was found in the older
stages of the Romance languages ; cf. O.Ital. *Non vi
rimasse un sol non lacrimassi* (' There remained none
did not cry ') ; O.Fr. *Or n'a baron ne li envoit son
fil* (' There is no baron does not send him his son ').
Nor must we suppose that this construction is one
peculiar to the Indo-European languages, and entirely
inherited from an early stage in their development.
Its use in Teutonic languages becomes more general
towards the end of the Middle Ages than before that
time.   But even in Semitic languages like Arabic, we
meet with expressions such as ' I passed by a man
slept.'

In the above instances, we have seen that the
finite verb could sink into the position of a mere
attributival determinant.   In other words, in such a

sentence as 'There is a devil haunts thee,' the very words show that the important word, in which the chief information lies, is *devil*, while the verb *haunts* might almost as well be expressed by an adjectival attributive, as 'haunting.' It is plain that if a verb could thus easily lose its predicatival character, a predicate bearing no distinguishing marks of its verbal character could, with even more facility, be similarly degraded. The border-land between *meus* in 'liber meus' (=the book is mine) and *liber meus amittitur* is a very narrow one.

It is very necessary to distinguish between the various functions of the determinant—the differences in which, however, commonly remain undenoted by us by any corresponding verbal difference, though they are, logically speaking, of the greatest importance. The determinant may leave the extent of the subject untouched; in other words, the epithet may apply to all the objects or ideas which the substantive by itself, or limited as it is by other circumstances, denotes: this is the case in *mortal man; the almighty God.* On the other hand, it may serve to restrict the meaning of the substantive; as when we say, *old houses, an old house, a* (or *the*) *son of the king, the journey to Paris, Charles the Great.* Similarly, if we say, *the old house,* meaning to contrast it with *the new one,* it is obvious that we individualise the meaning of *house:* while the expression would come under the first head in a sentence like *Lo, the place where I was born! Humble as it it, I love the old house.* In the latter class of instances, the determinant must be expressed, because without it the predicate is meaningless or untrue. If we say, *A journey obliges us to cross the channel,* we ascribe by these words to all journeys what is true of some only, *e.g.,* of a journey to Paris. In the first category, in

considering the epithet, we may notice that it may
already be known as commonly attached to the word to
which it is appended, as in *This red wine* (the speaker
holding it up) *I prefer to many more expensive ones ;* or
it may tell us something new, as in the case of *That
poor man has no children,* where the sentence without
poor would state the same fact, the word *poor* conveying
additional information.   In this case it approaches the
nature of a true predicate, and we often employ a
relative sentence to express it : thus, instead of saying,
Poor Charles has had to emigrate ; if we wished to
emphasise the adjective, we should say, *Charles, who
was poor, etc.* Again, the determinant need stand in no
direct relation to the predicate, as in our above example,
where the fact that the man has no children is
independent of his being poor ; but it may also stand
to the predicate in the relation of cause and effect, as
in *The cruel man would not listen to his victim's prayers,*
where the determinant 'cruel' is applied *owing to* the
fact mentioned in the predicate.

We have now seen that attributes are degenerated
predicates.   There are sentences in which the determinant has, as yet, a somewhat greater independence
than is the case with the ordinary attributes, and which,
therefore, may be said to represent a transition
stage.   In a sentence like *He arrived safe and sound,*
the determinant *safe and sound* is still predicate, in the
wider sense of the term, to *he,* but subordinate to the
other predicate *arrived,* which alone in present grammar
would bear this name.   *Safe and sound* are, IN COM-
PARISON WITH *arrived,* a mere attribute to *he,* and
nowadays such determinants are, for the linguistic
consciousness, what has been very correctly termed
PREDICATIVE ATTRIBUTES.   These are distinguished
from ordinary attributes by a greater freedom in the

place they may occupy in the sentence, and thereby manifest their greater independence.

Predicative attributes are very frequently, but not always, adjectives : we might, *e.g.*, replace the one in our example by a prepositional phrase like *in safety and in good health.* In Modern High German, where the attributive adjective is declined in agreement with its noun, the near affinity of this construction to the predicate shows itself in the use of the uninflected form of the adjective as in the case of the predicate. Thus we say, *Er is gesund nach Paris gekommen :* just as we say, *Er ist gesund.*

When once all these various determinations have been developed from original subjects or predicates, the sentence may become further complicated, (1) by a combination of a determined and a determining element becoming determined by a new element,—as in *All good men* (i.e. *good men + all*) ; *John's eldest daughter* (i.e. either *eldest daughter + John's* or *John's daughter + eldest,* according to circumstances) ; *He falls easily into a passion,*—to be understood, *He falls into a passion + easily :* (2) this combination may itself serve as a determinant,—as in *Very good children* (i.e. *children + very good*); *An all-sacrificing love* (i.e. *a love + all sacrificing*) ; *He speaks very well* (i.e. *He speaks + very well*) ; or (3) several determining elements may be joined to one determinate,—as in *Bad gloomy weather ; He walks well and fast :* or (4) several determinate elements may be joined to a single determinant, just as several subjects may be joined to one predicate, or several predicates to a single subject,—e.g., *John's hat and stick ; He hits right and left.*

These constructions are not always distinctly separable : for instance, a phrase like *big round hats* may be understood as *hats that are big and that are also round* (constr. No. 3,) or we may take it as *round hats that are big* (constr. No. 1). Though the results of both constructions would be the same, the ways in which these results are obtained are logically distinct ; just as the result of 3×5 is identical with 5×3, though the genesis of that result varies according as we have groups of five and take three of such groups, or as there are groups of three and we put five of them together.

We have now considered the simple sentence and its extensions according to the formula $a+b+a$ (see p. 110) in all their bearings and consequences. We said, however, that besides extensions on this plan, there were others in which some combination of subject and predicate became itself the predicate or subject to another member of a sentence.

This we may symbolise by $(a+b)+a$.[1]

We here enter on the ground covered by the complex sentence ; but if the reader has understood what has been already said, he will see that, if we consider this division into simple and complex sentences from a historical and psychological point of view, no clear line of demarcation is to be found. It is indeed true that, as long as we agree that no set of words shall be called a sentence unless it contains a finite verb, a definite criterion exists. If, however, we fully realise that a combination of noun and adjective, for instance, is as much subject and predicate as noun and verb (cf. *homo vivus* with *homo vivit*), we shall likewise feel that ' The good man lives ' is a complex sentence, one predicate of which has degenerated : it must accordingly be admitted to differ in degree, but not in kind, from ' The man who is good lives,' where, again, the complexity is of precisely the same nature as in the

[1] Paul $(a+b)+c$.   See note on p. 110.

phrase *round straw hats*, if we were to say, for instance, 'Round straw hats are pretty, but round felt hats are ugly.'

Combinations on the plan $(a + b) + a$ are common enough : *I think you are mistaken ; The doctor saw I was not well ; Remember you owe me sixpence:* in which cases the subject and predicate $(a + b)$ serve as object to another predicate.

There are, however, other constructions conceivable which would be more strictly conformable to the scheme ; such as *I owe you sixpence is true*, or *You are in danger grieves me ;* where we now use the so-called conjunction *that*, which is originally a pronoun standing as a repetition or a resumption of the subject —'*That* I owe you sixpence is true' being originally 'I owe you sixpence ; *that* is true.'

To find such constructions as *I owe, etc., is true* in actual use, we must go back to older stages of language, *e.g.*, to Hans Sachs, the German shoemaker —poet—dramatist (1494–1576), who framed such sentences as *A couple (man and wife) lived in peace for seventy years vexed the devil*, for *A couple lived, etc., and this vexed, etc.;*[1] *The afflicted woman stabbed herself tells Boccaccio.* In the former of these the sentence is subject, in the latter, object. A sentence $(a + b)$ serving as actual predicate we might illustrate by remembering that in Latin *Imperator felix* may mean 'The emperor *is* happy,' and then using *Imperator qui capite est operto* for the emperor's answer in the well-known anecdote—'The emperor *is* he who has his hat on his head.'

Remembering this, and always carefully remembering the extended meaning of the terms subject and

---

[1] Not to be understood as if it were English : *A couple, who lived . . . . vexed.* See the next example.

predicate, we realise that in the common construction like *You are always grumbling, a bad habit*, we have really, in the so-called apposition *a bad habit*, a predicate.

In this way we can follow up the development of the sentence from its simplest to its most complex form. After thus studying the hypotaxis in all its bearings, we need only touch briefly on the subject of parataxis.

Though, of course, it may occur that we have reason to make in immediate succession two or more statements which are absolutely independent of one another, this will be naturally rare; and, when it happens, we are not likely to combine these statements into one compound clause. Even in the nearest approach to such a case, where we enumerate different but analogous or contrasting facts, the sentences are not absolutely disconnected and independent: cf. *She is crooked, he is lame.* Here, undoubtedly, more is expressed by means of the parataxis than the mere enumeration of the two facts; an additional significance being given to each by the very analogy between the two cases. Similarly in *He is laughing, she weeps*, where the contrast is an additional fact expressed by the coupling of the sentences. Still, the approach to independence is here undoubtedly very close. We already depart a step further from mere co-ordination in the case where —in grammatically absolutely identical manner—two or more sentences are co-ordinated in a story; as, e.g., *I arrived at twelve o'clock; I went to the hotel; they told me there was not a single room to be had; I went to another hotel*, etc., where each sentence to a certain extent expresses a cause or defines the time of occurrence of the fact which is mentioned in the next. Now, though this additional meaning is clearly there, it is a meaning which at the moment of uttering each clause is not necessarily, nay not probably clearly present in the speaker's mind : we might more fully and perhaps more correctly, though undoubtedly very clumsily, express the course of thought by : *I arrived . . ., and when I had arrived, I went . . ., but when I had gone to the hotel, they told . . ., and because they told . . . I went to another, etc.*

We have, then, in our example a combination of independence with interdependence which is the first step on the road towards subordination of one member to the other.

Instead of the clumsy method of repetition which, if ever, is of course but very seldom employed, we give partial expression to this mutual relationship by demonstrative pronouns or verbs. (1) *I arrived . . ., then I went . . ., there they told . . ., etc.* (2) *I met a boy ; he told me. . . .* (3) *He bought a house ; that was old.* (4) *He told a lie ; that was a pity.* A careful study of these examples,—in the third of which the demonstrative pronoun refers (as in the second) to one part only of the preceding sentence, whilst in the fourth it relates to the whole statement made in the former part,—will show (*a*) the method of development of demonstrative into relative pronoun; (*b*) that of demonstrative pronoun into conjunction—*It was a pity that he told a lie;* (*c*) the concomitant change from parataxis to hypotaxis—from *He bought a house,* + *that* (*house*) *was old,* to *He bought a house that was old* = 'which was old.'

A peculiar kind of paratactical subordination occurs where an imperative or interrogative clause loses its independence and becomes an expression of condition ; e.g., *Go there yourself,* (*and* or *then*) *you will see that I am right,* or *Do you want to do it? then make haste.*

CHAPTER VII.

CHANGE OF MEANING IN SYNTAX.

WE have considered, in Chapter IV., the different ways in which words change their meanings: and have remarked that change of meaning consists in the widening or narrowing of the scope or application of each word. We wish, in this chapter, to point out that these processes are not confined to words, but that whole syntactical combinations are constantly undergoing changes of meaning of a similar nature. It may be well to give at the outset an instance illustrative of such difference. Let us take the sentence, 'The book reads like a translation.' In this sentence the meaning which we attach to the word *book* has developed from that attached to A.S. *bóc*, a beech tree.[1] The word *read* has been specialised in meaning from the more primitive signification 'to interpret.' In the same way, *translation* meant originally nothing more than a *transference* of any kind, but has been specially applied to a transference of the ideas expressed by one language into those of another. Such, then, are examples of changes of meaning which have occurred in words.

But besides these changes, it is obvious that we have here a sentence in which the relation between

---

[1] See Skeat, s.v. *book.*

the subject and predicate differs considerably from that which is the *usual* one. We do not in the aforesaid sentence mean to say that the subject *book* performs the action *reads*, but we wish to assert that the subject is of such a nature as to admit of some person performing the action in question. This usage of the subject and predicate, though, when employed circumspectly, it need cause no obscurity, yet is an exceptional usage, or, as we have elsewhere called it, an *occasional* one. Such a construction might, however, easily spread, and become habitual or *usual*. In that case we should have to admit that the meaning of the general syntactical relation between subject and predicate connected by a verb in the active voice had widened in extent, and contracted in content. Instead of stating that the subject *does* the action, we should now have to adapt the statement to the wider but more indefinite relation—the subject either *does or admits of* the action. We shall have occasion to return to these and similar phrases later on.

Now let us take the phrase ' He reads himself into the mind of his author.' In this case we shall find that the meaning of *reads* is the same as that which we usually attach to it; the peculiar meaning lies not in the separate words, but in the phrase taken as a whole. The particular, *occasional* use of the accusative *himself*, together with the combination of the words, is what expresses the whole thought implied ; and thus we have here an instance of a specific construction in which the force of the accusative connected with the word is different from the force of the case in more common usage. Though the application of the accusative in the way we have just mentioned must originally have been an *occasional* one, yet the phrase, though it has indeed become specific, has become so common,

that we may *in this combination* call its meaning *usual.*
We have, then, in studying change of meaning in
syntactical relations, besides the classification of *occa-*
sional and *usual,* another *distinction* to draw ; that
between (*a*) a change of meaning in a general relation,
without reference to the individual terms which happen
to stand in that relation (such as subject and predicate,
verb and object, noun with accompanying genitive, preposition and its régime), and (*b*) a change in meaning
of a case, or other syntactical relation, with regard to
a specific word or expression, in connection with which
it has come to express a new shade of thought. These
two classifications are independent of each other, and
cross one another. It is further to be noticed that,
just as it is impossible to draw a hard and fast line of
distinction between the *occasional* and *usual* in the
meaning of a word, so it is impossible to always clearly
formulate when the change in meaning of a syntactical
relation is *general* or *special;* nay, it would in many
cases be difficult to decide whether a change of meaning in a group of words is owing to a change of meaning in the words, or in their syntactical relations. Yet
it is necessary to keep the distinction in view.

Instances of these syntactical changes are common
in all languages. We might take, as a simple instance,
from the Latin, the syntactical change which is brought
about in the relationship of the transitive verb and
its accusative. Transitive verbs commonly take the
accusative of the direct object ; as, *Grecia capta ferum*
victorem cepit. But many words not originally transitive become so when composed with a preposition ; as,
accedere, præcellere, transgredi, just as *to forego* in
English is transitive, while *to go* is intransitive. This
construction was then felt as *usual.* But besides
these we find a quantity of verbs strictly intransitive

employed with the accusative ; as, *ambulare maria* (to walk the seas: Cicero, de Finibus, ii. 34) ; *ludere Appium* (just as we say, *to play the fool:* Cicero, ad Quint. Fratr., ii. 15) ; *saltare Cyclopa* (to dance the Cylops dance: Horace, Sat. I. v.) ; *stupere donum* (Vergil) ; etc. It was felt that the relationship between *ambulare* and *maria*, e.g., was closely enough related to that of *regere currum* on the one hand, and to that of *ambulare super maria* on the other, to enable analogy to become widely operative in extending this use. The result was that some of the constructions passed into regular usage ; some stood out longer, and must always have appeared as exceptional or occasional ; as, *sudare mella* (Vergil, Eclogue iv. 30).

One of the most ordinary changes brought about by relations in syntax is that due to the relationship of what is commonly called the governing word and its case. The signification, for example, borne by an accusative standing in the relation of object to a verb may cause the verb to bear a meaning more special than its ordinary meaning. Thus, in the case of such a phrase as *I beat*, it is clear that in *to beat a dog, to beat the enemy, to beat the air,* different values are attached to the meaning of the word '(to) beat,' and the word thereby is narrowed in its definition and correspondingly enriched in its contents. It seems natural to examine a little more in detail the relationship borne by the cases to the word which governs them : there seems no objection to the use of the word *governs*, provided only that it be understood with due limitations that certain particular forms are commonly devoted to the expression of certain ideas or relationships, and that the idea be not entertained that there is anything in the nature of the meanings of the words indissolubly connected with a particular form.

To deal with the *Cases* first. It is impossible to set together the different uses of the genitive, and to draw from these by induction any certain proof of the functions which this case fulfilled in the primitive Indo-European languages. For instance, the use of the genitive when it depends on verbs seems to have nothing in common with that of the same case when connected with substantives. In the former case, for instance, in the Classical languages, we find merely a few isolated instances of the genitive regularly governed by verbs, especially those verbs which signify *ruling over, remembering, lacking,* etc. The genitive with nouns, on the other hand, seems most probably to have been used in Indo-European for the expression of any relation between two substantives, as indeed it was in classical Greek, and, to a less extent, in Latin ; cf. such different usages as *Cæsaris horti ; docendi gratia ; reus Milonis ; urbis instar ; me Pompeii esse scio* (Cicero, Fam., ii. 13) ; *Germanicus Ægyptum proficiscitur cognoscendæ antiquitatis* (Tacitus, Annals, xi. 59); *hoc præmii ; ut adhuc locorum* (Plautus, Captivi, 382). In modern English, on the contrary, the function of the genitive in connection with substantives is greatly restricted. Many usages possible in Anglo-Saxon are at the present day obsolete ; for instance, *Criste is* ALLRE *kinge king* (Orm., 3588), MÁDMA *mænigo* (Beowulf, 41), *ðaer wæs* MÁDMA *fela* (ibid., 36), RINCA *manige* (ibid., 729), *he* ðAES WÆPNES *onláh sélran sweord-frecan* = *he lent the weapon to the brave hero* (ibid., 1468–69), *tó gebídanne* ÓðRES YRFEWEARDES = *to expect another heir* (ibid., 2453, *he ʒef Horse* MÁDMES *inoʒe* (L.I. 163, Fiedler and Sachs, ii. p. 277).[1] The genitive at the present day is confined to certain characteristically special usages, and possesses

---

[1] A good collection of examples will be found in Sweet's Anglo-Saxon Reader, introd., p. lxxxvii.

several apparently independent significations. It must, however, be noticed that the true inflectional genitive in English is that which characterises the possessive case; as, *John's hat.* In other cases in Modern English, we have commonly dropped the inflection, and are accustomed to render the genitival relation by a periphrasis with the preposition *of.* Using the word *genitive* in this sense, we may say that the typical usages of the genitive in modern English are the possessive genitive (*the man's brother*), the partitive genitive (*a cup of wine*), and the genitive denoting that the governing substantive is what it is in virtue of what depends upon it (*the writer of the work*). This last division falls naturally into two sub-divisions in the case of nouns of action: the *subjective* genitive (*surly Gloster's governance*—Shakespeare, 2 Henry VI., I. iii.) and the *objective* genitive (*the government of the country*). These usages have survived the various original methods of the application of the genitive, and they must thus be counted amongst genuine grammatical categories.

The relation of the accusative to its governing verb resembles the relation of the genitive to its governing substantive. The most general definition of the meaning of the accusative might be that it denotes any and every kind of relation that a substantive can bear to a verb, except that of a subject to its predicate. It is, however, true that, in English, we are unable to employ it in every case to denote such relation: nor, indeed, does this use seem to have been permissible in the original Indo-European languages; though it is true that the accusative was used more freely and commonly in old Greek and Latin, for instance, than in later times: cf. such constructions as ἄπορα πόριμος (Æsch., Prom. Vinctus); *Quid tibi hanc rem tactio est?* (Plautus, Pœnu-

lus, V. v. 29), *humeros exsertus uterque* (Statius, The-
bais, v. 439).   Hence, in considering the different uses
of the accusative, we must at the very outset place
those meanings side by side which have gradually
become independent.

The first distinction which we must remark in the
use of the accusative is that between the *free* accusative,
or accusative which is independent of the nature of the
verb which it follows,—as, *to buy a hat*,—and the *attached* accusative, which is connected with a few verbs
only by a close tie, and in each case with a restricted
signification,—as, *to blow a gale, to row a race*.   The
free accusative is more freely used in English than in
French or German ; many of the relations which in
those languages are expressed by the genitive and
dative are in English expressed by the case under
consideration.

One of the original usages of the *free* accusative
was the expression of an extension *over space and time ;*
and in this case, it is not always found with verbs. We
have in Latin, *Cæsar tridui iter processit* (Cæsar, Bell.
Gallic., i. 38) ; *Unguem non oportet discedere* (Cicero,
ad Att., xiii. 20) : and, in English, such uses as *To
write of victories next year* (Butler, Hudibras, II., III.,
173) ; *My troublous dream this night* (Henry VI.,
Part II., Act. II., ii.) ; where the dative was usual in
Anglo-Saxon (see Koch, ii., p. 94 ; Mason, p. 147).
As instances of the *attached* accusative, we must
especially consider the accusative of such substantives
as are ETYMOLOGICALLY CONNECTED with the verb ; as,
*to fight a hard fight ; to see a strange sight ; sangas
ic singe* (Ps. xxvi. 7).[1] This 'cognate accusative'
most probably furnishes the cue to such constructions as *Come and trip it as you go*, where *it* seems

---

[1] Cf. Mätzner, iii. 202.

to replace some noun, as, e.g., *tripping*. Once established, this use of *it* instead of a cognate noun in
the accusative, would easily be extended to cases like
to foot it for *to dance a dance*, where the use of the verb
to foot is but an ' occasional ' one, and apparently too
unusual to admit of the formation of the noun *footing*
in the sense of *dance*. We must, then, suppose that the
word *it* stands for a *dance*, i.e. for an accusative not
cognate with the verb actually used, but with another
and synonymous verb. The use of the accusative of
towns in Latin, in answer to the question *Whither ?*—
as, *Ire Romam, Tarentum*, etc., further illustrates the
attached accusative with which we may compare expressions in English, as *to go west ; flying south*, etc.

The usage, now common in English, whereby a
predicative adjective is connected with an intransitive
verb seems to be of later origin. Cf. *to cry one's eyes
red ; to wash one's forehead cool ; to eat one's-self full; to
dance one's-self tired ; to shout one's-self hoarse*. In these
cases the predicatival force of the accusative must be
regarded as a widening of the signification. No doubt,
however, special factors must have aided to bring this
construction into use : such as the survival of the
memory of the general signification of the accusative,
as representing the goal of the verbal action ; and,
again, the analogy of such cases as *to shoot a man
dead ; to buy a man free ; to strike a man dumb ; to beat
black and blue ;*—where the accusative serves to define
the verb, and indeed, almost enters into composition
with it, as it in fact actually does in many cases in
German, like *tot schlagen ;* cf. the English *dumb-
foundered*. There are a large number of colloquial
phrases which are similar,[1] such as *to talk a person's
head off ; to worm one's-self into another's confidence ; to*

---

[1] Cf. Koch (ii., p. 95), who cites a number of examples.

read one's-self into an author ; to laugh a man down, etc.

There is, next, the case of the accusative after *compound* verbs, where the simple verbs are intransitive or govern a different kind of accusative from that taken by the verb when compounded. Such are *circumdare* and *præcellere* in Latin, and, in English, *to forego, to underrate, to withstand, to outlast ;* or, A.S. *ofer-swimman, forestandan,* etc. ; e.g., (hé) *oferswam sioleða bigong* — *He swam across the sea* (Beowulf, 2368) : *Wið ord and wið ecge ingang forstód*—*He withstood entrance against sword and spear* (ibid., 1550).[1] These are on the border line of ' free' and 'attached' accusatives.

There are certain verbs composed with certain prefixes which, in virtue of their composition, receive a transitive force; as, *belabour, begrudge, bewitch, belie, befleck,* etc., and which, in some cases, receive in addition the power of adopting a different kind of object, generally calling in the aid of metaphor to extend their meaning ; as, *embody, encompass, enthral, overrule.*

An 'attached' accusative, or one properly attached adverbially, in a defining and qualifying sense,[2] to one definite individual verb, has, as a rule, only one single meaning, limited by use. But sometimes we find that in this case, too, several applications have set in ; such may have been in some cases original, and in others due to the fact that the one 'usual' signification has extended by 'occasional' transgression. Take such cases as *to blow a gale, to blow a sail, to strike a blow ; to*

---

[1] See Vocabulary to Beowulf, by Heine, under *standan, gangan, lácan,* etc., and their compounds. Also Koch, ii., p. 3, verbs from A.S. which are transitive and intransitive, e.g., *winnan,* to fight ; *fleogan,* to fly ; etc.

[2] See King and Cookson, Comparative Grammar of Greek and Latin, p. 177.

strike a man, to strike terror; to run a race, to run a man down; to stone a man, to stone cherries; pacing the ground, the morrice pacings; to keep a man from harm, to keep harm from a man; to stick a man with a knife, to stick a stamp; and in Latin, *defendere aliquem ab ardore solis, defendere ardorem solis ab aliquo; prohibere calamitatem a provincia, prohibere provinciam calamitate; mutare equum mercede, mutare mercedem equo.* So, too, in Greek: ἀρκεῖν τινα ἀπὸ κινδύνου: ἀρκεῖν κίνδυνον ἀπό τινος.

Poetry has a strong tendency to aid such 'occasional' constructions to become 'usual:' for it is a part of the technique of poetry to produce strong impressions by using its material in a fresh and striking way: thus we find in Latin, *vina cadis onerare* (Vergil, Æneid, i. 199: a variation for *cados vinis*); *liberare obsidionem* (Livy, xxvi. 8), instead of *liberare urbem obsidione; vina coronant* (Vergil, Æneid, iii. 526) instead of *pocula vinis coronant:* δάκρυα τέγγειν = 'to stain tears,' instead of 'to stain with tears' (Pindar): αἷμα δεύειν = 'to stain blood,' instead of 'to stain with blood' (Sophocles). Thus, in English, we have *The Attic warbler pours her throat* (Gray); *to languish a drop of blood a day* (Shakespeare, Cymbeline, I. ii.) The relation expressed by the accusative may in itself be more than a single one; and thus the connection of a single verb with several accusatives to express different ideas is quite natural.

It seems hardly true to state that the Indo-European prepositions governed any particular case. The case which followed the preposition was actually referred to the verb; the general meaning of the verb was still felt and was merely specialised by the preposition; whence it comes that the same preposition is followed by different cases, each bearing its own special meaning. The Greek language offers good examples of this, and seems to stand nearer the original state, as far as usage goes. Take, for instance, a preposition like παρά. Its general meaning may be defined as 'from:' when followed by the genitive it signifies 'proceeding from;' when followed by the accusative, 'to,' reference to the source not being overlooked: similarly with κατά, μετά, etc. In English, more than in most European languages, the tendency has been to multiply the use of prepositions, and to employ them independently of any feeling for the case. The case has thus become more and more independent of the preposition: the connection of the latter with the case has become merely matter of custom; and the consciousness of the original signification of the case has become fainter. With regard to the Latin prepositions which govern one case only (like *ex, ab*), or which govern more than one without affecting the sense (like *tenus*), the employment of the case is merely traditional, and no value can be attached to it. Between the absolute fixity of the one use and the original freedom of the other use stands the employment of *in, sub,* and *super*, sometimes with the ablative, sometimes with the accusative, but with different meanings for the respective cases.

The changes that have appeared in Syntax in the case of prepositions are very well exemplified in English, in which language their use has so greatly spread, and plays such an important part. They were, in the first place, prefixed to the verb, which they qualified adverbially,[1] forming, in fact, a compound with it; as, 'to *over*take,' '*over*reach,' '*over*look.' They were next detached from the verb, but not prefixed to the noun; as, 'to take *over*,' 'to reach *over*,' 'to look *over*;'

[1] Mason's Grammar, p. 107.

and the difference in meaning between these three pairs of phrases will show us how the preposition came to lose memory of the proper signification of the case. In a later stage still, they appear prefixed to nouns, and serve to particularise the relations of actions to things—relations which, in the inflected state of language, were expressed by the case endings of nouns ; cf. *Bigstandað me strange genéatas* (Cædmon)=' Stout vassals bystand me ;' *He heom stód wið* (Layamon) = ' He them stood against;' or *Again the false paiens the Christens stode he by* (P. Langtoft) = ' Against the false pagans the Christians he stood by ;' *i.e.* ' He stood by the Christians.'

We sometimes find the partitive use of the genitive replaced by apposition. The simplest and most natural example of this is where the apposition is made up of several members which are collectively the equivalent of the substantive to which they are appended ; for instance, ' They went, one to the right, the other to the left ;' ' Postero die terrestrem navalemque exercitum, non instructos modo, sed hos decurrentes, classem in portu, simulacrum et ipsam edentem navalis pugnæ ostendit' (Livy, xxix. 22). ' Duæ filiæ harum, altera occisa, altera capta est' (Cæsar Bell. Gallic., i. 53) ; ' Diversa cornua, dextrum ad castra Sammitium, lævum ad urbem tendit' (Livy, x. 41); ' Capti ab Iugurtha, pars in crucem acti, pars bestiis objecti sunt' (Sall., Iug.). But the same appositional construction appears when the whole apposition represents only a part of the expression or phrase of which it is the expansion ; as, ' Volsci maxima pars cæsi,' (Livy) : ' Cetera multitudo decimus quisque ad supplicium lecti' (Livy) ; ' Nostri ceciderunt tres (Cæsar) ; ' My arrival, although an only son, unseen for four years, was unable to discompose, etc.' (Scott Rob Roy, i.) ; ' Tuum, hominis simplicis, pectus

vidimus' (Cicero, Phil., ii. 43).   This is also the case
where the subject is expressed only by the personal
termination of the verb; as, 'Plerique meminimus'
(Livy); 'Simoni adesse me quis nuntiate' = 'Tell
Simo, one or the other of you!' (Plautus). Similarly, in
the case of the designation of materials, we find an
apposition taking the place of the partitive genitive ;
thus we find, in Latin, 'aliquid id genus' for 'something of that kind ;' 'Scis me antea orationes aut aliquid
id genus solitum scribere' (Cicero, Att., xiii. 12) ; 'Pas-
cuntur omne genus objecto frumento maxime ordeo'
(Varro, de Re Rustica, iii. 6) ;[1] 'arma magnus numerus'
(Livy).   Thus, 'He gained the sur-addition Leonatus'
(Shakespeare, Cymbeline, I. i.).

This more simple and primitive appositional construction is very common in modern German ; as, *ein
stück brot, ein glas wasser:* in Middle High German
it was rarer; in modern Scotch it is common in such
instances as *a wee bit body, a curran days* (a number
of days): it was common in Anglo-Saxon; as, 'scóp him
Heort naman' (Beowulf, 78) ; *Emme broðer ðe queene*
(Robert of Gloucester) ; *The Duke of Burgoys,
Edmonde sonne* (Wa., i. 87) ; *David Kingdom* (R. of
G., i. 7.) :[2] and is found in Chaucer,—*Gif us a busshel
whet or malt or reye* (Canterbury Tales, 7328) ; *half
a quarter otes* (ibid., 7545) : and has survived even
in modern English, in such cases as *The Tyrol passes*
(Coleridge, Picc., i. 10) ; *Through Solway sands,
through Tarras moss* (Scott, Lay of Last Minstrel,
i. 21).   We must regard this method of apposition
as the most primitive in language ; the two words in
apposition are simply placed side by side like two
Chinese roots, and must be looked upon as the simple
stems without any inflection.

[1] See Zumpt, § 428.   [2] Fiedler and Sachs, ii. 273.

Even the subject of a verb may deviate from previous usage in the way whereby it denotes a relation: cf. such phrases as *The cistern is running dry ; The roof drips with water ; The trees drop honey.* Thus we can say, *The river is running over ; The wood is resonant with song ; The window will not shut; The fire will not draw ; The kettle boils; This sample tastes bad ; The hall thick swarming now with complicated monsters* (Milton): in Italian, *Le vie correvano sangue* (Malespini): in Spanish, *Corrieron sangue los rios : Sudare mella* (Vergil, Ecl. iv., 30) ; cf. also, the use of *sapere*, in Latin, in such cases as *cum sapimus patruos* (Persius, Sat. i., 11) ; *sentir*, in French, as *Cela sent la guerre.* In these cases we should expect the subject and object to be inverted.

A similar departure from ordinary usage occurs in the case of what we commonly speak of as 'transferred' epithets; *i.e.* adjectives referring to merely indirect relations with the substantive to which they are attached. Such are expressions like *wicked ways; quiet hours; in ambitious Latin* (Carlyle, Past and Present, ii. 2) ; *the blest abodes* (Pope, Essay on Man, iii. 259). Many of these linguistic licences have become quite usual, and it is forgotten that the epithet attached to the word does not strictly fit it : thus we speak quite commonly of *the happy event, a joyful surprise, happy hours, a learned treatise, an intoxicated condition, in a foolish manner, a gay supper, a bright prospect,* etc. ; and we can even say, *He gives us an unhealthy impression, a stingy gift,* etc. The word *secure* in English, like *sûr* in French, refers in the first instance to a person who need not be anxious ; in the second place, to a thing or person about whom no one need be anxious. Thus we can say, *I am safe in saying that he is safe.* As soon as these freer combina-

tions are apprehended as an ordinary epithet applied
to its substantive, we may state that a change in word-
meaning has occurred.

Such licence occurs in the case of the participles and
nouns in *-ing* even more than in that of adjectives ; thus
we can say, *in a dismantled state* (Dickens, Pickwick,
2) ; *a smiling answer; this consummation of drunken
folly* (Scott, Rob Roy, 12) ; *a dazzling prospect; the
selling price ; the dying day ; a parting glass ; writing
materials ; sleeping compartment ; dining room ; singing
lesson ; falling sickness ; waking moments ; the ravished
hours* (Parnell, Hesiod, 225). So, too, we speak of
a talented man ; cf. also the common French expressions, *thé dansant, café chantant.* Tacitus has such
uses as *Muciano volentia rescripsere* (Hist., iii. 52) for
volenti, etc.

We may probably compare with this use that of the
so-called 'misrelated participle,' a freely attached predicatival attribute, which is indeed condemned as
ungrammatical and careless, but which still occurs very
commonly in even the best authors. Cf. When *gone*
we all regarded each other for some minutes with
confusion ' (Goldsmith, Vicar of Wakefield, 13) ;

> ' Thus *repulsed*, our final hope
> Is flat despair'
>   (Milton, Paradise Lost, ii. 142) ;

'*Amazed* at the alteration in his manner, every
sentence that he uttered increased her embarrassment'
(Miss Austin, Pride and Prejudice, ch. xliii.).[1] We
are, indeed, accustomed to say that in this case we must
supply a subject, and that the full expression would
be 'Amazed *as she was,*' in the last instance cited. But

---

[1] Numerous instances are given in Hodgson, p. 105, and in
Mätzner, vol. iii., p. 80.

if we use such an expression as 'a *pitying* tear,' we
might maintain as well that it is necessary to explain
this as, 'with a tear, shed in sign of his pity.' The fact
is, that these loosely appended predicatival attributes
answer to a need felt in language, just as much as
such words as *regarding, during, vu que, instar,* supply
a requirement in the prepositional category.

In the case of participial constructions, the
participle expresses formally the time-relation in which
the condition or action denoted by the participle stands
to the finite verb. Thus, '*Being frightened* he runs
away' expresses formally nothing more than the
temporal relation between the fright and what follows
it. It is, however, possible to understand different
relations as implied by this participle; thus there
would, in this instance, be a connection of cause and
effect. There are many cases in which, were we to
extend the participial construction into a separate
sentence, we should have to employ different conjunctions; sometimes those denoting the reason,—as, '*Since*
he was frightened he ran away;' sometimes we should
have to employ such conjunctions as denote an opposition,—as, 'Notwithstanding that;' thus, supposing
that the sentence in question ran, 'Being frightened
he did *not* run away,' this would naturally be broken
up into '*Notwithstanding* that he was frightened, he
did not run away.' Sometimes, again, the participle
expresses a condition, as in such common cases as
'*Failing* an heir, the property passes to the crown.'

Still it is unnecessary to assert that the participle, as
such, denotes these different meanings—such as cause,
condition, opposition, etc. These relations are only
accidental and *occasional.* When, however, we have
dependent sentences introduced *by a temporal conjunction,* like *quum, since,* the accidental relation of this

conjunction to the governing sentence may come to attach itself and become permanent; in this case, the conjunction will experience a change of syntactical meaning. Take the case of *since*, formed by the adverbial genitive suffix *es*, from *sin = sithen* (from *síð*, þam, after that). *While*, again, from meaning 'the time that' (a thing occurred,) has come to denote 'in spite of the fact that,' in such phrases as '*While* you pretend that you love me, you act as though you did not.' In the case of the modern German *weil*, the temporal signification has completely disappeared ; and in the same way prepositions, such as *through* and *by*, which possess strictly speaking a local or temporal meaning, pass into a causal meaning.

The instances given above may serve to show the way in which changes are constantly occurring in syntax, and will aid in pointing out how language is constantly aiming at supplying, in an economical fashion, its needs as they successively present themselves.

CHAPTER VIII.

CONTAMINATION.

We have discussed, in Chapter V., the force of analogy
and its effect. We have now to study a phenomenon
of language which may be called 'contamination,' and
which, though widely differing from analogy in the
most characteristic instances of both, is yet so closely
allied to it as to render it a difficult matter to draw
any hard and fast line of demarcation between the two.

We call the process 'contamination' when two
synonymous forms or constructions force themselves
simultaneously, or at least in the very closest succession, into our consciousness, so that one part of the
one replaces or, it may be, ousts a corresponding part
of the other; the result being that a new form arises
in which some elements of the one are confused with
some elements of the other.

Thus, for instance, to take an imaginary case, a
person seeing a book on the table might wish to exclaim, 'Take that thing away!' Just, however, as he
is uttering the word *thing*, the consciousness that it is
properly called a *book* forces itself upon him, and he
utters the word *thook*. Of course such a form is a
mistake, and a mistake so palpable and, indeed, so
absurd that the speaker will at once correct it. Every
one, however, who is in the habit of watching closely

the utterances of others, and indeed of himself, will be
aware that such slips of the tongue are extremely
common ; and it is clear that, though such formations
are, in the first instance, sudden and transitory, and
generally travel no further than the individual from
whom they proceed, yet they may, by repetition on
the part of the same individual, or, it may be, by
imitation, conscious or unconscious, on the part of
others, end by becoming 'usual.'

Contamination manifests itself not merely in the
form of words, but also in their syntactical combination. In the case of such a curious mixture of two
words as that which we took for our example, the
very grotesqueness of the result would probably bar
the way to the spreading of the word, though, as we
shall see, traces are to be found of cases hardly less
grotesque than this. In syntactical combinations,
however, the results have far more frequently proved
permanent ; or, in any case, the results do not commonly appear in such jarring contrast to received
usage as to challenge immediate correction, and, consequently, instances can be more easily found in
literature of syntactical than of verbal contamination ;
some cases of such contamination pass into language
and become 'usual ;' some are refused admission into
normal language and are set down as the peculiarities
of the individual writer or speaker, or, it may be, as
his mistakes.

We saw that formation by analogy manifests itself
as the alteration of one form in compliance with a rule
more or less consciously abstracted from a number of
examples drawn from a group to which that form does
not, strictly speaking, belong. Contamination is the
alteration of one form on the model of another synonymous form. The difficulty of distinguishing between

the two arises from this—that the contaminating
form or construction often derives additional force
from being associated with other members of its
group, so that it may be doubtful whether the rule
or the one synonym gave the impetus to the new
formation. Nevertheless, we may lay it down that
for analogy we must demand a sufficient number of
examples on which to base a rule ; while for contamination, a single form or construction may suffice. If
we bear in mind these main points of distinction, we
shall commonly find no difficulty in deciding to which
of the two classes we should refer any particular case.[1]

Among the results of contamination in single
words, we must naturally expect that those have the
best chance of becoming permanent which least
deviate from the correct form ; *i.e.* where the synonymous[2] forms confused resembled each other, and the
form due to their contamination consequently bore
sufficient resemblance to both to enable it to arise
repeatedly in the mouth of several speakers, and,
when formed, to escape observation. Thus the word
milt (the soft roe of fishes) is a substitute for *milk* (it
appears in Swedish as *mjölke*) ; this was probably due
to contamination with *milt* (spleen), which is a different
word.[3] Again, the English combination *ough* is due
to the contamination of three distinct forms, viz., *ugh*
(A.S. *-uh*), *-ogh* (A.S. *-áh*), *-oogh* (A.S. *-óh*) ; whilst, at
the same time, the loss of the *gh* has affected the

---

[1] A strict attention to this difference would involve the transference of some of Professor Wheeler's examples, in his admirable
pamphlet on Analogy, to the head of ' Contamination.'

[2] ' Synonymous ' must here be understood in a wide sense, em-
bracing sets of words which, though really distinct in meaning as
well as origin, become confused, and consequently become synonymous merely by misunderstanding (see our first example).

[3] Skeat, Principles of English Etymology, p. 357.

quality of the preceding vowel by the principle of
compensation. Thus the word *through* should have
appeared as *thrugh*, A.S. *ꝥruh* (for *ꝥurh*) ; but it has
been altered to *through*, as if from A.S. *ꝥrúh*, or else
to *thurgh* (A.S. *ꝥurh*), which has been lengthened to
thor(ou)gh.[1]

A.S. *byrꝥen*, 'a load,' became *burthen*, and is now
burden, the change being assisted by confusion with
burden (Fr. *bourdon*), 'the refrain of a song.'[2] The
word *anecdotage* is a wilful contamination of *anecdote* +
dotage, with a side glance at *age* (time of life), though
in *dotage* the suffix *age* has no connection with the
noun of same sound. *Another-gaines*, which was used
by Sydney in his Arcadia (1580) seems to have
resulted from the confusion of *anotherkins* (of another
kind), which survives in the Whitby dialect, and
anothergates (of another gate, manner). On these
instances, see Murray's Dictionary, s.v.

In this and similar instances, where the fact that
the word occurs in more than one meaning is due to
confusion or misconception, it is often difficult to say
whether we have to deal with contamination proper,
as we defined it and illustrated it by the example on
page 140. There exist, however, in many languages
words and forms which can be explained in no other
way. Such is the O.Fr. form *oreste*, a contamination
between *orage* and *tempeste;* and again, the O.Fr.
triers seems to be a contamination between *tres* (trans)
and *rier* (retro).[3]

The confusion was rendered easier in the case of
forms which may easily pass into a grammatical para-
digm. Thus, from the Italian *o* of *sono* and the perfect termination in *-ro* (= *runt*), the *o* was transferred

---

[1] Skeat, Principles of English Etymology, p. 361.
[2] Cf. ibid., p. 368.   [3] Cf. Gröber, p. 630.

to the other third person plural forms; whence such forms as old Tuscan *fecérono* (modern *furono*) are contaminations between the forms *fecéro* and *amano*.

The confusion of words belonging to the same etymological group is more common : an instance may be seen in the Italian *trápano* (τρύπανον), whose form seems to have been affected by *traforare*.[1] In Old French the form *doins* is due to a contamination between *dois* and *don*. In Provençal, the form *sisclar* seems a contamination between *sibilare* and *fistulare*.[2] The English *yawn* represents a fusion of two Anglo-Saxon forms, *géonian* and *gánian*.[3] The word *minnow* is a contamination between M.E. *menow* and the O.Fr. *menuise*. Both of these are ultimately from the same base, *min* (small),[4] but underwent a different development. We might add as an instance the jocular coinage *squarson* = Squire + Parson.

Our word *ache* offers a further curious illustration. There was in Anglo-Saxon a verb *ácan* with past tense *oc*, past participle *acen*, which gave us the verb *ake* (to hurt)—now erroneously spelt *ache*, but still correctly pronounced. The noun in Anglo-Saxon was *œce*, in which the *k* sound was palatalised into the sound of *ch* (in church), whilst it remained *k* in the verb.[5] Accordingly we find still in Shakespeare the distinction between the verb *ake* and the noun *ache* (pronounced with *tch* as in *batch*, etc.). The confusion began about A.D. 1700, when the verb began to replace the noun in pronunciation, and occasionally the spelling *ache* was used for both noun and verb.

[1] Gröber, p. 524.   [2] Ibid., p. 629.
[3] Skeat's Etymological Dictionary, p. 363.   [4] Cf. ibid., s.v.
[5] As in the case of many other verbs : cf., e.g., *make* with *match ; bake* with *batch ; wake, watch ; break, breach ; speak, speech ; stick, stitch*. Cf. Murray, Dictionary, s.v. *ache*, upon which the discussion of the above example is based.

The prevalence of this spelling at present is mainly
due, it appears, to a mistaken derivation from the
Gr. ἄχος;—the pronunciation to confusion, or to contamination of the noun by the verb.

We reach the borderland of 'Analogy,' if we do
not actually enter it, in those cases where a word—
under the influence of a modal group with a synonymous function—assumes a suffix or prefix whose modal
significance was already expressed by the word in its
simpler form.   Thus it has been considered a case of
contamination of the comparative *worse* with the modal
groups of the other comparatives in *er*, when we find
the double comparative *worser*.   Similarly, the Latin
frequentative *iactare* (*iacio*) was extended into *iactitare*
under the influence of the modal group composed of
words like *volitare*, etc. : again, in English, the form
lesser has, as an adjective, almost entirely superseded
the form *less;* just as, in the colloquial language of the
uneducated, we find *leastest* by the side of *least*.   There
is, in Gothic, a superlative *aftuma*, beside which we,
however, find even there the double superlative *aftu-
mists*.   This appears in Anglo-Saxon [1] as *æftermest*,
M.E. *eftermeste*, and in Modern English as *aftermost;*
where the *o* in the last syllable is due to the mistaken
idea that the whole word was a compound of *most*,
though, as we have seen, it was really another instance
of a double suffix.

Contamination plays a far more important part in
the area of syntax.   It is easy to cull from the pages
of authors of repute instances of anomalies which have
no permanent influence on language : cf. 'Amazed at
the alteration in his manner, every sentence that he

---

[1] Of course, Anglo-Saxon is not *derived* from Gothic. The Anglo-
Saxon forms are of common origin and cognate with Gothic, but not
derived from them.

uttered increased her embarrassment' (Miss Austen,
Pride and Prejudice, ch. 43,[1]—a confusion between
'She was amazed at the alteration,' etc., and 'Amazed
as she was.') There are many similar constructions
in Shakespeare: cf. 'Marry, that I think be young
Petruchio' (a confusion of 'That I think *is*' and 'I
think that *be*,' — Romeo and Juliet, I. v. 133); so,
again, 'Why do I trifle thus with his despair is done
to cure it' (a confusion between '*Why* I trifle is *to cure*'
and 'My trifling is done to cure,'—Lear, IV. vi. 33).[2]
The following are instances of syntactical contamination from various quarters:—'Showering him with
abuse and blows' (Mary L. Booth, Translation of
'Abdallah' by Laboulaye, p. 4,—from 'Showering
abuse and blows upon him' and 'Overwhelming him
with abuse and blows').

> 'Let us once again assail your ears . . .
> What we have two nights seen.'
> (Hamlet, I. i. 31),

(from 'Let us once again tell you' and 'Let us assail
your ears with what we . . . ').

> 'Jhone, Andrew, James, Peter, *nor* Paull
> Had few houses amang thame all'
> (Sir David Lyndsay, The Monarche, Bk. III. i. 4541–42),

(from 'John, Andrew, etc. *and* Paul had few houses
among them all' and 'Neither John, Andrew, etc. *nor*
Paul had many houses').

> 'Thare ryches, rentis nor tressour
> That tyme, sall do thame small plesour'
> (Ibid., Bk. IV., 5504–5; see Skeat, 'Specimens,' iii.),

(from 'Riches, rent, *and* treasure shall give small

---

[1] Quoted by Hodgson, Errors in the Use of English.
[2] See Abbott's Shakespearian Grammar, p. 297.

pleasure' and 'Riches, rent, *nor* treasure shall give much (or great or any) pleasure').

> 'What with griefe and feare my wittes were reft'
> (Cf. Th. Sackville, Mirrour for Magistrates—Skeat,
> Specimens, iii., p. 287—stanza 18),

(from 'What with grief and what with fear my wits' and 'With grief and fear my wits, etc.').

'She was not one of *those* who fear to hurt *her* complexion' (W. Besant, The World went very well then, ch. 26). 'What Castilla insists' (= What Castilla pretends + upon which Castilla insists),—Ibid. 'If our eyes be barred that happiness' (= If our eyes be debarred from that . . . + If (to) our eyes be denied that happiness),—Comus, 343. 'On attempting to extract the ball, the patient began to sink' (= On attempting . . . ball, the doctors saw that the patient, etc., + when the doctors attempted, . . . the patient began, etc.),—Nichol and M'Cormick, p. 56. 'I must insist, sir, you'll make yourself easy on that head' (She stoops to conquer, ii. 1,—a confusion between 'I must insist upon your making yourself easy,' and 'I hope, or demand, that you will make, etc.'). 'Was ever such a request to a man in his own house?' (ibid.,—a confusion between 'Was ever such a request made to a man?' and 'Did ever you hear such a request to a man?'). 'A very troublesome fellow this, as ever I met with' (ibid.,—A very troublesome fellow this + As troublesome a fellow as ever I met with). 'There can be no doubt but that this latest step . . . has been the immediate result of . . .' (President's Address, Mechanical Section, British Association, Manchester;—a confusion between 'There can be no doubt that' and 'It cannot be but that'). 'I prefer to go to London rather than to Paris,' (a confusion between 'I prefer going (to go) to London to going to Paris,' and 'I would go to London rather than to Paris').[1]

In many cases the contamination has become usual. We say in English, *I am friends with him*, from 'I am friendly with him' and 'We are friends.' The Danish popular idiom is similar : *Han er gode venner med dem* (He is good friends with them). Compare too, the following expressions : 'a friend *of mine;*' *Fare thee well* (a confusion between 'Keep thee well' and 'Fare well'). *On my behalf* arose out of a confusion of the A.S. *on healfe*, 'on the side of,' with a second common phrase *be healfe*, 'by the side of.'[2]   In Greek we find expressions like ὁ ἥμισυς τοῦ χρόνου, a confusion between ὁ ἥμισυ χρόνος and τὸ ἥμισυ τοῦ χρόνου, etc. ; in Spanish, *muchas de virgines*, instead of *muchas virgines* or *mucho de virgines :* in Italian, *la più delle gente* (Boccaccio). We have a similar instance of contamination in the case of the Latin gerund : *Pœnarum solvendi tempus* (Lucretius), from *Pœnarum solvendarum* and *pœnas solvendi; nominandi istorum quam edundi erit copia* (Plautus, Captivi, IV. ii. 72). Cicero, again, writes, *Eorum partim in pompa partim in acie illustres esse voluerunt*, in which there is a confusion between *eorum pars* and *ii partim*. Occasionally, a contamination results from the confusion of the active and passive constructions ; e.g., *I care na by how few may see* (Burns's song, 'First when Maggie was my care').

Sometimes an inaccuracy arises owing to the idea of a word which might have been used displacing the word which actually was used by the writer. Thus, for instance, the idea of the inhabitants displaces that of the town or the country : cf. Θεμιστοκλῆς φεύγει ἐς

---

[1] See note at end of chapter.

[2] Cf. Skeat, Etymological Dictionary, s.v. *behalf*.

Κέρκυραν, ὧν αὐτῶν εὐεργέτης (Thuc., i. 136) : *Auditæ
legationes quorum* (Tacitus, Annals, iii. 63). Cf. *The
revolt of the Netherlands* (for *the Netherlanders*) *from
Spain;* 'That faction (for *the partisans*) in England
who most powerfully opposed his pretensions' (Mrs.
Macaulay.)[1] Here belongs the pleonastic use of
pronouns, common in English : cf. 'I bemoan Lord
Carlisle, *for whom*, although I have never seen him,
and he may never have heard of me, I have a sort
of personal liking *for him*' (Miss Mitford, Letters
and Life, 2nd Series, 1872, vol. ii., p. 160).[2] In
Latin and Greek we often find the relative referring
to a possessive pronoun, as if the personal pronoun
had preceded : cf. *Laudare fortunas meas qui natum
haberem* (Terence, And., I. i. 69) ;[3] Τῆς ἐμῆς ἐπεισόδου,
ὃν μήτ' ὀκνεῖτε ('The approach of me whom neither
fear ye'—Sophocles, Œd. Col., 730).

We have next to note confusions of the comparative
and superlative manner of expression, resulting in combinations like 'Hi ceterorum Britannorum *fugacissimi*'
(Tacitus, Agricola). Cf. 'The climate of Pau is perhaps
the *most genial* and the *best suited* to invalids of any
other spot in France' (Murray, Summer in Pyrenees,
vol. i., p. 131). 'Mr. Stanley was the only one *of his
predecessors* who slaughtered the natives of the region
he passed through' (*London Examiner*, Feb. 16,
1878, p. 204).[4]

A case of contamination sometimes results from the
idea of the past time rising into memory simultaneously with that of present time : cf., in Latin, the
use of *iamdudum* when joined to the imperative ; as

---

[1] See other instances in Hodgson, p. 74.
[2] Numerous other instances are given in Hodgson, p. 195.
Cf. Zumpt, § 424.
[4] Numerous other examples are given in Hodgson, p. 72.

iamdudum sumite pœnas (Vergil, Aneid, ii. 103),—a
confusion between *iam sumite pœnas* and *sumite pœnas
iamdudum meritas*, i.e. between the thoughts 'pray
take' and 'you should long ago have taken.' Cf. *Those
dispositions that of late transform you from what you
rightly are* (Lear, I. iv. 242), and *He is ready to cry
all the day;* cf., also, such instances in Latin as *Idem
Atlas generat* and *Cratera antiquum quem dat Sidonia
Dido* (Vergil, Æneid, ix. 266), where the *effect* of the
action once performed is intended to be brought out by
the use of the present.

We often find in English an interrogation with the
infinitive, where we should expect a finite verb; as,
I do not know what to do; where we should rather
have expected *I do not know what I should do.* This
construction seems a confusion between cases in which
the infinitive was directly dependent on the verb
without any interrogative, as, *Scit dicere* (He can say);
Il sait dire: and such constructions as *What to say?
I do not know.* Other instances are *Shelley, like Byron,
knew early what it was to love* (Medwin's Memoirs of
Byron, p. 9); *How have I then with whom to hold
converse* (Milton); *then sought where to lie hid* (ibid.);
hath not where to lay his head. This construction is
common in the Romance languages; as in French,—
je ne sais quel parti prendre; Italian,—*non ho che dire;*
Spanish,—*non tengo con quien hablar;* Latin,—*rogatus
ecquid haberet super ea re dicere* (Aul. Gellius, iii. 1).

Another form of syntactical contamination is when
an interrogative sentence is made dependent on a
verb, and, at the same time, the subject of this interrogative sentence is made the verb's nominal object;
as, *I know thee who thou art: You hear the learned Bel-
lario what he writes* (Merchant of Venice, IV. i. 167):
cf., also, Lear, I. i. 272. This usage is common in

Latin; as, *Nosti Marcellum quam tardus sit* (Cicero):
in Italian an instance occurs in *tu'l saprai bene chi è*
(Boccaccio).

Similarly, we have cases in which the subject of an
objective clause introduced by *that* becomes a nominal
object of the principal verb; as, *All saw him, that he was
among the prophets:* so, too, the *object* of some subordinate clause may be also object of the main verb;
e.g., *They demanded £400, which she knew not how to
pay.*

We find in English such phrases as 'SUCH of the
Moriscoes might remain WHO demeaned themselves as
Christians' (Watson's Life of Philip III.)[1] We find
in common use such phrases as *such as I saw* side
by side with *the same which I saw,* or *that I saw.*
Bacon writes *such which must go before;* and Shakespeare, *Thou speakest to* SUCH *a man* THAT *is no
fleering tell-tale* (Julius Cæsar, I. iii). So Fuller: *Oft-
times* SUCH WHO *are built four stories high are observed
to have little in their cockloft.* In Latin, we similarly
find *idem* followed by *ut,* as in *eadem sunt iniustitia
ut si in suam rem aliena convertant.* In English, again,
we find sentences like—

'But scarce were they hidden away, I declare,
   Than the giant came in with a curious air'
          (Tom Hood, Junr., Fairy Realm, p. 87);

It is said that nothing was so teasing to Lord Erskine
THAN *being constantly addressed by his second title of
Baron Clackmannan* (Sir H. Bulwer, Historical Characters, vol. ii., p. 186, Cobbett). We say 'each time
when' and 'each time *that*' (similarly, in French we
find 'au temps *où*,' and, at an earlier period, 'au
temps *que*'); 'the rather *because*,' as well as 'the
rather *that*.'

[1] Quoted by Crombie, Etymology and Syntax, p. 256.

In English we frequently find constructions like 'Mac Ian, *while* putting on his clothes, was shot through the head' (Macaulay, History of England, vii., p. 24); 'I wrote an epitaph for my wife *though* still living' (Goldsmith, Vicar of Wakefield, ii.). In these cases, the predicatival attribute has the same function as a dependent sentence introduced by a conjunction; and consequently the circumstance described is rendered more exact by the placing of certain conjunctions before the simple adjective. So, in French, we say, *Je le fis quoique obligé;* and, in Italian, *benchè costretto.* Similarly, in Latin, many conjunctions are placed before the ablative absolute; cf. *quamvis iniqua pace, honeste tamen viverent* (Cicero): *etsi aliquo accepto detrimento* (Cæsar).

Conversely, the fact that dependent sentences and prepositional determinants may have the same function, causes prepositions to be used to introduce dependent sentences. This use is especially common in English: cf. EXCEPT *a man be born* (St. John iii. 5); FOR *I cannot flatter thee in pride* (Shakespeare, 2 Henry VI., I. iii); AFTER *he had begotten Seth* (Genesis); sometimes this usage extends to cases where the strict written language hesitates to accept it as usual; as, '*without* they were ordered' (Marryat); 'I hate him *for* he is a Christian, but more for that—he lends' (Merchant of Venice, I. iii. 43). *Till* and *until* are specially common in this use. Indeed, the prepositional use of these words has almost died out in Modern English, but is frequent in the literature of the Elizabethan age; cf. Shakespeare, 'From the first corse *till* he that died to-day' (Hamlet, I. ii. 105), where *he* should, strictly speaking, be *him.* Other instances are quoted by Abbott, § 184. It must, however, be particularly noticed that the constructions *for that, after that,* etc.,

may be used instead of *for, after*, when these words
are used as conjunctions.   A preposition also stands
before indirect questions : cf. '*at* the idea of how sorry
she would be' (Marryat) : 'the daily quarrels *about*
who shall squander most' (Gay).

The result of contamination in syntax is often a
pleonasm.   Thus, in Latin, we frequently meet with
several particles expressive of similarity ; as, *pariter
hoc fit atque ut alia facta sunt* (Plautus) : and, again, we
find expressions like *quasi si ; nisi si*.[1]   Thus, in English, we meet with the common but incorrect expression
like as if.   We can connect a preposition either with
a substantive or with a governing verb : we can say,
the place I am in, or, *the place in which I am*.   The
two even occur in combination : cf. *That fair* FOR
which love groaned FOR (Shakespeare, Romeo and
Juliet, I. v., chorus), and, *In what enormity is Marcus
poor in . . .?* (Coriolanus, II. i. 18).   Nay, we often
find such expressions as *of our general's* (Shakespeare,
Antony and Cleopatra, I. i. 1), instead of *of our general* or *our general's ;* 'If one may give that epithet to
any opinion *of a father's*' (Scot, Rob Roy, ch. ii.) ;
'He is likewise a rival *of mine*, that is my other *self's*'
(Sheridan) : cf. also the common pleonasm *of ours.*
Sometimes, to adverbs of place — themselves denoting the direction whence—is added a preposition
with a similar meaning ; as, *from henceforth* (Luke
v. 10) : cf. 'I went *from thence* on to Edinburgh' (Life
of George Grote, ch. ii., p. 187).

Other instances of pleonasms arising from syntactical contamination are : 'He saw that *the reason why*
witchcraft was ridiculed was *because* it was a phase of
the miraculous, etc.' (Lecky, History of Rationalism,
vol. i., p. 126); "*The reason why* Socrates was con-

[1] Zumpt, § 340.

demned to death was *on account of* his unpopularity'
Times, February 27, 1871).[1]

Double comparatives and superlatives pleonasti-
cally resulting from syntactical contamination are not
unusual in English : cf. 'Farmers find it far *more
profitable* to sell their milk wholesale *rather than* to
retail it' (Fawcett, Pauperism, ch. vi., p. 237) : 'Still
it was on the whole *more satisfactory* to his feeling to
take the directest means of seeing Dorothea *rather
than* to use any device,' etc. (Middlemarch, vol. iii.,
bk. vi., ch. lxii., p. 365). Thus we have in Shakespeare,
more kinder, more corrupter, and *most unkindest* (Julius
Cæsar, III. ii. 187) ; and *thy most worst* (Winter's
Tale, III. ii. 180). In poetry, again, we find adjectives with a superlative sense compared ; as, *perfectest,
chiefest* (Shakespeare), *extremest* (Milton), *more perfect*
(English Bible), *lonelier* (Longfellow).[2]

In Latin and Greek, we find the comparative where
we should expect the positive ; as, *ante alios immanior
omnes* (Vergil, Æneid, iv.) ; αἱρετώτερον εἶναι τὸν καλὸν
θάνατον ἀντὶ τοῦ αἰσχροῦ βίου (Xenophon). In Scotch it
is usual to say *He is quite better again* for *He is quite
well again*. We find the positive where we should
expect the comparative, as in St. Mark ix. 43 ; Καλόν
σοι ἐστί . . . ἤ (It is good for thee than, etc.). We
also find the superlative used where the comparative
would be regular : cf. Theocritus, xv. 139 : Ἕκτωρ,
Ἑκάβας ὁ γεραίτατος εἴκατι παίδων.[3]

Pleonasm arising from contamination occurs most
extensively in the case of *negations*. Cf. 'There was
no character created by him into which life and reality
were *not* thrown with such vividness that the thing

---

[1] See Hodgson, p. 215, where more instances are given.
[2] Cf. Morris, p. 106.
[3] Cf. Berliner Wochenschrift, No. 52, p. 1622.

written did *not* seem to his readers the thing actually done' (Forster's Life of Dickens, vol. ii., ch. ix., p. 181). In older stages of English, as of German and French, this usage was very common. Cf. *Parceque la langue française cort parmi le monde est la plus délitable à lire et à oir que nulle autre* (Martin da Canale);[1] *Wird das hindern können, dass man sie nicht schlachtet?* (Schiller). In Chaucer and Shakespeare the use of the double negative is common : *First he denied you had in him no right* (Comedy of Errors, IV. ii. 7). *You may deny that you were not the cause* (Richard III., I. iii. 90).[2] With this we may compare the redundant negative in Greek after verbs of denying: οὐκ ἀπαρνοῦμαι τὸ μή; and, in Latin, *non dubito quin:* cf. also the use of the double negative in Plautus, *neque illud haud objiciet mihi* (Epid., V. i. 5). In these cases a negative appears with an infinitive where the main verb itself contains a quasi-negatival force : numerous instances may be found in Shakespeare; cf. *Forbade the boy he should not pass those grounds* (Pas. Pilgrim, 9).

So we find a contamination of the two constructions : 'not—and not' and 'neither—not' in cases like Shakespeare's 'Be not proud, nor brag not of thy might' (Venus and Adonis, 113), = Be not . . . and brag not + neither be . . . nor brag.

Compare also, 'I cannot choose one nor refuse none' = I cannot choose one and I can (or may) refuse none + I can neither choose one nor refuse one.[3]

A pleonastic negation occurs in French and other languages after words signifying 'without:' cf.

---

[1] Chevallet, vol. i., p. 40.

[2] See other instances in Abbott, § 406.

[3] Abbott, § 406 and § 408.

Mätzner, Fr. Gr., § 165 : *Sans* NUL *égard pour nos scrupules* (Béranger) ; *Elle ne voyait aucun être souffrant sans que son visage* N'*exprimât la peine qu'elle en ressentait* (Bernardin de St. Pierre).[1] A curious pleonasm of the article occurs in the following sentence : *No stronger and stranger* A *figure is described in the modern history of England* (Justin McCarthy, History of our own Times, vol. i., ch. ii., p. 31) ; a contamination between *There was not a stronger figure,* and *No stronger figure.*

[1] Cf. also such sentences as *Il n'écrit pas mieux cette année ci qu'il* N'*en faisait l'année passée;* and *Il faut plus d'esprit pour apprendre une science, qu'il* N'*en faut pour s'en moquer.*

NOTE TO PAGE 148.

A very interesting and useful little book has been published by Professor Nichol and M'Cormick on English Composition. It came too late into our hands for us to make use of the many instructive and often amusing examples it contains. We subjoin one (from p. 76).

'The curses of Mr. A. B., like chickens, will come home *to roost against him*' (a contamination of ' will be brought up against him,' and ' will come home to roost ').

Contaminations will account for many irregularities noted by the authors.

CHAPTER IX.

ORIGINAL CREATION.

WE must not suppose that the conditions under which language was originally created were different from those which we are able to trace and to watch in the process of its historical development. We must not suppose that mankind once possessed a special faculty for coining language, and that this faculty has died out. Education and experience must have developed our faculties no less for the creation of language than for other purposes; and if we have ceased to create new materials for language at the present day, the reason must be that we have no further need to do so. The mass of linguistic material which we have inherited is, in fact, so great that it is scarcely possible for us to conceive a new idea for which, in the existing language, we could not find some word or form either ready to our hand, or capable of being made more or less suitable to express it, or at least able to supply some derivative for the purpose. On the other hand, we must admit that the process of new creation has never wholly ceased in language; and even in English we find a certain quantity of words whose derivation is unknown, and which seem to be unconnected with any Indo-European language; *e.g.*, dog, rabbit, ramble, etc.[1]

Again, we must not suppose that the history of

[1] Cf. Skeat, Etymological Dictionary, p. 761.

language falls into two parts—a period of *roots*, and another period when language was *built up* of roots. At first, indeed, every idea to be expressed demanded the creation of a new term; and even when the stock of existing words had already become considerable, new thoughts must constantly have arisen for which, as yet, there was no expression. Still, as the existing vocabulary grew larger, the necessity for absolutely new words, not connected with or derived from others already existing, grew less and less; and it would therefore seem as if the need for such formations would have gradually disappeared completely. But a little consideration will suffice to show that, at all stages in the history of language, there must have existed a certain necessity for new creations to express new ideas; and we have a right to assume that in later times, as civilisation grew more complex, the degree in which new creations were necessary remained a considerable one.

The essence of original creation consists in the fact that a group of sounds is connected with a group of ideas, without the intervening link of any association already existing between a similar, related sound-group, and a similar, related idea. When the Dutch chemist, Van Helmont, conceived the novel idea of a category which should embrace all such substances as *air, oxygen, hydrogen*, etc., he invented a new term, 'gas,' which, unless the fancied connection with the word 'geest' (ghost) was indeed present in his mind, was a 'new creation.' If, on the other hand, some one were now to invent some entirely new process of treating gases, or of treating other substances with gases, and to indicate such an operation by some such form as *gasel*, the word *gasel* would no doubt be quite new, but we should not speak of it as an 'original creation' in the sense in which we use the words in this chapter. It would be a new *derivative*.

Original creation is due, in the first instance, to an impulse which may disappear and leave no permanent traces. It is necessary, in order that a real language may arise from this process, that the sounds should have operated upon the mind so that memory can reproduce them. It is further necessary that other individuals should understand the sounds which thus constitute a word, and should be able to reproduce them as well.

We find that the new is named in language after what is already known; in fact, the old and the new stand related to each other as cause and effect: in other words, the new is not produced without some kind of connection with the old. This connection generally consists of some pre-existing association between cognate words and cognate ideas. In the case, then, of original creation, the essence of which we declared to be the absence of that link, some other connection must exist ; and this will generally be found in the fact that the sounds and their signification suggest each other. The sounds in that case will strike the generality of hearers as appropriate to the meaning intended to be conveyed, and the speaker will be conscious that those sounds are peculiarly fitted to express the idea which is in his mind. As an instance, we might take the barbarously constructed word 'electrocution,' now in use in America to denote the new method of inflicting the death penalty in that country. The word *electric* is understood ; and so is the word *execution :* the barbarous new word is the effect of our previous comprehension of these two words. Such appropriateness will secure the repetition of the new creation by the same speaker, and make probable the spontaneous creation of the same term by various speakers living in the same mental and material surroundings, both which effects are essential conditions for the common acceptance of the new expression.

The most obvious class of words to illustrate this connection between sound and meaning is what is known as 'onomatopoietic;' *i.e.* names which were plainly coined in order to imitate sounds. The most common of these are such as seem to be imitations of noises and movements. Such are *click, clack, clink, clang, creak, crack, ding, twang, rattle, rustle, whistle, jingle, croak, crash, gnash, clatter, chatter, twitter, fizz, whiz, whisk, whiff, puff, rap, slap, snap, clash, dash, hum, buzz, chirp, cheep, hiss, quack, hoot, whirr, snarl, low, squeak, roar, titter, snigger, giggle, chuckle, whimper, croon, babble, growl.*[1] Those with the suffix *le* are used to express iteration, and so to form frequentative verbs. These suffixes are specially noticeable in words of imitative origin, such as the list given in Skeat, English Etymology, p. 278. Some verbs denote at once a noise and an explosion, like *bang, puff;* French, *pan, pouf:* others a noise and motion, as *fizz, whirr.* These are words which appear to date from comparatively modern English. There would be no difficulty in gathering from Greek and Latin parallel instances, namely of words imitative of sounds, which seem to be new creations and have no apparent connection with any other Indo-European language, such as *gannire,* χρεμετίζειν.

It would seem, therefore, that, as far as we can

---

[1] In O.Fr. we find *baer,* Prov. *badar,* 'to open the mouth,' properly speaking to 'utter the sound *ba;*' *bouffer,* from a French interjection *buf.* The word *piquer* comes from an interjection representing the sound uttered on giving a prick, *pic!* Other examples are O.Fr. *glapir,* 'to bark;' *ronfler, miauler, chuchoter, caqueter; toutouer, vonvonner, pouf.*

judge, the original creations of language must have consisted in words expressive of emotion on the one hand, and of sounds on the other.

Because, in such words as we have been considering, we recognise an intimate affinity between the sound and the signification, it does not however follow that all these words must necessarily have been in their origin onomatopoietic. There are some cases in which the words have been consciously modified so as to imitate the sound; as, *hurtle, mash, smash. Some* may thus, perhaps, only *seem* to be 'new creations,' but it is very unlikely that this is generally the case. Nay, we may say it is certain that most of such words as we have been considering are 'new creations,' and we are further strengthened in this conviction by the fact that we frequently find words of similar meaning, and very similar forms, which cannot, according to the laws of sound, be referred to a single original; such are, e.g., *crumple, rumple, crimp; slop, slap, slip; squash, gash; grumble, rumble.* These seem to support the idea that they were formed as imitative of sound.

Strictly speaking, however, the only absolutely certain original creations are interjections. True interjections, at least those usually employed, are as truly learnt by tradition as any other elements of language, and it is owing to their association that they come to express emotion. But, as reflex-utterances to sudden emotions, they essentially belong to the class of words we are now considering. Once existing, they become conventional, and hence it is that we see different sounds employed to express the same emotions in different languages. Thus we have in English to express surprise, *Dear me!*—in Greek, Παπαί——German, *Aha!* The Englishman says *Hulló* with rising, where the Portuguese would say *Holà* with

falling intonation.   To express pain, we have *Alas!*
Welladay! Woe's me!—in German, *Ach! Weh! Au!*
—in French, *Oh! Hélas! Ciel!*—in Gaelic, *Och! Och
mo chreach!*   To express joy, we have in English,
Hurrah, Good!—in German, *Heida! Heisa! Juch!
Juchheisa!*—in Greek, Εὖγε!—in Latin, *Evax!*—in
French, the old expression, *Oh gay!* (Molière, Mis.,
Act. I., sc. iii.).   Hence it is, too, that individuals
employing the same dialect employ different interjections to express the same emotion.   Thus, different
individuals in the same linguistic community might
employ, to express disgust or disbelief, *Pshaw! Fudge!
Stuff! Nonsense!* etc.

Of the interjections cited above, it may be noticed
that some, like *Pshaw!* and *Pooh!* seem to be a
primitive and simple expression of feeling.   Most
interjections, however, seem to be made up of existing
words or groups of words; cf. *farewell, welcome, hail,
good, welladay, bother, by 'r Lady, bosh*: and this is the
case in the most various languages.   In many cases,
their origin is quite concealed by sound changes; as in
hélas, which is really derived from the natural sound
hé, and *las*, 'weary,' and has come to be pronounced
'hélas.'   Other instances are *Welladay! Zounds!* (i.e.
God's wounds), *Jiminy* (i.e. *Jesu Domine*).   Some of
these have been assimilated by popular etymology to
words existing in the language; such as *Welladay!*
into which meaningless expression the old form
wellaway (A.S. *wá lá wá = wo! lo! wo!*) has been
turned.   Other instances are *harrow*, in Chaucer, from
N.F. *haro*; *goodbye*, from *God be wi' ye*; *palsangguné =
par le sang béni* (Molière); *cadedis*, in Gascon, (= *cap
de Dieu* = caput Dei).   Some, again, have come to be
used as expressions of emotion, being in their origin
foreign words whose signification is partially or wholly

forgotten; such are *Hosannah!*[1] (Save, we pray),
Hallelujah![2] (Praise ye Jehovah).

There seems, however, to be a certain number of
words which owed their origin immediately to reflex
movements, and which come to be employed when we
happen to again experience a similar sudden excite-
ment. Such words as these are *bang, dash, hurrah,
slap, crack, fizz, boom.* There are, probably, 'interjections' which, in single cases, are natural productions,
and in all cases lie near the field of natural production;
e.g., the sign of shuddering, or shivering with cold,
horror, fright (often written *ugh!*). It accompanies the
shiver of the body and is itself the result of an expulsion
of air from the lungs through the vocal passages
where all the muscles are in a state of sympathetic
contraction. *Aau!* may also be, in single cases, a
natural production. *Aautch* is a sort of diminutive
of it. Again, the sound used in clearing the throat is
a purely natural production. Coupled with closure
of the lips, forcing an exit by the nasal passages, it
assumes the form *hm!*—or *hem!* as commonly written.
As commonly appearing preparatory to speaking, it
comes by association to have value in attracting attention.

Many of these words are, at the same time, substantives or verbs as well; and in this case it is often
difficult to say whether the interjectional use, on the
one hand, or the nominal and verbal on the other, is
the original. For us, however, this is at present
immaterial; as long as in the one we have a real 'original

---

[1] Heb. *hôshî' a,* 'to save,' hiphil (*i.e.* active causative) of
yásha'; and *ná,* a particle signifying entreaty. (Skeat, Etymological
Dictionary, s.v.)

[2] *Halelú,* 'Praise ye,' (from verb *halal,*) and *jáh,* short form of
Jahve = Jehovah. See ibid., s.v.

creation,' the other meaning may be a derived one. Duplication and triplication of sounds is often employed, and often the vowel sounds belonging to the different syllables are differentiated by *ablaut*. Thus *chit-chat, ding-dong, snip-snap* (Shakespeare, Love's Labour 's lost, V. i.), *tittle-tattle, kit-kat* (in 'the Kit-kat Club'), *sing-song, see-saw, gew-gaw, tick-tack ;* French, *clic-clac, cric-crac, drelin-drelon, cahu-caha* (used to express the jolting of a vehicle). Words used as substantives only, are formed in somewhat similar pairs as *hurly-burly, linsey-woolsey, hotch-potch ;* and so also are adverbs such as *helter-skelter, higgledy-piggledy.* Old language material, too, is often employed in the formation of such words as *sing-song, ding-dong, boohoo, rub-a-dub, zig-zag.* We may compare also such formations as *ring-a-ching-a-chink-chink.* There are other words due to the same imitative impulse, which, however, are formed according to the regular laws of language. Such are combinations of several words echoing the sound, and differing only in their vowels : such as *flicker and flacker, crinkle-crankle, dinging and donging.*

Nursery language. Most nursery language is imitative of natural sounds, and reduplication plays an important part in the words in this ; cf. *bow-wow, puff-puff, gee-gee,* etc.[1] This language is not invented by children, but is received by them like any other, and welcomed by those who have to teach infants, as facilitating the efforts of the teacher. The relation of the sound to the meaning which often still exists therein, facilitates the acceptance of the word by the child to be taught. Indeed, the words of the language of culture are

---

[1] The relation of sound to meaning in *gee-gee* is, *for infants*, no clearer than between *horse* and its meaning. This offers the best proof of the conventionality of much nursery talk.

sometimes actually compounded with words of nursery
language, as in the case of *moo-cow, baa-sheep, coo-dove*.
It must further be remarked that, when a language
has developed into a state of culture and finds it
necessary to create new words, these words accom-
modate themselves to the forms already existing in
the language, and undergo processes of formation
similar to those which have operated on the words
already existing in the language.   They appear with
the derivation and flection syllables common in the
language at the time when they were created.   For
instance, supposing *cackle* and *chuckle* to be words of
this sort, *cack*, and *chuck* or *chugh* are the only parts
due to original creation;—the termination *le* seems a
regular iterative form, and the words have come to be
classified with others of the same formation, and
treated in the same way.   Similar instances are αἰάζω
(αἰαί) οἰμώζω (οἴμοι), etc.

Roots.   We are led to see, then, from such forms
as *cackle*, that what we regard as a *root* need not
necessarily ever have existed as a bare root, as
an independent element; but immediately upon its
appearance, it is naturally provided with one or more
suffixes or prefixes in accordance with the exigencies
of the language.   Thus, for instance, in the Middle
ages a belfry was called *clangorium*.   And further,
the *function* of new creations is determined by the
analogy of other words existing in the language; and
thus the new words, as soon as they appear in the
language, conform to the laws of language, and an
element appears in the words which does not depend
upon original creation.   So φεῦ forms a verb in
Æschylus, Agamemnon: τί ταῦτ' ἔφευξας (1194; see
also line 960); cf. *ächzen* in N.H.G., and the use of
such words as *crack, crackle, crackling*.

In what has been said hitherto, we have mainly considered the form in which language appears ; but neither in this nor in its syntax must we suppose that the first creations with which language began were operated upon by any such influences as analogy. We must suppose them to have been entire conceptions, condensed sentences, as when we cry out *Fire! Thieves!* They are really, it will be seen, predicates ; and an impression unspoken but felt by the speaker forms their subject. The impressions made by noises and sounds would be those that would naturally strike first upon man's consciousness ; and to express these he creates the first sounds of language. The oldest words, therefore, seem to have been imperfectly expressed conceptions partaking of an interjectional character.

Again, it must be remembered that the new creations of primitive man must have been made with no thought of communication. Until language was created, those who uttered the first sounds must have been ignorant that they could thereby indicate anything to their neighbours. The sounds which they uttered were simply the reflection of their own feelings, or when they came by observation to associate with their neighbours' feelings. But as soon as other individuals heard these reflex sounds, and at the same time had the same feelings, the sounds and feelings were in some way connected, and must have passed into the consciousness of the community as in some measure connected as cause and effect. We must also suppose that gesture language developed side by side with the language of sounds : and, indeed, it is not until language has reached a high degree of development that it can dispense with gesture language as an auxiliary. The Southern nations, which use most interjections, employ also most gesticulations. The Portuguese language, for instance, is exceedingly rich in interjections, and moreover these interjections are in common use, to an extent which at first strikes a foreigner as excessive and almost unpleasant, but which he soon learns to appreciate. Conversation in Portuguese often derives a peculiar charm and picturesqueness from the frequency with which one of the speakers expresses his meaning, quite clearly, with some interjection (e.g. *ora*) and some gesticulation.[1]

We must further remember that, as soon as a speaker has recognised the fact that he can, by the means of language, communicate his thoughts, there is nothing to prevent the sounds uttered consciously as the vehicles of communication from attaching themselves to those which are merely involuntary expressions of feelings. Whether the group of sounds so produced shall disappear or survive must depend on its suitability to fill a need, and on many chance circumstances.

It should also be noticed that we must suppose the original human being, who had never as yet spoken, to have been absolutely unable to reutter at his will any form of speech which he had chanced to produce. He would slowly and gradually, after repeatedly hearing the sound, acquire the capacity for reproducing it. The children of our own day hear a certain number of definite and limited sounds repeated by persons in whom identical motory sensations have developed.

We are driven, therefore, to assume that language must have begun with a confused utterance of the most varying and uncertain articulations, such as we never find combined in any real language. We may thus

[1] See also an article of S. Mallery on Gesture Language among Savages, in Techmer's Internationale Zeitschrift, vol. i., p. 193.

gather that the consistency in motory sensation necessary to a language must have been very slow in
developing.

The result, then, at which we arrive is that no
motory sensation can attain to a definite form and
consistency except for such sounds as are favoured by
their natural conditions. The sounds most open to be
acted on by such conditions are those immediately
resulting from the attempt to express natural feelings ;
in the endeavour to express these, nature, which
prompted the feelings, must have prompted some
uniformity of utterance. The traditional language
must at its outset have contented itself with comparatively few sound signs, even though a large quantity
of different sounds were, on different occasions, uttered
by the different individuals.

The process of utterance must have been long and
tedious before anything worthy to be called a language
could come into existence. A language cannot be
produced until individuals belonging to the same
linguistic community have begun to store up in memory
the product of their original creations. When they
can draw upon their memory at will, and can count
upon reproducing the same sound-groups to represent
the same ideas, and can likewise count upon these
sound-groups being understood in the same sense, then,
and not till then, can we speak of language in any true
sense.

If this be the true test of the existence of a language,
it is no doubt true that we must admit that many beasts
possess language. Their calls of warning or of entice-
ment are clearly traditional, and are learnt from those
around them. They utter the same cries to express
the same emotions, and this consistently. But the
language of beasts suffices only for the expression of a

simple and definite feeling. The language of man consists in the grouping of several words so as to form a sentence. Man thus develops the power of advancing beyond simple intuition, and of pronouncing judgment on what is not before him.

CHAPTER X.

THE process of forming our modal and material group-ings of ideas, and of the terms which we use to express those ideas, is essentially a subjective one, and is, as such, productive of results which would seem at first sight to be incapable of scientific generalisation. Within the limits, however, of any given linguistic community, the elements of which such groups can be formed are identical, and—with all possible divergence of width and depth of intellectual development in the members of that community—there is a certain uniformity in the manner in which each individual member employs that part of the common stock of ideas and terms of which he is master. Hence it inevitably follows that the groups which are formed will, IF THE AVERAGE be taken, prove about equal, and we are thus justified in abstracting from the individual, and in generalising concerning such grouping at any given period, in exactly the same manner as we do in speaking of the language of a community or of the pronunciation of a given word by a community. In this process, we may for our purpose neglect individual peculiarities or deviations from that abstract and always somewhat arbitrary norm.

And just as the language of any two periods of

time shows that differences arise which permeate the whole, so, if we compare the groupings of which we can prove the existence in former times by the influence they exerted on the preservation or destruction of different forms in the language with those we can observe at present in our own linguistic consciousness, or with those which were prevalent at any other period of time, we notice (1) that what formerly was naturally connected by every member of the linguistic community is no longer felt to belong together, and (2) that what once formed part of different and disconnected groups has been joined together.

It is the former of these two events which we have to discuss in this chapter :[1] its chief causes are change in sound and change in, or development of, signification. The effects of the latter in isolating more or less completely some word or some particular use or combination of any word from the group with which, owing to parallelism in meaning, it was once connected, we have already illustrated in Chapter IV. Sound-change has or may have similar effects, and even the influence of analogy, which, as we have seen in Chapter V., is mainly effectual in restoring or maintaining the union between the members of a group, sometimes contributes to the opposite effect when any one particular member happens, from whatever cause it may be, to be excluded from its operation.

Thus, for instance, our present word *day* is found in Anglo-Saxon as—

Nom. and Acc. Sing. *dæg*	Plur. *dagas*
Gen.	,, *dæges*	,, *daga*
Dat.	,, *dæge*	,, *dagum,*

---

[1] The latter, the formation of new groups, forms the subject of the next chapter.

where *æ* was pronounced as the *a* in *man, hat*, etc.,
and *a* as *a* in *father: æ* is therefore a 'front-vowel,'
like the *a* in *fate, ee* in *feet*, etc., while *a* of *dagas* was
a 'back-vowel,' as are *o* or *u*.

The phonetic development of final or medial *g*
differs according to the vowel which preceded it. If
this was a front-vowel the *g* became *y* (vowel),[1] if it
was a back-vowel the *g* became *w*. Thus, *e.g.*, A.S.
hnægan, E. *neigh ;* A.S. *wegan*, E. *weigh ;* A.S. *hálig*,
E. *holy :* but A.S. *búgan*, E. (*to*) *bow ;* A.S. *boga*, E.
bow ; A.S. *ágan*, E. *to own*. Accordingly *dæg*, etc., in
the singular became *day*, whilst in the plural we find
in M.E. *dawes*, etc. As soon, however, as analogy
had established the 'regular' *s* plural to the sing. *day*,
plur. *days*, the verb (*to*) *dawn*, A.S., *dagian* was thereby
isolated completely, and no speaker who is not more
or less a student of the history of English, connects
the verb with the noun.

Another instance may be found in the word *forlorn*.

To understand the history of this word we must
know what is meant by Verner's law.

Among the first illustrations of the regular correspondence of the several consonants in Latin and in
the Teutonic languages are such pairs as *mater,
mother ; pater, father ; frater, brother ; tres, three ;
tu, thou :* in all of which a *th* is found in English
where the Latin shows a *t*. This and other similar
regular interchanges were generalised by Grimm and
formulated by him as a law, part of which stated
that if the same word was found in Latin, Greek,
and Sanscrit, as well as in Teutonic, a *k, t, p*, in the
first three languages appeared as *h, th, f* in Low German, of which family English is a representative.

---

[1] *I.e.* the *sound* of *g* was replaced by the *sound* of the (vowel) *y ;*
the *spelling* varies, as is shown by the given instances.

All our sets of examples seem to illustrate and confirm this law. If, however, we trace the English words back to older forms, we see that this absolute regularity is disturbed. In Middle-English almost invariably, and in Anglo-Saxon invariably, we find *fader*, *moder*, *brother*, A.S. *fæder*, *môdor*, *brôðor*, in perfect agreement with O.S. *fadar*, *môdar*, *brothar*, and Goth. *fadar*, *brothar* (cf. Mod. Ger. *vater*, *mutter*, but *bruder*). It was Karl Verner who explained this irregularity, and proved that it was connected with the place of the accent in the Teutonic languages, not as we find it now, but as it can be proved to have existed in those languages, where it corresponded generally with the Greek accents, or more closely still with the accent in Vedic Sanscrit. There we find that in the corresponding forms *pitar*, *mâtar*, and *bhratar*, the accent or stress lay on the FIRST syllable in *bhratar*, but on the LAST in *pitar* and *mâtar*. Verner proved by numerous examples that only where an ACCENTED vowel preceded the *p*, *t*, *k*, Teutonic showed the corresponding *f*, *th*, *h*; but that, on the other hand, where the preceding vowel was UNACCENTED, instead of *f*, we found *b*, and *d* instead of *th*, *g* instead of *h*. And also, instead of *s*, which was elsewhere found both in Latin or Sanscrit as well as in Teutonic, *z* was found, which *z* further changed into *r* in Anglo-Saxon.

Thus—to give one more instance—the suffix *ian*, used to form causatives in Teutonic, once bore the accent, which afterwards was placed on the root-syllable. Accordingly, the causative of the verb *rís-an* (to rise) was once *rás-ian*,[1] which, with *z*, and, later on, *r*, instead of *s*, changed into *rǽr-an*, Mod. Eng. *to rear*.

---

[1] The *á* and *í* have here the acute accent to indicate *length* of the vowel, not the *stress* or 'accent.'

The so-called Grammatical change in Anglo-Saxon (and other Teutonic languages) now becomes clear:

The verb	in past sing.	plur.	p. part.
céosan (to choose) has	*caés*	*curon*	*coren*
sniðan (to cut; Scotch, *sned*) has	*snáð*	*snidon*	*sniden*
téon (to drag) has	*téah*	*tugon*	*togen*

and all this series of regular sound-change depends upon the fact that in the past plural and in the past participle the accent fell ORIGINALLY on the termination. Similarly, (*for*) *léosan,—léas,—luron,—loren,* from which last form we have our word *forlorn,* meaning, therefore, 'completely lost.' Already, however, in Anglo-Saxon, in very many verbs all traces of this grammatical change have disappeared, and the history of the strong conjugation in Middle-English shows the gradual supersession of the consonants in the past plural and past participle by those found in the present and past singular. Hence those forms in which these older consonants remained were more and more isolated from the groups with which they are etymologically connected; and as little as in popular consciousness *to rear* is grouped with *to rise,* so little is the adjective *forlorn* thought of as a member of the group *to lose, lost,* etc.

We have had already more than one occasion to point out that not only words, but also syntactical combinations and phrases can and do form matter groups. Nay, even the various meanings of a syntactical relation are thus combined.

Such a relation, for instance, is that expressed by the genitive. Though we employ — and formerly employed more generally than now—this case with various meanings, all these meanings are more or less (rather less) consciously felt as one, or at least are closely related—and they continue to be so felt, *i.e.* the grouping remains a close one—as long as these various usages remain general and what we may call living. When, however, any one of these usages becomes obsolete, and the relation indicated finds another form of expression in some other syntactical arrangement, some few examples of the older mode of expression, strengthened as they are by, *e.g.*, very frequent employment, remain, but cease to be felt as instances of that relation.

Thus, though the meaning of the genitives in *This is my father's house*, and in *God's goodness* is essentially different—the one expressing an ownership of one person with regard to a material external object, the other the relation between a being and an immaterial inherent quality,—both are felt as one kind of relation ; nay, the superficial thinker has some difficulty in fully realising that they express really TWO meanings. More easily felt is the difference between the Latin and French 'genitivus subjectivus' and 'genitivus objectivus :' *amor patriæ, l'amour de la patrie* (the love for our fatherland, *ob. gen.*), and *amor matris, l'amour de la mère* (the love which our mother feels for us, *sub. gen.*). Yet, once more, even this difference is not always realised by every one who uses both constructions. Another use of the genitive once was to form adverbs. As long as any genitive could be thus employed, we may be sure that the ordinary speaker will have grouped, when thus using it, not only the particular form with other cases of the same noun, etc., but also the genitives, as such, with other genitives. When, however, other modes of forming the adverbs prevailed, the old genitival adverbs which remained were no longer felt as

genitives, and became isolated and no longer productive as examples for other formations. A remnant
of this genitive survives in *needs*, and perhaps in
Shakespeare's *Come a little nearer this ways* (Merry
Wives, II. ii.; ed. Collier);[1] in *straightways*, and
certainly in M.E. *his thankes, here unthankes* (libenter,
ingratis), or A.S. *heora ágnes δoances* (eorum voluntate).
It further survives in adverbs derived from adjectives: *else* (from an adj. pron. *el*) *unawares, inwards,
upwards*, etc.

Similarly the preposition *of*, which early began to
serve as a substitute for the genitive, has been
employed in some adverbial and other expressions.
This usage, however, if it ever was really "alive,"
is now completely dead. We find *I must of force*
(Shakespeare, 1 Henry IV., II. ii.) and *my custom
always of the afternoon* (Hamlet, I. v.); and still can
say *of an evening; all of a sudden;* but not, e.g., *of a
moment*. Nor should we now imitate Shakespeare's
not be seen to wink of all the day (Love's Labour's lost,
I. i. 43); *Did you not of late days hear* (Henry VIII.,
II. i. 147), though we still have *of late, of old*.

Many other prepositions offer in their constructions
illustrations of isolation. Thus, *e.g.*, the combination
of any preposition with a noun without an article was
exceedingly common in the older language, and we
still possess a numerous collection of such combinations in almost daily use. Thus we find *indeed, in
fact, in truth, in reality, in jest*, etc., a construction
which perhaps may yet be considered a living one
when the noun is an abstraction. Adverbs of place,
however, such as *in bed, in church*, are no longer
formed at will: no one would say *in house, in room*.

So, again, we have *at home, at sea, at hand*, but

[1] Mätzner, i., p. 380.

not *at house*,[1] *at water, at foot.* We can throw something *overboard*, but not *over wall* or *over river.* We can stand *on shore, on land, on foot, on board*, but do not speak of standing *on bank, on ship.* We can sit *at table*, not *at sideboard.* One may come *to grief, to ruin*, but cannot omit *his* or *her* in *come to . . . death.* We can say *by night, by day, by this day week*, but not *by spring, by winter.* Lastly : we travel *by land, by sea, by water, by rail ;* we send a packet *by parcel delivery ;* we communicate *by letter*, or *by word of mouth*, but should not ask for information by saying, *Let me know by line* (instead of *by a line*), *will you ?*

In the isolation of the genitives, which we discussed above, and in all similar syntactical isolations, it would perhaps be correct to distinguish two phases of development, or—as they are not necessarily chronologically separated—two sides of the same process. For while in course of time, as we have seen, one of the SYNTACTICAL MEANINGS OF THE GENITIVE CASE became isolated from the other relationships expressed by that same case, we must, on the other hand, also remember that this involved an isolation of certain formal or modal groups (in this case, of —s forms) from their historical nominatives, which in most cases in its turn caused, or was accompanied by, a more or less clearly marked separation in development of meanings. When the genitive case was no longer generally employed to form adverbs from nouns and adjectives, words like *needs, straightways, else, upwards*, were no longer felt as genitives, and we now feel that the adverb *needs* is not in our consciousness grouped with the noun *need*, in the same way as, for instance, the nom. plur. *needs* with the sing. *need ;* nay, if we carefully examine the meaning of the adverb, we find that its material

---

[1] Cf. Fr. *chez* = (in) casis.

meaning no longer completely coincides with that of the noun.

The various meanings of the NOUN *need* are *urgent want, poverty, position of difficulty, distress, necessity, compulsion;* the ADVERB answers only to the last two : *He must needs go* could not be used for *He must go on account of urgent want,* or *as a consequence of poverty or distress,* but only for *He must go of necessity, indispensably, inevitably.*

Such formal isolation, then, is almost always at the same time a material one. Thus, we may say that the noun *tilth* is not so intimately connected with the group *I till, tilling, well tilled,* etc., as, e.g., *writing* is connected with *to write,* etc. ; and this because the suffix *-ing* is a living and productive one, *i.e.* one which still forms verbal nouns at our will, whenever the need arises, and from whatever verb ; whilst the suffix *th* is no longer so used, being at the present day comparatively rare in English (*health, wealth, strength, length, breath, width*), and, indeed, more often occurring as an adjectival than as a verbal suffix.

The closest groups are naturally always those consisting of the different inflected forms of the same noun or verb, and the ties connecting the members of such a group are undoubtedly stronger than those between words of different functions, etymologically connected, but whose mode of formation or derivation is not so vividly realised by the ordinary speaker. This is so true, that the same form, when used as present participle, must be said to be more closely connected with the other parts of the verb than when used as an adjective; and this can be proved by the fact that often such an adjective has undergone changes in meaning in which the verb and even the present participle, as such, has not participated. Thus, *e.g.,* the present part. *living*, in 'he is living,' whether we mean this for 'he is alive' or 'he is dwelling in . . .' has the same usage as the verb *he lives*, and no more.   This is, however, no longer true of the ADJECTIVE *living*, in a phrase like 'I give you living water.' To realise this we need but replace the adjective by a relative clause, 'which lives,' when we at once feel that we extend the use of the verb in an unusual way.   Thus, again, the NOUN *writing*, in 'These are the writings of . . .' for 'These are his (perhaps printed) works,' has an application which we could not give to the verb *to write*.

This illustrates the fact that a development in meaning of a derivative is not necessarily shared by or transferred to the primary word, whilst any extension of usage of such parent-word is likely to spread to its derivatives.   The same is of course true of simple and compound words.   Hence the process of isolation of derivative from primary, or compound from simple, generally originates in change of meaning in the former of each of these groups.   Thus, the noun *undertaker* is isolated from the verb *to undertake* in consequence of a restriction of its meaning to the person who makes it his profession to undertake the management, etc., of funerals.   So, again, though the noun *keeper* = guardian, watchman, protector, is applied to a certain gold ring, we could hardly say that such a ring *keeps* the others.   A *beggar*, originally 'one who begs,' is now one who 'habitually begs and obtains his living by doing so,' while, if ever we do apply the term in the wider and older sense, we often indicate— in writing at least—the closer connection with the verb *to beg* by using the termination *er*, the characteristic termination of the nomen agentis *begger*.   There is, in German, a very interesting word which illustrates this fact to an extent which it would be difficult to parallel completely in English. By the side of the verb *reiten*, 'to ride,' a noun *ritter* exists, of which the original meaning was merely *a rider*. Like our word 'beggar,' this *ritter* was specialised in meaning, and applied to one who rides habitually and as a profession, *i.e.* a warrior who fights on horseback. When these warriors began to form a privileged body (an order to which many were admitted who never, at least professionally, rode) the noun attained a meaning to which no verb could correspond.

Again, some adverbs, especially such as emphasise our expressions, have developed in meaning often much further than the primary adjective has followed them. Thus *very*, as adverb a mere emphatic word, has, as adjective, retained much more fully its original meaning of *true*: cf. *this is very true, very false*, with, *a very giant*. It is the same with the adverb *awfully*, now indeed common, but noted by Charles Lamb as a Scotticism, and with the adjective *sore*, and the adverb *sorely*.

It is, however, not *always* the derivative which, in its isolation, assumes the modified signification. The primitive may change, and the derivative remain stationary. Thus the English *shop*, as a place for retail trade, has been displaced in America by *store*, while *shop* comes to have the value of *work-shop*, *machine-shop*, etc. Yet the derivative *shopping*, a much-used word in America, retains a reminiscence of the older value of *shop*.

To return for a moment to the example which we gave from German : the verb *reiten* (pronounced with a vowel sound closely resembling that of *i* in *to ride)* and the noun *ritter (i* nearly like *i* in *rid*, or, more correctly, like *ee* of *need*, but shortened), show a gradation of vowel-sound, of the same nature and origin as that in such pairs as *write, wrote ; sing, sang ; give, gave.* This change in vowel-sound without doubt co-operated in effecting the isolation, and so facilitated the change in meaning in the one form ; a change in which the other did not participate. Thus, speaking generally, phonetic development, by creating numerous meaningless distinctions, loosens the modal and material groups, and serves to forward isolation of meaning. Thus, again, the special meaning which we now attach to the verb *to rear* would have been more likely to transfer itself to the primary verb *to rise,* or—*vice versâ*—the meaning of the primary *to rise* would have almost certainly prevented the special development of *to rear,* if the etymological connection had not been obscured by the phonetic development which we formulate as Verner's law, *i.e.* if the grouping had not been loosened.

It is, moreover, clear that if, from whatever cause, an interchange of certain sounds becomes less frequent in a language, those words which do preserve that interchange become *ipso facto* more strongly separated. Thus,*e.g.*, the *umlaut,*i.e. the change of *u* (sounded as *oo*) to *ü* (sounded as *u* in French, the Devonshire *u ;* more like English *ee* than like English *u*), or of *a* (*a* as in *father*) to *ä* (sound much like *a* in *fate,* but without the *ee* sound which in English follows it), etc., is in German so common that in no case is its presence or absence alone sufficient to effect the isolation of any form from its related group. In English, this interchange has almost completely disappeared, and the few traces of it which we preserve in the plural formation (*foot, feet ; tooth, teeth ; mouse, mice ; man, men,* etc.) are only preserved as so-called 'irregularities,' and no longer form a model or pattern for other formations.

Hence in English, where, besides *umlaut*, we have difference in function (*e.g.* adjective and noun), the isolation has often been complete. Thus, no ordinary speaker groups the adjective *foul* with the noun *filth ;* and the connection, though still felt, between *long* and *length*, *broad* and *breadth*, is undoubtedly less clearly felt than between, e.g., *long* and *longer*, or *broad* and *to broaden*, *high* and *height :* similarly, the difference in vowel between *weal* and *wealth*, (*to*) *heal* and *health*, has facilitated isolation of these forms.

If phonetic development were the only agent in the history of language, we see that, shortly, an infinite variety of forms, absolutely unconnected, or at best but loosely connected, would be the result. But here, as always, we have action and counteraction.[1] This counteracting influence is chiefly exerted by analogy, as we explained in Chapter V. It is, however, not always analogy which brings about the readjustment or unification.

We have already had occasion to point out that our word-division, though undoubtedly based on real and sufficient grounds, is not consistently or even commonly observed in SPEAKING. Our thoughts are, indeed, expressed not in words but in *word-groups ;* and letters, even though they stand at the end or at the beginning of words, have often had a special phonetic development, in cases where these words occurred in very frequent or in very intimate connection with other words. The differences so created have very commonly, though not by any means universally, found expression in writing. As an instance of a differentiation of which the written language takes no cognisance, we may take the French

---

[1] We choose this term in preference to 'reaction,' which, in the physical sciences, has a specific meaning not applicable here.

indefinite article.   Few are unaware that when *un*
stands before a consonant the *n* is not pronounced,
leaving in the spoken word only a trace of its existence
in the fact that the vowel is nasalised. When *un* comes
before a vowel, on the other hand, the vowel is much
less strongly, if at all, nasalised, and the *n* is clearly
pronounced.   Thus (using the circumflex to indicate
the nasal quality of the vowel and *ö* for the sound of
u in *un*), *un père* = *ô père*, but *un ami* = *ön ami* or *ön
ami*.   The corresponding difference which exists in
English is expressed in writing : *a father*, *an aunt*.

Just as the article is closely connected with the
noun, so preposition and noun, or preposition and
verb, are very intimately connected in pronunciation.
Hence—though many, who have never carefully observed either their own pronunciation or that of others,
may dispute or deny the assertion—in ORDINARY conversation, in the phrases, *in town*, *in doors*, we employ
the *n* sound ; but when the word *in* stands before *Paris*
and *Berlin*, we use an *m* sound, just as we say *impossible* by the side of *interest*.   Similarly, we pronounce
generally 'in coming' with *ng* for *n*, just as we speak
of a man's *ingcome*.   This differentiation of the pronunciation of the preposition *in* into three forms—*in*, *im*,
ing—is not, however, consistently expressed by us in
writing. The Greeks, on the other hand, who similarly
differentiated the terminal consonants of the prepositions in their spoken language, but on a much larger
scale (accustomed as they were to a far closer
correspondence between their spoken and their written
language than the Englishman observes), did actually, in
many cases, write as they spoke : κάδ δὲ,—κὰκ κεφαλὴν,
κὰγ γόνυ—κὰπ πεδιόν, etc., instead of employing the normal form of the preposition, κατά. So we find in inscrip-
tions τὴμ πόλιν, τὴγ γυναῖκα, τὸλ λογόν, ἐμ πόλει, etc.

The first step on the road towards unification is
frequently that the external reason which caused the
difference in form, disappears or loses force, and one
form is found in connections where, historically or
phonetically speaking, the other is correct. We may
instance this by the common mistake of children when
they say, e.g., *a apple* instead of *an apple*. In this case,
however, the correct form is so very frequently heard
that the encroachment of *a* on the domains of *an* is not
likely to lead to permanent confusion. Where, however, circumstances are less favourable to the preservation of the historically correct usage, it happens that
either form encroaches on the domain of the other, or
else it may result that the encroachment is reciprocal,
—when, after a period of confusion in which both forms
are used indifferently, one becomes obsolete and falls
into oblivion, not without often leaving some striking
form or phrase to testify to what once existed. Thus,
for instance, our word *here*, Old High German *hier*,
or *hêr*, was, in the period of transition from Old to
Middle High German, differentiated in accordance
with a phonetic law of that time, viz. that final *r* was
dropped after a long vowel. If not final however, *r*
remained untouched, and this whether it stood in the
body of a word or within a group of intimately connected words. Of the two forms *hie* and *hier*, the
former, as the form employed when the word was used
independently, was in Middle High German often set
before words beginning with a vowel ; and we find *hie
inne* (= here-in) or even, by contraction, *hinne*, for *hier-
inne*. On the other hand, it is probably owing to the
frequency of combinations similar and equivalent to
our *here-in*, *here-upon*, etc., that the form *hier*
encroached successfully upon the domain of *hie*, and
finally supplanted it. *Hie*, however, remained, singu-

larly enough, in the one expression *hie und da* (here and there), where the form without *r* is not and has never been, phonetically speaking, correct. An excellent example of this differentiation is furnished by *one, an*.

The best example of the process is furnished by the history of the working of Verner's law, and of the gradual disappearance of its effects. We have before (pp. 172, 173) explained this law and quoted instances of forms created in agreement with it, which have now been replaced by others. To repeat this explanation here with other examples would be superfluous; to give a full history, even confining ourselves to an enumeration of all the various ways in which it has been operative and the areas of its influence, would transcend the scope of this work. To carefully note all instances of its occurrence and its neglect, and to closely investigate the possible courses of the latter, is a task which may most usefully challenge the attention of philologists. We will illustrate the truth of this by a single example: (though even this we cannot discuss exhaustively). The forms which we employ at present as the past tense of the verb *to be*—sing. *was* and plur. (with grammatical change according to the law) *were*, belong to a root which in old English and Anglo-Saxon furnished a complete verb: pres. *wese*, past. *wæs*, p. part. *wesen*. Now we should naturally expect that in a time when the grammatical change was still preserved in

> *freóse, fréas, fruron, froren*, (to freeze) etc.
> *ceóse, céas, curon, coren*, (to choose)
> *seóðe, seáð, sudon, soden*, (to seethe, to boil)

we should also find that change here, and that accordingly the past participle should be *weren. That such a form once existed is proved by the past participle *forweorone* (cf. Sievers, Anglo-Saxon Grammar, § 391). Everywhere, however, in Anglo-Saxon, in the past participle of this verb and in that of all similarly conjugated, such as *lesan*, *læs*, *lesen* ; *genesan*, *genæs*, *genesen*, etc., the *s* has once more been fully established. The fact that *these* past participles had already so far proceeded on the road to unification, while the others as yet remained isolated, may be explained in this way,—the latter, IN ADDITION to the differentiation in accordance with Verner's law, showed a difference of vowel-sound, which in the case of others did not exist. Hence the forms differentiated in two distinct ways were able to resist the tendency towards unification long after those which differed only in one respect had succumbed. In fact, of the former we still have such remnants as *forlorn*, from *to lose* ; *sodden*, from *to seethe*. We may formulate the result which we have illustrated, thus : *The greater the phonetic distance of two differentiated forms, the greater is the power of resistance against unification and equalisation.*

But the ORDER in which we see the traces of the working of Verner's law disappear one after another, and the study of such few remnants as still exist, brings out two other general truths concerning unification. We may without hesitation affirm that, close as is the etymological connection between the various tenses of the same verb, or, to speak perhaps more correctly, that clearly as that connection is felt by the speech-making community, it is still more strongly felt as between the various forms of the same tense, or the various cases of the same noun. Now, it is against the differentiation between the members of these most intimate groups that unification first takes place. In the declension of the noun, where nothing but the operation of

Verner's law had separated the various cases, the re-assimilation first took place, and though we can prove that, in this case also, the differences actually once existed—in the historic periods of the Teutonic dialects almost all traces thereof have been obliterated.   In the past tenses of the verbs they are still at first found, supported as the differentiation had been by that other force—the gradation of vowels (the 'ablaut').[1]   But again : unification between the singular and plural of the past tense took place first in cases where the vowels were alike in both, and next in those where the vowels differed—and again, this occurred *before* the unification of the past participle with the whole group. In agreement with this same rule, that very difference of vowel-sound has completely disappeared in all past singulars and plurals, even where—as, *e.g.*, in German generally—the past participle still preserves the 'ablaut.'

We can then lay it down as a second rule, *that the closer the etymological connection is between differentiated forms, the sooner will unification be effected ;* whilst a consideration of such rare instances as the preservation of the interchange of *s* and *r* in *I was, we were*, which is clearly due to the very exceptional frequency with which these forms must always have been used, and the consequent firmness with which they are impressed on every speaker's memory, exhibits a third law, viz. *that the greater the intensity with which differentiated forms are impressed upon the minds of the community, the greater will prove their power of resistance against unification.*

It is further evident that in cases where the dif-

---

[1] And by the expectation thus created of the regular occurrence of such differentiation between past singular and past plural, even where this ablaut did not show different vowels.

ferentiation of form had been accompanied by one in meaning, the tendency towards unification was counteracted, or rather can never have existed. Thus, the pair of words *glass* (etymologically = the shining substance) and *glare* (to shine) is separated once and for ever. We have seen the plur. *dawes* re-united to sing. *day;* the verb *to dawn* has not followed suit.

Though thus much is clear, and when once apprehended, almost self-evident, we must acknowledge that much is as yet obscure and unexplained. It is often already very difficult to find any reason why in one case unification has taken place and not in another, which apparently presented the same conditions : it is generally harder still to find an answer to the question why in any given case one form has prevailed over another, instead of the converse having happened. Omniscience alone could answer all such questions : but here, again, a few general observations may serve to explain some points, though, as we have said, much as yet remains inexplicable. Thus, for example, when unification replaces the confusion which followed differentiation, members of the same formal or modal group (that is to say, for instance, the same parts of speech) are likely to follow in the same direction. Thus, *e.g.*, in the original Teutonic, when the suffix *no* was preceded by a vowel, that vowel varied in the different (strong and weak) cases of the declensions of nouns, adjectives, and participles, according to fixed rules, between *u* and *e*. This *u* developed into *o* or *a*, and *e* into *i*. Soon unification took place, in some cases in one, in others in another direction, so that we find, for instance, in Gothic a form like *þiudᴀɴs* (king) by the side of *maurgɪɴs* (morning), whilst now, the past participles (formed with this same suffix) all have *ans* throughout; such participles as became pure adjectives

or nouns have often *ins*, e.g. *gafulgins* (adj. 'secret'),
past participle, of *filhan*, 'to hide,' with *fulhans* as
past participle, = hidden; *aigin* (neuter, hence without *s* in nom.) = property, is past participle of *aigan*,
'to have.'

Sometimes—as, for instance, in the singular and
plural of past tense in strong verbs—a differentiation
coincides with difference in function, though its origin
was independent of any such functional divergence.
This, of course, strengthens the phonetic differentiation, and, if such a coincidence affects simultaneously
a formal group of large extent, and thus becomes a
model for analogical formations (Chap. V.), the originally
meaningless phonetic divergence may become indissolubly associated with difference of function, and so
become expressive of the latter.

Thus, for instance, the words *tooth*, *foot*, and *man*
form their plural *teeth*, *feet*, and *men* by *umlaut*, and by
umlaut alone. This modification of the vowel is, then,
here expressive of plurality. Originally, however, it
was not so. In Anglo-Saxon the declension was—

Singular Nom. and Acc.	*fót*	*tóð*	*mann*
Gen.	*fótes*	*tóðes*	*mannes*
Dat.	*fét*	*téð*	*menn*
Plur. Nom. and Acc.	*fét*	*teð*	*menn*
	fóta	*tóða*	*manna*
	fótum	*tóðum*	*mannum*

When once the combined force of nominative, accusative, and genitive had ousted the modified vowel
from the dative singular, the whole singular exhibited
ó (*a*) in contrast to the nominative and accusative
plural with *é* (*e*). This caused the transference of the
latter to the genitive and dative plural also, and thus

invested the modification with a force originally quite foreign to it.

In English, no doubt owing to the mixed influence upon that language of two very different grammatical systems (the Teutonic of Anglo-Saxon, and the Romance of Norman-French), unification has proceeded to a far greater length than in most other Teutonic dialects.   In German, *e.g.*, the history of the *umlaut* and the origin of plurals in *er*—of which English has no trace but the provincialism *childer*, or the "correct" form *children*—furnish examples of what we have said ; and students of German will find a careful investigation of that history both interesting and instructive.

CHAPTER XI.

THE effect of sound-change is to produce differences in language where none previously existed ; but it likewise tends to cancel existing differences, and to cause forms originally distinct to resemble each other or actually to coincide. Now, symmetry and uniformity are clearly an aid to the memory, when attained by the abolition of useless and purposeless differences. It is, for instance, in English, far simpler to state, and far more easy to remember the statement, that all plurals are formed by adding *s* to the singular, than that some are formed in -*n*, or -*en*, or by such modifications as *man, men ; foot, feet ;* etc. : and it is therefore a gain to language when such forms as *shoon, eyen,* etc., disappear in favour of such forms as *shoes, eyes,* etc. On the other hand, the cancelling of such differences when they serve to mark different functions is naturally disadvantageous and tends to obscurity. When a sound which marked such a functional difference disappears, or when of two words or forms which had different meanings one becomes obsolete, and the other is employed to do service for both, it is clear that language cannot but be the loser by dispensing with an important aid to clearness and distinction. Thus, of the two forms *mot* and *moste,* the former has now disappeared, and the latter, in the form *must*, serves to indicate both the present and the past tense. The effect of this ambiguity is that where we wish to clearly indicate the past of *must*, we have to employ some idiom in which *must* has no place ; as 'was obliged to,' 'had to,' 'was constrained to,' etc. Similarly, the loss of the plural *s* in very many French nouns (which *s*, though still written, is seldom sounded) would create ambiguity were it not that the difference of the article attached to the noun marks the difference, and to a large extent remedies the evil ; cf. *l'ami, les amis*.

The remedy, however, for such obscurity is not always to be found in the context. Sometimes, indeed, the evil brings its own cure ; changes arise which enable the necessary distinctions to be once more felt and maintained, creating new forms by analogy with other forms (see Chapter V.) : but, on the other hand, it frequently occurs that the evil remains, and a confusion follows in the grouping of the words ; which grouping, as we have seen, is all-important in the life history of the members of the group.

We must in this chapter endeavour to study some of the results of this confusion, and consequent rearrangement in the groups ; and to distinguish the cases where similarity caused by phonetic development affects the matter-groups from those where the modal-groups are influenced.

I. i. There are many cases where words connected neither by etymology nor by signification fall into the same form.

Still, in spite of this similarity in form, the words remain perfectly distinct in the linguistic consciousness of a speaker of ordinary intelligence. Such are, *e.g.*,—

1.   *a. Hale*, in such a phrase as *hale and hearty*.

This word is of Scandinavian[1] origin (cf. Icelandic *heill*), and represents the Anglo-Saxon *hál*, to which word we owe the misspelt word *whole*. *b. Hale*, 'to drag,' found in Middle-English as *halien*.

2. *a. Whole* = A.S. *hál;* see above. *b. Hole* = A.S. *hol*, 'a cave.'[2]

3. *a. Grave* (A.S. *gráfan*). *b. Grave* (Fr. *grave*, Lat. *gravem*).[3]

4. *a. Cope* (O.Fr. *cape*). *b. Cope* (Dutch *koopen* = to *bargain, to chaffer, to buy, to vie with*).

5. *a. Stile* (A.S. *stigel*). *b. Stile* (commonly misspelt *style*, Lat. *stilum*).

6. *a. Well*, adverb (A.S. *wel*). *b. Well*, noun (A.S. *wella*).

7. *a. Arm* (Lat. *arma*). *b. Arm*, the limb, cognate with Ger. *arm*.

8. *a. Lay* (A.S. *lecgan*). *b. Lay* (O.Fr. *lais*, 'song').

9. *a. Pale* (Fr. *pal*, Lat. *pālum*). *b. Pale* (Fr. *pâle*, Lat. *pallidum*).

10. *a. Elder*, the tree (A.S. *ellarn*). *b. Elder*, 'older.'

---

[1] Thus says Professor Skeat, Etymological Dictionary, s.v.; others maintain that it is due to Northumbrian preservation of *a*, which in the South became *o*.

[2] Professor Skeat (Principles of English Etymology, p. 411) draws a useful distinction between *homographs* and *homophones*, or words spelled alike and those sounded alike. For our purpose, as students of the spoken language, the homophones alone are of importance. A homograph is commonly, but not invariably, a homophone; cf. 'I *read* now' and 'Yesterday I *read*.' We need not here further consider such vagaries of English spelling.

[3] It is unnecessary to point out in the text that we must bear in mind that French nouns or adjectives are almost always derived from the accusative case as representative of the oblique cases. For the full explanation of this see Brachet's Grammaire Historique, Introd.

It would, of course, be possible to extend this list to almost any length ; but this would be useless for our purpose, which is to investigate solely those cases in which similarity causes confusion. This happens where the difference in origin and meaning is lost sight of. It is naturally impossible to draw a hard and fast line of demarcation between the case just discussed and that which we are about to exemplify, as one speaker may keep distinct what another may confuse or treat as identical. Still, no one, we may fairly say, unless he be a student of language, or unless he has been expressly informed, is aware that in a phrase like *The ship is bound for London*, the word *bound* employed by him has absolutely no connection with the past participle of the verb *to bind*. In the first case, *bound* is of Scandinavian origin, and meant originally *ready, prepared;* cf. the Icelandic verb *búa*, perf. part. *búinn*, ' to prepare.' Similarly, few ordinary speakers can explain, or indeed realise, the existence of the distinction in meaning between *shed*, ' a hut' (a doublet of *shade*), and *shed* in *water-shed*, when derived from the A.S. *scéadan ;* or that between *sheer*, allied to Icelandic *skærr*, 'bright,' and *sheer*, akin to Dutch *scheren*, ' to shave.' Thus, again, many might suppose that some etymological connection existed between *hide*, ' a skin' (A.S. *hýd*, akin to Ger. *haut*), and *hide*, ' to conceal' (A.S. *hídan*) ; while others, when told that *hide* also served as the name for a certain measure of land, might naturally even suspect some allusion to the famous legend of the foundation of Byrsa or Carthage. The A.S. noun *setl* (a seat) and the verb *settan* survive both in the word *settle* and in *to settle*. In employing, however, the word in ' to settle a dispute,' we have a word of very different origin : the A.S. *sacu*, ' a quarrel,' ' dispute,' ' lawsuit' (surviving in ' for my *sake*,' etc.),

existed side by side with a verb *sacan*, ' to strive,' or
' dispute :' akin to this, we find *saht*, a substantive
which owes its meaning, ' reconciliation,' to the development *lawsuit, adjustment by lawsuit*, etc.   Again,
derived from this we have the verb *sahtlian*, ' to
reconcile,' which, at a later period, occurs in the forms
saztlen and *sattle*.[1]   When this verb ceased to be
understood, confusion with the other verb *to settle* =
to fix, to arrange, arose, and the two forms ' flowed
together, just as two drops of rain running down a
window-pane are very likely to run into one.'[2]
Another instance of this nature is discussed by Professor
Skeat, s.v. ; viz., *sound* = A.S. *sund*, akin to the Ger.
(*ge*)*sund ; sound*, ' a strait of the sea,' and *sound*, M.E.
soun, Anglo-Fr. *soun* or *sun*, Lat. *sonum*.

ii. Such forms, where phonetic development brought
about merely a close resemblance without producing
perfect similarity, and where, as a next step, one or
other of the set of words underwent some change more
or less violent in consequence of its supposed connection with the rest, are peculiarly instructive, proving as
they do the confusion which arose in the minds of the
speakers who thus combined what was distinct and
unconnected.   In these cases we have entered upon
the domain of ' popular etymology,' to which we have
already incidentally alluded.

It does not, however, always follow that the
supposed connection in meaning—in other words, the
coalescence of elements of different origin into a single
material group, brings about the further change in
form ; at this period nothing but the linguistic consciousness of the speaker can decide whether the

---

[1] See Skeat, Etymological Dictionary, s.v. *settle ;* Stratman, s.v.
sahtlen.

[2] Skeat, Principles of English Etymology, p. 410.

'popular etymology' is or has been at work. Of course, as long as the etymology of the different words in the set is clearly understood by the speaker, there can be no question as to the connection, but when one or more of the members of the set is no longer understood in its historical bearings, it is possible for a new grouping to arise.

Let us take, as an instance, the word *carousal*. This bore originally the sense which it bears in the Parisian name of the *Place du Carrousel*, viz. a tournament or festival. It was confused with the word *carouse* (Ger. *gar-aus* = properly 'quite out,' *i.e.* 'empty your glasses'); and at present our word *carousal* represents both. The Anglo-Saxon word *bonda* meant a boor, or householder. His tenure appears expressed in Low Latin by the word *bondagium*, and it is only to a supposed, but wholly erroneous connection with *bond* and the verb *to bind*, that our present word *bondage* owes its sense of *servitude*.

The Fr. *sursis* gave us, before its final *s* had ceased to be pronounced, our verb *surcease*, which most speakers now look on as a compound of *cease* (Fr. *cesser*).[1] *Wiseacre*, really derived through the Dutch from the Ger. *wizago* (A.S. *witega*, 'a prophet'), was already, while on its way to England, misunderstood in Holland, and taken to be a compound of *wise*. In Dutch, a verb *wys-seggen* and a noun *wys-segger* ('to speak wisely' and 'a wise sayer') were formed,

---

[1] Or rather Fr. (*je*) *cesse*. Just as, in the French language, we must explain most nouns from the Latin accusative form, so in English most of the verbs which we owe to French can only be explained by the 'strong' forms, *e.g.* first person singular of the present tense; as *complain* from *je complain*, and not from *complaindre;* to *despise*, O.Fr. *tu despis*, not infinitive *despire;* to *prevail, je prévail,* not *prévaloir;* to *relieve, je (re)lieve,* not from *relever;* to *acquire, j'acquier,* not from *acquérir*.

and modern German as well possesses the word
weissagen, 'to prophesy.' This *wys-segger*, when it
reached England, could no longer be understood as a
derivative from the verb *secgan*, which in English had
already lost its guttural and had become (*to*) *say ;* and
thus popular etymology altered the second part of the
supposed compound into the meaningless *acre*. The
Fr. *surlonge*, the piece of meat 'upon the loin' (Lat.
super, Fr. *sur*, and Lat. **lumbea*, from *lumbus*, Fr.
longe), became in English the *surloyn* in the time of
Henry VI. This was no longer understood ; the word
was accepted as a compound with the word *sir*, and thus
the fable was invented of the 'merry monarch' knight-
ing the loin.[1] The *berfroit* or *belefreit* of Old French
is of German origin, and signifies a watchtower. The
word had ceased to be understood, and its origin was
forgotten ; but, as many towers contained a bell or a
peal of bells, a supposed connection with these bells
caused the word to be changed into *belfry*. The
spelling is affected in *sovereign*, where the *g* is due to
a supposed connection with *to reign* (*régner*, *regnare*) ;
the real derivation being from *soverain* (*superaneum*),
and the word being correctly spelt *sovran* by Milton.
Further instances are *lance-knight* (= *lanz-knecht* =
landes knecht = 'the *knight*, *i.e.* the *man*-of the *land*,'
'the servant of his country') ; *cray-fish* (= *écrévisse*) ;
shamefaced (really *shamefast*, like *steadfast*), etc.

In other cases of rarer occurrence than those which
we have discussed, a significant part of a compound
assumes the form of a mere derivative. This has
occurred in the case of the word *righteous*, taken to be
a derivative from some French adjective in *-eux*, Lat.
-osus, though really due to *right-wise*, a compound like
otherwise. It is natural that Proper nouns, where

[1] See Skeat, s.v.

there is no connection or only a fanciful one between the word and its meaning, should be more liable to such transformations than others; so the *Rose des quatre saisons* appears as the *quarter-sessions rose*, the *asparagus* appears as *sparrow grass*, the ship *Bellerophon* becomes the *Billy ruffan*,[1] the *Pteroessa*, the *tearing hisser*. We may perhaps add here a word like *liquorice*, which, though the name, rightly understood, is descriptive, has become a mere proper noun. Originally from *liquiritia*, itself a corrupt form of *glykyrrhiza* = 'a sweet root,' it has, as its spelling shows, become connected with *liquor*,[2] while those who deemed this impossible preferred to explain the word as connected with *to lick*.[3]

II. Important, then, as the part played by phonetic development is in bringing about the formation of new material-groups, it has made its influence felt more widely still in the modal grouping of the various systems of inflection.

Here, again, two cases should be distinguished: (1) when forms which have had identical functions come to coincide: (2) when such coincidence occurs in the case of forms that have had different functions.

1. The cancelling of diversities in form or in inflection when such inflection indicated no difference in function must obviously on the whole be set down as a gain to language: simplicity is gained thereby without any loss in clearness. This gain, however, is only effected

---

[1] It appears that this, and not *Billy ruffian*, is the form used by sailors. It would thus seem that *Billy ruffian* is a further popular etymology, due to 'scholars.'

[2] See Palmer, Folk Etymology, s.v.

[3] This derivation is given in a certain well-known SCHOOL edition of Milton's Comus: *liquorice = something which makes one lick one's lips !*

when the abolition is complete; should the abolition be partial only, simplification may be gained at the expense of a new confusion.

We have an example of such a complete process of cancelling in the terminations *er* and *est* in the comparative and superlative of adjectives. In Gothic the comparative was formed either with the suffix *iz* or *ôz*, the superlative with *ist* or with *ost;* and, except, indeed, that the forms in *iz* and *ist* were more common than those in *ôz* and *ôst*, and that the latter are found only with stems in *a*, no rule can be given for their occurrence. Thus *mānags* (an *a* stem) has in its comparative *managiz-a*, superlative *managists;* *alðeis* (*ja* stem) *alðiza*, *alðists;* *hardus* (*u* stem), *hardiza*, *hardists;* but *frôðs*, *frôdôza*, *frôdôsts;* *arms*, *armôza*, *armôsts.*[1] In Old High German there was a similar uncertainty. Here the *z* of Gothic appeared as *r* in the comparatives,[2] and while *salîg* has for its comparative *salîgôro* and its superlative *salîgôsto*, we find (*h*)*reini*, (*h*)*reiniro*, (*h*)*reinisto*.[3] In Anglo-Saxon we find already but a single termination for the comparative, viz. *ra;* but the two forms of superlative are still extant in *ost* and *est;* *earm*, *earmra*, *earmost;* *heard*, *heardra*, *heardost;* but *eald* *ieldra* (with *umlaut* or modified vowel),[4] *ieldest.* Our forms *hard*, *harder*, *hardest;* *old*, *older*, *oldest;* *silly*, *sillier*, *silliest*, etc., are clearly a further step in the right direction of simplicity in system.

The convergence is, however, not always complete: sometimes it happens that two systems coincide; and

---

[1] Braune, Goth. Gram., § 135–137.

[2] For similar interchanges of *r* and *z* (*s*), cf. Latin *Venus, Veneris* for **Venesis; arbos, arboris* for **arbosis*, etc.

[3] Braune, Alt-Hochdeutsche Gram., § 260 sqq.

[4] The term *umlaut* is more convenient than 'modification of the vowel sound.'

this coincidence may be (1) in ALL FORMS but only in
SOME WORDS belonging to each system ; or, again, (2) it
may manifest itself in ALL WORDS but only in SOME
FORMS ; and, lastly, this coincidence may affect (3) only
SOME WORDS in SOME FORMS of two converging systems.

In the case of (1) the convergence is complete and
irrevocable, and words which formerly belonged to one
system have simply parted company with it, and have
definitely joined the other to which they were assimilated.   In the cases, however, of (2) and (3), confusion
must arise, and further development must be looked
for.   We find a good illustration of this confusion and
of its development in the history of the Teutonic
declensions.   In the case of these, as of other Indo-
European languages, the declensions differed as the
stems of the words terminated in a consonant or a
vowel ; and amongst the latter, again, we must draw
distinctions between the declension of stems in *a*, (*o*), *i*,
and *u*.   In the *a* declension, again, a subdivision arose
for *pure a, ja, wa,* and *long ā* stems.   These different
terminations of the stems are, for instance, clearly preserved in Gothic dat. and acc. plur. *dags, dagam,
dagans ; gasts, gastim, gastins ; sunus, sunum, sununs ;*
and (with Gothic *ō* instead of *ā*) *gibā, gibōm, gibōs.*
In the oldest forms of Scandinavian, the so-called
Ur-Norse, also, we find the vowels preserved in the
nominative singular, *holingar, erilar,* etc., *gastir, staldir,*
etc., *haukoδur, warur :* [1] but even in these, the oldest
forms of the Teutonic dialects accessible to us, the
various systems were confused ; and it is the study of
Comparative Grammar that we have to thank for the
distinction between the different classes ; and, again, it
is only owing to the light shed on the subject by the
comparison with Latin, Greek, and Sanskrit cognates,

---

[1] Noreen, Altisl. Gram., § 266, 299, 307.

that we are enabled in some instances to decide to which
of these classes any given word belongs.   The 'wearing down' of the various terminations produced here
identity, elsewhere close resemblance of many cases in
many words, while in other cases the influence of the
preceding letter made itself felt, and a difference in
declension arose for the *a* stems : this difference depending on whether the *a* was preceded by a consonant *i* (*j*) or *w*.   Where phonetic development had
caused some of the cases to agree, other cases soon
followed suit, and thus we find, for instance, that even
in Gothic the entire singular of *i* declension has already
become identical with that of the *a* stems :—

		a stem.	*i* stem.
Sing.	Nom.	*dags*	*balgs*
	Gen.	*dagis*	*balgis*
	Dat.	*daga*	*balga*
	Acc.	*dag*	*balg*
	Voc.	*dag*	*balg*
Plur.	Nom.	*dagôs*	*balgeis*
	Gen.	*dagê*	*balgê*
	Dat.	*dagam*	*balgim*
	Acc.	*dagans*	*balgins.*

As a consequence of this, numerous words which
cognate languages prove to belong to the *i* declension
are nevertheless entirely declined like *a* stems in
Gothic ; and even in the very few Gothic texts which
we possess, and though these are derived from one
source only, we meet with words evidencing the fact
that Ulfilas himself (or, it may be, his copyist) was
sometimes confused as to the declension usually
followed by some word in his own language.   Thus,
in case of *wêgs* (a wave), we find nom. plur. *wêgôs*, but
dat. plur. *wêgim* ; so too, the dat. plur. of *aiws* is

aiwam, while the accus. is *aiwins*.   In Old High German the coincidence in termination between these two schemes goes further, and extends over *all cases ;* but since—in such words as had *a, o,* or *u,* in the preceding syllable—*umlaut* had been produced in the plural by the *i* of the stem, only those words whose stem vowel would not admit of *umlaut* or *modification* became throughout identical with the *a* declension. Where the reverse was the case, the words naturally remained distinct in the plural, and a further development arose ; viz. that this *umlaut* in the plural began to be regarded as a sign of that number, and to be used for the purpose of marking it even in words whose etymology afforded no justification for the change, *e.g.* in *hand, hände,* which word originally belonged to the *u* declension.   See also our remarks in Chapter V. pp. 87 and foll.

2. So far, in every case which we have discussed, we have had to do with similarity arising from phonetic development of forms with identical functions : one or more cases of one system *converged* with the same cases in another system.   Often, however, this same phonetic development creates a similarity between forms which were originally distinct and served distinct purposes ; and we have a good instance of this in our personal pronouns, and one which is instructive as to the consequences of this phenomenon :—

The Gothic	*ik*	*meina*	*mis*	*mik*
	ðu	*ðeina*	*ðus*	*ðuk*
	weis	*unsara*	*uns*	*uns*
	jus	*izwara*	*izwis*	*izwis*

already shows no difference in the forms of accusative and dative plural ; but in Anglo-Saxon we find that a further stage has been reached :—

In *ic*	*mín*	*mé*	*mé*
ðú	ðín	ðé	ðé
wé	úser	ús	ús
gé	eówer	eów	eów

we see (though separate forms for accusative still
occur) that dative and accusative have become identical
throughout, and so it is in the modern language with—

I	*mine*	*me*
thou	*thine*	*thee*
we	*our*	*us*
ye (*you*)	*your*	*you*

The double form of the nominative *ye* (*you*), and more
especially the history of the pronoun for the third
person, illustrate one of the consequences of such con-
incidence, viz. that the language-producing community
becomes accustomed to use the same form for certain
sets of functions, and transfers this similarity to cases
which it would not reach—or, at least, has not yet
reached—by the aid of phonetic development alone.
Let us consider first the pronoun of the third person.
In Anglo-Saxon we find—

	Sing. Masc.	Fem.	Neuter.
Nom.	*hé*	*heó*	*hit*
Gen.	*his*	*hire*	*his*
Dat.	*him*	*hire*	*him*
Acc.	*hine*	*hí*	*hit.*

The forms which we now use for the plural are derived
from a different stem,[1] which in Anglo-Saxon gave us
the following plural for all three genders :—

Nom.	ðá
Gen.	ðára, or ðǽra
Dat.	ðǽm
Acc.	ðá

---

[1] So, indeed, is our present nom. sing. fem. *she.*

and here we find distinct forms for dative and accusative, the latter of which has now disappeared, so that here, too (as in the case of the other personal pronouns), we use one form only (the original dative form) for both dative and accusative. But we have only reached this stage after a period of confusion and uncertainty, during which the historically correct form of the accusative and the new form (that of the old dative) strove for permanence.

It is the very marked difference between *ic* (*I*) and *me* (accus.), ᚦ*u* (*thou*) and ᚦ*e*, *we* and *us*, which has protected the members of these pairs from becoming identical in form, notwithstanding the important fact that such a process had long since identified the nominative and accusative of all nouns and adjectives. To this influence, indeed, *ye* and *you* (both of which, when unemphatic, become *ye*, where *e* is pronounced as in *the* before a consonant) have succumbed.

Not only in this way, moreover, does such convergence of forms with different functions show its effect: it also causes the ordinary speaker to lose sight of such difference in function altogether. As students of Latin, and especially teachers of that language, know by sad experience, it is extremely hard for the untrained English mind to realise the function of the accusative case ; and the difference between this case and the dative may be fairly described as nonexistent for the Englishman who has not learnt it from the study of other languages. This, again, influences syntax, so that a phrase like *I showed him the room* can be turned in the passive into *The room was shown* (*to*) *him*, etc., or *He was shown the room*, etc.

CHAPTER XII.

ON THE INFLUENCE OF CHANGE IN FUNCTION ON ANALOGICAL FORMATION.

THE careful consideration of such a form as *I break-fasted* will lead us to understand another phase in the life history of our words, and in the development of their syntactical combinations. It is well known that the word (*to*) *breakfast* is really a compound of the verb *to break* and the noun *fast* (ieiunium). Accordingly, we find, about the year 1400 A.D., 'Ete and be merry, why *breke* yee nowt your *fast;*' in 1653, Izaak Walton wrote, 'My purpose is to be at Hodsden before I *break* my *fast;*' and as late as 1808, Scott writes in his Marmion, 'and knight and squire had *broke* their *fast.*'[1] In these and similar cases, the words have retained their full and original meaning of 'to put an end to fasting by eating;' and the natural apprehension of this compound when employed as a noun was in the sense of the meal whereby this process is effected after the night's fasting, *i.e.* the first meal taken in the day. When once the verb had thus acquired the meaning of 'to take the first meal in the day,' and was next applied even in cases where so little food had been taken before that meal as to be hardly worth considering a 'meal,' the meaning of

[1] Murray, Dictionary, s.v. 29 c.

'breaking the fast' had been effaced by the new sense of *eating the first* IMPORTANT *meal of the day.* The change of meaning, coupled with the change in function, disconnected the compound from the linguistic groups to which it had hitherto belonged, and so it came about that, after the analogy of other verbs formed from nouns, *to breakfast* was conjugated as a weak verb. Thus, in 1679, Everard writes, *After breakfasting peaceably;* and about a century later, the word is used transitively in the sense of 'to entertain at breakfast,' e.g., *They will breakfast you,* or *I was breakfasted.*[1]

This and all the following examples to be discussed in this chapter illustrate the point that, in the unconscious grouping of our words into material and modal groups, it is mainly the function of the word which causes such grouping; and that a change of function, entailing, as it does, a change in the grouping, will often expose the word which has thus altered its meaning to the influence of analogy with other groups, though as long as it preserved its original meaning it stood quite apart from them. No doubt, however, similarity of form conduces also sometimes to this end. The group to which the word once belonged will then follow its own path of development, while the detached member will go on its new way.

We have a similar instance in *vouchsafe : The king vouches it* SAUE (Robert of Brunne, early in fourteenth century), where we should now say : *The king vouchsafes.* The verb *to backbite* is most probably a derivative from the compound nouns *back-biting* (of which the earliest instance dates from 1175) and *backbitter* (which is found as early as 1230); while in the Early English Psalter (A.D. 1300) the past tense

---

[1] Cf. Murray, s.v.

is still formed *bac-bate*.   Gower (1393) already formed
the past participle *back bited*.[1]   Again, the noun *brow-
beating* (from 'to beat one's brows,' *i.e.* 'to lower the
brows,' 'to frown'), found as early as 1581,[2] became,
from a compound noun, a simple one with the meaning of scolding or teasing; and gave rise to a verb *to
browbeat*, of which the earliest known instance dates
from 1603.   It is, however, doubtful whether this verb
has hitherto been definitely separated from the group
to which etymologically speaking it belongs.   The
past participle *brow-beat* (1803 ; Jane Porter, Thad-
deus) occurs, it is true, but the more usual form is as
yet *browbeaten*.

The most ordinary results of this process are, of
course, all the numerous formations from nouns that
have been pressed into the service of verbs ; as, *I box,
He boxed;* (*to*) *dust,* (*to*) *soap,* (*to*) *dog,* etc., etc. : in the
case of all which, the change of function must have
preceded all forms due to analogy with the groups
into which the word entered solely in consequence of
that change.   So, again, as long as a word has an
adjectival function, and even when it is used substantively, but retains its original attributive meaning,
it is, in English, not declined : as *the* POOR *men ; the*
POOR *ye have with you always ; the* BLUE *hats*.   When,
then, only certain individuals belonging to the class
designated by the adjective have to be indicated—and
not, as in the case of *the poor*,—all the individuals
possessing the quality of poverty,—we resort to the
addition of the word *ones* : as, *I do not like those green
hats ; I prefer the blue* ONES.   As soon, however, as
the word loses its real signification, and passes into a
proper noun, it is at once declined : as, *the Grays, the*

---

[1] Murray, s.v.

[2] Ibid., s.v. ; and Skeat, Etymological Dictionary, s.v.

Pettys, the Quicklys; the Blues, the Liberals, the Conservatives, etc.[1]

It may happen that the position of the accent aids to produce change of function, as in the case of *prófecto* (*pró facto*), and in the very interesting case of *igitur,* which has been shown to be the enclitic form of *agitur,* originating in the common Plautine phrase (*Quid agitur*) *Quid igitur.*[2]

The case is similar with the adverbial termination *ment* in French and *-mente* in Italian, from the Latin *mente. Cruellement (crudeli mente)* and *fièrement* are intelligible formations; but *solidement, lourdement,* etc., are formed upon their analogy. At first applied only to adverbs of manner, the termination was transferred to adverbs of time and space; as, *anciennement, largement.* Our English termination *-ly* (from *like*) is a familiar instance of the same degradation of the final syllable: cf. *godlike,* by the side of *godly.*

The word *self* was originally an adjective meaning in Anglo-Saxon and Middle-English 'the same,' and declined in apposition with the noun or personal pronoun to which it was attached to mark emphasis. It then stood in the same case, number, and gender, *he selfe, his selfes, him selfum, hine selfne,* etc., gen. and dat. sing. fem. *hyre selfre,* etc. The history of the development from this usage to our present one is not quite clear; but we should remember that the terminations of the adjective were among the first to wear off completely, or at least to become confused and indistinct; and, further, that the accusative of the personal pronouns, was at an early date merged into

---

[1] Used very often in a sense quite distinct from *the Liberal ones: the Conservative ones,* etc.

[2] Cf. King and Cookson, Principles of Sound and Inflexion, p. 285.

the dative. We thus obtain the following schematic declension :—

SINGULAR.

Nom.	*I self*	*thou self*	*he, she, it self*
Gen.	*my self*	*thy self*	*his, her, his self*
Acc.⎫ Dat.⎭	*me self*	*thee self*	*him, her, him self*

PLURAL.

Nom.	*they selve*
Gen.	*their selve*
Acc.⎫ Dat.⎭	*them selve*

Now, if we bear in mind that in these combinations the accent fell upon the word *self* (or *selve*), and that consequently the proclitic forms *my*, *me*, and *thy*, *thee*, in the genitive and dative had the same sound respectively,—and, further, that in the feminine of the third person singular (*herself*), these two cases were also alike,—it does not seem strange (1) that these two cases (genitive and dative) became confused, and (2) that the word *self* became a noun, as exemplified in such phrases as *I said it to herself*. Once having changed its function, the word assumed the flection of the new group to which its new function had attached it, and a plural form, as of a noun, arose— *themselves, ourselves, theirselves*.[1] When once a single form served in three (genitive, dative, accusative) of the four cases, it not unnaturally succeeded in ousting the last, and succeeded all the more easily as *I self* was, of course, wrong, if *self* was a noun.

It is not, however, an invariable rule that the new

---

[1] This last ungrammatical form, like the singular *his self* (now a vulgarism), testifies to the confusion of dative and genitive.

associations into which a word enters in consequence
of its change of function entail a change of form in the
word. In Latin the word *frugi* was originally the
dative case of a word *frux*, gen. *frugis*, meaning
fruit, profit, advantage; and is actually employed by
Plautus, with the full consciousness of its origin, in
the phrase *bonæ frugi esse* (Asin., III. iii. 12). In fact,
this use is exactly parallel to the use of *usui* in *bono
usui estis nulli*, in Plautus, Curculio, l. 499; but in
this case, *usui*, owing to its frequent occurrence,
preserved the memory of its origin fresh. Cicero,
however, treats *frugi* simply as an indeclinable
adjective: *Homines et satis fortes et satis plane frugi et
sobrii* (In Verrem, v. 27). Instances are also frequent
where a change in meaning brings about a change in
syntactical construction. Thus, for instance, in Latin
we find that the nominative *quisque* is coupled with
the reflective pronoun in the plural almost in the
signification of *singulatim*.[1] In Plautus we find
præsente testibus (Amphitruo, II. ii. 203), and, in
Afranius and Terence, *absente nobis* (Eunuchus, IV.
iii. 7); in these cases the participles approach the
characteristics of prepositions. A similar development
gave to the present participle *considering* its present
prepositional force. *Macte* is used similarly. *Age!* in
Latin is used as generally as *Come!* in English, irrespective of the number of persons addressed; *cave* is
used in the same way. *Paucis* is used for 'a little' in
ausculta paucis (Terence, Andria, 536). *Hélas* is used
in French by women equally as by men; φέρε, ἰδού,
in Old Greek, are addressed to either one or many
persons indifferently. In the same way, in late Greek,
ὤφελον and ὤφελε were employed simply as conjunctions, without any consideration of number or person,

---

[1] Cf. Roby, Latin Syntax, p. xxiii., and §§ 1069, 1073.

the original construction having been Ὀλέσθαι ὤφελον
τῇδ᾽ ἡμέρᾳ = 'Would that *I* had perished on that day!'
In English *albeit* is used simply as a conjunction, and
may be, in the sense of perhaps, is showing a tendency
to fuse into one word, as it is actually written in
American conversational language *mebbe*.

In German we find expressions like *Heb hinten
über sich das glas*, 'Raise your glass high' (Uhland,
Volkslieder) instead of *über dich*.   In the same way
we find in Latin *suo loco*, etc. ; and in Latin law
formulæ, *Si sui juris sumus*, where we should expect
Si nostri juris sumus (*i.e.* 'If we stand in our own
rights').   In Old Norse a middle and passive is formed
by the aid of a reflective *-sik* (sese), which is, of
course, properly applicable to the third person only :
it appears later as *st;* thus, *at kalla*, 'to call;' *at
kallast*, 'to be called.'   In the same way, we have
in English the words (*to*) *bask* and (*to*) *busk*,[1] where
the proper meaning of the termination has so completely died out that it is possible to write *busk
ye*.   The passive is similarly formed in the Slavonic
languages.

Again, change of meaning influences the construction in the case of numerous verbs in Latin, which
are properly intransitive, but are used as transitives.
Such are *perire*,[2] *deperire ; demori*, used in the sense of
'to be mortally enamoured of;' *stupere*, 'to marvel at;'
ardere, 'to love with fire:' the last-mentioned two
words approximate in sense to *mirari* and *amare*
respectively, and hence the instinct of language
employs them in the same government.

The verb *to doubt*, in the etymological signification
of hesitating between two beliefs, was, and is still

---

[1] Morris, Historical Outlines, p. 6.
[2] See Roby, Syntax, p. 51.

constructed with *whether*. If, however, Spenser (Faëry Queene) says—

> 'That makes them doubt their wits be not their aine,'

it is because the word is employed in this case, as indeed it frequently is in Shakespeare, in the sense of 'to fear.'

The verb *to babble*, originally used intransitively, means *to prattle* or *to chatter*. When, however, it is employed in the sense of 'to speak foolish words,' or of 'to reveal by talking,' it is used with an object in the accusative case, and a passive is formed of it; e.g., *Griefs too sacred to be babbled to the world*. Again, compound words, as long as they are felt as such by the speakers, are naturally treated as such; cf. the Latin word *respublica*, which, though we write it as a single word, was declined in both its parts, *respublica, reipublicæ*, etc. But, when it had once become an indivisible unit—when the form *république* in French, or the English word *republic*, was formed with its various meanings, all closely resembling, but not identical with, that of the original compound, the word came to be treated after the analogy of other nouns, and the same derivatives are formed from it as from a simple form; cf. *republican*, etc. This fact is, again, instanced by such forms as *high-spirited* (high-spirit + ed, and not high + spirited), *gentleman-like* (gentleman + like, not gentle + manlike), *good-natured* (goodnature + ed, not good + natured).

Similarly, the Latin compound *i* (a demonstrative pronoun) + *pse* was at first declined as *eumpse* (*e.g.*, Plautus, Truc., I. ii. 64), *eampse, eopse, eapse*, etc., all which forms are found in Plautus.[1] When, however,

---

[1] Nay, we even find the suffix *-pse* attached to other parts of speech; cf. *sirempse*, Plaut., Amphit., Prol. 73.

the word came to be looked on as a simple word, it was declined as such : *ipsum, ipsam, ipso, ipsa,* etc.

In German there are many instances of words compounded with adverbs of place which are specially instructive as to the way in which a word may become detached from its previous use by a change of meaning. For instance, in modern German the usage is to say *wirken* AUF *etwas*, and not IN *etwas*, which was the usage even in the last century. In the same way, we speak of influence *over* as much as of influence *on*, showing that we have forgotten the significance of *in*.[1]

The word *welcome* in such phrases as *I made them welcome* is employed as an adjective, as, indeed, it is commonly apprehended to be. It was originally a substantive, and was derived from the infinitive mood of the verb, its meaning being *pleasure-comer*. The word is popularly supposed to derive from *well* and *come;* but the first element in the compound is really related to *will*—the true sense being the *will-comer*, i.e. *he who comes to please another's will.* (Cf. Ger. *willkommen*.) The change in meaning seems due to Scandinavian influence, for in the Scandinavian languages the word is *really* composed of the adjective *well* and the past participle *come ;* cf. Danish *velkommen* (welcome).[2]

The expression *Quin conscendimus equos* (Livy, i. 57) is properly *Why do we not mount our horses?* but is understood as *Let us mount our horses ;* and in accordance with such usage *quin* may take after it an imperative, as *quin age;* or a hortative subjunctive, as *quin experiamur?* The sense of *cur* in some cases approximates to that of *quod;* and hence we find the word followed by a similar construction, in Horace,

---

[1] See Mätzner, vol. ii., p. 313, 314, etc.
[2] Cf. Skeat, Etymological Dictionary, s.v.

Ep. I. 8. 9;—*irascar amicis, Cur me funesto properent arcere veterno*. The O.Fr. *car* underwent a similar change. Derived from *quare* it meant, in the first instance, *then;* as, *Cumpainz Rolond, l'oliphant* KAR *sunez* (Chanson de Roland), i.e. *Compagnon Roland sonnez* DONC *l'oliphant;*[1] it next came to be used like *que* or *parceque* after phrases like *la raison est;* and it then comes to be used with the conditional and imperative in the sense of *utinam* (*cf.* Diez, iii. 214).

In O.Fr. the word *par* (*Latin per*) was used for *much*. It took this sense from its use in combinations like *perficere, perraro*, etc., but it was detached from the verb, and was habitually used in O.Fr. in such combinations as *par fut proz = il fut très preux;* and in some cases coupled with other adverbs, like *moult* and *tant;* as, *tant par fut bels = il était si beau*, literally *tant beaucoup* (Chanson de Roland). The phrase survives in *par trop*.

The Greek οὐκ οὖν, originally *not therefore*, like the Latin *nonne,* serves to introduce a question expecting an affirmative answer. It then comes to be used to introduce direct positive assertions; thus, οὐκοῦν ἐλευθερία ἡμᾶς μένει; from meaning 'Does not, then, freedom await us?' comes to mean simply 'Therefore freedom awaits us.' The word *nanu* in Sanskrit has gone through a similar development. *Ne* in Latin, properly the interrogative particle, comes to be used as the correlative of *an :—faciatne an non faciat;* or even *faciat, necne*. Similarly, in Russian, the interrogative particle *li* comes to be used as the correlative of *ili* (or); as *ugodno-li vam eto?* ('Is this agreeable to you?'); but we then get combinations like *dyélaet-li, ili ne dyélaet* ('whether he does it or no').

---

[1] See Clédat, Grammaire de la Vieille Langue Française, p. 261.
[2] Clédat, p. 253.

The accusative with an infinitive could originally only stand in connection with a transitive verb as long as the accusative of the subject was regarded as the object of the finite verb, as *audio te venire ;* but the accusative and infinitive came to be regarded as a dependent sentence with the accusative as its subject, and then we find the construction after words like *gaudeo, horreo* (Livy, xxxiv. 4. 3), *doleo* (Horace, Odes, iv. 4. 62), etc., which can properly speaking take no accusative of the object connected with them ; as *gaudere, dolere, infitias ire ;* nay, we find it after combinations such as *spem habeo,* etc. The accusative and infinitive construction then passes into sentences which depend on another accusative and infinitive, as (1) into relative sentences loosely connected ; e.g. *mundum censent regi numine Deorum—ex quo illud natura consequi* (Cic. de Fin., iii. 19, § 64) : (2) into sentences of comparison ; e.g. *ut feras quasdam nulla mitescere arte sic immitem ejus viri animum esse* (Livy, xxxiii. 45) : (3) into indirect questions ; e.g. *quid sese inter pacatos facere, cur in Italiam non revehi* (Livy, xxviii. 24) ;[1] (4) into temporal and causal sentences ; e.g. *crimina vitanda esse, quia vitari metus non posse* (Seneca, Epist., 97. 13). A similar extension of the use is found in Greek.

The possessive cases *mine, thine, his, her, its, our, your, their* have passed into the category of adjectives, as in the case of *Shall I not take mine ease in mine inn ?* (1 Henry IV., III. iii. 93). The instinct of language regarded *mine, thine,* etc., as the equivalents of *of me, of thee,* etc. ; and marked the function by the addition of the possessive preposition *of,* as in *this inn of mine.* Thus, again, a gerund like *killing,*[2] from having the

---

[1] See Dräger, Historische Syntax, vol. ii., p. 436.

[2] Cf. Mason, English Grammar, p. 64.

same form as the participle, can be used in expressions like *the killing a man*, instead of *the killing of a man*.

We not only find that the word which changes its function undergoes the consequent changes in form or in syntax, but it also often happens that, owing to functional changes participated in by a certain group of words, such a group becomes detached, and thereby gains independence enough to influence other words that have cognate meanings. There are in Old English, as in German, many adverbs which are in their origin the genitives singular of strong masculine and neuter substantives, such as *dæges* (*by day*); but the origin of the termination has been forgotten, and the *s* has come to be looked upon as a merely adverbial termination. Consequently we find the adverb *nihtes* (*by night*), though *niht* is really feminine, and its genitive case is properly *nihte*. Similar formations are *here-abouts*, *inwards*, *othergates* (Shakespeare, Twelfth Night, V. i. 198), *towards*, *whereabouts*, etc. In the same way, the genitive plural of Anglo-Saxon substantives in *-ung* (later *-ing*) could be used adverbially; as,— *án-ung-a*, *án-ing-a*, (altogether), genitive plural of *án-ung*, a substantive formed from *án* (one) : after this analogy others were formed : as, *hedling*, afterwards altered to *headlong ; darkling*, etc.

CHAPTER XIII.

DISPLACEMENT IN ETYMOLOGICAL GROUPING.

We have already more than once had occasion to point out that, in our individual vocabularies, two classes of words are inextricably confused. In the first place, we employ such words and derivatives of words as we REPRODUCE by the aid of MEMORY, which recalls to us what we have frequently heard from those with whom we have intercourse. In the second place, another part of our stock of words and verbal derivatives is FORMED by us on the MODEL OF OTHER FORMA-TIONS of the first class.

Only in a very few cases is it possible for any speaker to decide, with absolute certainty, whether any particular form which he may employ with perfect familiarity belongs to the former or the latter group. If, for instance, we hear the simple sentence, 'He is walking,' there is nothing which can help us to determine whether the speaker is merely reproducing the word *walking* just as he has learnt it from others, or whether he is forming the present participle of and from the word '(to) walk' after the model of other similar derivatives. In the chapter on Analogy, we considered principally cases falling under the second class, in which the result of such a process as we have described proved at variance with other forms already existing in the language, *i.e.* where *Analogy* brought about certain changes.   The cases in which the result was the mere production of what we should have reproduced by the simple aid of memory, we considered as of very small importance for the purpose of illustrating the operations of Analogy.

But it is far from true that they have no significance.   Every time that we consciously or unconsciously form words 'by analogy,' our habit of doing so is strengthened, and our confidence in the results is increased ; and the more we enter upon domains of thought where we are comparative strangers, the more confidently and the more consciously do we proceed 'to make our own words.'   In this process of word-making, we follow certain models ; in fact, we derive one form from others which exist in our own vocabulary.

In words and forms reproduced by memory (though only in the case of such as these) it is, strictly speaking, correct to say of each form—tense, person, singular or plural, or of each case—that it is derived, not from what our grammars call the standard forms (such as infinitives or nominative-singulars), but from the corresponding older form of that tense, person, etc., in the language as it existed before.

In words and forms produced, not from memory, but by analogy, *i.e.* by derivation according to a certain model, and from words which already exist in our own vocabulary, even where our result does not differ from what we might have produced by memory, it does not at all follow that our process of derivation has been the same as that by which former speakers reached their results.

For instance, suppose that there exists a class of adjectives really derived from verbs.   In the course of development of the language, these verbs approach in form to the cognate nouns, or—for whatever reason—some of the verbs become obsolete. The effect will be that, in the consciousness of the ordinary speaker, the adjective appears as derived from the noun.

It is our object in this chapter to study the phenomenon of such displacements in the etymological connections and the consequences which follow therefrom.

A good instance may be found in the history of the suffixes *ble*, *able*, and their application.[1] Both these suffixes we owe to the French language, which, in turn, derived them from Latin.

In this latter language we find the suffix *bili-s*, *bilem*, forming verbal adjectives. Where the stem of the verb ended in a consonant, the connecting vowel *i* was inserted: *vend-e-re*, *vend-i-bilis*. Where the stem ended in a vowel this insertion was of course unnecessary: *honora-re*, *honora-bilis*, *dele-re*, *delebilis*, *(g)noscere no-bilis*, etc. By far the greater number of these words in *ble* were derived from verbs in *are*, of which the present participle ends in *ans*, *antem*. Hence, though the words in *ble* were in reality not immediately derived from this participle, a feeling arose that such a connection existed. Among 'the matter-groups' in French their existed numerous pairs, such as *aimant*, *aimable*, etc. In time, all present participles in French came to end in this termination *ant*, after which an adjective in *able*, derived from such participles, nearly always supplanted the older and correcter forms in *ible*, etc. Hence came forms like *vendable*, *croyable*, etc.

The suffix *able*, introduced into English in enormously preponderating numbers, was there at first

[1] Cf. Murray's Dict., *-ble* and *-able*.

confined to words of French origin, but soon, by analysis of such instances as *pass-able, agree-able, commendable,* was treated as an indivisible living suffix, and freely employed to form analogous adjectives, being attached not only to verbs taken from French, but finally to native verbs as well, e.g., *bearable, speakable, breakable.* These verbs have often a substantive of the same form, as in *debat(e)-able, rat(e)-able,* etc. Owing to this, a new displacement such as we are here studying occurred, and such words, treated *as if* derived FROM THE NOUN, became the models for others where *able* is added to nouns, such as *marketable, clubbable, carriageable,*[1] *salable.*

Another suffix, the history of which affords an instance of similar displacement is *ate* as verbal formative.[2]

We find in French several past participles, some due to regular historical development of the popular language, others to deliberate adoption by the learned classes, all of which differ only from their Latin prototypes in having lost the termination *us:* e.g., *confusus,*

---

[1] That 'carriageable' is a very unusual word does not matter at all, the point is that it *is* formed and that it *cannot* be derived from a verb.

[2] What follows is almost entirely taken from the article in Murray's Dictionary dealing with the suffix. Our excuse for reproducing it is the unavoidably high cost of the work, which places it beyond the reach of the ordinary student, so that a mere reference to it would be useless; and, secondly, that we believe that in Murray's otherwise admirable treatment of the subject, one not unimportant side of the question has been overlooked. To avoid misunderstanding, we ought perhaps to assure the reader that what we give is not simply a copy of the article in question ; this will appear to any one who will take the trouble to compare the two. Our object being different, we lay more stress upon some points which are less material to Dr. Murray ; we, however, use his facts, and wish to acknowledge our indebtedness.

Fr. *confus; contentus, content; diversus, divers*. This analogy was widely followed in later French in introducing new words from Latin, and, both classes of French words (*i.e.* the popular survivals and the later accessions) being adopted in English provided English in its turn with analogies for adapting similar words directly from Latin by dropping the termination. This process began about 1400 A.D., and the Latin termination *atus* gave English *at*, subsequently *ate*, e.g. *desolatus, desolat, desolate*. The transition of these words from adjectives and participles to verbs is explained by Dr. Murray by a reference to the fact—

(*a*) That in Old English verbs had been regularly formed from adjectives: as, *hwit, hwitian* ('white,' 'to whiten'); *wearm, wearmian* ('warm,' 'to warm,'); etc.

(*b*) That with the loss of the inflections, these verbs became by the fifteenth century identical in form with the adjectives, e.g., *to white, to warm*.

(*c*) That, as in Latin, so in French, many verbs were formed on adjectives; whence, again, English received many verbs identical in form with their adjectives, e.g., *to clear, to humble, to manifest*.

These verbs, though formed immediately from participial adjectives already existing in English, answered in form to the past participles of Latin verbs of the same meaning. It was thus natural to associate them directly with these Latin verbs, and to view them as their regular English representatives. This once done, it became the recognised method of Englishing a Latin verb, to take the past participle stem of the Latin as the present stem of the English, so that English verbs were now formed on Latin past participles by mere analogy and without intervention of a participial adjective; e.g., *fascinate, concatenate*, etc. These English verbs in *ate* correspond generally to

French verbs in *er*,—e.g., *separate*, Fr. *séparer ;* this, in turn, gave a pattern for the formation of English verbs from French,—e.g., *isoler* (Ital. *isolare*, Lat. *insulare*), Eng. *isolate*, etc.

To this lucid and apparently adequate explanation we must, however, add another fact, which has demonstrably aided in the formation of the enormous number of English verbs in *ate*. From the fourteenth century onward, we find again and again such pairs as *action* (1330), *to act* (1384) ;[1] *affliction* (1303), *to afflict* (1393) ; *adjection* (1374), *to adject* (1432) ; *abjection* (1410), *to abject* (1430), etc.[2]

Such pairs led to the supposition that the verbs were derivable from the nouns in *tion* by merely omitting the *ion*, and this was done with many nouns in *ation* even where another verb (itself the ground-word for that form in *ation*) existed by the side of it. Thus we find, e.g., *aspiration* (1398), *to aspire* (1460), the verb *aspirate* (1700) ; *attestation* (1547), *to attest* (1596) *to attestate* (1625) ; *application* (1493), *to apply* (1374), *to applicate* (1531).[3]

[1] The number in brackets behind these words gives the date of the earliest quotation found for their use in Murray's Dictionary.

[2] It will help us to realise the strength of the ties which united these groups, if we remember that the modern pronunciation of the ending, *tion* as *shun* IS really quite modern, *i.e.* that, formerly, the *ti* was in such words pronounced as *tea* and not as *sh*. The verb *abject* consisted therefore of the first two syllables of the noun *objection*, WITHOUT ANY ALTERATION.

[3] A carefully compiled list of *all* forms in *ation*, past participles in *ate*, verbs in *ate*, found in Dict. Murray, sub. let. *A.*, has given the following results :—

Forms in *ation* 219. Of these the first instance belongs to the fourteenth century in 11, fifteenth in 26, sixteenth in 49, seventeenth in 76, eighteenth in 23, nineteenth in 34 cases.

Among the 219, the form in *ation* is the *only* one in 89 cases, distributed over the same centuries as follows,—fourteenth, 2

The suffix *full* forms adjectives from nouns : *baleful*, A.S. *bealofull* from *bealu* (woe, harm, mischief) ; *shameful*, A.S. *sceamfull* from *sceam* (shame).   This ending was also added to nouns of Romance origin ; e.g., *powerful*, *fruitful*.   In both classes, however, the word might, in very many cases, be just as well derived from a verb as from a noun, so that, e.g., *thankful*, which originally undoubtedly was *= full of thanks*, could equally well be apprehended as *he who thanks ; respectful*, as *he who respects;* etc.   It is similar with such words as *harmful*, *delightful*, etc.   That such a grouping has actually been made, is proved by the occurrence of such forms as *wakeful, forgetful*, and the dialectical *urgeful;* so also the form *weariful* seems more likely to be interpreted as *that which wearies*, than as a derivative from the adjective *weary* as Mätzner seems to take it.[1]   So, again, the form *maisterful*, found in Lydgate and Chaucer,[2] seems more likely to be taken as 'he who is always mastering,' than 'as he who is full of master,' which gives no sense.   The suffix *less*, originally and still as a rule only added to nouns, could not have been used with the verb to *daunt* (—O.Fr. *danter*, Modern French, *dompter*, Lat. *domitare*, 'to tame,') if in such compounds as *restless, sleepless, hopeless, useless*, the noun had not been identical in form with the verb.

fifteenth, 9 ; sixteenth, 10 ; seventeenth, 31 ; eighteenth, 15 ; nineteenth, 22.

There are 138 verbs in *ate*, 20 of which stand alone.   Distribution : fourteenth century, 0 ; fifteenth, 4 ; sixteenth, 53+7; seventeenth, 53+13; eighteenth, 13 ; nineteenth, 15.

Of all cases where we find both the noun in *ation* and the verb in *ate*, the noun is older in 74 and the verb in 34 cases.   It seems plain therefore that we may say that in English the verbs in *ate* are in very many cases formed from the nouns in *ation*, and that both are chiefly due to the sixteenth and the seventeenth centuries.

[1] Vol. i., p. 433.   [2] Goeders, p. 9.

The history of the suffix *ness*, is also especially instructive for our purpose. If we go back to the oldest records of the Teutonic languages, Gothic, we find a noun, *ufarassus*, literally ' overness,' used in the sense of ' abundance,' superfluity,' from *ufar*, ' over : ' similarly formed was *ibnassus*, ' equality,' from *ibns*— ' even,' ' equal.' This suffix *assus* was very frequently added to the *stem of verbs* which, in their turn, were derived from nouns. Thus, for instance, besides the noun—

lekeis (leach), we find	*lekinon* (to cure),	*lekinassus* (leachdom).
shalks (servant), „	*shalkinon* (to serve),	*shalkinassus* (service).
gudja (priest), „	*gudjinon* (to be priest),	*gudjinassus* (priesthood).
frauja (Lord), „	*fraujinon* (to rule),	*fraujinassus* (dominion).
ðiudans (king), „	*ðiudanon* (to be king),	*ðiudinassus* (kingdom).

In all these and similar cases, however, etymological consciousness might equally well operate otherwise. It might, for instance, derive a noun meaning *kingdom* from another noun denoting *king*, or one meaning *priesthood* from one denoting *priest*. That this has been done is proved by the fact that the *n* has coalesced completely with the suffix *assus*, forming *nassus*, or, in its more modern form, *ness*. Even in Gothic, this coalescence has already been powerful enough to produce *vaninassus* (want) from *vans* (adjective = ' wanting,' ' less ; ' found, *e.g.*, in *wanhope* = ' lack of hope,' ' despair : ' *wanton*, = ' uneducated,' ' untrained,' ' unrestricted,' ' licentious : ' and *wane* = ' to grow less ').

In Anglo-Saxon, adverbs were formed from adjectives by means of the termination *e :* for instance, *heard, hearde*, (' hard ') ; *sóð, sóðe*, (' true,' cf. *soothsayer* and *forsooth*) ; *wíd, wíde*, (wide). Adjectives in *lic* were formed first from nouns : *eorð, eorðlic*, (' earth,' ' earthy ') ; *gást, gastlic*, (' ghost,' ' ghostly '), etc. ; and

then, also, from other adjectives, as *heard-heardlic,
æðele-æðelic,* (for æðel-lic), etc.

By the side of these adjectives, we naturally find
adverbs in *lice,* normally formed from them by the
addition of *e;* as, *æðelice,* etc. ; but as soon as, owing to
phonetic decay of the terminations, the adjectives and
adverbs in both sets of words (both in those with and
without *lic*) came respectively to coincide,—when, for
instance, *heard* and *hearde* had both become *hard,* and
adjectives in *lic* and adverbs in *lice* had both come to
terminate in *ly,*—then the adjective that had never
ended in *lic* came also to be grouped with the adverb
in *lice,* or rather *ly,* and *ly* became the special and
normal adverbial termination : as in *prettily, care-
lessly,* etc. Thus were produced a great quantity of
adverbs, the adjectives corresponding to which never
had the termination *ly.*

Modern English possesses remnants of all the
above original formations; as, for instance, the adverbs
(with loss of adverbial *e*) *hard,* in 'to hit hard,' *loud,*
in 'to speak loud,' etc. ; or, again, the adjectives
heavenly, earthly, kingly, goodly, etc.

CHAPTER XIV.

ON THE DIFFERENTIATION OF MEANING.

LANGUAGE develops by the development of the vocabulary of individual speakers in the same linguistic
community : their tendency is to produce synonymous
forms and constructions in addition to those already
at their disposal. Each individual is, in fact, constantly engaged in increasing the number of synonymous words, forms, and constructions in the language
which he speaks. One source of this superfluous
development depends on analogical formation : as
when in English the imperfect is assimilated to the
participle, or the participle to the imperfect ; as where
forms like *spoke* and *broke* appear beside *spake* and
brake or *held*, beside *holden*.

A second source of the same superfluity depending on synonyms arises from the fact that of two
words, each may develop its meaning on its own lines,
and the meanings may come to converge so as to
become one and the same. Thus, for instance, the
two words *relation* and *relative*, the former originally
the abstract verbal noun, the latter an adjective, have
converged in the meaning 'a related person ;' and it
has thus happened that owing to this process there
arise two terms for one and the same idea. To the
above a third source may be added ; viz., the accept-

ance of a foreign word into a language where a native
word already exists to express the same idea.   Of
course English is especially rich in words of this kind,
owing to the large number of Norman-French words
imported at the Conquest and maintained as an integral part of the language; though the process of
borrowing from French has been also active since the
epoch of the Conquest: such are the pairs *nude, naked ;
pedagogue, schoolmaster; poignant, sharp ; peccant, sin-
ning; sign, token* : other familiar instances are *tether*,
derived from the Celtic at an old date; and *loot*,
adopted from the Hindi, by the side of *plunder*.   The
case is, of course, similar where a synonym is adopted
from another dialect, as *vetch* by the side of *fitch, vat*
beside *fat* (a vessel), etc.

But though such superfluities in language are continually appearing, they have a constant tendency to
disappear on the earliest possible occasion.   Language
is a careful housewife, who is constantly endeavouring
to keep nothing on hand but what she can use, and
carefully to retrench the superfluous.   We must, of
course, never suppose that any body of speakers combine to admit a word into the common language which
they employ, and that then, finding that the word or
form has its meaning already expressed in their
language and is therefore unnecessary, they proceed
to discard it.   These new words and forms proceed in
each instance from individuals, who overlook the existence in their own language of a term already in use
for some meaning which they need to express, and so
introduce a new form : this is then employed by others,
who, hearing the new form and the old, employ both
alike indiscriminately.   Superfluity in language, then,
must be regarded as spontaneously arising, and without the aid of any voluntary impulse on the part

of any individual or individuals.   The language of
common life is, as might be expected, most ready in
freeing the vehicle of ordinary communication from
superfluities, and in the differentiation of synonyms.
The language of poetry and, in a less degree, of
written prose, demands a store of synonyms, on which
an author may draw at will, thereby forming an individual style and avoiding monotony.   It is as useful, nay, as indispensable to the poet that he should
have a store of words with similar meanings which he
may employ for the purposes of his artificial style,
as it is for the ordinary speaker or writer to have a
distinct shade of meaning attached to each of the
synonyms which he employs.   And as poetry makes
greater demands upon the taste and powers of an
author than prose, we find that the language of poetry
preserves archaic forms and words which in prose
have been practically obsolete.   In fact such words
become the stock in trade of all writers of poetry,
appearing, of course, most frequently in those who
seek to invest their work with a peculiarly archaic
caste.   Thus, the diction of Spencer must have appeared almost as archaic to his contemporaries as to
ourselves.[1]   Poetry will also maintain constructions
which have a tendency in prose to become obsolete:
as, *meseems ; Time prove the rest*.   The metaphors employed in old Norse poetry are very instructive on
this head.   They have been treated at great length
in the 'Corpus Poeticum Boreale' by Vigfusson and
York Powell, from whose work [2] we cite the following
instances.   The breast is spoken of as *the mind's*

[1] Cf. Abbott and Seeley, English Lessons for English Readers,
p. 55.
[2] Vol. ii., p. 446, 467, Figures and Metaphors (Kenningar) of
Old Northern Poetry.

*house, memory's sanctuary, the lurking-place of thought,
the shore of the mind, the bark of laughter, the hall
of the heart.*   The eye is *the moon or star of the brows,
the light or levin of the forehead, the cauldron of tears, the
pledge of Woden.*   Herrings are *the arrows of the sea, the
darts, the tail-barbed arrows of the deep.*   Ships are
characterised by a host of metaphors ; as, *the tree or
beam, the sled, the car, the beam or timber of the sea or
waves ; the steeds of the helm, oars, mast, sail, yard :* and
numerous other specimens of 'pars pro toto.'

The most simple and obvious case of retrenchment
in language is where, out of several similar forms and
phrases, all disappear and are disused except a single
one ; as where *to grow* is used instead of *to wax; to go,*
instead of *to fare,* etc.   We must look upon these
retrenchments in language as mainly due to individuals ; each speaker expresses himself more or less
unconsciously with a certain consistency, and uses,
generally speaking, what we may properly call his own
dialect.   It is owing to such individual influence that
the distinctions in language which we call dialects
arise, and thus the different opportunities for choice
form a main source of the distinctions of dialect.

In addition to this negative process of simply
dropping what is useless, there is the positive process
of utilising what is superfluous in language by differentiation of meaning in the case of synonymous words
and phrases.   This process is no more the result of
conscious purpose than the other.   Since each individual has gradually to learn the different senses of
words, inflections, particles, etc., it is clear that when
there are several synonyms in use—each of which has
several shades of signification—he will almost certainly
hear one of them used in one, and another in another
of these meanings.   If, for instance, we represent the

full meaning of a word in its different shades by the letters $A + B + C + D$, and, similarly, that of its synonym by $a + b + c + d$, the probability almost amounts to certainty that when a learner first hears the former word, the shade of meaning (say B) in which it happens to be employed will differ from that (say d) in which he first learns the use of the latter. He will then inevitably, though perhaps unconsciously, attach by preference these particular shades of meaning to the two words; and will continue to do so, unless stronger impulses, such as frequent use in other meanings by surrounding speakers, force him to discard the differentiation which he has established. But from the moment when he begins to use, and as long as he uses the word consistently in one sense, he will influence others in the same linguistic community, and lay the basis for definite acceptance of the word in a particular or special sense.

Nor, again, must we assume that a differentiation in sound was purposely and consciously made by speakers with a view to differentiate meanings. Cases taken from modern languages may serve to show the unreasonableness of such assumptions. Especial attention has been paid by writers on Romance Philology to the 'doublets' occurring in their own languages. By 'doublets' we mean the double derivative forms of one and the same word (such as *raison*, 'reason,' and *ration*, 'allowance,' both coming from *rationem*): forms commonly appearing in a language at two different periods in the history of the language, and invested, in spite of their common origin, with distinct and special senses. The name of 'doublets' was first applied to them by Nicolas Catherinot, who, as early as 1683, published a list of those which he had observed in French, but without giving the reasons for the phenomenon. How imperfect the philological knowledge of his day was may be seen from the following specimens of 'doublets' which he gives: from BATTUERE, Low Latin for 'to fight,' he derived both *battre* (to fight) and *tuer* (to kill): from GRAVIS (heavy), *grave*, serious; *brave*, brave: from MARMOR (marble), *marble*, marble; *marmot*, guinea-pig.[1] A. Brachet has collected many other specimens in the work cited below: Coelho has made a collection from the Portuguese in the Romania, II. 281, sqq.[2]

It must, however, be noticed that many of the doublets cited in these works stand outside of the class of those with which we have to deal, and such cannot be taken as real cases of differentiation. For instance, a loan word may immediately upon its introduction have been accepted in a sense different from that borne by the word of the same origin which already existed in the language: as in the case of *chantée* (sung, fem. past. part.) and *cantata* (cantata, a piece which is sung, as distinguished from a sonata, a piece which is sounded or played), borrowed from the Italian by the French; of *sexte* (term in music and 'the sixth book') with its doublet *sieste* (the hour of rest) borrowed from the Spanish *siesta*, both derived from the Latin *sextam*; of *façon* (manner) with its doublet *fashion*, borrowed from the English, both from Latin *factionem*, 'a making.' Thus, again, the French

---

[1] See Brachet, Dictionnaire des Doublets, Appendice. Paris, 1868.

[2] Other works on doublets are *Romanische wortschöpfung*, by Caroline Michaelis, Leipzig, 1876. *Latin doublets*, by M. Bréal, in the *Mémoires de la Société de Linguistique de Paris*, i. 162, sqq. (1868). For German, O. Behagel, *Die Neuhochdeutschen Zwillingswörter*, *Germania*, 23, 257, sqq. For English doublets, cf. Mätzner, *Englische Grammatik*, i. 221; and Skeat, *Principles of English Etymology*, p. 417; besides the appendix to his Lexicon.

chose (a thing) and *cause* (a cause) alike owe their
origin to the Latin *causam*, but the meanings were not
differentiated in France : *cause* was borrowed as a law-
term long after *chose* had developed into the general
meaning of *thing*. It is the same, moreover, with
such English doublets as *ticket, etiquette: army,
armada: orison, oration: penance, penitence*. Such
doublets as these, and *guitar, zither, cithara* may be
called pseudo-doublets, producing as they do the *effect*
of differentiation, but serving really as labels to
designate a foreign idea or object. Nor, again, must
we include cases in which a word became grammatically
isolated and then received a special meaning ; such as
where ' besch*ei*den,' in German, is now employed with
the signification of ' modest,' while ' besch*ie*den ' is used
as the true participial form, and never means, or has
meant, ' modest.' Similarly, in French, we have
savant (a scholar) originally used as synonymous with
present participle *sachant* (knowing) but in modern
French as an adjective or noun only, whilst *sachant*
has always remained present participle and no more :
amant, the present participle of *amare* (to love) is used
as a substantive only.[1]

There are, however, other cases in which words
are really differentiated ; that is to say, cases in which
two words, whose meaning we know to have been
identical, have come to be accepted in different
meanings. This is a genuine process of economy in
language. In French *s'attaquer à* and *s'attacher à*
at one time were used with identically the same
meaning and employed indifferently. *Attaquer* is
used in the sense of ' *attacher* ' in this line of the fourteenth century—*Une riche escarboucle le mantel ataqua*
(' a rich carbuncle attached (= held) the mantel ')

[1] See Mätzner, Fr. Gr., p. 223.

(Bauduin de Sebourc, i. 370). On the other hand, *attacher* is used in the sense of 'to attack:' as in the following passage, quoted by M. Brachet[1] from a letter of Calvin to the regent of England,—*Tous ensemble méritent bien d'estre réprimés par le glayve qui vous est commis, veu qu'ils s'attaschent non seulement au roy, mais à Dieu qui l'a assis au siège royal,* = 'All together deserve to be put down by the sword which has been entrusted to you, seeing that they attack not merely the King, but God who has set him on the royal seat.' (Lettres de Calvin recueillies par M. Bonnet, ii. 201). In modern French *attacher* is used exclusively in the sense of 'to attach' 'to fasten;' *attaquer* = 'to attack.' Another instance is found in *chaire* and *chaise*, both of which words came into French from *cathedram*, and both of which once signified the same thing (Theodore Beza, in 1530, complains of the faulty pronunciation of the Parisians who say *chaise* instead of *chaire*). At the present day, of course, *chaise* means 'chair,' and *chaire* is confined to the signification of 'pulpit' or 'professor's chair.' In English, *shoal* and *shallow* seem to have been used synonymously, and to have become differentiated.[2] Other instances are *of, off; naught, not; assay, essay; upset, set up; Master, Mister (Mr.); Miss, Mistress, Mrs.* (pronounced *Missus*). In these cases, the differentiation took place within the given language; and such cases should be carefully distinguished from those cases in which the differentiation

---

[1] Page 28.

[2] *Shoal*, the substantive from A.S. *scólu*, meaning either 'a school' or 'a multitude' (see Skeat, s.v.), seems to have been used convertibly with *school*, and indeed, the meaning of *shoal* has survived in the fisherman's phrase a 'school of mackerel;' while the adjectives *shoal* and *shallow* likewise had the same meanings; but they have become so far differentiated that the latter form alone can be employed metaphorically; as when we say, 'a man of shallow intellect.'

was made *outside* of the language. For instance, in *squandered* and *scatter*, both of which seem to have signified the same thing, simply 'to disperse'; cf., *squandered abroad* (Merchant of Venice, I. iii. 22). *Indict* and *indite* seem to have borne the same meaning, but are now differentiated.

To these may be added the German doublets *reiter* (a rider) and *ritter* (a knight), which may be paralleled by the use of the English *squire* and *esquire;* of which the latter word has lately come into use simply as a title of society, whereas both forms were once used as in Scott's *nine and twenty squires of fame.* Other instances are *scheuen*, 'to fear,' and *scheuchen,* 'to scare:' *jungfrau*, 'maiden,' and *jungfer*, 'virgin.'

Double forms arising from the confusion of different methods of declension are often used in different senses, as in the case of the Latin *locus*, whose plurals `loca` and *loci* mean 'places,' and 'passages in books' respectively: the German *Franke*, the Franconian *franken*, 'a franc' (9½*d.*): this difference is utilised, together with a difference of gender, in the German *der lump*, 'the worthless fellow;' *die lumpe,* 'the rag;' etc. The difference of gender cannot be utilised in English, but is thus utilised—in German—in such cases as DER *band*, 'volume;' DAS *band*, 'ribbon:' DER *see*, 'the lake;' DIE *see*, 'the sea:' DIE *erkenntniss*, 'the act of judging;' DAS *erkenntniss*, 'the judgment:'—in French, UN *foudre de guerre*, 'a thunderbolt of war' (personified); UNE *foudre*, 'a thunderbolt:' UN *critique*, 'a critic;' UNE *critique*, 'a criticism:' UN *office*, 'a duty;' UNE *office*, 'a pantry:' LE *mémoire*, 'memorandum;' LA *mémoire*, 'memory;' LE *politique*, 'politician;' LA *politique*, 'politics:' LE *Bourgogne*, 'Burgundy wine;' LA *Bourgogne*, 'Burgundy:' LE *paille*, 'straw colour;' LA *paille*, 'the straw.' To these must be added the cases in which double plural formations are differentiated, as in English *clothes, cloths ; brothers, brethren ; cows, kine* (poetical) *; pence, pennies:*—in German, *Band*, 'bond' and 'ribbon;' *Bande*, 'bonds :' *Bänder*, 'ribbons :' *Bank*, 'bench' and 'bank;' *Bänke*, 'benches ;' *Banken*, 'banks :' *Gesicht*, 'face' and 'vision ;' *Gesichte*, 'vision ;' *Gesichter*, 'faces :' *Laden*, 'shop' and 'shutter ;' *Läden*, 'shops ;' *Laden*, 'shutters :' etc.[1] In French, we have *l'aïeul*, 'the grandfather ;' *les aïeux*, 'ancestors;' and *aïeuls*, 'grandfathers :' *les travaux*, 'works ;' and *les travails*, 'a minister's reports :' *l'œil*, 'eye ;' *les yeux*, 'eyes ;' and *les œils* (small oval windows commonly called *œils de bœuf*). The singular *appât* means 'bait ;' *les appas* signifies 'charms,' and has a doublet, *les appâts*, meaning 'baits.' In Russian, the accusative plural is the same as the nominative in the case of inanimate objects : it is in the case of animate beings identical with the genitive form. In Dutch, the plurals in *-en* and *-s* are used in the case of some words indifferently, as *vogelen* and *vogels*, 'birds :' in the case of some others, one alone is commonly used, as *engelen*, 'angels,' but *pachters*, 'farmers :' again, in the case of others, both forms are used, but with different meanings ; thus *hemelen*, 'the heavens ;' but *hemels*, 'canopies of a bed :' *letteren*, 'letters,' or 'literature ;' *letters*, 'letters of the alphabet ;' etc. From the Danish, we may cite *skatte*, 'treasures ;' *skatter*, 'taxes ;' *vaaben*, 'weapons ;' *vaabener*, 'armorial bearings.' From Italian, we may instance *braccia*, 'the two arms of the body ;' *bracci*, 'arms of the sea ;' *membra*, 'the members of the body ;' *membri*, 'the members of an association.' Similarly, in Spanish the neuter of the second declension takes in many cases a feminine form

[1] See Meyer's German Grammar, paral. series, p. 18.

in the plural; and in Portuguese this manner of differentiation is more common than in any other European language: cf. *serra*, 'saw,' 'mountain ridge;' *serro*, 'a high mountain;' etc. In Russian, *synovya* means 'descendants'; *synui*, 'sons;' etc. The words (*to*) *purvey* and (*to*) *provide* have arisen from the same original form, as have *respect* and *respite; deploy* and *display; separate* and *sever*.

The word *as*, like *also*, took its rise from the A.S. *ealswâ;* it is simply a short form of *also;* and an intermediate form exists in O.E. *alse* and *als*. In Maundeville, p. 153, we find the two forms used convertibly: *As foule as thei ben, als evele thei ben* = *so evil they are;* and again, *als longe as here vitaylles lasten, thei may abide there*, p. 130.

Than and *thanne* were used in Chaucer's time where we should use *then: Now thanne, put thyn hond down at my bak* (Chaucer, Cant. Tales, 7721); and in comparisons *then* was used where we should employ *than*, as: 'I am greater *then* (i.e. *than*) you.'

In German, the word *verdorben* means 'spoiled' in a material sense: *verderbt* is employed in a moral sense only. It is the same with *bewegt*, 'moved,' and *bewogen*, 'induced.' In English we employ *aged* mostly as a participle proper, but *agèd* as an adjective; cf. also *molten* and *melted*.

The words formed with the suffixes -*hood*, -*ness*, -*dom* generally cover the same ground in English as in Anglo-Saxon. There are, however, here also, a few cases in which differentiation seems to have set in. Such are *hardihood* and *hardiness; humble-hede, humble-ness, humility: young—hede, youth*. In German, *klein-heit* and *neuheit* were used convertibly with *kleinigkeit* and *neuigkeit:* now the former = *smallness, newness*, the latter = *trifle, novelty*.

In the case of adjectives, we may see the same process in *mobile, movable*: and in German, in *ernstlich* and *ernsthaft* which were once used convertibly, but are now differentiated.

Sometimes a word originally of a different meaning encroaches on the domain of another word, and gradually arrogates the latter's meaning to itself. Thus, in French, the meaning of *en*, the form taken in French for the Latin *in*, has been encroached upon by the preposition *à*, and by the adverb *dans* (O.Fr. *denz* = *de intus*), and *dans* has completely ousted the prepositional meaning of *dedans*. Molière could still write *dedans ma poche* = 'in my pocket.' *Böse*, in German, is now almost restricted to the sense of 'morally bad' by the encroachments of *schlecht* (originally 'smooth, 'straight') English *slight*. The English word *sick*, once the general word for *ill*, has been restricted in meaning by the encroachments of the latter word.

Sometimes a newly formed word encroaches on the domain of meaning covered by a word in existence, as *to utilise* on *to use; serviceable* upon *useful; gentlemanly* upon *genteel* and *gentle; magnificence* on *munificence:* [1] *mainly* is encroached upon by *chiefly, pursuer* by *persecutor* and *prosecutor:* and sometimes it practically ousts it from its previous meaning, as in the case of *methodist, naturalist, purist,* etc.

The above examples may serve to show us some of the main factors in the differentiation of meaning, and with how little conscious design on the part of the speakers they were carried out.

[1] See Trench, Select Glossary, p. 129, numerous other instances may be found in this work.

CHAPTER XV.

CATEGORIES : PSYCHOLOGICAL AND GRAMMATICAL.

THE divisions into which grammarians have distributed words, such as gender, number, and, in the case of verbs, voice and tense, are based upon the function which each word discharges in the sentence. Now, these functional differences rest ultimately upon psychological categories : that is to say, upon differences which depend upon the view taken by our mind of the natural grouping and classification of ideas. In other words, the divisions formed by grammarians depend ultimately upon the classification of the relations in which the ideas suggested by words stand to each other, as it appears to our imagination. Grammatical classification was, in fact, originally nothing but an attempt to express and group the order and connection of ideas as they were conceived of by the human mind. Immediately that this influence of imagination has made itself felt in the usage of language, it becomes a grammatical factor : and the groups which it forms become grammatical categories. But the action of the psychological category does not cease when it has thus produced the grammatical; and the difference between the two kinds is that, whereas the grammatical categories become, so to speak, stereotyped and fixed, those created by the imagination are ever changing;

just as the human mind itself is ever changing its
ideas. Besides this, changes in sound-groups are always
occurring, and are constantly operating to prevent
the grammatical categories coinciding with the psychological. Then, as a tendency makes itself felt to bring
about a coincidence of the two categories, the grammatical category suffers a displacement, whence arise
what we are accustomed to call grammatical irregularities. A consideration of the way in which these
irregularities arise may help us to understand the
origin of the grammatical categories, to which we now
proceed.

GENDER.

The foundation of grammatical gender is the
natural distinction between the sexes in mankind and
animals. Fancy may endow other objects or qualities
with sex ; but sex, whether fanciful or real, has no
proper connection with grammar. The truth of this
may be well seen from the English language, in which
we have in most cases discarded the use of grammatical
gender. In order, therefore, to study the conditions
of gender, we have to turn to languages more highly
inflected than English.

The test whereby we now recognise the grammatical gender of a substantive is the *concord* existing
between the substantive and its attribute and predicate,
or between it and a pronoun representing it—*Domus
nigra est*, 'The house is black;' *Domus quam vidi*, 'The
house which I saw ;' *It is the moon ; I ken her horn*
(Burns) ; etc. The rise, therefore, of grammatical
gender is closely connected with the appearance of a
variable adjective and pronoun. One theory to explain
this is, that the difference in form, before it yet marked
the gender, had become attached to a particular stem-

ending : as if, *e.g.*, all stems ending in *n-* admitted the
ending *-us*—as *bonus,* 'good,'—and all those in *g-* the
ending *-ra*—as *nigra,* 'black ;'—and that the ending
may have been an independent word which, while yet
independent, had acquired a reference to a male or
female.[1]   Gender appears in English, in the first place,
as an artificial and often arbitrary personification, as
when the sun and moon are spoken of as *he* and *she*
respectively, under the influence of the ideas attaching
to Sol and Luna : Phœbus and Diana, etc. : and, again,
as an expression of interest in objects or animals, it
frequently occurs in the language of the people and of
children ; though it sometimes enters into the language
of common life, as when a dog is referred to as *he* and
a cat as *she*, in cases where sex is not spoken of.   (See
Storm, die lebende Sprache, p. 418.)

In the pronoun, as in the adjective, the distinction
of gender may appear in the stem-ending : as 'un*e*'
('one,' 'a ') ; 'qu*æ*,' ('which'). It may, however, also
be expressed by distinct roots, such as *er, sie ; he* and
she.   It is, indeed, probably in substantive pronouns
that grammatical gender was first developed, as in
fact it has longest maintained itself ; as in English,
where, in adjectives and nouns, it has almost entirely
disappeared.

Grammatical gender probably corresponded originally to natural sex.   Exceptions to this rule must
gradually have come about, partly through changes of
meaning setting in,—as where a word is used metaphorically, like *love* (neuter, abstract), *love* (masc. or
fem. — 'the beloved object') ; or where it has
'occasionally' modified its meaning, like Fr. *le guide*,
strictly 'the guidance,' and so used in Old French ;

[1] Cf. Sayce, Principles of Comparative Philology, p. 268 (3rd
edit.).

your fatherhoods (Ben Jonson). Consequently we find
natural sex again influencing the genders as fixed by
grammar. Thus, in German, *Die hässlichste meiner
kammermädchen* = 'the ugliest of my chambermaids'
(Wieland), where the article *die* is of the feminine
gender, though the word *kammermädchen*, being a
diminutive in *chen* is, like all others of that class,
neuter. In French, we have UNE (fem.) *brave enfant*,
'a brave girl.' The word *gens*, again, is, properly
speaking, feminine, like the word *la gent*, which still
survives in the restricted sense of 'a race:' but in
combinations like '*tous* les braves gens' ('all worthy
people') the grammatical gender is neglected; and
this neglect is fostered by the use of such a word as
braves, which in form might apply to either sex. On
the other hand, in combinations like 'les *bonnes* gens,'
('good people'), where an adjective with a specifically
feminine termination is joined to the substantive, the
grammatical gender maintains itself. Cf., also, instances
like '*un* enseigne' ('an ensign'), '*un* trompette' ('a
trumpeter'); and, in Provençal, '*lo* poestat,' for 'the
magistrate' ('*il* podestà'). In Latin and Greek, these
so-called violations of the concord in gender are very
common; we are familiar with them as constructions
πρός σύνεσιν, i.e. *according to the sense;* cf. *Thracum
auxilia* (neuter) . . . *cæsi* (masc.) (Tac., Ann., iv.
48), 'The Thracian auxiliaries were killed;' *Capita*
(neut.) *conjurationis virgis cæsi* (masc.) *ac securi
percussi* (masc.) (Livy, x. 1), ' The heads of the con-
spiracy were slain and their heads cut off;' *Septem
millia* (neut.) *hominum in naves impositos* (masc.)
(Livy, xl. 41), 'Seven thousand men put on board
ships;' *Hi* (masc.) *summo in fluctu pendent . . . tres
Notus abreptas* (i.e. *naves* — fem.) *in saxa latentia
torquet* (Vergil, Æn., i. 106–8), 'Some (of the ships)

hang on the crest of the waves . . . ; three, swept
away, the South wind whirls upon hidden rocks.'   In
Greek, ὦ φίλτατ', ὦ περισσὰ τιμηθεὶς (masc.) τέκνον
(neut.) (Eur., Tro. 735), 'O dearest, O much honoured
child ;' τὰ τέλη (neut.) καταβάντας (masc.) (Thuc., IV.
xv. 1), 'The magistrates having descended :' and
similar instances frequently in Thucydides.

We next find cases where the grammatical gender
has completely changed. Thus, in Greek, masculine
designations of persons and animals are turned into
feminines by simply referring them to female objects :
thus, we have either ὁ or ἡ ἄγγελος ('messenger'),
διδάσκαλος ('teacher'), ἰατρός, ('healer'), τύραννος
('ruler'), ἔλαφος ('deer'), ἵππος ('horse' or 'mare'),
etc.   In Christian times, a form ὁ παρθένος ('an un-
married man') was constructed (Apocal., xiv. 4),
translated into Italian by *Vergine.* Neuter diminu-
tives in German readily become masculine or feminine
when the diminutive meaning has been obscured : as,
e.g., the occasional construction *die Fraülein,* 'the
young lady;' cf., also, in Latin, *Glycerium mea,
Philematium mea* (Plaut., Most., I. iii. 96), *mea
Gymnasium* (Plaut., Cist., I. i. 2).   In English, there
are a great number of words which would, in the first
instance, be thought of as masculines, as containing
a suffix commonly associated with masculine words.
These are, however, very frequently used as feminines ;
and, in some cases, even when a feminine termination exists side by side with the masculine one—as,
She is heir of Naples (Shakespeare, Tempest, II. i.) :
others are *enemy, rival, novice, astronomer, beggar,
teacher, botanist,* etc. Cf. *she is a peasant* (Longfellow) ;
The slave loves her master (Lord Byron); *His only
heir a princess* (Temp., I. 2) ; *She is his only heir*
(Much Ado, I. i.) ; *The daughter and heir of Leonato*

(ibid., I. iii.) ; *She alone is heir to both of us* (ibid., V. i.) ; etc.

If collectives or descriptions of qualities become descriptions of persons, the result may be a change of gender. The Fr. *le garde* ('the watchman') was once identical with *la garde* ('the watch,' *vigiliæ*) ; cf. further, in Spanish, *el cura* ('the priest'), *el justicia* ('the magistrate'): the Old Bulgarian *junota* ('youth'), as a masculine, means 'a youth.' The Russian *Golova* means 'a head,' and, in the masculine, 'a conductor.' Portuguese furnishes numerous instances of this; as, *a bolsa* (fem.), 'the purse,' 'exchange ;' *o bolsa* (masc.), 'the treasurer :' *a corneta*, 'the cornet ;' *o corneta*, 'the trumpeter :' *a lingua*, 'the tongue ;' *o lingua*,' 'the interpreter :' etc.[1] In Italian, *podestà* ('magistrate') is an instance of this. Feminine surnames, again, are frequently added to masculine personal names : cf. Latin *Alauda, Capella, Stella ;* Ital. *Colonna, Rosa, Barbarossa, Malespina*, etc. So, in French, we find names like *Jean Marie*.

A word often takes a particular gender from the fact that it belongs to a particular category. The gender of the type of the species, in fact, fixes the gender for other members classed with it. Thus, in English, the word for *beast* comes from the O.Fr. *beste* (bête), which is feminine : but this word, and the names of beasts generally, are treated in poetry as masculines, because the Teutonic usage is to treat beasts generally as masculine. Cf. *The beast is laid down in his lair* (Cowper) ; *And when a beste is deed he ne hath no peyne* (Chaucer, Cant. Tales, 1321) ; *The forest's leaping panther shall hide his spotted hide* (Bryant). Numerous other instances are given by Mätzner.[2] It is probable that personification aids in fixing the gender in these

---

[1] See Gröber, p. 788.　　　　　[2] Vol. i., p. 250.

cases. Similarly, in French, *été* ('summer'), from *æstatem*, has become masculine because the other seasons of the year were masculine. *Minuit* ('midnight') has followed *midi* ('midday'); *val* ('valley') has followed *mont* ('mountain'), *font* ('fount') *fontaine* ('fountain'); *aigle* ('eagle') is masculine because *oiseau* ('bird') is masculine; *brebis* ('wether') is feminine because *ovis* ('sheep') is feminine; *sort* ('lot') is masculine because *bonheur* ('happiness') is masculine; *art* ('art') is masculine because *métier* ('profession') is masculine : *mer* ('sea') is feminine because *terra* ('land') is feminine. In German, again, the names of *Tiber* and *Rhone* have followed the model of most German river names, and appear as feminine. In Greek, many names of plants and trees have become feminine, following the model of δρῦς ('tree') and βοτάνη ('grass'); cf. ὁ κύανος ('steel'), ἡ κύανος ('the corn-flower'), so called from a fancied resemblance between the plant and the metal. Towns, again, in Greek, show an inclination to follow the gender of πόλις, 'a city:' cf. ἡ Κέραμος, from ὁ κέραμος, 'clay;' ἡ Κισσός, from ὁ κισσός, 'ivy;' ἡ Μάραθος, from ὁ μάραθος, 'fennel.'

In other cases *formal* reasons have brought about a change in gender. We have a striking example of this in the feminine gender assumed by abstract nouns in -*or* in the Romance languages, to which *flos* ('flower') has also added itself. The fact was felt that most abstract substantives were feminine, *e.g.* those terminating in -*tas*, -*tus*, -*tudo*, -*tio*, -*itia*, -*ia*; and, especially, the feminine termination -*ura* sometimes was employed as an alternative to -*or*; cf. *pavor* ('fear'), Ital. *paura*. Again, in Latin, words in -*a*, when these were not, like *poeta*, the names of males, were commonly feminine. Consequently, we find that

Greek neuters in -μα appear in popular Latin as feminines, a gender which they have in many cases preserved in the Romance languages. Examples of this are seen in *schème, dogme, diademe, anagramme, énigme, épigramme*, etc. In the same way, in Modern Greek, the old Greek feminines in -os have in many cases became masculine, as ὁ πλάτανος, ὁ κυπάρισσος, 'the plain,' 'the cypress."

Sometimes the termination appears altered to suit the gender; thus the Lat. *socrus* ('a father-in-law') produces the Spanish word *suegra* ('a mother-in-law') : and, again, sometimes the traditional was the natural gender; and this was an additional reason why the word should alter its termination, instead of being modified by the gender,—thus, in Greek, the α stems which have become masculine, like νεανίας ('a youth'), have adopted the characteristic *s* of the masculine nominative.

The way in which natural gender, as viewed by imagination, has affected grammatical gender may be well seen in English. The personal pronouns give the only real traces of grammatical gender left in English, *he, she, it ; his, her, its*, etc. On the other hand, substantives are very commonly referred to one sex or another by writers, and to some extent personified. In these cases sometimes a faint tradition of their Anglo-Saxon gender seems to have lingered, as when, for instance, mammals and reptiles are in poetry spoken of as masculine ; e.g., *Like the roe* (A.S. *rá*, fem.) *when he hears* (Longfellow) ; *I have seen the hyena's* (Lat. and Fr. fem.) *eyes of flame, and heard at my side his stealthy tread* (Bryant). Birds, on the other hand, are treated very often as feminines, irrespective of the grammatical gender possessed by their Anglo-Saxon or French original ; cf. *But the sea-*

fowl has gone to her nest (Cowper) ; *A bird betrays her nest by striving to conceal it* (Byron) ; *Jealous as the eagle of her high aiery* (ibid.) ; *The raven flaps her wing* (ibid.) ; *A hawk hits her prey* (Halliwell, s.v. *ruff*) ; *The swan rows her state* (Milton).

We must mention one more point which ought not to be overlooked, though, owing to the scanty survival of grammatical gender in modern English, it cannot easily be illustrated by English examples. We have indicated some of the causes which have been active in producing a change of gender; but, besides these, there is a negative one, viz., the absence of impediment to such change, which, in a certain sense, may be said to have contributed to the same effect. The distinction in gender which is even yet marked in French and German by the different forms of the singular article (*le, der,* masc.; *la, die,* fem.; *das,* neut.) has long since disappeared in the plural. We find *les, die* for all genders. And hence it is clear that such words as were most frequently used in the plural were least closely associated with a particular gender, and were therefore more especially amenable to the influence of any force tending to group them with words of a gender different from their own. For instance, most feminine nouns in German form their plural by adding -*en* to the singular, while few masculine and only six or seven neuter nouns do the like; as a result of which many nouns, formerly masculine, are now feminine, and this especially applies to cases where the plural was in frequent use.

The neuter, the sexless, owes its origin as a grammatical category merely to the development and differentiation of the two other genders.

NUMBER.

As in the case of gender, so, before number passed into a grammatical category, concord must have been developed. Even in languages which, like English, would naturally express the plural by some plural termination, we find words denoting a plurality, and, indeed, a definite number, conceived and spoken of as a unity. Such are *a pair, a leash, a brace, a triplet, a trio, a quartette, a dozen, a score.*

We find similar cases in the most varied languages: cf. the Fr. *une dizaine* ('a collection of ten'), *une douzaine* ('a dozen'), *centaine* ('a collection of a hundred'), etc.; Ital. *una diecina, dozzina,* etc.; *trave,* in Danish, means 'a *score* of corn sheaves;' *schock,* in German, means 'sixty;" *tchetvero,* in Russian, means 'a set of four.' We may add, the curious Latin word *quimatus,* 'the age of five years.'

Thus, in like manner, so-called collective nouns are simply comprehensive singular designations of plurality. Now, the speaker or writer may choose to think of the collective of which he is speaking as a unity or as a plurality, and the way in which he chooses to regard it may affect the concord; nay, it may even affect the gender.

The most common case is where a plural verb follows a singular collective noun: as, 'The whole nation *seem* to be running out of their wits' (Smollett, Humphrey Clinker); 'The army of the Queen *mean* to besiege us' (Shakespeare, 3 Hen. VI., I. ii.);[1] cf. 'Even until King Arthur's *table*, man by man, had fallen in Lyonness about *their* Lord' (Tennyson, Idylls of the King); '*Pars perexigua*, duce amisso, Romam *inermes delati sunt*' (Livy, ii. 14) = 'A very small part,

---

[1] Mätzner, vol. ii., p. 143 (edit. 1864).

their leader lost, *were brought unarmed* to Rome ; '*Cetera classis*, prætoria nave amissa, *fugerunt*' (Livy, xxxv. 26) = 'The rest of the fleet, with the loss of the prætorian ship, fled (plur.).' Sometimes there is a mixture of singular and plural, e.g. '*Fremit improba plebes* (sing.) Sontibus *accensæ* (plur.) stimulis' (Stat., Theb., v. 488) = 'The *impatient people murmur* (sing.), *inflamed* (plur. part.) etc. :' cf. the following examples from the Greek—Μέρος τι (sing.) ἀνθρώπων οὐκ ἡγοῦνται (plur.) θεούς (Plato., Leg., 948) = 'A *portion* of mankind *do* not believe in gods ;' Τό στράτευμα ἐπορίζετο (sing.) σῖτον, κόπτοντες (plur.) τοὺς βοῦς καὶ ὄνους (Xen., Anab., II. i. 6) = 'The army provided itself with food (by) cutting up (plur. part.) the oxen and asses.'

In A.S., when ꝺæt or ꝺis is connected with a plural predicate by means of the verb 'to be,' the verb is put in the plural : 'Eall ꝺæt sindon micle and egeslice dæda' ('All *that* are great and terrible deeds.') Conversely, where we should say 'each of those who *hear*,' the idiom in Anglo-Saxon was to say 'each of those who *hears*:' as, 'Ælc ꝺára ꝺe ꝺás míne word *gehyrꝺ*' (= 'Each of those who *hears* these my words', where the verb is made to agree, not with ꝺara ꝺe, but with *ælc*. Cf. Sweet, Anglo-Saxon Reader, p. xci.).

We find many words so commonly combined with the plural, that we more naturally apprehend them as plural than as singular ; such a word is the English 'people,' which we instinctively connect with a plural verb. In such cases, we sometimes even find that the grammatical form actually assimilates itself to the psychological number, as when we speak of *folks ;* cf. also *sheeps* in Shakespeare (Love's Labour's lost, II. i.) ; while from the French word *gent*, which was used in Old French with the plural, we find formed, in the same way, the word *gens :* in Italian we find *genti* beside *gente*. In

Anglo-Saxon, -*waru* denotes 'a nation,' 'a defence :'
the plural -*ware*, 'citizens ;' as *Rómware*, 'the men of
Rome ;' *Cantwáre*, 'the men of Kent,' etc.   In Gothic,
there is a collective neuter *fadrein*, which we may illustrate or parallel, though not exactly translate, by the
word 'fathership.'   In the singular (genitive) it is used
in the meaning of 'race' or 'family' (Eph. iii. 15), thus
showing its original abstract and then collective sense ;
and again it is found (Luke viii. 56) still singular but
with a plural verb : *jah usgeisnodedun fadrein izos = and
were-astonished fathership* (i.e. PARENTS) *her = and her
parents were astonished*.   We even find the singular
noun with the *article* (*i.e* demonstrative pronoun) *in the
plural : Andhofun ꝺan im ꝺai fadrein is jah qeꝺun =
Answered then to him those fathership his and said = Then
answered his parents and said* (John ix. 20).   It is, thus,
this *plural meaning* which caused the word to be used
in the *plural form*, exactly as we use *folks* quoted
above, while the etymological meaning as abstract collective was overlooked.   For example : *Ni auk skulun
barna* FADREINAM *huzdjan, ak* FADREINA *barnam = not
eke shall bairns for* FATHERSHIPS *hoard, but* FATHERSHIPS
for bairns, i.e. *For the children shall not hoard for
the parents, but the parents for the children* (2 Cor.
xii. 14).[1]

The converse of this also happens.   A plural
expression receives the function of a singular when the

---

[1] In Hungarian, the plural ending is -*k*. But many nouns are
thought of as collectives, and have no plural. And if the noun be
preceded by a numeral, or by an adjective or pronoun of quantity, it
does not take the plural form unless the number embraces the
whole ; as, *tíz apostol* (ten apostols), but *á tizenket apostolok* (the *twelve*
apostles).   In the former case, the individuals are thought of *indefinitely*, and so the sense of the individual is weak ; in the latter case,
definitely, and therefore it is strong. Byrne, Principles of the Structure
of Language, vol. i., p. 435.

parts thus indicated are thought of as a whole. Thus we can talk of *another sixpence, another hundred yards;* or even use phrases like *There's not another two such women* (Warren); *this seven year* (Shakes., Much Ado, III. 3.); *What is six winters?* (Rich. II., I. iii.). *Amends, gallows, sessions, shambles* are plurals, but are generally treated as singulars; e.g., *a shrewd unhappy gallows* (Love's Labour's lost, V. ii. 12). So, too, *works, scales,* etc. : e.g., *that crystal scales* (Rom. and Jul., I. ii. 101); *Stoppage of a large steelworks* (Weekly Times and Echo, August 19, 1888); *Fire in a Liverpool chemical works* (Liverpool Daily Post, June 30, 1884, p. 7); *This is good news;* etc. Finally, such plurals become singular, not only in sense, but even in form, and are treated and declined as such. Thus, in English, we talk of *an invoice* (Fr. envois, plur.). In Latin, *castra* (plur.) sometimes formed a genitive of singular form, *castræ* :[1] the plural *litteræ*, in sense of 'an epistle,' has passed into the French *lettre* as singular, with a new plural, *lettres;* the Latin plural *vela,* 'sails,' into French *une voile: minaciæ* has become the French *menace,* 'threat,' and the Italian *minaccia: nuptiæ,* 'nuptials,' has become, in French, *noce,* 'a wedding,' as well as *noces: tenebræ,* 'darkness' has become, in Spanish, *tinieblas,* as well as *tinieblas; deliciæ,* 'delights,' in French, *délice,* as well as *délices. Pâques,* 'Easter,' *Athènes,* 'Athens,' are used as singulars.

Pronouns referring to abstract expressions stand sometimes in the plural; as, *Nobody knows what it is to lose a friend till* THEY *have lost him* (Fielding). Again, the predicate may stand in the plural ;[2] as, *Quisque suos* PATIMUR *manes* (Verg., Æn., 743)—'We each suffer our own ghostly punishment,' where *quisque*

[1] Accius apud Non., iii. 65.
[2] Cf. Roby, vol. ii., p. 183.

'each' in singular, but the verb *patimur* is plural.
Similar are *uterque educunt* (Cæs., C., iii. 30); *uter*
ERATIS (Plaut., Men., 1119); *neuter ad me* IRETIS;
Every one of these letters ARE *in my name* (Shakespeare,
Twelfth Night, II. v.); *Neither of them* ARE *remarkable*
(Blair); *Every one to rest* THEMSELVES BETAKE (Rape of
Lucrece, 125); *when neither* ARE *alive* (Cymb., IV. ii.
252). Most Indo-European languages possess pairs
of pronouns, in each of which sets one properly denotes
the singular, the other plurality; as in English *all*,
every; or *each*, and *any :* and these are readily inter-
changed; e.g., *without all doubt* (Shakes., Hen. VIII.,
IV. i. 113), *less attemptable than any the rarest of our
ladies* (Cymb., I. iv. 65). Thus, even in Latin, the
singular *omnis* is used where we should have expected
omnes ; as, *militat omnis amans* (Ovid, Amor., I. ix. 1).
Tu pulses omne quod obstat (Hor., Sat. II., vi. 30).
Thus *totus* has passed into the French *tout*, 'all.' We
find *both* in Shakespeare, connected with the singular;
Both our remedies within thy help and holy physic lies,
i.e. *the remedy for us 'both* (Rom. and Jul., II. iii.
51). Thus, also, *autrui*, 'others,' in French, really
the oblique case of *autre*, is in fact a singular, but is
looked upon as a plural; as, *la rigueur envers autrui*
(Massillon).

Number, in the sense of singular or plural, cannot,
again, be properly predicated of the simple names of
materials. We do not think of them as individuals,
except in connection with form as well as matter,—in
fact, till we think of substances as divided as well as
divisible. Hence it is that the names of materials
occur mostly in the singular number; the fact being
that if there were a *neuter number*, i.e. a grammatical
form expressive of neither plural nor singular, we
should naturally employ it.

But the name of a material is readily used as that
of an individual object, and, on the other hand, the
name of an individual object may easily come to be
the designation of a material. The imagination
supplies or withdraws, as it may be, the form and
definite shape which, as we have seen, is essential to
number. Take such instances as *hair, grass, bloom,
fruit, weed, grain, cloth, stone, wood, field, meadow,
marsh, heath, earth, land, bread, cake*, etc. Similarly,
when we talk of *fowl* as a viand, we individualise and
give form to a general conception; as, in French, when
we talk about *du porc, du mouton*. In the same way,
we have in Latin such expressions as *leporem et
gallinam et anserem* for '*the flesh of* the hare, the fowl,
and the goose;' and *fagum atque abietem* for 'the beach
tree and the fir-tree' (Cæsar, Bell. Gall., v. 12). In the
same way, we must explain the singular in cases like
The enemy is approaching; The Russian is within hail.
Similarly, Livy uses the singular, as *Romanus* for 'the
Romans,' *Poenus* for 'the Carthaginians,' *eques* for
'the cavalry,' *pedes* for 'the infantry,' etc.; nay, he even
goes as far as to combine *Hispani milites et funditor
Balearis* (xxvii. 2).

Thus, too, Horace ventures on the combination
miles nautæque (Sat. I., i.). Vergil has *plurima mortis
imago*, 'many an image of death' (Æn., ii. 369); in
Seneca, we even find *multo hoste*, 'many an enemy.'

In German, the singular of many words stands
constantly after numerals; as, *tausend mann*, 'a thousand
men,' *zehn stück Pferde*, 'ten head (lit. pieces) of horses.'
Similarly it was usual to write in English such expressions as *many score thousand: twenty score paces.*[1]
The fact is, that there is no need for any special
designation of plurality to follow a number; the plu-

[1] On 'abstract' v. 'concrete,' see p. 45.

rality is already sufficiently denoted by the number itself.[1] We thus see that the form taken by such a word would naturally be *numberless*, or *absolute*, in fact, would be treated in the same way as it would have been treated before the rise of grammatical number.

TENSE.

It is the function of the various 'tenses' to express the temporal relation of an event, when considered with regard to a certain moment. At the outset, however, we must observe that the tenses actually existing in any given language do not by any means perfectly correspond to the varieties possible and logically distinguishable in these relations. We will first consider what would be indispensable to a logically complete system.

Any event whatever must necessarily be anterior, contemporary, or posterior, to the moment with respect to which it is considered; and this moment must itself be past, present, or future. Hence, according as the moment of comparison is varied, we get the following sets :—

I. *Moment of comparison* PRESENT.
    The event is stated as—
        (a_1) NOW *past*.
        (b_1) NOW *present*.
        (c_1) NOW *still to come*.

II. *Moment of comparison* PAST.
    The event is stated to have been—
        (a_2) THEN *already past*.
        (b_2) THEN *present*.
        (c_2) THEN *still to come*.

---

[1] Accordingly, in Welsh, the noun is invariably in the singular when preceded by a numeral.

III. *Moment of comparison* FUTURE.

It is stated that the event—

(a_3) *will* THEN *be past.*

(b_3) *will* THEN *be present.*

(c_3) *will* THEN *be still to come.*

The above nine subdivisions exhaust all possibilities as long as we employ but a single 'moment of comparison' in each case; and it is so important that this point should be fully realised, that, simple as it appears, we proceed to illustrate each division as follows :—

(a_1) Cæsar once *said,* ' Veni, vidi, vici.'

(b_1) I now *believe* that this is true.

(c_1) I expect that he *will come.*

(a_2) When I entered, he *had gone.*

(b_2) When I entered, he *was speaking.*

(c_2) When I entered, he *was going to speak.*

(a_3) On New Year's day I *shall have completed* my fiftieth year.

(b_3) I *shall* then *receive* a letter.

(c_3) I *shall* then *be going to write.*

It is at once apparent here that in some of these cases we are forced to have recourse to periphrasis, and that in some we use tenses which might also serve in other divisions. This, for instance, may be seen by comparing b_2 and a_1, or, at any rate, c_1 and c_3. But before discussing these points we must pay a little more attention to the above scheme, not, indeed, as it actually exists, but as it might conceivably exist.

It is by no means inconceivable, and quite in accordance with logic, that we should wish to employ *two* moments of comparison instead of *one,* especially in some of the cases falling under II. and III. In c_2, for instance, the event might be *then* still to come, but *now* (a) past, (β) present, (γ) even yet to come.

This at first seems fanciful ; but while the example we employed to illustrate c_2 does not necessarily convey as much, still most hearers would naturally interpret it as follows : "When I entered, his speaking was still in the future, but now (unless some hindrance, as yet unstated, has intervened) it belongs to the past." Again, if, on the other hand, we take a sentence like *He has promised to do so ;* in the first place, it is found to STATE that the promise was given in the past, when as yet the action of fulfilment belonged to the future ; and, secondly, to IMPLY that this action of fulfilment belongs to the future *still*.

Further, it is logically possible, and often necessary, to make a statement about some event without any reference to time ; when, for instance, a statement is true at any time, or at no time at all. The form employed in such cases ought, in strict agreement with our definition of 'tense,' to be called 'tenseless' or 'absolute;' but it is well known that, in English and all Indo-European languages, the 'present' is the tense employed. In *Man is mortal* the copula *is* cannot justly be called 'present' tense, for the statement is wholly abstract, and applies equally to past, present, and future; yet it is customary and convenient to apply the term 'present' even to the word *is* as thus used.

This use of the present sometimes gives rise to a certain ambiguity. If, in speaking of a child, we say *He is very troublesome*, the statement may mean *He is at this moment very troublesome*, in which case the verb *is* is *present* tense proper; or it may mean *He is a troublesome child*, whence the sentence becomes *abstract-concrete* [1] and the verb *is* tense *absolute*.

If, as in the case of grammatical gender and

---

[1] On 'abstract' v. 'concrete,' see p. 45.

number, these distinctions of form are to be regarded as later developments in the case of the grammatical tenses of the verb, we must assume (i.) that the same form must once have served indifferently for all tense relations, and (ii.) expect that the tenses actually differentiated will (*a*) correspond only incompletely with the scheme of logical distinctions, (*b*) will in various languages show various deviations from the ideal scheme, and (*c*) will, in the same language at different periods of its history, show similar variations in those deviations.

i. Though the conclusion under head i. is actually inevitable, it seems, at first sight, improbable and doubtful; but, in addition to the use of the present tense discussed and exemplified above, there is much in modern English which may help to illustrate and enable us to realise it, while older languages afford much more material for the same purpose. A usage closely akin to that of the *present* tense for tense *absolute* occurs when the *present* is used for the *future*, and more especially when some other word in the sentence definitely refers the event to the future. Thus, in *I am going to London to-morrow*, we actually employ that specially English periphrasis which is never used in the *absolute* sense, but, as a rule, emphatically expresses that the action belongs to the present time.[1] Nay, where circumstances are sufficiently unequivocal to absolutely preclude the meaning of the present tense, the addition of such words as *to-morrow*, etc., is not even needed. If two friends, for instance, were speaking about some coming holidays, and the one had said, *I think I will go to Wales*, the other might answer, *I don't care for Wales, I am going to*

---

[1] In a sentence like *I am going out; I thought you were*, even the past tense refers to future.

London; or, again, without such explanatory circumstances, or any special words, the *present* in a subordinate clause can stand for a *future* event, provided
that the main clause grammatically expresses the
future; e.g., *I will call you when he comes.*

We also sometimes use the PRESENT TENSE FOR
THE PAST. This we do (*a*) where the event is equally
true of the past as of the present; e.g., *I know that* =
I know it, and knew it some time ago—a case in which
the present tense expresses past AND present together:
or (*b*) where the event belongs, indeed, entirely to the
past, but the result is represented as actually *present.*
Of (*b*) these are instances: 'Master *sends* me to tell
you,' 'He *tells* me that he is going away,' 'I *hear* he
is better now.' This usage approaches closely to a
third (*c*), the so-called *Historic present*, which, however,
we should probably not consider as a present tense expressing the past, but as a simple present, whose use
is due to the vivid imagination of the speaker, when it
leads him to regard the past as actually present.

We have said that the consciousness of the result
of an action sometimes causes the use of a present
tense for a past event. The same cause may also
lead to an exactly opposite usage, viz., that of a past
tense for an event in the present. Thus, as the result
of *seeing* is *knowing*, it came to pass that a form
originally signifying *I have seen* acquired the meaning
I know; the Ger. *Ich weisz* means 'I know,' but is
derived from the same root as the Lat. *Video,* 'I see.'
Thus, again, the root which we find in Lat. *gno-sco*
(= *I begin to learn, I get to know*) appears in the
English *I can,* which, exactly as the Lat. *novi* (for
**gnovi,* cf. *agnovi* for *ad-gnovi*), meant *I have got to
know* (= *I know*), has developed its present meaning,
I am able, from one expressive of something like *I have*

S

become able, or *I have learned*. It is thus that arose
the so-called 'præterito-presentia,' *can, must, will, shall,*
etc., which still betray, one and all, their origin from a
former grammatical past tense, by absence of *s* as a
characteristic termination of the third person singular
—a termination which we add to the stem in the case
of all other present tenses.

Logically, the relation between some tenses of the
same verb, as, *e.g.*, the present TENSE *cognosco* ('I get
to know') and the perfect TENSE *novi* ('I have got to
know'), which is used as a present tense to express the
result, is identical with that between many sets of
verbs. In fact we might translate *cognosco* by I LEARN
and *novi* by I KNOW. Similar sets are *to step, to stand,
to fall, to lie;* etc. But here, again, this distinction
need not to be expressed, or, at least, is not always
expressed ; the same form may serve for both. Not
to refer to dead languages or obsolete forms, it is
sufficient to quote the well-known schoolboy's ex
pression, *He stood him on the form*, for *He made him
stand on the form*. So, also, *He stood the candle on the
floor* (Dickens).[1]

Now, all this confusion of·past for present, present
for past, effect for cause, cause for effect, present for
future, present for every relation, causes in practice
as we have already seen, little or no ambiguity. If
we remember this, it becomes easy for us to realize
how conversation and intelligible statement may once
have been quite possible without further aid than that
afforded by what we call the tense *absolute*, i.e. a form
of the verb expressive of the action only, without any
indication of its time. A glance at a tense system
very different from our own, will enable us to do this

[1] Cf. Storm, p. 217, for other instances, such as *Sit you down*
(Shakespeare, Measure for Measure, 366), etc.

even more fully, and at the same time will to some
extent illustrate our statement that, in different languages, the actually existing tenses correspond vari-
ously with the logical scheme. In Hebrew, the verb
has three different forms, called respectively (*a*) imperative, (*b*) perfect, (*c*) imperfect; which terms, however, might be replaced for the occasion by (*a*)
command tense, (*b*) *finished* tense, (*c*) *unfinished* tense,
lest they should mislead readers who have not studied
Hebrew. Instead of 'tense,' we might as correctly
call them 'moods.'

The context is the sole guide as to whether the
event spoken of belongs to past, present, or future.
In narrative, the perfect and imperfect serve very
much the same purposes as the tenses similarly named
in Latin; but the *imperfect*, as tense or mood of *unfinished* action, serves also for our present and future,
while a future which is to represent something as
certainly expected, is supplied by the *perfect* or *finished*
tense. Again, the imperfect serves for the optative
(*wish* mood), and also sometimes replaces the imperative, since the latter is essentially a mood of action as
yet unperformed. In this latter use of the imperfect
there is sometimes a slight differentiation of form.

ii. *a*. The fact that the grammatical tenses correspond very incompletely with the logical distinctions,
has already been very fully illustrated by all we have
said in this chapter, and it only remains to add a few
words on what are termed in our grammars 'the compound tenses.' Strictly speaking, these are not tenses
at all of the verbs to which they are said to belong:
of tenses, *i.e.* forms derived from the verb itself, and
expressive of definite relations of time, there are but
two in English—the present, and the past or imperfect. The enumeration of the so-called compound

tenses amongst the tenses proper is due to a confusion
between logic and grammar, only slightly removed
from the fiction which gave us the still lingering
potential mood (*I can write*), or which might with
equal correctness have given us an obligatory mood
(*I must write*), a desiderative mood (*I like to write*),
an obstinate mood (*I am determined to write*), etc., etc.
In English we now employ various periphrases for all
relations but the present and that indicated by the
imperfect; and the line which separates a 'future
tense' *I will write*, from a phrase like *I have the intention of writing*, is a perfectly arbitrary one.

ii. *b.* Our short and necessarily very incomplete
discussion of the Hebrew tenses furnished an instance
of what we stated under ii. *b*, p. 256; and there is no
need to further illustrate this, especially as any reader
acquainted with a foreign language knows how much
care is requisite in translating the various English
tenses in their different applications. Any student of,
say, French or German will recognise this; while, in
the case of those who know English alone, no amount
of illustration of the point in question could raise their
knowledge above mere acceptance on authority, or
belief at second hand.

To illustrate ii. *c*, we shall only give a few instances of (*a*) the use in English (Modern English
and Anglo-Saxon) of a present tense where we should
now employ a future (which latter was then, as now,
non-existent as a tense, the only difference being that
the present periphrasis had not then yet become customary), and of (*β*) the use of a simple past tense
where we should now employ the plu-perfect:—

a. Æfter ðrím dagon ic árise = 'After three days
I *arise*' (Matt. xxvii. 63); *Gá gé on mínne wíngeard,
and ic sylle eow ðæt riht bið* = 'Go ye into my vine-

yard and I *give* (= *shall give*) you what right is'
(Matt. xx. 4).

β. *Hé mid ðám léohte his gást ágeaf ðam Drihtne ðe
hine to his ríce gelaðode* = 'He with the light his spirit
gave-up to the Lord who him to his Kingdom *invited*
(i.e., *had invited*)' (Ælfric; cf. Skeat, Anglo-Saxon
Reader, i., p. 86): *Hé ne grétte hi oð ðæt héo cende hyre
sunu* = 'He not knew her until that she *brought forth*
(= *had brought forth*) her son.'

In our preceding remarks, we have had occasion
to mention that, in Hebrew, the categories of tense
and mood are scarcely differentiated. Similarly—to
some extent—in Sanscrit, the distinction between
what we call tenses and moods is less clearly defined
than in, *e.g.*, Latin or Greek. Of this confusion, or
rather absence of distinction, we preserve some traces
in modern usage. Thus, as the imperative is essentially significant of something still to come, we can
understand how a future TENSE can come to be employed instead of an imperative MOOD. Such a phrase
as *You will do that at once*, especially when aided by
accent or emphasis, can be used for 'You *shall*, etc.'
Nay, the future is occasionally used as OPTATIVE; e.g.
Sic me di amabunt, = *So the gods will love me*, for *May
the gods love me:* and even as DUBITATIVE, as in the
Scottish *Ye'll no be o' this country, freend?* (Scott,
Mannering, ch. i.) = 'You will not be of this country,'
i.e. 'I suppose you are not, etc.'

VOICE.

We have seen that what in formal grammar appears as the 'object' of a verb is often, from a psychological point of view, the subject of a sentence (cf.
Chap. VI.). The use of the passive voice enables us
to do away with this incongruence: the object of the

action becomes the subject of our sentence, and the grammatical construction is thus made to harmonise with the psychological instinct. For instance, if, in answer to the question *Whom does he prefer as companion?* we say *John he would prefer*, we overcome, by a construction somewhat alien to the genius of the English language, the difficulty of expressing that John, the object of the verb to prefer, is in our mind the subject of a statement: *John is the person whom he would prefer.*

But such an inversion as *John he would prefer* is not always possible; while such an extension as *John is the person whom he would prefer*, though, indeed, always a possible construction, would be felt as very awkward and needlessly lengthy. This difficulty is evaded by the use of the passive voice: and the use of this voice serves to give clearness and elegance to style.

It is, however, perhaps not superfluous to point out that, whether we employ the active or the passive voice, the ACTUAL relation existing between the subject and object of our sentence remains the same. Whether we say *John loves Mary*, or *Mary is loved by John*, the person *John* is in either case described as the agent; the person *Mary* is the object of the feeling expressed by the verb. It is the *form* only of the two sentences which differs; it is the *syntactical*, and not the *real* relation of subject and object which varies. Hence we may say that the distinction of voice in the verb is to some extent purely syntactical in its nature. It is, moreover, clear that the distinction implied in voice could not arise before the distinction between the grammatical subject and object had been established. Until such was the case, mere juxtaposition of substantive and verb must have served equally as the expression of the active and of the passive relation between subject and predicate.

A somewhat similar phenomenon, possibly a survival of this prehistoric stage, is observable in the nominal forms of the verb, which, though indeed already specialised in the earliest stages of those languages with which we are acquainted, contain nothing in their actual formation which can assign them to either voice. And, again, if we consider fully the Latin genitives known in grammar as *objective* and *subjective*, we find a similar indefiniteness of expression prevalent as to relationship active or passive. *Amor patris* ('love, father's') can, according to the context, signify either the love which the father feels, or that which is felt for the father by some one else.

The present participle, now always called *active*, is even yet sometimes used in a passive meaning, and this use was formerly much more common. We hear, even at the present day, such phrases as *Do you want the tea making? I want my coat brushing*, etc.[1] Again, we have expressions like *One thing is wanting*, common now as in Shakespeare's time;[2] *so much is owing*, etc. Other instances not less striking have become obsolete: as, *his unrecalling crime* (Rape of Lucrece, l. 993) for *unrecalled* = 'not to be recalled;' and *his all-obeying breath* (Ant. and Cleop., III. xiii. 77) = his breath obeyed by all. We find, also, *Relish your nimble notes to pleasing ears* (= pleased ears) in Rape of Lucrece, l. 1126.

---

[1] Cf. Earle (Philology of the English Tongue, p. 536), who cites these phrases as provincialisms to be heard in all classes of society in Yorkshire. Every careful speaker will agree with him in deeming them "one of the finest of our provincialisms."

[2] Cf. Cor., II. i. 217 ; Rich. II., III. iv. 13 ; 1 Hen. VI., I. i. 82.

In Gothic there is a remarkable and indeed unique instance of this use (Mark xv. 15): *Atgaf Jesu usbliggvands*, i.e. (*Pilate*) *gave Jesus scourging* = *gave up Jesus to be scourged*, or *for being scourged*.

The so-called gerundives in Latin have commonly a passive meaning; thus, *amandus* usually means 'fit to be loved.' But here, again, we meet with exceptional uses which prove that what is now regarded as the 'regular' meaning is in reality but accidental and adventitious. *Oriundus* means 'arising' and, in somewhat older Latin, we find forms like *pereundus*, 'perishing,' *placendus*, 'pleasing,' etc.

Little as the distinction of voice is expressed in the *nomen actionis*, it is equally little inherent in the infinite. In such a sentence as *I gave him a good beating*, the meaning of *beating* is active; in the sentence *He got a good beating*, it is decidedly passive. Similarly, in such a sentence as *I can read*, the infinitive is active, but this is owing to the context: for instance, in such a sentence as *This is not easy to read*, it is clearly passive. Yet no one would call these phrases ambiguous. We can therefore easily imagine that infinitives may have existed long before they were differentiated into separate forms to mark the two voices. We still employ many infinitives which might be called neuter, neither active nor passive: such as, for instance, 'Is it better *to say* yes or *to say* no?' 'fair *to see*;' 'a marvel *to tell*.'

In Gothic, however, we find many instances of infinitives which, being commonly employed as actives, are conveniently considered as belonging to that particular voice; but which, in special sentences, have a very clearly defined passive sense. Thus, *qêmun ðan môtarjôs daupjan* = *Came then publicans* (*to*) *baptise* = *to be baptised* (Luke iii. 12); *Untê sunus mans*

skulds ist atgiban in handuns mannê = For (*the*) *son*
(*of*) *man due is* (=*must*) *deliver into hands* (*of*) *men =*
shall be delivered into. (Luke ix. 44); *Varᵭ ᵭan gasviltan*
ᵭamma unlêdin jah briggan fram aggilum in barma
Abrahamis = (*It*) *happened then* (*to*) *die* (*to*) *the beggar*
and (*to*) *bring from* (=*by*) *angels into* (*the*) *bosom* (*of*)
Abraham = It came to pass that the beggar died and was
carried, etc. (Luke xvi. 22); *du saihvan = to see = for*
being seen (Matt. vi. 1), etc.

Though, then, in these and similar cases we find
infinitive forms with unquestionably passive meanings,
it would not be quite correct to assign them in formal
grammar to the passive voice.

A grammatical passive is only acknowledged in
cases where that passive has been formed from the
same stem as the active, and has been marked off from
it by a special method of formation, as in such cases
as *amo,* ' I love,' *amor,* ' I am loved.'   The relation of
an intransitive verb to its corresponding causative,
resembles that of a passive to its active, as in such
cases as *to fall, to fell ; to drink, to drench ; to sit, to set :*
and the pairs from roots etymologically unrelated, *to*
make, to become; to kill, to die.   In the case of the
intransitive verbs, however, as compared with that of
the grammatical passive, we do not dwell so much in
thought upon an operating cause as constituting the
difference between active and passive.   But this distinction is so slight, that we actually find intransitive
verbs used with a sequence such as we should expect
after a passive, as in *He died by the hand of the public*
executioner; He fell by his own ambition.   On the
other hand, we can see the transition from the passive
to the active in the case of the Russian—where the
active form is employed to express a passive sense,
—and of the so-called deponent verbs.   We have to

translate a form like the Latin *verti* by 'to turn,' employing the middle voice.   A case like *Jam homo in mercaturâ vortitur*, 'The man is now busy with merchandise' (Plautus, Mostellaria, III. i. 109) may serve to show how nearly allied is the middle or passive voice to the deponent proper.   No doubt a true deponent differs from a verb used in the middle voice, by the fact that the deponent takes an accusative after it; but how nearly the two touch one another, may be gathered from such instances as that given above, by the side of *adversari regem* (Tac., Hist., iv. 84,), 'to oppose, or to oppose one's-self to, the king.'

One of the most common ways, in which the passive takes its origin, is from the middle voice, which is sometimes seen to be formed from the composition of the active with the reflective pronoun.   We have in English two examples of this method of formation, in the words (*to*) *bask and* (*to*) *busk*: *to bask* means 'to bathe one's-self;' *to busk*, 'to prepare one's-self,' or 'get ready.'[1]   The *sk* stands for *sik*, as it appears in Icelandic, the accusative case of a reflective pronoun of the third person.   The Russian often, in like manner, employs a reflective form in *-sya* instead of the passive, just as does the French; thus, *Tavárni prodáutsya, les hardes se vendent*, 'The goods are sold,' lit. 'sell themselves:' cf. *Rien ne s'y voyait plus, pas même des débris* (De Vigny).[2]   'Nothing more was to be seen, not even the ruined remains.'

In these cases, one element of the signification of the middle voice is discarded.   The middle voice denotes that an action starts from a person, and returns to him.   In *I strike myself* the action '*strikes*'

---

[1] Skeat, Principles of English Etymology, p. 468.
[2] See Mätzner's Fr. Gr., p. 176, for more examples.

starts from the speaker, but visits him again with its effects; in *I am struck* the action is visited upon the subject, but does not originate therewith. There are some reflective combinations, even in English, where the consciousness of the activity of the subject has practically disappeared: as in *How do you find your-self? I bethought me; He found himself in an awkward position :* but these, it will be seen, approach more to the use of the simple intransitive, by means of the relationship which this bears to the passive; cf. *s'exciter* with *être excité;* 'to be excited:' *moveri*, with *se movere*, 'to move.' There are certain uses of the verb, in French and German, in which the operation of the subject is almost effaced: as, *sich befinden*, in *Wie befinden sie sich* ('How are you?'); *cela se laisse dire* ('that may be said').

CHAPTER XVI.

DISPLACEMENT OF THE SYNTACTICAL DISTRIBUTION.

THE reader who remembers and fully apprehends the wider meaning, which in Chapter VI. we assigned to the terms (Psychological) 'subject' and 'predicate,' must realise how comparatively seldom the grammatical categories of the same name coincide with the corresponding parts of the thought to which the sentence is to give utterance. We defined the subject as the expression for that which the speaker pre-supposes known to the hearer, and the predicate as that which indicates what he wishes the hearer to think or learn about it. Hence, as we saw, the sentence theoretically consists of two parts; but, as each of these parts may be extended, we get—if we indicate subject and predicate by the letters S and P respectively, and the extensions by a, b, c, etc.—the following scheme for a simple sentence: $Sabc + Pdef$.

Now, in such a sentence, the grammatical subject, with all its extensions, will correspond with the psychological subject, and the grammatical predicate and its extensions with the psychological predicate, *only in case* the extensions of the subject are really no more than additions made in order to specify the *known* or *presupposed*, and if the predicate contains nothing which serves any further purpose than to convey the

thought about that subject.   But as soon as to the
subject-noun, for instance, an adjective is added which
conveys *new* thought about the subject; or, again, as
soon as the object is indicated by a noun accompanied
by a similar 'additional' qualification, then these
additions or extensions become *ipso facto* psychological predicates, and the sentence, grammatically
simple, becomes a psychologically complex one.
Thus, suppose a good Charles and a wicked Charles
have been spoken of, and the latter is known to have
done something with his thick stick to the speaker;
then, and then only, can a sentence like *The wicked
Charles has beaten me with his thick stick* be a psychologically simple one.   In this sentence then, *The wicked
Charles* is subject, *has beaten* is predicate, and *with his
stick* extension, and the psychological and grammatical divisions coincide completely.   But suppose
that it was known that the same person had beaten
the speaker, but that the instrument was not known;
or that the action and the instrument were known,
but not the recipient of the blows : in this case the
sentence, though remaining a simple one, would at
once cease to correspond in its grammatical parts to
the psychological divisions of (*a*) *Charles has beaten me*
(subject) + *with his stick* (predicate), or, (*b*) *Charles
has beaten with his stick* (subject) + *me* (predicate).
In fact, if we wished to make the grammatical form
correspond to the divisions of that psychologically
simple statement, we should have to adopt a form
grammatically complex *;* such as *The instrument with
which Charles has beaten me is his thick stick*, or, *The
person whom Charles has beaten with his thick stick is
I*, according to the circumstances of the case.

In any of the cases enumerated above, the psychological subject and predicate were simple.   But

suppose that the hearer was not aware that anything had happened, nor could be supposed to have any predisposition to call the individual in question 'wicked.' Then, though the sentence remains grammatically a simple one, we really get the following complex PSYCHOLOGICAL analysis : —

1. Subject : *Charles*
   Predicate : *is (in my opinion) wicked.*
2. Subject : *The wicked Charles*
   Predicate : *has beaten.*
3. Subject : *The object of that beating*
   Predicate (with copula) : *is I.*
4. Subject : *The instrument with which that beating was inflicted upon me*
   Predicate (with copula) : *is a stick.*
5. Subject : *That stick*
   Predicate (with copula) : *is thick.*

While, therefore, the scheme could grammatically be symbolised $aS + Pbc$, we should have to symbolise the psychological analysis somewhat as follows :—

$$P + S$$
$$\underbrace{}$$
$$S' + P'$$
$$\underbrace{}$$
$$S'' + P''$$
$$\underbrace{}$$
$$S''' + P'''$$
$$\underbrace{}$$
$$S'''' + P''''$$
$$\underbrace{}$$

At first sight this may seem far-fetched and useessly refined, but the student will find that it is desirable to force himself in some such manner to fully realise the absolute inadequacy of our grammatical terms and distinctions when we apply them to psychological questions: and to realise, also, the vagueness with which long habit has taught us to be satisfied in our modes of expression, and in our constructions for various thoughts, differing essentially, though perhaps not always widely.[1] It is the full conception of the somewhat haphazard nature of our constructions which will help us to understand how uncertain and how different in various speakers must, on the one hand, be the correspondence between the grammatical and psychological subject and predicate; and, on the other, how vague must often be the distinctions between the parts of our sentences, and how varying the grouping of these parts, as we more or less consciously conceive of them as connected or as 'belonging together.' All is here fluctuating and indefinite. Thus, as a rule, the word *is* in sentences like *He is king, He is subject,* is mere copula, and *king* the real predicate; though, when we utter the same words in order to state that *he* and no one else occupies the throne, *he* becomes psychologically predicate, and *king*, or rather *is king*, becomes subject, whatever the

---

[1] It is altogether unimportant that, in the case of such a sentence as the one which we took for our example, the ultimate result, as far as the understanding of the meaning goes, makes practically very little, if any, difference. Thus, we teach a child that three times five and five times three are the same, because the ultimate result of bringing together three fives or five groups of three each is identical. Still, no one will deny that, for correct conception of the operation, there is an important difference between—

    . . . .

and— . . .   .

or maintain that the understanding of this difference is of no importance for the theory. Nay, even in practical life there would be a great difference between going thrice, *e.g.*, to fetch five apples at a time, and making five journeys for three apples each time. Yet every one admits that $3 \times 5 = 5 \times 3$ is a 'truth' generally quite 'true enough.'

grammatical form of the sentence may seem to prove to the contrary. Again, in *He* IS *king* (*i.e.* now, and not only going to be so), *he as king* is subject, *is* (*now*) predicate.

Psychologically, the idea of the copula as mere link between subject and predicate is far more extensive than ordinary grammar admits. Thus, in *What is the matter with him? He has got the toothache*, the predicate of the latter sentence is *the toothache, has got* is copula.

In *Will he be quick, do you think? Oh yes, he was running very quickly*, the words *was running* are a mere copula, unless, emphasised by stress of accent, they are made to convey the specially desired statement that the person spoken of *ran*, and did not walk slowly or ride, etc., in which case they are a true predicate.

We have here illustrated how one of the means for distinguishing the predicate from the other parts of the sentence is found in *accent* or *stress*.

But we do not invariably thus emphasise our predicate. An interrogative pronoun, for instance, is always a psychological predicate. If we ask *Who has done this?* we usually lay our stress on *done* or on *this*, though these words, being mere expressions for the observed and known fact, contain the psychological subject, and the unknown person indicated by *who* is the predicate sought for by the questioner.

There exist other elements of speech which are regularly subjects or predicates; for instance, a demonstrative referring back to a substantive previously expressed and commencing a sentence, is necessarily a psychological subject, or part of it : *I know those men are my enemies : them I despise*. A relative pronoun, of course, has the same function :

there is a man whom I respect highly.   Again, every
element of a sentence whose connection with the rest
is denied by means of a negative particle is generally
a psychological predicate; as, *Yield not me the praise*
(Tennyson) = 'The person to whom praise is due is
not I.'   *But not to me returns day* (Milton, Par. Lost,
iii. 41) = 'Day returns to many, but among those
is[1] not I.'

This, of course, includes any words expressing the
contrast with the negatived element: *Give not me but
him the praise* = 'The person to whom praise is due
is not I, (but) he.'

Besides emphasis, we have, in so-called inverted
constructions, the means of characterising any part of
a sentence as subject or predicate.   Thus: *One thing
thou lackest* (Mark x. 21) = 'One thing there is which
thou hast not.'   '*No pause of dread Lord William
knew* (Scott, Harold, v. 15) = 'Not a pause of dread
existed which Lord William knew' = 'Not a pause
of dread was made by Lord William.'

A means of establishing correspondence between
the grammatical and psychological predicate has been
incidentally illustrated in the foregoing discussion.   It
is the periphrastic construction with *is*, of which
instances are very numerous.   *It is to you, young
people, that I speak ; What I most prize in woman, is
her affections, not her intellect* (Longfellow); *It is thou
that robbest me of my Lord* (Shakespeare, 2 Hen. VI.,
IV. ii.); *It was not you that sent me hither, but God*
(Gen. xlv. 8).

This construction is quite common in many other
languages: French—*C'est a vous que je m'adresse*
(= 'It is to you that I myself address); German—
Christen sind es, die das getan haben (lit. 'Christians

---

[1] *Is* rather than *am* here, to symbolise the sense of *I* as predicate.

T

are it, that that done have ' = 'It is (the) Christians that have done this ').

In English, another construction often serves the same purpose : *As to denying, he would scorn it ; As for that fellow, we'll see about him to-morrow.* Or (with the psychological subject simply in the nominative, without any verbal indication of its connection with what follows), *Husband and children, she saw them murdered before her very eyes ; My life's foul deed, my life's fair end shall free it* (Shakespeare, Rape of Lucr.) ; *The prince . . . they will slay him* (Ben Jonson, Sejanus, III. iii.) ; *That thing, I took it for a man* (Lear, IV. vi. 77). *Antipholus, my husband . . . this ill day a most outrageous fit of madness took him* (Com. of Errors, V. i. 138). When, in this construction, the words which head the sentence stand for the same thing as the subject pronoun of the following clause, the result, of course, is not a readjustment of the parts, but an (often useless) emphasis : cf. *John, he said so ; The king, he went*, etc. When the psychological subject would, in the simpler constructions appear as a genitive, this is indicated by the pronoun standing, in that case, e.g., *'Tis certain every man that dies ill, the ill is upon his head* (Henry V., IV. i. 197). *That they who brought me in my master's hate, I live to look upon their tragedy* (Rich. III., III. ii. 57) *; And vows so born, in their nativity all truth appears* (Mid. Night's Dream, III. ii. 124).

In Chapter VI. we have discussed the point that in reality an adjective is psychologically a predicate : an expression like *The good man* containing, in fact, a statement that the man is good. There is a construction, however,—and one, too, not unfrequent,—in which the adjective contains the psychological and logical subjects; e.g., *The short time at my disposal prevented me from calling upon him*—' The shortness of the time prevented,' etc. Though this construction may perhaps be due to a contamination between, say, *The shortness of the time prevented* and *The short time did not allow,* it still remains certain that in the construction, as it stands, a displacement has occurred.

It might *a priori* be expected that all this uncertainty and vagueness would cause parts of a sentence which grammatically belong together to cohere but loosely, and eventually to get separated, whilst other grammatical connections, which at first did not exist, would thereby arise. It is clear, for instance, that in the sentence *I sit on a chair,* the preposition *on* is as closely connected with the verb *to sit* as with the noun *a chair.* Nay, it may be said that the ties which connect it with the noun in this and similar cases must once have been, and perhaps in the linguistic consciousness of some speakers still are, stronger than those between the preposition and the verb. This would appear from the fact that the various prepositions used to govern in English—as they still do in German, for instance—various cases, while these ties would be strengthened by the common occurrence of the preposition with a noun, unaccompanied by any verb; e.g., *That book there on the chair; The man in the garden,* etc. It is, however, evident in many constructions that the noun has separated from the preposition, and that the latter has entered into closer connection with the verb. We owe to this, *e.g.,* the Latin and German 'compound verbs,' as *excedere,* ' to go out from,' *anliegen,* ' to be incumbent on,' etc., which used to govern, or still do govern the case which would have followed the preposition if used immediately before the noun and detached from the verb. In English, this or a similar displacement has given rise to such constructions as *And this rich fair town we make him lord of* (K. John, II. i. 553); *a place which we have long heard of; Washes of all kinds I had an antipathy to* (Goldsmith); *Logic I made no account of* (Smollett, Rod. Random, 6); *This house I no more show my face in* (She stoops to conquer, IV.); *The false paiens stood he by* (P. Langtoft).

A careful study of the above examples will show that in these and several of the following, the construction has the effect and is most likely due to a desire of bringing the psychological subject to the head of the sentence. It is at present chiefly employed in relative and interrogative clauses, and in sentences in the passive voice: *The intended fire your city is ready to flame in* (Coriolanus, V. 2); *An idle dare-devil of a boy, whom his friends had been glad to get rid of* (Green, Short History, p. 732); *Stories of the lady, which he swore to the truth of* (Tom Jones, bk. xv., ch. 9); *He was such a lover, as a generous friend of the lady should not betray her to* (ibid., xiii. 2); *A pipe in his mouth, which, indeed, he seldom was without* (ibid., ii. 2): *The eclipse which the nominal seat of Christianity was under* (Earle, Anglo-Saxon Liter., p. 25); *Such scruple of conscience as the terrors of their late invented religion had let them into* (Puttenham, Arte of Poesie, Arber's reprint, p. 24); *An outrage confessed to on a death-bed* (Liv. Daily Post, Aug. 1, 1884, p. 5, col. a.); *He was seldom talked of*, etc. *What humour is the prince of?* (Hen. IV., II. iv).[1]

[1] It would be worth investigating—a question which only the most extensive statistical collection of earlier examples of this construction could decide—whether the very extensive use of this construction in English is not due to, or has not been at least promoted by, the existence of the so-called pronominal prepositions in Welsh, and their construction. The personal pronouns are used in Welsh as suffixes to the prepositions: *e.g.*, prep. *at* = to; *ataf*, 'to me;'

In the sentence *I will never allow you to read this book*, there is no doubt that every speaker feels *this book* as object of *read*, and *read this book* as object of *allow*. If, however, in order to make *this book* if it is psychological subject, appear also as the grammatical subject, we say *This book I shall never allow you to read*, we can very well understand how a speaker's linguistic sense may come to connect *this book* directly as object with the entire group *allow to read*, nay more, with the verb *allow;* as if it stood for *I will never allow you this book to read.* This may arise all

atat, 'to thee ;' *ato,* 'to him ;' *ati,* 'to her ;' *atom,* 'to us ;' *atoch,* 'to you ;' *atynt,* 'to them ;' *imi,* 'to me ;' *iti,* 'to thee ;' *iddo,* 'to him ;' *iddi,* 'to her ;' *ini,* 'to us ;' *ichwi,* 'to you ;' *iddynt,* 'to them ;' etc. (Rowland's Welsh Grammar, §§ 374–381). These forms were used especially in relative clauses ; *e.g.,* instead of—

    Y   cyfaill at yr hwn yr afonais lythyr,
    The friend   to whom   I-sent   letter,

we might say more elegantly—

    Y cyfaill yr hwn yr afonais lythyr ato.
    The friend whom I sent letter to (him).

Similarly—

    Efe yw'r gwr yr ysgrifenaist ato.
    He is the man thou wrotest   to (him).

    Rhoddwch i'r hwn y cymmerasoch oddi arno.
    Give   to whom you took   from (him).

Even the present occasional (and vulgar) repetition of the pronoun is found :—

    AR yr hwn y gwelwch yr ysbryd yn disgyn   ac yn
    ON *whom you see   the spirit (in) descending and (in)*

    aros   arno
    remaining ON *(him).*

A careful study of the translations here given will enable even one who has never seen any Welsh to judge of what is at least a possibility ; viz., that our construction began with the relative clauses, and is, even in its present more extensive use, a remnant of Celtic origin.

the more easily that, in a clause like *I have to read
this book*, the words *this book* are historically the object of *have* and not of the infinitive *to read*, and that,
in the form *this book I have to read*, the noun is in
close proximity to its historical government *I have*.
Hence, such transference of government from the infinitive to the group *finite verb + infinitive* and finally
to the *finite verb* has occasionally really taken place,
as can be shown by the way in which such clauses
have sometimes been turned into the passive voice.
A sentence like *The judge allowed them to drop the
prosecution* can, strictly speaking, be turned into the
passive only in one or other of the following ways:
They were allowed to drop the prosecution, or, *The
judge allowed that the prosecution should be dropped;*
in each of which cases, the object of the verb has
become the subject of the same verb in the passive
voice.   If, however, aided by such constructions as
The prosecution which the judge allowed them to drop,
the object (*prosecution*) of the verb *to drop* becomes,
first, object of the syntactical combination *allow to
drop*, and, finally, in the illogical thinker's consciousness or linguistic sense, object of the verb *to allow*,—
there may arise a passive construction something like
the following: *The prosecution which was allowed to be
dropped*.   This construction is indeed incorrect in
English, but its parallel may be occasionally heard
from careless speakers, and a careful study of it will
illustrate and make intelligible such phrases as the
German, *Hier ist sie zu spielen verboten*, literally =
' Here is she (*i.e.*, Minna v. Barnhelm, *i.e.*, the play of
that name) to play forbidden ' = 'Here it has been forbidden to play her (*sc.* it),' as passive of ' They have
forbidden to play it here;' *Die stellung des fürsten
Hohenlohe wird zu untergraben versucht* = 'The position

of the Prince Hohenlohe is to undermine attempted'
= 'An attempt is being made to undermine the position, etc. ;' or again, the Greek χιλίων δράχμων ἀπορ-
ρηθεισῶν λαβεῖν (Demosthenes), lit. 'One thousand
drachms having been agreed to receive' = 'It having
been agreed that I should receive one thousand
drachms.' Similarly, the Latin *Librum legere cœpi* =
('I begin to read the book') is turned into the
passive, *Liber legi cœptus est* = ('The book to be read
has been begun'), the perfect parallel of our somewhat fictitious English example.

In our examples, 'He has got the toothache,'
etc., we saw that the grammatical predicate often
has, in reality, no other psychological function than
that of mere copula, or, as it is often called, connecting word. The regular and constant use of
certain words in that manner has led some grammarians to group these together as a separate grammatical category, a grouping or distinction to which
many others vigorously object. The view which one
takes in this question is mainly influenced by (*a*) what
we call a 'connecting word,' and (*b*) a clear distinction
between the grammatical form and the function of a
word. Now, a connecting word is a word which
serves to indicate the connection between two ideas
or conceptions, and which accordingly can neither
stand alone, nor have any definite sense if placed with
only one such conception. Such a connecting word
between subject and predicate we have in the verb
to be, the copula, in most of its uses. It is said by
some that the word *is* never has any other function
than that of true predicate, and that the predicatival
adjective or noun is always to be considered a determinant of the predicate. This, whilst true as to grammatical *form*, is certainly incorrect as to *function*. In

the first place, we have already discussed (Chap. VI.) how sentences like *Borrowing is sorrowing*, contains no less, but also no more than *Borrow sorrow*, in which the latter word contains the true psychologic predicate.   Further, if we were to attribute to the word *is* in such sentences the same force as, for instance, in *God is*, i.e., *God exists*, we should necessarily have to explain a sentence, *This is impossible*, as 'This exists as something impossible;' which every one will at once perceive to be nonsense.

We must recognise in sentences like *Borrow sorrow* an original construction, by the side of which there sooner or later arose clauses truly denoting existence, such as *God is*, or even *God is good*, in which, at first, *is* had its full meaning of *exists*, and *good* had consequently much the function of an adverb.   When once, in the latter and similar sentences, a displacement and redistribution of the function began to take place, and the adjective *good* (or, *e.g.*, the noun *king* in *He is king*) acquired the force of a true logical predicate, the fuller construction with the copula *is* more and more frequently ousted the shorter one, which had no such link between subject and predicate.   The reluctance of some grammarians to admit this is perhaps partially due, also, to the fact that the copula has always retained the full inflectional forms of a true predicatival verb.   Hence they did not so easily realise the displacement which had occurred—a displacement which, in other sentences, where the part thereby affected is flectionless, is easier to demonstrate.

We shall first discuss one more instance of how a displacement affects inflected parts of speech, and then one or two in which the words concerned have no longer any inflection to connect them with other forms, and to protect them from isolation and change of function.

In the sentences *I make him* and *I make a king*, we have two accusatives of slightly different functions : the one indicating the OBJECT of the action (*him*), and the other indicating the RESULT of the action (*a king*). If the two statements be now combined, then, applied as they are to convey to the hearer the two distinct pieces of information as to the object and as to the results of the action, both of which were previously unknown to him, we have undoubtedly one verb with two distinct and equipoised accusatives. But assuming that either the object of the action or the result is already known, it is then only the other member of the pair which has the full predicatival force, whilst the former inevitably enters into a closer relationship with the verb. The member which retains the full force of a predicate becomes predicate to the group ; nay, even—as in our example, where the verb cannot be taken in its literal meaning—the one noun becomes almost a predicate to the other, *I make him king* being very similar in meaning to *He becomes king through my agency*. If this is the correct explanation of the origin of similar constructions, we must perhaps consider the use of an adjective as second accusative as due to analogy with this use of the noun. We must not forget, however, that the line of demarcation between adjective and noun was once very much more vague and indefinite than it is now.

In a similar way, the sentence *I teach him to speak and I declare him to be an honest man* must be a combination, with consequent displacement of relation, of two independent clauses—the one with a noun, or the equivalent thereof, and the other with an infinite as object. It is thus we explain the origin of the Latin accusative with infinitive.

An example of displacement, or re-arrangement of

relations, is next furnished by the origin and history of our correlatives *either, or, both, and*. *Either* means originally (A.S. *ægðer*, contracted from *æghwæðer* = *á* + *ge* + *hwæðer*) *one of two*, so that *either he or you* is really = *one of the two ; you or he*, where the word *either*, as it were, sums up or comprehends the whole of the following enumeration. It stands, therefore, in syntactical relation to both the members of the clause which are connected (or contrasted) by *or ;* but is now usually felt as connected with the first only, the sentence being divided as *either he* + *or you*. Similarly, *both* means *two together*. Hence *both you and I* originally had the full force of *the two together*, i.e., *you and I*. The word which stood in syntactical relation with the pair has therefore, as in the former case, become co-ordinate with the word *and*, which once formed part of the group it governed, and we now feel and explain expressions like our examples as consisting of the two groups, *both you* + *and I*.

In the last two examples the words are now flectionless, and have become, when used in such constructions, connecting words, a change entirely owing to such displacement of relationship between the parts of the sentence as we have been studying in this chapter.

In the discussion of our example on page 270 we noticed how even a grammatically simple clause might in reality be a logically complex one. *Vice versâ*, a clause logically simple may be expressed by a grammatically complex sentence. *I asked him after his health*, as an answer to *What were you asking him ?* is a psychologically and grammatically simple sentence.[1]

---

[1] The grammatical and the psychological distribution, however, differs. Grammatically : subject, 'I ;' predicate, 'asked ;' etc. Psychologically : subject, 'I asked him ;' predicate, 'after his health.'

The answer might, however, without in the least degree altering the thought expressed, have been cast in the form *I asked him how he was*—a grammatically complex sentence.

Again, logical independence and grammatical co-ordination do not by any means necessarily go together — a sentence like *He first went to Paris, whence he proceeded to Rome, where he met his friend* being in form complex with main and subordinate clauses ; in meaning, however, equivalent to an aggregate of three co-ordinate ' main ' clauses : *He went + from there he proceeded + there he met.*

Nay, it occasionally happens that syntactical form and logical function are in direct opposition. Thus, *e.g.*, in *Scarcely had he entered the house, when his mother exclaimed, There is John !* what is logically the main clause has the grammatical or syntactical form of a subordinate one.

It cannot now, therefore, seem strange that in syntax we also meet with the parallel of the process which gave birth to such words as *adder, orange, newt,* and *nickname. Adder*, cf. Ger. *natter*, Icelandic *naðr*, was in Anglo-Saxon *nædre*. Similarly, *orange*, derived from the Persian *nâranj*, was originally preceded by an *n*. In the combination with the indefinite article *a* or *an* (the older form) this *n* was thought to belong to the article only, and the sound-groups *anorange, anadder* were wrongly split up into *an + orange, an + adder*. On the other hand, the groups *anekename* (really *an + ekename*) and *anewt* (really *an + ewt*) were erroneously broken up into *a + newt, a + nickname.*[1]

A precisely similar occurrence in syntax has given

---

[1] Compare ' the tother,' *e.g.* in Wycliffe, Matt. vi. 24 ; ' love the tother,' which took its rise from ' that other.' The word ' ewt ' also survived under the form *eft*.

us our conjunction *that*. *I know that* (= ' I know this
thing') + *he can sing*, when combined into the group of
subject *I*, predicate *know*, object (double, the one part
being explanatory of the other) *that* and *he can sing*,
gradually became divided, or divisible for the linguistic consciousness, into *I know* + *he can sing*, with
the conjunction *that* for connecting word.

In some cases the correspondence between psychological and grammatical distribution is so incomplete,
the subordinate and main clauses are so interwoven in
the grammatical form, that it becomes impossible to
separate the parts in our ordinary analysis.   This
happens more especially when a part of the grammatically subordinate clause really contains the psychological subject, and when, consequently, that part, with
a construction similar to that discussed on page 274 is
put at the head of the clause.   When, in the sentence
I believe that something will make you smile, the word
something expressed the psychological subject, Goldsmith emphasised this fact by writing, *Something, that
I believe will make you smile:* cf. Milton's *Whereof I
gave thee charge thou shouldst not eat; With me I see
not who partakes*, etc.   This arrangement, then, places
the main clause between parts of what is grammatically
the subordinate one.   In not a few cases confusion
or uncertainty may, then, arise as to whether the
words which head the sentence must be considered as
belonging to the subordinate clause or as governed by
the verb of the main clause.   If we say *The place
which he knew that he could not obtain*, we may hesitate
as to whether *place* is really object to *knew* or to
obtain.   We can, and often do, avoid this ambiguity
and intermixture of main and subordinate clauses by
a kind of double construction, like *The place, of which
he knew that he could not obtain it.*

CHAPTER XVII.

ON CONCORD.

IN inflectional languages, words relating to the same thing in the same way are commonly made to correspond formally with each other. This correspondence we call grammatical concord. Thus we find concord in gender, number, case, and person subsisting between a substantive and its predicate or attribute, or between a substantive and a pronoun or adjective representing the latter. Similarly we find a correspondence in tense and mood within the same period, or complex of sentences. This concord can hardly be said to be the necessary result of the logical relation of the words; the English collocation, *the good father's child*, where no formal concord is established between 'the good' and 'father's,' seems as logical as *des guten vater's kind*, where the article and the adjective have their respective genitive forms as well as the noun. Concord seems to have taken its origin from cases in which the formal correspondence of two words with each other came about, not owing to the relation borne by the former to the latter, but merely to the identity of their relation to some other word. Thus we should have an example of primitive concord in *fratris puer boni*, if felt by the speaker's linguistic consciousness something like *of (my) brother (the) child of* (*the*) *good* (*one*), i.e., *the child of* (*my*) *brother*, *the good*, i.e., *the child of* (*my*) *good brother*.

After such correspondence began to be regularly conceived of as concord, *i.e.*, as a habit natural to language, we must suppose that, owing to the operation of analogy, it extended its area to other cases to which it did not logically belong. We shall be confirmed in our theory that such was the procedure, if we examine certain cases in which the extension of concord can still be historically followed.

In the first place, let us take such a case as *Ce sont mes frères*. In English we translate this by *Those are my brothers*. The subject, however, in this case merely directs attention to something unknown until the predicate states what has to be known: the English pronoun, therefore, should strictly speaking stand in the neuter singular, as, indeed, it habitually did in A.S. *ðæt sindon*, etc., and as it does in Modern German to the present day—*Das sind meine brüder*. Even in Modern English we have cases like *It is we who have won; 'Twas men I lacked ; Is it only the plebeians who will rise?* (Bulwer, Rienzi, i. 5); but commonly, in Modern English and elsewhere, it appears brought into concord with the predicate, as *These are thy glorious works* (Milton): in Italian— *È questa la vostra figlia?* = 'Is this (fem.) your daughter?' Spanish—*Esta es la espada* = 'This (fem.) is the sword' (fem.): in Greek—Αὔτη τοι δίκη ἐστι θεῶν (Homer) = 'This (fem.), then, is the judgment (fem.) of the gods:' and in Latin this use is extremely common; as, *Eas divitias, eam bonam famam, magnamque nobilitatem, putabant* (Sall., Cat., 7),[1] = 'These (fem. plur.) they considered riches (fem. plur.), this (fem. sing.) a good name (fem.), and great nobility (fem.) ;'

[1] See Roby, Lat. Gr., vol. ii., p. 28.

i.e., 'This they looked upon as true riches; by such means they strove for fame; that was what they thought conferred true rank:' *Patres C. Mucio agrum dono dedere quæ postea sunt Mucia prata appellata* (Livy, ii. 13) = 'The fathers (senate) gave to C. Mucius *a field* as a present which (neut. plur.) afterwards *were* called the Mucian fields (neut. plur.).'

On the other hand, we find instances like *Sabini spem in discordia Romana ponunt: eam impedimentum delectui fore* (Livy, iii. 38) = 'The Sabines base their expectations on the domestic quarrels of the Romans; (they hoped) that *this* (fem. sing. agreeing with *spem*) would be a preventative (neut. sing.): and so *Si hoc profectio est* (Livy, ii. 38) = If this (neut.) is a setting-out (fem.).' It seems that, in the former cases, the subject has been made to agree with the predicate just as the predicate in other cases conforms to the subject.

We sometimes find, in Latin, words which commonly occur in the singular only, placed in the plural when connected with words used in the plural only; as, *summis opibus atque industriis* (Plautus, Mostellaria, 348) = 'with the greatest means (exertions) and *zeals* (for *zeal*):' *neque vigiliis neque quietibus* (Sallust, Cat., 15) = 'neither during watchings nor during *rests* (for *rest*):' *paupertates—divitiæ* (Varro,[1] Apud Non.) = '*poverties* (for *poverty*)—riches.' Similarly, we find *She is my goods, my chattels* (Shakespeare, Tam. of Shrew, III. ii.), where the singular would be the natural form for *chattel;* but *good* in the singular would have a different meaning from *goods*, and *chattels* is made to conform to *goods*.

The so-called predicatival dative in Latin seems to have started from cases like *quibus hoc impedimento*

---

[1] Cf. Dræger, § vii. 4.

erat = 'to whom this was for a hindrance:' *Mihi gaudio fuit* = 'It was for a joy to me:' etc.

It was felt that the ordinary predicate was put in the same case as its subject, and the concord was analogically extended to the dative. Thus Cicero (Dom., 3) writes *Illis incuria inimicorum probro non fuit* = 'To them (dat.) the negligence of their enemies was not (*for a*) *reproach*' (dat.), *i.e.*, 'was no reproach,' as contrasted with *tuum scelus meum probrum esse* = 'that your wickedness (acc.) should be my reproach (acc.).'

In a sentence like *They call him John* the name *John* ought strictly speaking to have no case; the simple stem should stand: and we might even expect the vocative to occur after verbs of naming, as it actually does sometimes in Greek; as, Τί με καλεῖτε κύριε; (Luke vi. 46), translated, in the Vulgate, *Quid vocatis me domine?* [1] and in the authorised version, *Why call ye me lord, lord?* Thus in Latin, too: *Clamassent ut litus Hyla, Hyla, omne sonaret* (Vergil, Eclogue vi. 43), 'They were shouting so that the whole shore was echoing Hylas! Hylas!' (voc.); *Matutine pater seu Jane libentius audis* (Hor., Sat. II., vi. 10), 'O Father Matutinus, or Janus, if thou givest readier ear thus addressed.' But the most common usage at the present day is the accusative; which is already found at least once in the few remnants of Gothic literature which we possess: in Luke iv. 13, we read: *Jah gavaljands us im tvalib, ðanzei jah apaustuluns namnida* = 'and choosing out (from) them twelve whom also apostles (acc. plur.) (he) named.' This accusative seems to be an analogical transference from such cases as the common construction, *Izei ðiudan sik silban taujið* = *Qui regem se facit* = *Who king himself makes.*

[1] Cf. Ziemer, p. 71.

In cases like *He bears the name John*, the pure
stem, or the nominative which most nearly represents
it, should stand ; as it does in the instance given.   In
English, we often use phrases like 'the name of John,'
after the analogy of 'the city of Rome,' etc.   In
Latin, we find merely exceptionally such cases as
Lactea nomen habet (Ovid, Metam., i. 168) = 'It (the
Milky Way) has the name milky,' where *milky* is
nominative.   In classical Latin, concord is observed
by placing the nominative side by side with *nomen*
when this word stands in the nominative ; as, *Cui
nomen Arethusa est* (Cicero, Verr., iv. 53) = 'Whose
name is Arethusa ;' *Ei morbo nomen est avaritia*
(Cicero, Tusc. Disp., iv. 11) = 'To that malady the
name is avarice.'   But we not uncommonly find in
Latin that, while the word *nomen* is in the nominative,
the name itself is made to agree with the noun or
pronoun expressing the person who bears it ; as,
Nomen Mercurio est mihi (Plautus, Amph., Prol. 19)
= 'The name is Mercury (dat.) to me (dat.),' *i.e.* 'My
name is Mercury ;' *Puero ab inopia Egerio inditum
nomen* (Livy, i. 34) = 'To the boy (dat.) from his
poverty Egerius (dat.) was given the name,' *i.e.* 'The
name of Egerius was given to the boy from his
poverty.'   Nay, we find a similar vacillation in concord
where *nomen* is in the accusative case ; as, *Filiis
duobus Philippum et Alexandrum et filiæ Apamam
nomina imposuerat* (Livy, xxxv. 47) = 'To his two sons
he had given the names Philip and Alexander, and to
his daughter, Apama.'   In this sentence, we have *nomen*
in the accusative plural and the names *Philip*, etc., also
in the accusative, though singular ; so that the latter
agree in case with *nomen*, and not with the datives
(*filiis duobus* and *filiæ*) of the persons bearing them.
In the following instance the reverse is the case : *Cui*

Superbo cognomen facta indiderunt (Livy, i. 49) = 'To whom (dat.) Superbus (dat.) the name (acc.) his deeds have given,' *i.e.* 'To whom his deeds have given the name Superbus.' This very vacillation proves that the speakers recognised no logical necessity for employing one case rather than another; but, in default of an absolute stem, chose a case which seemed to tally with some existing principle of concord already prevailing in language.

A similar vacillation occurs in cases of the predicatival noun or predicatival attributive with an infinitive, as in *It suited him to remain unknown.*

In English no doubt could arise, as the adjectives maintain an absolute form; but even in German, where the adjectives when used as predicates have different forms from those which they bear when used as epithets, it is correct to say, *Es steht dir frei als verständiger mann zu handeln* = 'It stands thee free as sensible man to act,' *i.e.* 'You are free to act as a man of sense,'—in which case we find the declined nominative 'verständiger,' used as it is whenever the adjective is followed by a noun, and when, consequently, according to the rules of German grammar, the undeclined form cannot be employed.

In Latin the nominative stands if it can be connected with the subject of the governing verb: as, *Pater esse disce* ('Learn to be a father'); *Omitto iratus esse* ('I cease to be angry'); *Cupio esse victor* ('I desire to be victor'). In poetry we find expressions like *ait fuisse navium celerrimus* (Catullus, iv. 2) = 'Says that it was the fastest of ships,'—a construction copied by Milton in 'And knew not eating death' (Par. Lost, ix. 792 :) '*Sensit medios delapsus in hostes*' (Vergil, Æn., ii. 377) = 'He perceived that he had fallen into the midst of enemies.' In these cases, *celerrimus* and *delapsus* are nominative, instead of the usual accusative; and similarly, in Greek, we find the nominative coupled with the infinitive used substantively, though this may be in another case : as, Ὁπόθεν ποτὲ ταύτην τὴν ἐπωνυμίαν ἔλαβες τὸ μανικὸς καλεῖσθαι, οὐκ οἶδα ἔγωγε (Plato, Symp., 173 D), 'Whence ever thou didst take this name the-to-be-called *mad* (nom. sing. masc.), I don't know;' Ὀρέγονται τοῦ πρῶτος ἕκαστος γίγνεσθαι (Thucydides, ii. 65), 'They wish for the (gen.) first (nom.) each (nom.) to become (gen.),' *i.e.* 'They all wish to become first.' Nay, in Greek, it is possible to connect with the infinitive even a genitive or dative depending on the governing sentence ; as in Εὐδαίμοσιν ὑμῖν ἔξεστι γίγνεσθαι (Demosthenes, Dem. iii. 23), 'It is permitted *you* (dat.) to become *happy* (dat.) ;' Ἐδέοντο Κύρου ὡς προθυμοτάτου γενέσθαι (Xenophon, Hell., I. v. 2), 'They were begging *Cyrus* (gen.) to show himself as *energetic-as-possible* (gen.).'

In Latin we find the connection with a dative, though not so widely as in Greek : as, *Animo otioso esse impero* (Terence, Phorm., II. ii. 26) = 'Mind (dat.) easy (dat.) to be I command (myself—*dative understood*),' *i.e.* 'I order my mind to be at ease ;' *Da mihi fallere, da justo sanctoque videri* (Hor., Ep. I. xvi. 61), 'Grant me to deceive, grant *me* (dat.) to seem *just and holy* (dat.) ;' *Vobis necesse est fortibus viris esse* (Livy, xxi. 44), 'It is necessary for you (dat.) to be brave men (dat.) ;' and commonly with *licet* ('it is allowed,') as *in Republica mihi neglegenti esse non licet* (Cicero, ad Att., i. 17), 'In politics I dare not be indifferent.'[1] To take this last example, for instance, we have (1) the governing sentence *Non mihi licet* ('It is not lawful *for me*,' dat.), (2) the infinitive *esse* ('to be'), and (3)

---

[1] Roby, vol. ii., p. 23.

the dative (depending on the governing sentence, and connected with the infinitive), *neglegenti* ('indifferent').

There are a few exceptions to this customary usage.[1] The accusative is sometimes found after *licet*, as in the passage *Si civi Romano licet esse Gaditanum, etc.*, 'If it is allowed a *Roman Citizen* (dat.) to be *a citizen of Gades* (acc.).' This use depends on the fact that the accusative is the ordinary case of the subject with the infinitive, e.g. *Permitto civem Romanum esse Gaditanum,*[2] 'I permit a *Roman Citizen* (acc.) to be *a citizen of Gades* (acc.).'

There are, again, other cases in which no concord is expressed ; in which concord, indeed, is almost incapable of being carried out. In these cases, in default of the pure stem which—were it possible to employ it —would be the only natural form to employ, the place has been supplied by the nominative. In English, for instance, we are familiar with such phrases as *My profession as teacher, his position as advocate.* In Latin we find such constructions as *Sempronius causa ipse pro se dicta damnatur* (Livy, iv. 44.), 'Sempronius is condemned, *his cause having been defended* (abl. abs.) *himself* (nom.) ;' *Omnes in spem suam quisque acceptis prælium poscunt* (Livy, xxi. 45), 'All they having been accepted after their own hopes, each demand battle' (here *omnes* ('all') is nominative, while *acceptis* ('having been accepted') is ablative absolute) ; *Flumen Albin transit longius penetrata Germania quam quisquam priorum* (Tacitus, Annals, iv. 45), 'He crosses the river Elbe after penetrating Germany further than any of his predecessors,' lit. 'Germany having been penetrated (abl. abs.) further than any (nom.) of his predecessors (*i.e.* had penetrated it).'

---

[1] See Roby, vol. ii., p. 145.

[2] Cf. Ziemer, p. 96 : Madvig Kl. Schr.

In these cases, no doubt *ipse* and *quisquam*, 'himself' and 'any,' depend, *grammatically* speaking, on the subject of the finite verb, but they belong *logically* to the ablative absolute only, with which they cannot be brought into concord.

Variation of concord exists between two parts of the same sentence in various languages, as in the case of 'What *is* six winters?' (Shakespeare, Rich. II., I. iii.), as against 'What *are* six winters?' 'Such *was* my orders,' as against 'Such *were* my orders;' 'She *is* my goods;'[1] 'What *means* these questions?' (Young, Night Thoughts, iv. 398). Bacon (Advancement of Learning, II. ii. 7) has 'A portion of the time wherein there *hath been* the greatest varieties.' The original rule was that the copula, like every other verb, followed the number of the subject, as in the first-named instances; and as, again, in French, in such cases as *C'est eux*, 'It is they;' *Il est cent usages*, 'There is hundred usages;' *C'était les petites îles*, 'It was the little islands.' In Latin, also, *Nequam pax est indutiæ* (A. Gellius), 'A truce (lit. *truces*) is a bad peace;' *Contentum rebus suis esse maximæ sunt divitiæ* (Cicero, Pro. Ar., vi. 3), 'To be content with one's circumstances are the greatest riches.' In these cases it is indifferent which substantive be considered the logical subject.

In German, on the other hand, it is common, when the predicate is plural, to put the copula in the same number; as, *das sind zwei verschiedene dinge* = 'That are two different things.' Other languages have corresponding usages; thus, in Modern Greek, Ἔπρεπε νὰ ἦναι τέσσαρα, 'There behoves to be four.' In Old Greek we find Τὸ χωρίον τοῦτο, ὅπερ πρότερον Ἐννέα ὁδοὶ ἐκαλοῦντο, 'This spot which *were* before *called* the

---

[1] Cf. Mätzner, ii. 147 ; Abbott, § 335 ; Hodgson, p. 142.

nine ways' (Thuc., iv. 102); and in French we find
such expressions as *Ce sont des bêtises*, 'This are
stupidities.' Even in English we find such phrases as
'Their haunt *are* the deep gorges of the mountains.'[1]
The usage seems due to the fact that the plural makes
itself more characteristically felt than the singular.
On the other hand, in several languages the converse
usage is possible; *i.e.* the copula in the singular stands
with a plural subject and before a singular predicate:
as, in Greek, Αἱ χορηγίαι ἱκανὸν εὐδαιμονίας σημεῖον
ἐστι, 'The services is a sufficient token of prosperity:'
in Latin — *Loca quæ Numidia appellatur* (Sallust),
'Places which is called Numidia;' *Quas geritis vestes
sordida lana fuit* (Ovid, Ars Am., iii. 222), 'The
clothes you wear was dirty wool:' in English—*Two
paces in the vilest earth is room enough* (Shakespeare,
1 Hen. IV., V. iv. 91); *Forty yards is room enough*
(Sheridan, Rivals, v. 2). We also find the curious
instance of 'Sham heroes, *what* are called quacks'
(Carlyle, Past and Present, ii. 7): in Spanish we have
Los encamisados era gente medrosa, 'The highwaymen
(lit. 'shirtclad') was a cowardly lot' (Cervantes).

　　Similarly, we find in the person of the verb a
corresponding usage: *It was you; Is that they?* in
French—*C'est moi* ('It is I'); *C'est nous* ('It is we');
C'est vous ('It is you'): in Old French it was possible
to say *C'est eux* ('It is they'). On the other hand, in
Modern German we find such forms as *Das waren sie*
('That were you'); *Sind sie das* ('Are you that'):
and in Old French, *Ce ne suis je pas* = 'This no am I
(at-all);' *C'estez vous* ('This are you); but *C'ont été*
('This they have been); *Ce furent les Phéniciens qui
inventèrent l'écriture* (Bossuet), 'It were (3rd plur.) the
Phenicians who invented writing.'

[1] Cf. Hodgson, p. 131.

In sentences beginning in English with *there*, and in French with the (neut.) *il*, we find that commonly in English the verb agrees in number with the subject which follows it, whilst in French it agrees with the pronoun *il*, as *Il est des gens de bien* (' There *is* good people '); *Rarement il arrive des révolutions* (' Rarely there happen*s* revolutions '). In English we more commonly find the plural; cf. Mätzner, vol. ii., p. 106—*There were many found to deny it:* but we also find *There is no more such Cæsars* (Shakespeare, Cymb., III. i.).[1]

A participle employed as a predicate or copula may agree with the predicatival substantive instead of the subject; as, Πάντα διήγησις οὖσα τυγχάνει (Plato, Rep., 392 D), ' Everything happens to be an explanation,' where the part. οὖσα (lit. ' being ') agrees with διήγησις (' explanation '); *Paupertas mihi onus visum* (Terence, Phorm., I. ii. 44), ' Poverty (fem.) to me a burden (neut.) seemed (neut. part.) ' = ' Poverty seemed to me a burden ; ' *Nisi honos ignominia putanda est* (Cicero, pro Balb., 3), ' Unless honour (masc.) is to be thought (fem.) shame (fem.).' On the other hand, we find *Semiramis puer esse credita est* (Justin, i. 2) = ' Semiramis was thought to be a boy,' where the part. *credita* (' thought ') takes its gender from *Semiramis*, and not from *puer*.

The predicate, again, which would naturally follow the subject, may follow some apposition of the subject: as, Θῆβαι, πόλις ἀστυγείτων, ἐκ μέσης τῆς Ἑλλάδος ἀνήρπασται (Æschines v. Ctes., 133), ' Thebes (plur.) a neighbouring city, *is torn* from the centre of Greece; ' Latin—*Corinthum totius Græciæ lumen extinctum esse voluerunt* (Cicero, Leg. Man., 5), ' Corinth (fem.), the light of all Greece, they wished to be extinguished (neut.).' Again, though the subject is plural, we find

[1] See Mätzner, vol. ii., p. 141.

the verb agreeing with its distributival apposition, and placed in the singular; as, *Pictores et poetæ, suum quisque opus a vulgo considerari vult* (Cic., de Offic., i. 41), 'Painters and poets *each wishes* that his work should be examined by the public.'

The construction is more striking still in which the predicate is made to agree with a noun compared with the subject (1) in gender—as, *Magis pedes quam arma tuta sunt* (Sallust, Jugurtha, 74 [1]) = 'Feet (masc.) are safer (neut.) than arms (neut.):' (2) in number—*Me non tantum literæ, quantum longinquitas temporis mitigavit* (Cicero, Fam., vi. 4) = 'Me not so much *letters* as *length* of time *has* comforted:' (3) in gender and number—as, *Quand on est jeunes, riches, et jolies, comme vous, mesdames, on n'en est pas réduites à l'artifice* (Diderot), 'When *one* (sing.) is *young, rich, and pretty,* (fem.,plur.) as you are, *ladies,* one (sing.) is not reduced (fem. plur.) to artifice:' (4) in person and number—as, Ἡ τύχη ἀεὶ βέλτιον ἢ ἡμεῖς ἡμῶν αὐτῶν ἐπιμελούμεθα (Demosthenes, Phil., I. 12), 'Fortune always for us more than *we care for* ourselves.' In English we meet with many sentences like 'Sully bought of Monsieur de la Roche Guzon one of the finest *horses* that *was* ever seen.' The concord of the predicate with a second subject connected with the words *and not* is also curious; as, *Heaven, and not we, have safely fought to-day* (Shakespeare, 2 Hen. IV., IV. ii.).[2]

In Greek, an apposition separated from the noun by a relative sentence may follow the relative pronoun in case; as, Κύκλωπος κεχόλωται, ὃν ὀφθάλμου ἀλάωσεν, ἀντίθεον Πολύφημον (Hom., Od., i. 69), 'He is wrath with the *Cyclops* (gen.) *whom* (acc.) he deprived of an eye, *the divine Polyphemus* (acc.).'

---

[1] See Dräger, § 113, for more examples.
[2] Cf. Mätzner, vol. ii., p. 152.

A demonstrative or relative, instead of following the substantive to which it refers, may follow a noun predicated of it ; as, in Latin, *Leucade sunt hæc decreta ; id caput Arcadiæ erat* (Livy, xxxiii. 17), 'These things were decreed at Leucas (fem.) ; that (neut.) in the capital (neut.) of Arcadia ;' *Thebæ quod Bœotiæ caput est*, 'Thebes (fem. plur.) which (neut.) is the capital (neut.) of Bœotia ;' Φόβος ἦν αἰδὼ εἴπομεν (Plat.), 'Fear (masc.) which (fem.) we call modesty (fem.).'

A relative pronoun logically referring to an impersonal indefinite subject usually follows the definite predicate belonging to that subject ; and, of course, the predicate of the pronoun does the same. Thus we have to say '*It* was a *man who* told me,' and not '*It* was a *man which* told me :' 'It is the lord *Chancellor whose* decision is questioned.' It is the same in German and in French ; as, *C'est eux qui ont bâti* ('*It* is *they who* have built'). In French, too, the person of the verb in the relative sentence follows the definite predicate, as *C'est moi seul qui suis coupable* ('*It* is I alone *who am* guilty') ; and it is the same in English— '*It* is I *who am* in fault.' On the other hand, in N.H.G. the use is to say *Du bist es, der mich gerettet hat*, 'Thou art *it* who me saved *has*,' = 'It is thou that (who) hast saved me.'

In a relative sentence, the verb connected with the subject of the governing sentence goes into the first or second person, even though the relative pronoun belongs to the predicate, and the third person would strictly be natural : cf. *Non sum ego is consul qui nefas arbitrer Gracchos laudare* = 'I am not such a consul who *should think* (1st pers.) it base to praise the Gracchi' (Cicero) ; *Neque tu is es qui nescias* = 'Nor are you he who *would ignore*' (2nd pers.), *i.e.* 'Nor are you such a one as to ignore.'

In English, this construction is very common ; as,
'If thou beest he : but O how fall'n ! how changed
From him, who in the happy realms of light *didst*
outshine myriads' (Milton, Par. Lost, bk. i., 84, 85) ;
'I am the person who *have* had' (Goldsmith, Good-nat.
Man, iii.).   This construction was common in Anglo-
Saxon ; as, *Secga œnigum ðâra ðe tirleâses trôde
sceawode* = 'Of the men to any of those (plur.) who
of the inglorious the track looked at (sing.)' + 'To any
of the men who looked at the track (of the) inglorious
(man)' (Beowulf, 844).

So in French—*Je suis l'homme qui accouchai d'un
œuf* (Voltaire), 'I am the man who laid (1st. pers.)
an egg ; *Je suis l'individu qui ai fait le crime*, 'I am
the person who *have done* the crime ;' and Italian—*Io
sono colui chi ho fatto*, 'I am he who *have done.'*

The predicate or attribute, instead of agreeing
with the subject, or with the word which it serves to
define, may agree with a genitive dependent on that
subject ; as, Ἦλθε δ' ἐπί ψυχή Θηβαίου Τειρεσίαο χρύσεον
σκῆπτρον ἔχων (Homer, Od., xi. 90), 'The soul (fem.)
of the Theban Teresias (masc.) came having (masc.)
a golden sceptre.'   In English we find 'There *are*
eleven days' *journey* from Horeb unto Kadesh-barnea'
(Deut. i. 2).

In French it is customary to say *La plupart de ses
amis l'abandonnèrent*, 'The most part of his friends
abandoned (plur.) him ;' but *La plupart du peuple
voulait*, 'The most part of the people wished (sing.) :'
in the former case the quantity of individuals is
regarded ; in the latter the people are looked upon
as a totality divided.

The attribute sometimes in Latin and Greek,
referring to the person addressed, appears in the
vocative : as, *Quibus Hector ab oris Expectate venis?*

(Vergil, Æn., ii. 282), 'From what shores, Hector, O long expected, dost come?' *Stemmate quod Tusco ramum millesime ducis* (Persius, iii. 28), 'Because thou, O thousandth, dost draw thy lineage from an Etruscan tree.' Thus, in Greek, Ὄλβιε, κῶρε, γένοιο (Theocr., Id., xvii. 66), 'Mayst thou be happy, O boy,' lit. 'O happy, O boy, mayst thou be!'

Such examples as these may aid us to understand the way in which concord has spread beyond the area to which it strictly belonged. And we may gather from these some idea of the way in which this process grew up in prehistorical times. We must remember, however, that concord was not felt so indispensable in the earliest stages of language, because absolute forms without inflectional suffixes were then the rule.

The question now comes, What were the rudiments from which concord proceeded? We must suppose that a period once existed in which substantives coalesced with the stem of the verb, and in which pronouns could precede the stem, just as our actual verbal inflections seem to owe their origin in many cases to the coalition of pronouns with the stem. We must therefore suppose that, just as it was possible to say Διδω-μι ('Give I'), so it was possible to say 'Go father,' 'Father go' (for 'Father goes') ; and 'I go,' just as it was possible to say 'Go I,' 'Go thou,' 'Go he' (instead of 'I go,' etc.). There are actually some non-Indo-European languages in which the third person singular differs from the other persons by dispensing with any suffix. Such is Hungarian,[1] in which the root 'fog,' 'seize,' is thus declined—*fog-ok, fogo-s, fog*. Here, then,

---

[1] Another instance is furnished by Hebrew, where the root *pakad* is conjugated 1st *pakadti*, 2nd masc. *pakadta*, 2nd fem. *pakadt*, 3rd masc. *pakad*, 3rd fem. *pakdah*, 1st plur. *pakadnu*, 2nd masc. *pekadtem*, 2nd fem. *pekadten*, 3rd *pakdu*. (Cf. any Hebrew grammar.)

the original plan maintains itself, of coalition according to the formula ' Go-father,' or ' Father-go.' In the next stage, the subject is repeated, as, when we say Ἔγω δίδω-μι, we are really saying '*I* give *I*.' This process is very common in some modern languages, especially in poetry, when emphasis is to be given to the subject : as, *The night it was still, and the moon it shone* (Kirke White, Gondoline) ;[1] *The skipper he stood beside the helm* (Longfellow) : *Je le sais, moi ; Il ne voulut pas, lui ; Toi, tu vivras vil et malheureux,*—' I know it, I ;' ' He would not, he ;' ' Thou, thou shalt live vile and wretched.' Similar is the anticipation of the subject by an indefinite *il ;* as, *Il suffisait un mot,* ' There sufficed a word.' The pronoun was originally doubled only where it was specially emphasised, just as in uneducated conversation at the present day we hear such forms as *I says, says I.* But such pronominal reduplication must have spread, and have affected the verbal forms when they were completely formed, just as it, at an earlier period, affected the tense-stems. It is, however, by this time so far forgotten that the termination of such a word as *legit* represents a personal pronoun, that its most common use is to indicate its relationship with the subject by mere concord ; as *Pater legit,* lit. ' Father read—he,' *i.e.* ' father reads.' In fact, the personal endings at the present day merely serve to mark the verb as such, and sometimes to express the difference between different moods.

In the case of nouns, the concord of gender and number, at any rate, is first formed in the pronoun to which reference is made, to which gender, too, owes its origin, as in such cases as *illæ mulieres,* ' those women (nom.) ;' *illas mulieres* (acc.).

Concord in case appears first in apposition ; as, *Im-*

---

[1] A fuller list is given in Mätzner, ii. p. 18.

peratoris Cæsaris exercitus, 'The army of Cæsar (gen.) the commander (gen.),' where it serves to show that both nouns have the same relation to *exercitus*. But here there is no more actual necessity for employing the case-ending twice, than there is for repeating the pronominal suffix in the case of the verb. This we may see in such cases as *King Arthur's seat; La gloire de la nation française*, 'The glory of the French nation.' A concord in gender and number occurs, even at the present day, only where it is demanded by the nature of the case; as, *La dame sur le visage de laquelle les grâces étaient peintes* (Fénelon), 'The lady on the face of whom the graces were painted.'

The concord of substantives in apposition having been the first to form itself—as in *Cæsaris imperatoris Romani*, 'Of Cæsar (gen.) the Roman-commander (gen.)'—we must suppose the concord of the attributival and predicatival adjective to have been modelled upon that use; as, *Cæsaris domini potentis*, 'Of Cæsar (gen.) the powerful master (gen.),' or *Cæsaris invicti*, 'Of Cæsar (gen.) unconquered (gen.).' In other words, their origin reaches back to a time when the adjective still occupied the same category as the substantive, and was not yet thought of as occupying a category of its own. The transition is marked by such substantives as are called, in Latin grammars, *Mobilia*, which in the forms of their genders resemble adjectives. Such as *coquus*, 'cook' (masc.); *coqua*, 'cook' (fem.): *dominus*, 'lord;' *domina*, 'lady:' *rex*, 'king;' *regina*, 'queen.' As these substantives passed into adjectives, they maintained the concord, and it then came to be regarded as of the essence of the adjective.

CHAPTER XVIII.

ECONOMY OF EXPRESSION.

LANGUAGE, as a rule, employs no more material than is necessary to make the hearer or reader understand the meaning intended to be conveyed by the speaker or writer. This statement must be taken merely generally, for it admits of many exceptions. But, as a rule, language, like a careful housewife, husbands its resources, and tends rather to economy than to lavishness in their employment. Everywhere in language we meet with forms of expression which contain just so much as is needed to make the employer of language understood, and no more. In fact, the supply offered by language depends on the demand, and on this alone. A gesticulation may supply the place of a sentence ; a nod, a frown, a smile may speak as plainly as any words. Much, too, must depend upon the situation : on the relations of the speakers to each other ; their knowledge of what is passing in each other's minds ; and their common sentiments with regard to the subject discussed. If we consider a form of expression which shall convey a thought under all possible conditions to any possible hearer as the only correct standard, and measure all other forms with that standard, then all these will appear imperfect, or, as grammarians would say, elliptical.

Practically, however, ellipse should be assumed in a minimum of cases, and each form of expression should be referred to its origin. Otherwise, we must be content to regard ellipse as an essential part of language; in fact, we shall have to regard language as habitually containing less than ought rightly to be expressed, and hence we should have to regard most expressions as elliptical.

We will consider first the cases in which a word or phrase is said to be *supplied* from what precedes or what follows. It hardly seems that we are justified in using the word *supplied*. Take such a sentence as *Is Bushy, Green, and the Earl of Wiltshire dead?* (Rich. II., III. ii. 14). We can hardly contend that in the perfectly expressed sentence we should have to supply *dead* after *Bushy, Green*, and *the Earl, etc.* Again, in such a sentence as *He saw me and grew pale*, it seems unnecessary to supply *he* with *grew pale;* nor in such a combination as *in fear and hope* need we supply *in* before *hope* merely because we can also say *in fear and in hope.* It seems more correct to drop the notion of *supplying*, and to think of single *positing* with plural reference—regarding what usually is called a sentence, not as an independent self-contained integer, but as a link in a continuous series.

It is common to assume an ellipse in such cases as 'the German and French languages,' and still more in the form 'the German language and the French.' But we have really here a pair of elements standing in the same relation to a third. That this is so, we see by the fact that there are other languages in which the two elements are really treated as a unity and attached as such to the third, which then becomes strictly speaking the second. This is shown by the use of the plural. We say, for instance, in Latin—*quarta et Martia*

legiones (Brut. apud Cicero, ad Fam., ii. 19), 'the fourth
(sing.) and the Martian (sing.) legions (plur.),' beside
legio Martia quartaque, 'the legion Martian and fourth'
(both in Cicero); *Falernum et Capuanum agros*, 'the
Falernian (sing.) and Capuan (sing.) fields (plur.)'
(Livy, xxii. 15): Italian—*le lingue Greca e Latina*, 'the
languages Greek (sing.) and Latin (sing.),' besides *la
lingua Greca e Latina*, 'the language Greek and Latin:
in French—*les langues Française et Allemande* :—so,
*the fourth and fifth regiments; the second and third
days.*

In the same way, in the case of such sentences as
John writes well, James badly, we are prone to assume
an ellipse. But that the current assumption of an
ellipse cannot be always right is proved by the fact
that even in English we sometimes meet with a plural
predicate: as, 'Your sister as well as myself, said Booby,
are greatly obliged' (Fielding, J. Andr., iv. 7); 'Old
Sir John with half a dozen more *are* at the door,'
(Shakespeare, 1 Henry IV. II. iv.): as against, 'Ely,
with Richmond *troubles* me" (Rich. III., IV. iii.);
'Until her back, as well as sides, was like to crack'
(But., Hud., II. i. 85).[1]

In Latin, we actually find this construction with
the ablative absolute: *ille Antiocho, hic Mithridate
pulsis*, 'the former when Antiochus, the latter when
Mithridates WERE defeated' (Tacitus); *quod tu aut illa
queri possitis*, 'what thou or she require could' (the
verb plural)' (Tullia, ap. Cicero, ad Fam., iv. 5): cf.—

> 'Not the King's crown nor the deputed sword,
> 'The marshal's truncheon nor the judge's robe,
> 'Become them.

(Shakespeare, Meas. for Meas., II. ii. 60); 'For there

---

[1] For other examples, see Mätzner, vol. ii., p. 151.

nor yew nor cypress *spread* their gloom' (Th. Campbell,
Theodoric). So in French—' Ni l'or ni la grandeur
ne nous rendent heureux' (La Fontaine), ' Neither
gold nor grandeur *make* us happy :' and in Latin—
' Erant quibus nec Senatus gloriari nec princeps
possent,' lit. ' There were (some) of whom neither
Senate boast nor the Emperor *could* (plur.)' (Plin., Pan.,
75).[1] This plural has originated from cases where the
copulative connection could be substituted without
essential alteration of meaning—as, ' Yew and cypress
spread not there their gloom,'—and has thence been
extended by analogy. In fact, for the instinct of
language, the predicate has been posited once and not
twice.

In sentences like ' I will come and do it,' ' Who
steals my purse steals trash' (Othello, III. iii. 157),
' Who was the thane lives yet' (Macbeth, I. iii. 109), we
have instances of an element common to the principal
and subordinate sentence, and also in such sentences
as ' It is thy sovereign speaks to thee,' a variety of
sentences constructed ἀπὸ κοινοῦ. Sometimes also, in
German, we find such sentences as *Was ich da
traümend jauchzt und litt, muss wachend nun erfahren*
(Goethe), lit. ' What I there dreaming cheered-at and
suffered must waking now experience ;' with which we
may compare sentences like Milton's ' Thou art my
son beloved : in him am pleased,' and ' Here's a young
maid with travel much oppressed, and *faints* for
succour'[2] (Shakespeare, As You Like It, II. iv. 75).
It occurs frequently in dialogue that words of one
speaker are not repeated by another, and they are
ordinarily described as being *supplied*. Really, however,
dialogue must be regarded as a continuous whole, so

---

[1] Dræger, vol. i., p. 178.
[2] See Abbott, p. 166.

x

that, *e.g.*, the words of one speaker (or their contents) form subject to predicate uttered by the other. Cf.—

> 'O Banquo, Banquo !
> Our royal master 's murdered——
> (*Lady Macb.*) Woe ! alas !
> What, in our house ? '

If we take a sentence like ' *my* relatives and friends,' the common element *my* stands at the outset of the whole sentence ; it is then nearer indeed to *relatives*, but is without difficulty referred to *friends*. But insertion in the second part of the sentence is also possible : cf. ' It (*i.e.* love) shall be (too) sparing and too severe' (Ven. and Adon., 1155), ' Beggars (sitting) in their stocks refuge their shame that (*i.e.* because) many have (sat) and many must sit there' (Rich. II., V. v. 27) ; ' of such dainty and such picking grievances' (2 Hen. IV., IV. i. 198).[1] In this case, the first portion of the sentence remains incomplete until the common element has been spoken or written ; and this serves to complete the first and the second part of the sentence simultaneously.

Sometimes the common element stands in different relations to the two others with which it is connected. Then concord must be violated : and different languages try to avoid this breach of concord in different ways.

We, in English, admit the want of concord in such cases as ' She LOVES him not less than I (LOVE him) ;' ' He thinks so : not I ;' ' They are going to-morrow : I too.' The case is similar in French : *Vous partez—moi aussi* (= ' You depart—me also ') ; and in German, *Du gehst—ich auch* (=' Thou goest—I too'). The sequence of tenses is not observed in ' Therefore they thought it good you hear a play ' (Tam. of Shrew, Introduc. ii.

---

[1] For other instances, see Abbott, p. 281.

136) ;[1] ''Twere good you do so much for charity'
(Merch. of Ven., IV. i. 261). The infinitive has
to be borrowed from the finite verb in cases like 'He
has done as he was bound ; ' ' He is gone where he was
told.'

It is, of course, harder to find cases of discord in
gender in English than in more highly inflected
languages. In French, however, we find *Paul et
Virginie étaient ignorants* (B. de S. Pierre), 'Paul
and Virginia were ignorant [masc. plur.]:' and
also *Le fer, le bandeau et la flamme est toute prête*
(Racine), 'The iron, the bandage and the flame is
quite ready;' *C'est un homme ou une femme noyée*
(Boniface), 'It is a man or a woman drowned (sing.
fem.):' cf. Lat. *Visæ nocturno tempore faces ardorque
cœli* (Cicero, Cat., iii. 8). The case is similar in
Italian and Spanish. In English, we find such
sentences as 'I am happy to hear it was his horse and
not himself *who* fell in the combat.'[2]

A single word may actually stand in relation to two
or more verbs, and represent two or more cases ; as,
which (accusative to *spit* and nominative to *is*), *however, they pretend to spit wholly out of themselves, is
improved by the same arts* (Swift, Battle of the Books,
p. 29, Cassell's Edit.) : so in Latin—*Quibus insputari
solitumst atque iis profuit* (Plaut., Captivi), 'On whom
it is customary that it should be spat, and (this) has
been good for them.'

In Latin, again, we find a nominative actually
representing an accusative ; as, *Qui fatetur . . . et . . .
non timeo* (Cicero) = 'Who confesses . . . and . . .
(whom) I do not fear :' and, again, a dative represents
an accusative in *Cui fidem habent et bene rebus suis*

---

[1] See other instances in Abbott, p. 269.
[2] Hodgson, p. 81.

consulere arbitrantur (Cicero), 'In whom they trust and whom they deem to manage their affairs well.'

There are, again, cases in which the two principal notions are connected by a *link* which serves to define more closely the nature of the connection. Such links are often dispensed with, as in *Hectoris Andromache, Cæcilia Metelli;* or, *The Duke of Westminster's Ormonde.* It is misleading, in such cases, to say that *uxor,* 'wife,' or *filia,* 'daughter,' or *colt* is to be *supplied;* indeed, no definite expression of the kind could be supplied unless the hearer or reader were conversant with the situation; and even then it does not follow that any one of the three words which we have mentioned would actually be supplied. The truth is that the genitive, in these cases, denotes a connection which may be rendered more definite as our knowledge of the *situation* becomes more intimate.

Indications of direction were no doubt originally associated with verbs of motion only; as, *I am going thither.* But they are now found attached to verbs of preparing, wishing and the like: as, *Wo wollen sie hin?* = 'Where will you to?' (= 'Whither will you?' = 'Whither are you going?'); *He purposeth to Athens* (Shakespeare, Ant. and Cleo., III. i. 35); *I must to Coventry* (Rich. II., I. ii. 56); *To Cabin! silence,* (Temp., I. i.); *To horse! to horse!* (Rich. II., II. i.); *Back to thy punishment, false fugitive; Forward, brave champions, to the fight* (Scott, Lay of Last Minstrel, v. 20); *And thou shalt back to France* (Marlowe, Edward II., I. i.); *Let us across the country to Terracina* (Bulwer, Rienzi, iii. 1).[1] Similarly, the common Scottish phrase *to want in,* for *to wish to enter.* In these cases, we must suppose that the notions of preparing, wishing, etc., and of the *terminus ad quem*

[1] Abbott, p. 293.

present themselves at once to our consciousness, and that they are directly connected as psychological subject and predicate. Then the ordinary construction in such cases, as, *They are going home*, or *to Rome*, occurred to the recollection, and the analogy of this form of expression co-operated to produce the form in question. The form has now become so usual that it cannot fairly be described as elliptical. Other similar phrases are *I never let him from home ; I will not let you out ; Let me in ;* and, again, such as *He is away*, or *He is off to Paris ;* in which case *away* and *off to Paris* are to be taken as predicates, and *is* as copula. With this construction may be classed the so-called *constructio prægnans*, like *conditus in nubem* (Vergil, Georgics, I. 442) = 'Hidden into a cloud,' *i.e.* 'Having passed into a cloud and hidden itself.'

In Latin, a nominative case standing as subject is sometimes followed by an accusative standing without a verb ; as, *Cicero Cassio salutem*, 'Cicero to Cassius greeting :' similarly, *Unde mihi tam fortem ?* (Horace, Sat., II. v. 102) ; *sus Minervam ; fortes fortuna ; dii meliora* (Cicero, Phil., viii. 3) ; *Di vostram fidem* (Plaut., Captivi, 591).

In these cases, two notions are combined in the form of nominative and accusative because they stand in the same relation to each other as, in a more complete sentence, obtains between subject and predicate.

Similarly, in French, we find expressions like *Vite un flambeau !* (Racine), 'Quick ! a torch ;' *Citoyens, trève à cette dispute !* (Ponsard), 'Citizens, enough of this dispute.'

Sometimes, again, a nominative standing as subject is connected with an adverb ; as, *hæc hactenus*, ' this so far ;' *an tu id melius ?* ' or (do you know) this better ? *ne quid temere,* 'nothing rash;' *ne quid nimis,* 'nothing

too-much ;' ταῦτα μὲν οὖν δὲ οὖτως (= 'that thou therefore thus') (Plato). Similarly, we find in English,
one step enough for me (Newman's hymn, 'Lead
Kindly Light'). Many instances of such constructions
may be found in Pepys' Diary ; as, *I to bed*, etc.

Sometimes we meet with sentences like *I will
give you an example how to do the thing.* In this case,
the subordinate sentence is combined with a principal
sentence without some element of the sentence like,
of how or *as how you should do it.* Thus we find sentences like the following :[1] *To talk to a man in a state
of moral corruption to elevate himself.* Then sentences
like *You look what is the matter ;* where the sentence,
if fully expressed, would be *Look to see what is the
matter.* Similarly, in Greek, Ὄρη δίφρον, Εὐνόα, αὐτᾷ
(Theoc., Idyll., xv. 2), 'Look (for) a chair for her.'
Similarly, we have such phrases as *As far as that goes ;
As far as I know ; To be plain :* and, again, such com-
pressed sentences as *in short ; quant à cela* ('as for
that'), etc.

In cases like *to the right, to the left*, the situation
again stands instead of a substantive. Just so, in
Latin, *calida frigida (aqua)*,[2] 'warm, cold (*i.e.* water) :'
Hot or cold? (with reference to refreshments); *Burgundy, Champagne ; agnina, caprina (caro)*, 'lamb, goat
(*i.e.* flesh);' *Appia (via),* 'Appian (road);' *Martia (aqua)*,
'Martian (water) ;' *une première représentation*, 'a first
performance;' *a tenth; the Russian, French (language)* ;
la Marseillaise. In these cases, if we speak of ellipse
at all, we must remember that we could not in
many cases supply the ellipse without the situation. If we were to say, *Bring the old instead of the
new*, this would be meaningless unless we had the

---

[1] Hodgson, p. 189.
[2] For a full list, see Roby, p. 26.

wine before us : unless, indeed, we had something else,
as *clothes*, for instance, in which case likewise the
situation would supply the sense required.   The more
' usual' such ways of speech become, the less do they
depend on the situation.   When we speak of *Champagne, Bordeaux, Gruyère*, etc., the word has passed
from the position of an epithet into that of a true
substantive.

In the case of genitive determinants, we meet with
a similar development.   An Oxford student would
have no difficulty in understanding what was meant
by *We were beaten by St. John's* (*College*), nor a
medical man by *I am house surgeon at St. George's.*
Similarly, we find in French *la Saint Pierre* (*fête*),
' S. Peter's (day) ;' and, in Latin, *ad Vestæ* (*templum*),
' to Vesta's (temple) ;' and in German, *Heut ist Simon
and Juda's*, 'To-day is Simon and Juda's (feast)' (Sch.).
In these cases, no ellipse can be assumed, for it is
evident that the words are already apprehended as
simple substantives.

In such forms as *No further !* the psychological
predicate alone is expressed, the unexpressed subject
being the person to whom the words are addressed.
We may gather that these words are apprehended as
in the accusative case from parallel instances in other
languages ; as *Cotta finem*, 'Cotta (made) an end ;'
Keinen schritt weiter, No step further !   It is the same
with sentences like *Good day, My best thanks, Bon
voyage* (' Pleasant trip !'), etc.   In sentences like
Christianos ad leones (' The Christians to the lions ') or
Manum de tabula (' Hand from table'), we might
certainly take *Christianos* and *manum* as the psychological subject, and *ad leones* or *de tabula* as the predicate ;
but the accusative in *Christianos* and *manum* shows
that a subject is really conceived of as taken from the

situation, and that *manum, Christianos*, are regarded as the object of such subject. It is the same with cases: as, *Ultro istum a me* (Plautus), 'Spontaneously him from me;' *Ex pede Herculem*, 'From foot Hercules;' *Ex ungue leonem*, 'From claw the lion;' *Malam illi pestem*, 'To him the plague' (Cicero); *Tiberium in Tiberim* (Suet., Tib., 75), 'Tiberius into the Tiber.' In German we have cases like *Den kopf in die höhe* = '(The) head into the height' = 'Heads up!' and, in English, probably such cases as *Heads up! Hands down!* are conceived of as in the accusative case. Other cases also, as well as adverbs, can be thus used: as, *Sed de hoc alio loco pluribus* = 'But more of this hereafter;' *Hæc nimis iracunde* = 'This too angrily.' Similarly, *So Gareth to him* (Tennyson, Gareth and Lynette, p. 47); *Whereat the maiden petulant* (ibid., p. 77).

Sometimes, as in the rhetorical figure which we call aposiopesis, the psychological predicate as well is taken from the situation; in this case gesticulation and the tone of the speaker may do much to promote the clearness of the situation. Thus we have suppressed threats, like the well-known Vergilian, *Quos ego* (Æn., i. 135), 'Whom I!'[1]

Again, we find such expressions as, *To be thus is nothing, but to be safely thus* (*is something*).[2] Again, take such expressions as *the wretch! A maid and be so martial!* (Shakespeare, 1 Hen. VI., I. iv.); and, again, exclamations such as *So young and so depraved! To sleep so long!* and, *To throw me plumply aside!* (Coleridge, Picc., i. 2). Under this head will come the so-called Infinitive of exclamation in Latin. *Huncc ine solem tam nigrum surrexe mihi* (Horace, Sat., I. ix. 72), 'Oh that this wretched day (black sun) has risen for me!' This use is also very common in

---

[1] Cf. Minto.   [2] Cf. Abbott, p. 262.

French ; as, *Enfoncer ce couteau moi-même, chose horrible* (Ponsard),[1] ' To plunge this knife (into him) myself, horrible notion !'

Similarly, dependent sentences may become by us independent ; as, ' O *that* this too too solid flesh would melt !' *If I only knew ! O had we some bright little isle of our own !* (T. Moore). This use is similar in Anglo-Saxon.[2]

It is similar when conditional sentences are used as threats ; as, *If you only dare ! Verbum si Addideris !* (Terence), ' If you say another word !'—or when such are set down and left uncompleted ; as, *But if he doesn't come after all !* French is full of parallels : cf. *Et quand je pense que j'ai été plusieurs fois demander des messes à ce magicien d'Urbain* (De Vigny), ' And if I consider that I have several times asked this con-jurer Urbain for masses !' *Puisque je suis là, si nous liquidions un peu ce vieux compte* (Daudet), ' As I am here (what) if we settled this old account ?' *C'est à peine si ma tête entre dans ce chapeau* (Acad.), ' It is (only) with difficulty if my head gets into this hat ; ' *Passez votre chemin, mon ami. Que je passe mon chemin ? Oui, qui, qui le pourrait* (Regnard) = ' Go on, my friend !—I, go on ?—Yes, yes, if it were possible.' These sentences with *that* are originally predicates ; or, speaking from a grammatical point of view, objects. *That I might be there to see !* if fully expressed, would be *I wish that I could be there to see.* Cf. *I am the best of them that speak this speech, Were I but where 'tis spoken* (Shakespeare, Tempest, I. ii.) ; *Those other two equalled with me in fate, so were I equalled with them in renown* (Milton, Par. Lost, iii. 33) ; *Would to God we had died by the hand of the Lord* (Exod. xvi. 3).

---

[1] See Mätzner, Fr. Gr., p. 446, for more examples.
[2] Cf. Mätzner, p. 92, vol. ii.

CHAPTER XIX.

WE have in former chapters dealt with, and frequently alluded to, the fact that much which is new in derivation and inflection is due to analogy. *Much* is due to this, but not all; and we must now ask whence originated these processes of derivation and flection, which cannot be explained as due to analogy, *i.e.* those which, instead of being moulded on a given pattern, have, on the contrary, served as the model for others. It is clear that as soon as language arose, even in its most primitive state, words must have been combined syntactically, in however simple a manner. Groups of etymologically connected words, words derived the one from the other by suffixes (as *long, length ; king, kingdom*) or by flection (as *book, books ; go, goes*),—such groups need not have existed at once, nay, must have arisen only gradually, and in course of time. How did they arise ? Theoretically, three ways only seem possible.

Words formed independently for cognate ideas, might accidentally resemble each other so closely as to group themselves also phonetically, *i.e.* to be sounded more or less alike ; or—what is essentially the same, though not quite so improbable—words originally different and expressing different ideas, might, in course of time, so develop in meaning and sound as to become members of a group. A case somewhat of this nature we studied in our word *bound* (cf. page 194), which, originally different in sound and form from the then existing past participle of *to bind*, has come to resemble it so much in form, and was used in such a sense as to cause all but students of language to group these forms together.

A second way is a differentiation in sound, *i.e.* two forms may arise, under the influence of accent or other causes, from the same word, which two forms then come to be differentiated in meaning. We have in this way, for instance, the two forms of the past tense of the verb *werden* (to become) in German, *ward* and *wurde*. These arose absolutely independently of any difference in meaning; once having arisen, a custom sprang up of using the one (*ward*) as aorist and the other (*wurde*) by preference as imperfect tense.

That in the above examples, the form which later on became *bound* is not itself an original creation, or that, in German, the two forms of the past tense were due largely to analogy, does not affect their value as illustrative of our point. We readily understand that both these ways were and are possible, but, at the same time, that in only very few cases they have been followed.

Only one way of explaining the origin of flection remains—'composition.'

In order to explain how derivation and flection can have been derived from composition, we will go somewhat deeply into the nature and application of the latter. We shall then see how impossible it is to draw a sharp line between syntactical co-ordination, composition, derivation, and flection anywhere, and then—and only then—we shall acquire an insight into the true nature of the subject of this chapter.

If we study the composition of words in the various Indo-European languages, we soon learn to distinguish two different kinds. In one we find the so-called crude forms (that is to say, those forms of the words which, WITH THE CASE-ENDINGS, make up what we now consider the complete word) combined with other crude forms, the last of which alone assumes these case-endings. To illustrate this we must of course go back to ancient languages, in which this crude form is clearly distinct from the nominative or any other case. We have plenty of such compounds even now in English and other modern languages; but, in consequence of the wearing off of terminations, the most undoubted examples would illustrate (*i.e.* throw light upon) nothing. In Sanscrit, for instance, there are three plants which in the nominative singular would be called *çaças* (or *çaçaḥ*), *kuças* (*ḥ*) or *kuçam* (masc. or neut.), and *palâçam*. It is the crude forms of these nouns (without their nominative—*s* and *m*) which are used in the compound *çaça-kuça-palâçam*, which indicates a collection of the three. Again *râjâ* (with long *â*) is the nominative form of a stem *râjan* ('king') or *râja* (with short *a*). In the compound *râja-purushas* (*ḥ*) we again find the crude form, this time the shorter form of the base: *purushas* means 'man' and the whole (= 'king-man') stands for *king's man*. We might illustrate this kind by such words as our *tragi-comic, melodramatic* (*melos* = 'song').

In the other kind of compounds we find two or more fully inflected forms combined in one group. This is the method of composition which survives in our present linguistic consciousness, which sees compounds of the second kind even in those which are historically connected with the Indo-European type, illustrated in the former paragraph by *râja-purushas*.

The wearing off of well-nigh all case-endings has in the present language almost completely obliterated the difference between crude forms and nominatives of nouns and adjectives or the infinitives of verbs. Hence, at present, the ordinary speaker realises no difference between, e.g., *noon* in *noon-tide* and the word *noon* in *It is noon.* Yet the compound *noon-tide* belongs historically to the former class, and *noon* is there a 'crude form,' if we may still so call it. In our following study of composition as at present employed in the English language, we neglect the scientific origin, but base our classification on appearance; in the present case, on present linguistic consciousness. One of the fullest and best-known lists of compounds in the English language is perhaps that given by Morris (Histor. Outlines, p. 222). We shall largely draw upon it in the following study, though we have, in our enumeration, rather considered the character of the component parts than, as Mr. Morris does, that of the function of the compound.

I. Nouns are compounded with Nouns—

1. Both in the same case; *i.e.* in apposition, the one explanatory of, or defining the other (in which case one of the nouns has a function almost, if not quite, identical with that of an adjective). Instances are *spear-plant, noon-tide, church-yard, headman, oak-tree, master-tailor, merchant-tailor, prince-regent, water-course, watershed, head-waiter, plough-boy, bishopdom* (found in Milton, *dom* = 'jurisdiction'), *bishopric* (*ric* = A.S. *ríce*, 'power,' 'domain'), *bandog* (= *band* + *dog*), *barn* (*bere*, i.e. *barley* + *ern*, i.e. 'storehouse'), *bridegroom* (*bride* + *groom* = *goom* = A.S. *guma*, 'man'[1]), *bridal* (*bride* + *ale* = 'bride-feast'), *cowslip* (*cow* = *slip*,

---

[1] On *groom*, see the excellent article in Skeat's Etymological Dictionary.

A.S. *cu-slyppe* = 'cow dung'), *hussy* (= '*house-wife*'—Skeat, Prin. Eng. Etymol., p. 422), *Lord-lieutenant*, *earlmarshal*, *wer-wolf* ('man-wolf,' A.S. *wer* = 'a man'), *world* (*weoruld*, *wer* = 'man' + *ældu* = 'age,' 'old age,' 'age of man'), *yeoman* (= 'village-man'—see Skeat), *orchard* (A.S. *orceard*, *ortgeard*, metathesis = *wort-yard* = 'vegetable-garden'), *Lammas* (= *hláf-maesse* = 'loaf-mass,' 'day of offering,' 'first-fruits'), *handi-work* (*hand* + *geweorc* = 'hand-work'), *mildew* (= 'honey dew,' *mil* = 'honey,' A.S. *mele*), *penny-worth*.

2. Genitive + Nominative. *Doomsday*, *Thursday*, *Tuesday* (day of *Tiw*, the godhead), *kinsman*, *trades-union*, *calf's-foot* (calf's-foot jelly), *lady day* (*lady* as a feminine had no *s* in the genitive), *daisy* ('day's eye,' A.S. *dæges éage*), *Wednesday* ('Wodan's day'), *shilling's-worth*.

3. Noun + Verbal Noun (the former having the function of object to the verb cognate with the latter). *Man-killer*, *blood-shedding*, *auger* (i.e. 'nauger,' *a nauger* having been divided as if = *an auger*; A.S. *nafu-gár*, 'nave (of a wheel)' '-borer,' '-piercer'), *groundsel* (A.S. *grunde* + *swelge* = 'ground-swallower' = 'abundant weed;' already in the Saxon corrupted from *gunde-swilge* = 'poison-swallower,' with reference to healing effects),[1] *lady* (*hláf-dige*, 'loaf-kneader'), *soothsayer* (= 'truth-speaker').

4. Two Nouns in other relations: *nightingale* (A.S. *nihte-gale* = 'night-singer'), *nightmare* (*mara*, 'an incubus,' by night).

II. Nouns are compounded with Adjectives.

1. Adjective and Substantive.

a. Nouns. *Nobleman*, *upperhand*, *good-day*, *some-time*, *meanwhile*, *freeman*, *blackbird*, *long-measure*,

---

[1] Cf. Skeat, Prin. Eng. Etymol., p. 395, from which and from his Dictionary most of these 'obscured' compounds are taken.

sweet-william, lucky-bag, midday, alderman (*ealdor-man* = 'elder-man'), *Gospel* (*god-spell* = 'good-spell' = 'good tiding'), *holiday* (= 'holy day'), *halibut* (= 'holy but' = 'holy plaice for eating on holy days'), *hoar-frost, hoar-hound* (the hoar or greyish *húna*, i.e. the plant now called horehound), *hind-leg, neighbour* (= 'near-dweller'), *midriff* (*mid* + *hrif* = belly), *tit-mouse* (small sparrow; *mouse* here = A.S. *máse*, small bird, not the A.S. *mús* from which the common word *mouse*).

b. Adjectives. *Barefoot.*

2. Substantive and Adjective.

a. Nouns. *Furlong* (= 'furrow long' = 'the length of a furrow').

b. Adjectives. In many of these the noun has very much the functions of an adverb. *Blood-red, snow-white, fire-proof, shameful, beautiful, manly* (i.e. 'man-like'), *scot-free* (free from paying *scot*, i.e. a contribution).

3. Substantive and Participle.

a. *Earth-shaking, heart-rending, life-giving, blood-curdling.*

b. *Airfed, earthborn, moth-eaten.*[1]

4. Numeral + Substantive.

Sennight (= 'seven night'), *fortnight* ('fourteen night'), *twi-light* (= 'double light' = 'doubtful light').

III. Pronoun and Substantive. *Self-will, self-esteem.*

IV. 1. Substantive and Verb (or Verbal Stem).

---

[1] Forms like *fur-booted, blackeyed*, etc., do not, of course, belong here. They are derived, with the suffix *ed*, from compounds or groups like *fur-boot, black eye, eagle eye, cone-shape*, etc., or formed by analogy to such derivatives. Some, indeed, are true compounds, but then the second element is an adjective and not a past participle. In that case they should be ranged under the compound formed from two adjectives.

Verbs. *Back-bite, blood-let, brow-beat, hoodwink, caterwaul* (= 'to wail like cats ').

2. Verb and Substantive.

Nouns. *Grindstone, bakehouse, wash-tub, pickpocket, brimstone* (i.e. *brenstone* = 'burning stone '), *rearmouse* (*hrére-mús, hreran,* 'to flutter '), *wormwood* (A.S. *wermód = weremód, werian,* 'to defend,' *mód* = 'mood' = 'mind;' 'that which preserves the mind '), *break-fast, spend-thrift* (cf. *wast-thrift*—Middleton, A Trick to Catche the Old One, II. i.).

V. Adjective + Adjective (or Adverb + Adjective; it is not always possible to decide which).

1. *Old-English, Low-German, deaf-mute, thrice-miserable.*

2. Adjective (or Adverb) + Participle.

a. Deep-musing, fresh-looking, ill-looking.

b. Dear-bought, full-fed, high-born, dead-beat.

(In *well-bred, well-disposed,* etc., there is, of course, no doubt that the first element is an adverb.)

VI. Adjective and Verb. *White-wash.*

VII. Adverb and Verb. *Cross-question, doff* (do-off), *don* (do-on).

Further compounds we meet are made up of—

VIII. Pronouns with Pronouns. *Somewhat.*

IX. Adverbs with Adverbs. *Each* (= *á* (aye) + *gelic* = like, A.S. *aelc*).

X. Adverbs with Pronouns. *None* (= *ne + one*), *naught* (= *ne + aught*).

XI. Adverbs with Prepositions. *Therefrom.*

XII. Adverbs with Adverbs. *Henceforth, forth-with.*

XIII. Prepositions with their Case. *Downstairs, uphill, instead.*

XIV. Adverbs with Verbs. *Foretell, gainsay, with-stand,* etc.

We also find more than two members formed into one; such as *man-o'-war*, *will-o'-the-wisp*, *brother-in-law*, *nevertheless*, *whatsoever*, etc. Sentences and phrases coalesce; as in *good-bye* (= 'God be with you'), the provincial *beleddy* (= 'By our lady,' *i.e.* the Virgin Mary), *may-be* (provincially in America written *mebbe*), and, aided by metaphorical usage, *forget-me-not*, *kiss-me-quick*, etc.

The student should carefully go over these examples, and, in each of them, attentively study the full force of the compound, and see what is really expressed by the component part, and what implied by the mere fact that they are thus joined.[1] If he is acquainted with any foreign languages, he should also study all the various habits of these languages as regards composition. He will then gain a clear insight into the nature of the process, and see how impossible it is to fix a line of demarcation between compounds and syntactical combinations. This is further illustrated by the fact that much, which in one language is looked upon as a compound, in another is kept asunder; nay, in the same language one calls a compound what the other would count as two distinct words. Thus a German writes *derselbe* (= 'the self,' *i.e.* 'the same') as one word, whereas an Englishman writes *the same ;* an Englishman writes *himself* where the German has, in two words, *sich selbst.* Cf. the Eng. *long-measure* with the Ger. *langenmass ;* the Fr. *malheureux* (from *malum augurium*, 'evil omen') with the Eng. *ill-starred*, etc. It is this uncertainty, this vacillation, to which we owe the compromise of writing such combinations with a hyphen; e.g., *a good-for-nothing*. Though even this usage is not fixed and invariable;

---

[1] The great importance of this distinction will be shown later on, see page 324.

for one author will write, e.g., *head-dress*, another *headdress*, etc.

If there is no line of logical demarcation between compound and syntactical groups, no more is there a phonetic one. Misled by the fact that the words of a syntactical group are written asunder, and a compound written as one word, we might think that the members of such a compound were pronounced as though more intimately connected than those of a syntactical group. But combinations like those of article and noun, preposition and noun, are really pronounced as one continuous whole as much as any compound. Nor is there an essential difference in the accent, either in place or in force. Compare, for instance, *with him* and *withstand* or *withdraw;* the degree of strength (or perhaps rather the absence) of emphasis on the first word in *Lord Randolph, Lord Salisbury*, with that on the last 'syllable' in *landlord;* or, again, the quantity of stress we give to the preposition in the expression *in my opinion* with that on the first syllable of *insertion*. If the example of *Lord Randolph* v. *landlord* seemed to show that the PLACE of the accent has some significance, we have but to read the sentences *Not Lord Randolph but Lady R. Churchill*, or *Not the landlord but the landlady spoke to the lodger*, to find the accents in exactly the opposite relations and places. No special place of accent, then, is characteristic of a compound. A very instructive example we have in the compound *Newfoundland*. This is actually pronounced by various speakers in three different ways: one says *Néwfoundland*, another *Newfóundland*, and, again, another *Newfoundlánd*. What, then, makes every one feel this word, in all three pronunciations, to be compound? Nothing physiological, but simply and solely the psychological fact that the meaning of the group *new-found-land* has become specialised, and no longer corresponds to what once would have been a perfectly equivalent group, *land-newly-discovered*. Semasiological development and isolation is the criterion of a compound. What degree of such isolation is required cannot be stated in any hard and fast rule.

Such isolation can be effected in four different ways. (1) In the first place, the whole group, as such, can develop its meaning in a manner, or to a degree, not shared by the compound members. An example of this we saw just now in *Newfoundland*. (2) Or, again, the component parts, as separate words, may develop and change their meaning, without being followed in that development by the same words as part of the group. Thus, e.g., *with* originally meant *against*. This meaning it still has in *withstand*, whilst as a separate word it is not now used in that meaning. (3) Thirdly, the compound parts may become obsolete as separate words; as, for instance, *ric* in 'bishopric' (cf. supra, p. 317). (4) And lastly, the peculiar construction according to which the parts are connected or combined may become obsolete, surviving only in the formula, which thus becomes isolated. Thus, *e.g.*, the genitive singular of feminine nouns can no longer be formed without *s ;* hence *Lady-day* is now felt as a compound word, whilst *ladies'-cloak* or *ladies'-house* would not be so felt.

Though such isolation is necessary and may suffice to stamp a group as compound, we must not conclude that every group, where such isolation in one way or another has commenced, is *ipso facto* looked upon as a compound. Many considerations are here of importance, some of which will be brought out in a further study of some examples in which we can observe the commencement of the fusion.

The first step which a syntactical group takes on

the road towards complete isolation and consequent fusion into a compound, is commonly the one we described under No. 1. in the former section. We must here distinguish two cases, which, though perhaps not easily distinguished *in words*, are yet clearly different.

An example will best serve to explain it. We have already more than once stated that in *Lady-day* the grammatical isolation of the genitive *lady*, as against the present genitive *lady's*, serves to emphasise the fusion of the two parts into one compound. But we must not forget that this form of the genitive in this combination would not have been preserved if, at the time when the word *lady* by itself began to assume the genitive *s*—or, rather, began to follow analogically other genitives in *s*,—if, we say, the compound had not then already been isolated to a sufficient degree to protect the first component part against the influence which affected it when standing in other combinations. The absence of the *s* is therefore NOT the CAUSE of the isolation of the group, or the fusion of its parts. We must seek for that cause most likely in the fact that the genitive was, in this combination, used in a sense which always was or had become unusual. *Lady-day*, even when the form *lady* was still felt as genitive, would but mean 'the day consecrated to the service of our Lady,' or 'the day sacred to our Lady.' Now this use of the genitive must always have been an exceptional one. Never, for instance, could *a man's book* or *a lady's cloak* have had a similar meaning. It was therefore at first not so much the meaning of the component parts, as the MEANING EXPRESSED BY THEIR SYNTACTICAL CO-ORDINATION, which stood apart and became isolated. We see something of the same influence if we compare *St. John's wood* and *St. John's Church*. In the second group, the latter of the component parts has a meaning which suggests and helps to keep alive the correct meaning of the genitive-relation expressed by the flection of the former part. In *St. John's wood* this is not so. This compound is therefore felt to be more intimately fused together than the other, and, while every one who uses the expression *St. John's Church* thinks of the Saint who bore the name of *John*, but few speakers will do so in speaking of *St. John's wood*. There is a very clear instance of this at hand in the German *Hungersnot*, lit. = *hungersneed*, i.e. '*famine*' (need, suffering *caused by* hunger). Here the genitive with the word *need* has a very special sense, which, *e.g.*, could not be expressed by the otherwise equivalent construction with *of*. 'The need of hunger,' if ever used in German, would be a very forced and uncommon way of expressing the idea 'famine,' a way which only a poet could adopt (*die Not des Hungers*). Here, then, again, it is not the sense of the words, but the sense of their syntactical relation which stands isolated.

On the other hand, if we consider forms like *upstairs, always, altogether*, we shall find that it is not this relation, but the whole meaning of the group as such, which has become isolated by development or specialisation of meaning. *Upstairs* has become equivalent to 'on a floor of the building ₍higher than we are now;' *always* has been extended so as to include the relation of time, etc. This development has then generally given rise to what grammarians term 'indeclinabilia,' which sometimes, by secondary development have become capable of flection. Thus the German preposition *zu* (to, at), and the dative case *frieden* (peace), in a sentence like *Ich bin zufrieden*, gave rise to the compound *zufrieden* (lit. = 'at peace'), 'contented.' When once the prepositional phrase *at peace* had developed into the adjective *content*, the compound was declined like other adjectives: *ein zufriedener mann* = 'a contented man;' etc.

Again, when the groups *round-about* and *go-between* had become nouns, they could be treated as such, and we find the plurals *round-abouts* and *go-betweens*.

The more highly a language is inflected, the less liable will the parts of a syntactical group be to fuse into one. It is much easier for a combination like *Greenland* or *Newfoundland* to pass into a real compound than for one like the German (*das*) *rote Meer,* '(the) Red Sea,' though the amount of isolation of meaning is the same in both. Whether the group *Green+land* is nominative or dative or genitive, no change in the form of *green* occurs; in German, *das rote Meer* is nominative, *des roten Meeres* is genitive, *dem roten Meer* is dative. Every time one of the two latter cases is used, the addition of the flection *n* reminds us of the independence of the two words *rot* and *Meer*.

Just as by means of suffixes, etc., we derive new words from others, whether the latter are simple or compound forms (*love, love-able; for-get, forget-able;* etc.), so we sometimes find whole syntactical groups, which are not yet considered as having been fused into one compound, used with similar suffixes. Instances are: *good-for-nothingness, a stand-off-ishness, a devil-may-carish face; That fellow is such a go-a-header; He is not get-at-able,* etc., which no doubt scarcely belong to the literary language, but which show that the linguistic feeling of the speaker must have already apprehended these groups as unities; in other words, that the first step on the road towards welding them into a compound has been taken. A well-established instance appears in our ordinal numerals, such as *one-and-twentieth, five-and-fortieth,* etc.

A similar commencement of fusion we can observe in copulative combinations like *wind and weather* or *town and country*, as soon as the whole may be conceived as a single conception. In *wind and weather* this is the case, the two terms being in this combination SYNONYMOUS, describing the same object from different points of view. Other instances of this we have in *bag and baggage, kith and kin, moil and toil, safe and sound, first and foremost, house and home, far and wide.*[1] In *town and country*, on the other hand, we have two elements which, whilst CONTRASTING, supplement one another. Such groups are *old and young, heaven and hell, gown and town, big and small, rich and poor, hither and thither, to and fro, up and down, in and out.* In a few, the same member is repeated; as, *out and out, through and through, again and again, little by little.* A careful consideration of the real meaning of such groups will show that, strictly speaking, these form a subdivision of our second class.

Inflected languages like German afford a criterion not applicable to English, as to the fusion of such combinations. We find there, for instance, a group —*Habe und Gut* (Etymol. = *have*, as a noun, for 'property,' *and good* = 'chattels'), for 'all a man's possessions.' The first of these nouns is feminine, and consequently 'with all (his) belongings' would be 'mit all*er* Habe;' *Gut*, on the other hand, is neuter, and requires the form (dative after *mit*) 'mit all*em* Gut.' Goethe has treated the group *Hab' und Gut* as a neuter noun, and written 'mit all*em* mobilen Hab' und Gut' ('with all movable possessions').

We have seen that groups like *one and twenty, five and forty*, etc., were really far advanced on the way of

---

[1] It will be noticed that most of these formulative groups are alliterative.

fusion, as was shown by the formation of the corresponding ordinals. In the case of those which begin with *one*, we have a further proof of this in the use of the plural noun, *e.g.* 'one and twenty *men*.'

It will be readily felt that in expressions like *a black and white dog*, the group *black and white* really is in a similar state of fusion. We have but to separate the parts into two really independent words by the insertion of a second indefinite article, to see at once that 'black and white' is the description of *one* quality of *one* object, a compound word to express one (though not psychologically simple) conception.

So, again, the group *one and all* is sufficiently welded into one to resist, *e.g.*, the insertion of the preposition *of* before its second part. Thus we should say *It was for the good of one and all* (i.e. for the entire community) and not *of one and of all*.

We may assume that complete fusion between the parts of such copulative groups would be more common if it were not checked by the connecting particle *and*. In some of the most common of these the accent of *and* has become so much depressed that the word becomes almost inaudible : cf. *hare and hounds, half and half*, etc. In combinations where the connecting particle has become unrecognisable in consequence of such phonetic sinking, it no longer resists the fusion. Thus, *Jackanapes* has become to all intents and purposes one word. It stands [1] with the common preposition *on*, instead of *of* (cf. the very frequent use of this 'on' in Shakespeare and contemporaries), for *Jack-of-apes*, i.e., originally, 'the man of the (*or* with the) [performing] apes,' just as *Jack-a-lantern* stands for ' Jack of the (*or* with the) lantern,' etc. Combinations without any such connecting link pass, of course,

---

[1] See Skeat, Etymol. Dict., s.v. *Jack*.

all the more easily into compounds: cf. *Alsace-Lorraine*, as against such combinations as *Naples* and *Sicily*.

In the period of the Indo-European languages before inflections had taken their rise, or when they were not yet indispensable, the fusion into a 'copulative compound' (dvand-va) must have been simple and easy.

When a substantive has been *specialised* in meaning by being combined with an attributive, as *blackbird*, the combination may pass through all the changes of signification described in Chapter IV. without the uncombined substantive as such being affected. The result is commonly to make the combination richer in contents than the simple combination of the parts. Thus, by 'a blackbird' we understand the familiar songster to which we give the name, and no longer understand such birds as rooks, crows, etc., which *might* have been classed under the name 'blackbird.'[1] Further modifications may set in, which may cause the epithet, strictly interpreted, to become wholly inapplicable. Thus, 'a butterfly'[2] is applied to a whole class of insects quite irrespective of their colours. When we talk of the Middle Ages, we mean a strictly defined period of time, though no such definition is involved in the word *middle*. *Privy Councillor* denotes a definite rank ; and the idea of privacy hardly enters into our heads as we pronounce the word : cf. also such expressions as *the Holy Scriptures ; the fine Arts ; cold blood ; Black Monday ; Passion Week ; the High School ; the wise men from the East.* It must be observed that the substantival determinants are only able to fuse with the word defined if they are employed in an abstract sense. This restriction does not, however, apply in the case of proper names.

[1] A blackbird may be an albino and we still call it a blackbird.
[2] For the disputed derivation, see Whitney and Skeat, s.v.

A subdivision of this great class of words, thus *specialised*, is formed by common place-names which have become proper nouns by the aid of some determinant, itself possibly also unspecific. Such are *the Red Sea, the Black Forest, Broadway, the Sublime Porte, the Watergate, the Blue Mountains, High Town, Beechwood, Broadmeadows, Coldstream, Troutbeck, Dog-island*. It is similar, too, when an epithet attached as a distinguishing mark to a proper name comes to be apprehended as an integral portion of the proper name—in fact, as attaching to the individual; as, *Richard the Humpback, Charles the Bald, William the Conqueror, Alexandra Land, the Mackenzie River, Weston-super-mare*.

Compare also such compounds as *Oldham, Littleton, Hightown, Lower-Austria, Great Britain*.

The metaphorical application of a word is generally rendered intelligible by the context; especially and chiefly by the addition of a determinant: cf. 'the *head* of the conspirators;' 'the *heart* of the enterprise;' 'the *life* of the undertaking;' 'the *sting* of death.' Similarly, a determinant forming an element in a compound helps to render the metaphorical application intelligible; indeed, we are able by the aid of such a determinant to give to compounds a metaphorical sense, which we could hardly venture upon for the undetermined word alone: so, for instance, we give the name of *German-silver* to a material which we should not call merely *silver;* the name of *sea-horse* to what we would not call *a horse:* cf. further, *sea-cow, elder-wine, ginger-beer*, etc.

There are some cases, again, in which the compound has a proper, as well as a metaphorical meaning, and only as a compound acquires its metaphorical use: such are *swallow-tail, negro-head, mothers' joy, cuckoo-spittle, woolly bear*, etc.

We have now to consider how syntactical and formal isolation contributes to further the fusion of the determinant with the determinate. If we compare two combinations such as *kinsman* with *man-of-war*, or *man of deeds*, we shall find that whilst the one has become an undoubted composition, the others are still groups of more or less independent parts. This is of course due to the fact that even now the word *man* is inflected, and that consequently the plurals, *men of war* and *men of deeds*, remind us of the fact that the first member of the group is an independent word. Formerly, when the flection was far more elaborate, this was, naturally, much more the case, and this alone would have sufficed to establish the feeling that, in compounds, the genitive which remained the same in all 'cases' of the compound had to precede. Of course, as long as flection sufficiently indicated the cases, both orders *could* be used in any group, but as then only such groups in which the genitive *did* precede became 'compounds,' those compounds became models, and the practice arose gradually and gradually became a *rule*. Another force then came to exert its influence in the same direction. In such genitival combinations it is, as a rule, the genitive which has the accent. When, then, this genitive was placed first, the whole group thereby resembled in accent the existing composites of the oldest formation, and so was more easily considered in the same light as these. The main cause must, however, be sought in a syntactical isolation, *i.e.*, in our examples, an isolation in the construction of the article. As long as flectional terminations existed in their entirety, the Teutonic languages could dispense with the article before declined cases of nouns; in fact we may say the article did not exist, the demonstrative pronoun not yet

having been degraded into what it became later on—
a mere sign of case. Hence it was in old Teutonic
languages quite possible, and a frequent practice, to
use the genitive case of a noun alone without an
article at all. We may be sure that this has also
been true for the other cases. Phonetic decay, however, levelled the terminations of the other cases of a
noun long before the genitive; and accusative and dative
had long been alike (or very nearly so) at a time when
in the masculine and neuter singular the genitive *s* was
still preserved : in fact, as we know, in English it is all
that has remained to us of the old flectional endings,
with the exception of those *s*'s, in the plural which are
original and not due to analogy. In that older stage of
the language it was common to express an idea like *the
son of man* by constructions just as in Ancient Greek,
where the genitive stood between the article and the
noun, which were both, of course, in the same case.
Thus we find in Old High German, *ther* (NOM. SING.
masc.) *mannes sun* (= 'the man's son'[1]). In Anglo-
Saxon, *Heofona rice ys gelíc ðám hiredes ealdre* ('of
heaven's (the) Kingdom is like the (DAT. sing.) house-
hold's prince'). Gradually, however, the use of a
noun without the article, largely, no doubt, owing to
the levelling of all other cases, became more and
more rare even in the genitive. Such rare standing
expressions as remained without article, naturally assumed the appearance of compounds, and, especially in
the case where the article belonging to the second
noun preceded the genitive, the fusion was complete :
the + kin's + man became *the + kinsman.*[2]

[1] The student should note the difference : in the Old High
German the article is *nominative ;* in our English translation it is
genitive : 'the man's son' = '*a* son of *the* man.'

[2] It is, of course, not intended to say that this very combination was
thus formed. It is an example to illustrate the process, and no more.

We have already pointed out how the adjective and the noun entered into composition, and seen how, even in many combinations which we are not yet accustomed to look upon as fused into one, derivatives show that this fusion has at least partly been accomplished. Such are the many forms in *ed*, like *black-eyed*, etc., which are derived from the groups *black eye*, etc., and cannot be looked upon as compounds of *black + eyed*. We do not speak of an *eyed* person, for one who has eyes: cf. *left-handed*, *self-willed*, *one-handed*, etc.

In English, especially in Scottish dialects, many adverbs which commonly follow the verb, are occasionally made to precede it; as, *to uplift*, *to backslide*, etc. We may gather that in such forms no composition strictly so called has as yet set in, from the fact that the order is frequently transposed, as in *sliding back*, *to lift up*, etc. On the other hand, the fact that the words are joined in writing shows that the whole has begun to be apprehended as a unity.

In the case of most of these combinations we can trace the commencement of an isolation, which proves that the linguistic sense is ceasing to apprehend the elements as distinct. For instance, in English the old prepositional adverbs cannot be used independently and freely to form new combinations at will, but are confined to a definite group of combinations. Thus we can say, *enfold* and *entwine:* but not *enthrow*, for *throw in*. We can talk of *onset*, and *onslaught*, but not of *on-run :* of *overflow*, but not of *over-pour*. In many cases this isolation has led to a special development of meaning, and the word becomes still more definitely a compound ; cf. such words as *inroad*, *after-birth*, *offset*, *over-coat*. From the union of the verb with the adverb, there arise nominal derivatives in which the sense is yet more specialised, such as *offset, output, offal, under-writer*.

An adverb derived from an adjective sometimes fuses with the nominal forms of the verb. The first impulse to this fusion is often given by the metaphorical application of one part of the compound : cf. *deep-feeling, far-reaching, high-flying*. The combination becomes even closer when the first part retains a meaning which has become unusual to it in general. For instance, in such a combination as *ill-favoured, ill* retains a trace of the time when it could be used as synonymous with *bad*.

In German, the comparative and superlative forms are actually used, showing the completeness of the fusion ; as, *der tieffühlendste Geist* (Goethe), (lit.= 'deep-feelingest ghost,' *i.e.* 'spirit').

There are a few combinations of verbal-forms with an object accusative, which similarly occupy an intermediate position between the compound and the syntactic group; such as *laughter-provoking, wrath-stirring, fire-spitting*. No sharp line can be drawn between these instances of spontaneous and natural fusion, and the analogical formations coined by the poets ; as *sea-encompassed, storm-tossed*, etc.

Again, and even in English, where the application of the inflected comparative and superlative is of so very limited application, it is the use of the comparative or superlative which affords a test as to the degree of fusion. It is, of course, possible to analyse *most laughter-provoking*, as *provoking much laughter*. But few would adopt such an explanation in a sentence like *This is the most fire-spitting speech I ever heard*.

Besides this, there are many verbal combinations which must be apprehended as compounds, from the fact that they represent a single notion only ; such as

*with regard to, as soon as possible, forasmuch as,
seeing that, none the less,*—which must be considered to
stand on the same footing as *notwithstanding, nevertheless.* This fusion is sometimes accompanied by a
displacement of the psychological conception as to the
parts of the sentence, whereby the natural mode of
construction is altered, and the combination performs
a new function, and becomes practically a different
part of speech. For instance, we commonly hear *I as
good as promised it to them,* where 'as good as' is
nearly equivalent to 'almost,' and is construed like that
adverb. We even meet with sentences like *unclassified
and prize-cattle,* where a member of a compound is
placed on the same footing as an independent word.
Moreover, the first, or determinant member of the
compound may be followed by determinants, as if it
were itself independent; thus Milton can write *hopeless
to circumvent us ; fearless to be overmatched :* as if it had
been 'without hope to circumvent us ;' 'having no
fear to be overmatched.' All this shows over and
over again how completely impossible it is to draw the
line between syntactical groups and compounds.

In this manner, then, syntactical isolation favours
the fusion of a group into a compound. In our
discussion of the form *Jackanapes,* we had already
an instance how phonetic changes may have the same
effect. This we shall now investigate and illustrate
rather more in detail.

Though it would be impossible to prove the fact
historically, it seems involved in the nature of the case
that, for the most part, such phonetic changes at first
arose in EVERY case of such closer and more intimate
syntactical union ; that they were re-adjusted and
re-equalised later on, and were only preserved in
groupings which, as a consequence of development of

meaning, had become so far fused into one whole as to be capable of resisting the re-adjusting tendencies.

The simplest of such general effects of syntactical grouping is that the final consonant of a syllable is transferred in pronunciation to the next syllable. Thus, for instance, *an apple* is pronounced *a-napple*, without any pause ; *here + on* is pronounced *he + ron*, etc. If, then, as in French, this final consonant disappears from pronunciation, save when thus made an initial, *i.e.* save before a word beginning with a vowel, we may expect its presence to have an isolating effect, and consequently to be sufficient to stamp the group as a compound. This, however, is only the case if such a preservation is not sufficiently frequent to be realised as a rule of pronunciation for all similar cases. In French, *il peut* = 'he can,' is pronounced without the *t ;* in *peut-être* = 'may be,' 'perhaps,' the *t* is heard. Yet this has not isolated the form *peut* with *t* from the usual third person singular present indicative without *t*, because this *t* is preserved not in *peut-être* alone, or in a few such groups, but in *all* cases where the following word begins with a vowel ; e.g., *il peut avoir* = 'he can (may) have,' pronounced with the *t* likewise. If we suppose the French language to discard at some time this *liaison*, as it is called, and always to pronounce *peut* without *t* even before vowels, then, and not till then, would the pronunciation *peut-être* with *t* stamp the combination as a compound.

So, again, the well-known process of avoiding *hiatus* by contraction or elision, in the case of a word ending in a vowel preceding one that begins with a vowel, has been sufficient to fuse two elements into one compound in many cases (e.g., *about* = a + be + ut (an) : Lat. *magnopere* = *magno + opere ;* Gothic *sah*, 'this' = *sa + uh*), but has no such effect in the case of the French article, or of the French preposition *de*, because the elision of the unaccented *e* and *a* is there an almost invariable and still 'living' rule.

A third general effect of close syntactical combination is the assimilation of a final and initial consonant. This, in present European languages, is scarcely, if at all, noticed or expressed *in writing*. It is, however, an exceedingly common occurrence in the *spoken* language, a fact of which every one can and ought to convince himself by a little attention to his own and other's NATURAL pronunciation. It is only in cases where further reasons, in addition to this assimilation, such as, *e.g.*, isolation by development of meaning or other phonetic development, have welded the group into a compound, or at least have advanced it a considerable distance on the road towards complete fusion, that the written language sometimes takes cognisance of the change, and, by the very spelling, indicates the compound nature of the group. We say 'sometimes' takes cognisance; for while spelling in no living language follows all the variations in pronunciation, no European tongue is further from accurately representing the spoken—that is, the real—language in its writing than English. Hence the instances even of acknowledged compounds, in which the assimilation in sound is indicated by the spelling, are comparatively rare. Such are *gossib*, for *god + sib* = 'sib, or related, in God;' *leoman*, for *leof + man* = 'dear man;' *quagmire = quake-mire*, i.e. 'quaking mire.' Instances where the assimilation exists in pronunciation, but is *not* represented in writing, are plentiful : *cupboard*, pronounced *cub-board* (or *cubberd*); *blackguard*, pronounced *blagguard*, etc. In all these we must, on the one hand, admit with respect to the recognition of the group as compound, that, even if it has not promoted assimilation, it has at

z

least checked the tendency to restore the theoretically correct pronunciation of the final consonant of the former member in each group. On the other hand, however, it is as certain that the very facility thus afforded to the working of the assimilating tendency has aided the phonetic isolation of the group and promoted the fusion.

The most effective cause of phonetic isolation, however, lies of course in the influence of accent. This has been sufficiently illustrated in the course of the foregoing discussions.

In all these discussions we have mainly regarded the transition of a syntactical group into a compound. Several of our examples, however, well illustrate the fact that, just as the fusion between the two members of some group may be insufficient to stamp the combination as a compound, so, also, such a compound loses its character as such for the consciousness of all but the student of language, when the fusion proceeds too far. The compound then becomes, to all intents and purposes, a simple word ; it serves no more as model for analogical compounds with the same members, and at the very most gives the impression of having been 'derived' from its first member by a suffix. To instance this, we need only recall a few of our examples to the reader's mind—*bandog, auger, furlong,* etc., or (with the suffixes) *bishopric, kingdom,* etc.

A careful study of these and similar examples will show that in the first-class of compounds, no longer recognised as such, sometimes both members have become obsolete, and in both classes almost always one.

We have now reached a point whence we can observe the conditions necessary to give birth to a suffix, or, if the phrase be preferred, necessary to degrade an independent word into a suffix.

We have seen a suffix originate in a noun which either (as in a case of '-*ric*') became obsolete as an independent word, or whose connection with the etymologically identical independent form ceased to be felt in the linguistic consciousness of the community.

But such a fate may and does often befall a word without converting it into an acknowledged suffix. It has befallen the noun *ðyrl* ('a hole'), in *nostril* (= *nose-thirl*), or the word *búr* ('a dweller') in *neighbour* ('a near-dweller'), and yet neither -*tril* nor -*bour* have become recognised as suffixes in the English language.

What more, then, is required?

First of all, the first element must be etymologically perfectly clear; cf. *kingdom, bishopric* as against *nos-tril, gos-sip*.

Secondly, the second element must not occur in one or two combinations only, but in a sufficiently large group of words, in all of which it modifies the meaning of the first member in the same way; cf. *nos-tril, gos-sip*, as against 'king*dom*,' 'widow*hood*.'

This second condition can scarcely be fulfilled except in cases where—

Thirdly, the second element has originally, or in its combination with the others, some such abstract and general meaning as *state, condition, quality, action*, etc.

A few words on one of the best-known suffixes in English will make this clear. Though the phrase would hardly stand in written or literary language, we *might* indicate a dealer in pianos as the *piano-man*, i.e. 'the man who has pianos.' In the oldest stages of language, not only could a single noun be thus used with an almost adjectival force, but even a compound (or what was then still a syntactical co-ordination) of two or more nouns, or of adjective and noun, could be thus employed. Thus, *e.g.*, in Sanscrit, a *much-rice-*

king, would mean 'a king who possesses much rice,' *i.e.* 'is rich;' and the group *man-shape* (or its equivalent) might have been used for *man-shape-having*. Such compounds abound in Sanscrit, and could be formed at will. They were called *Bahuvrîhi* compounds. Now, without of course wishing to assert that the very combination *man-ly* is an original one, it is to such a combination of a noun with the *noun* which afterwards became *lic* in Anglo-Saxon that we owe the suffix *ly*. The phonetic differentiation and the development of meaning from *shape-having* to *appearance* or *quality-having*, isolated the member from its corresponding independent form (which in German and Dutch still exists as *Leiche* and *Lyk* = *body* or *corpse*), and gave us *lic* (later *ly*) as a suffix.

From all that we have said it must be clear that this process has gone on neither in prehistoric nor in historic times only, but is one which is repeated again and again, and consequently—seeing that prehistoric times are of unknown, but certainly enormous length—we must be on our guard against assuming that all these prototypes of Indo-Germanic suffixes must necessarily have existed at one time as independent words in the language, before the process which transformed them into suffixes began to operate. We may, nay, we are almost compelled to assume that there, too, they arose in succession, and that then as now, whenever phonetic decay or other causes had affected a suffix to such an extent as to take away the appearance of a derivative from what was once a compound, the suffix was no longer felt as such; it ceased to serve for new combinations, and another more weighty suffix took its function and supplanted it in all but a few remaining cases.

The most superficial knowledge of any modern

language, or of Latin etymology, is sufficient to show that it is as impossible to draw a line between suffix and flectional termination, as between syntactical group and compound. Even a Frenchman, unless he has had the true historical explanation pointed out to him, feels in a future tense like *j'aimerai*, a verb-stem *aim*, and a termination *-erai* indicative of futurity, though, nowadays, there are but few students of French grammar who ignore the fact that *aimerai* is a compound of the infinitive *aimer* and the first person singular, present, indicative, *ai* = (I) *have*. Similarly, we may safely assume that few Romans felt in a pluperfect *amaveram* a perfect stem *amav* and *eram* the imperfect of *sum*, much less in *amabo* a present stem *ama* and a suffix derived from the same root as their perfect *fu-i*. It is certainly useless to illustrate this further.

We may now conclude with three observations, the truth of which will be apparent from what has gone before.

First. Even when an inflected form, by means of comparative study of all its oldest forms and equivalents in cognate languages, has been brought back to its prototype, and analysed into what are commonly considered to be its component parts, we must remember that these parts cannot have been fused into the integer which we now find made up of them, and yet have retained their original form and original meaning. Just as *kingdoms* has certainly not arisen from *king + dom + s*, a Greek optative *pherois* is not a compound of *pher + o + i + s*, though, undoubtedly, each of these elements have their regular representatives in other words of the same function, and most probably had their prototypes in fuller forms, in a more independent state. We have no means of knowing what these forms were, or what their original function was when still independent.

Second. Many words which we now consider as " simple " may have been compound or derivative. Our inability to further analyse does not prove primitive unity.

Third. In the history of Indo-European flection we do wrong if we assume the separate existence of a period of construction and one of decay.

CHAPTER XX.

THE division commonly adopted of the parts of speech in the Indo-European language is convenient as a classification; but it must be borne in mind that it is not logically accurate, nor is it exhaustive. It is indeed impossible to divide words into sharply defined categories, seeing that, however we may divide them, we shall find it difficult to exclude some from each category which may fairly claim to be registered under some other category or categories, basing their claim upon at least certain uses.

The accepted grammatical categories have had their form determined mainly by the consideration of three points: (1) by the meaning of each word taken by itself; (2) by its function in the sentence; (3) by its capacity for inflection, and the part it plays in word-formation.

As regards the meaning of the word, we may notice that the grammatical categories of substantive, adjective, and verb correspond to the logical categories of *substance*, *quality*, and *activity*, or, more properly, *occurrence*. But here, at the outset, we find that the substantive is not confined to the denotation of substance, as there are also substantives denoting quality and occurrence as, 'brightness,' a 'rise.' There are also verbs which denote continuous states and qualities; as, 'to remain,' or the Latin '*cande*'='to be white.' Pronouns and numerals again have a right on the score of meaning to be separated as classes from substantives and adjectives : but these, again, must be separated from each other in their substantival as against adjectival use (e.g. *each* as against *each man ; Six went and six stayed* as against *Six men, etc. ; this and that* as against *this book and that one*), which forbids us to simply co-ordinate the classes : substantive, adjective, pronoun, numerals. And, on the other hand, it must follow that, if pronouns and numerals are to be regarded as distinct species of the noun class, the same separation must be extended to the adverb class : since *badly, there, twice*, are related to each other just as *bad, this, two*.

To come to the connecting words. The lines that define the class of the conjunctions are quite arbitrary ; *where*, for instance, is called an adverb even in passages like this : [1] " *Where*, in former times, the only remedy for misgovernment real or supposed was a change of dynasty, the evil is now corrected at no greater cost than a ministerial crisis." *As* and *while*, again, are called conjunctions. In the simple sentence, the test usually applied to distinguish prepositions from conjunctions is case-government. But it certainly is entirely illogical to call words like *before, since, after* prepositions when they occur in simple sentences, and to call them conjunctions when they connect sentences ;— for this function is in both cases exactly the same ; cf. *before my interview with you*, and *before I saw you*.

If we wished to classify words according to their function in the sentence, it might seem obvious to divide words (1) into those which can *of themselves*

[1] Quoted by Earle, p. 493.

form a sentence, (2) into those which can serve *as members* of a sentence, and (3) those which can only *serve to connect* such members.

In the first division we might, then, place the interjections, which, when isolated, are really imperfect sentences. But these also occur as members of a sentence, sometimes with and sometimes without a preposition ; as, *Woe to the land ! Out on thee ! Oh my !*

The finite verb in its original use better fulfils the idea of a perfect sentence. But in its present use it appears—if we except the imperative—as a mere predicate attached to a subject separately denoted. And the so-called auxiliaries are mainly used as mere connecting words.

Connecting words, again, such as conjunctions and prepositions, are, as we have seen, derived from independent words by a displacement as to the appreciation of the part which a word plays in a sentence (cf. Chap. XVI., pp. 282 and 284.). Such words are *during, in regard to, notwithstanding.* And there is this further reason why they cannot be sharply distinguished from other kinds of words—that a word may be an independent member of the particular sentence to which it belongs, and yet at the same time serve to connect this with another sentence. If I say, for instance, *The man who believes this is a fool*, the *who* is at once an independent member of the relative sentence and a connecting word between the principal and subordinate sentence. This is universally the case as regards the relative pronoun and relative adverb. It is true also of the demonstrative when this refers to the preceding or following sentence ; as, *I saw a man, he told me*, etc. But even if this first classification as to function could be consistently carried out, any further attempt at subdivision leads us into fresh difficulties, considering that the substantive, as opposed to the adjective and verb, is the part of speech which serves as subject and object. We might, indeed, be tempted to utilize this fact as the principle of our subclassification.   But we find in the first place that a substantive can also be used attributively and predicatively, like an adjective (cf. *We are men, We are manly*), and, on the other hand, other words may serve as the subject in such sentences as *Well begun is half ended ; Slow and steady wins the race ; Finished is finished.*   An adjective, too, may serve as object; as, *He takes good for bad ; Write it down, black on white ; to make bad worse.*

We have indeed seen that the use of prepositions to introduce subordinate sentences is very common in English ; as, *After he had begotten Seth*, etc.

The division which can be most systematically carried out is that which divides words according as they are inflected or not, and according to their mode of flection.   In this way three convenient divisions may be made of nouns, verbs, and uninflected words. But even here the nominal forms of the verb, such as the infinitive, *to love* (*amare, lieben*) and indeclinable substantives such as the Latin *cornu* and the English adjectives, resist the carrying out of the division. Pronouns, again, are differently inflected from nouns, and they differ among themselves.   In other languages, the system of inflection of the substantive is sometimes identical and sometimes not.   It might be alleged that the formation of degrees of comparison was a decisive mark of the adjective : but even here we are met by the fact that some languages, like Sanscrit, can compare nouns and even persons of the verb ; [1] and

---

[1] Cf. M. Müller, Sanscr. Gram,, § 249, which we here transcribe : The comparative is formed by *tara* or *iyas ;* the superlative by *tama* or *ishtha.*   These terminations, *tara* and *tama*, are not restricted

others, like Latin, can compare the substantive (cf. Plautus' use of *oculissimus*—Curc. I. ii. 28, etc.) *amicissimus* = '(my) best friend,' etc. This usage is seen in the English word 'top-*most*,' which is the substantive *top* with a double superlative ending (see Mätzner, vol. i., p. 270); the termination *most* superseded the O.E. *m- est*, which answered to the A.S. (*e*) *mest*, derived from a positive (*e*) *ma*, which itself had a superlative signification (cf. *optumus*). Again, the very meaning of some adjectives renders them incapable of comparison; as, *wooden, golden*, etc.

It is, then, clear that the current division of the parts of speech, in which all these three principles of classification are more or less embodied, leads to so many cross divisions that it cannot be consistently carried out. The parts of speech cannot be sharply and neatly partitioned off into eight or nine categories. There are many necessary transitions from one class into another; these result from the general laws of change of meaning, and from analogical formations which are characteristic of language in general. If we follow out these transitions, we at the same time detect the reasons which originally suggested the division of the parts of speech.

To consider, first, the division between substantive and adjective. The formal division is based in the Indo-European languages on the capacity of the adjective of inflections of gender and comparison. In individual languages still further distinctions have arisen. Thus, for instance, the adjective in the

in Sanscrit to adjectives. Substantives such as *nri*, 'man,' form *nritamah*, 'a thorough man;' *strî*, 'woman,' *strîtarâ*, 'more of a woman.' Even after case-terminations and personal terminations, *tara and tama* may be used. Thus, from *pûrvâhne*, 'in the forenoon,' *pûrvâhnetare*, 'earlier in the forenoon.' From *pachati* 'he cooks,' *pachatitarâm*, 'he cooks better,' *pachatitamâm*, 'he cooks best.'

Teutonic and Sclavonic languages admits of a double, nay we may even say a triple, mode of inflection: cf. *gut, guter, der gute;* in which declensions forms occur absolutely without analogy in the substantives. In Modern High German, we have to note the existence of the two declensions (the weak and the strong). On their uses and that of the third or undeclined form of the adjective in the predicate, the most elementary German grammar will give the student all information. As for the forms of adjectival (and pronominal) declension which are distinct from the noun declension, it is necessary to go back to Anglo-Saxon, or, better still, to Gothic. It is, of course, not necessary to master these languages thoroughly in order to simply compare their systems of inflection. Seeing that in English the adjectives have no flection, the test is no longer applicable to the language in its present form; though the test of capacity for comparison applies here still. But in spite of all differentiations of form, the adjective may receive, at first 'occasionally' then 'usually,' the function of a substantive: cf. *The rich and the poor, old and young, my gallants.*[1] From this substantival adjective a pure substantive may be derived by traditional use, especially if its form becomes in any way isolated as against other forms of the adjective; as, *sir* = Fr. *sieur,* from *seniorem* as against *senior.* The instinct of language shows that it apprehends the adjective definitely as a substantive when it connects it with an attributive adjective; as, *the powdered pert* (Cowper, Task); *a respected noble,* etc.: or with a genitive; as, *the blue of the sky.* In English the possessive pronoun is connected with

---

[1] Cf. also the (unusual) construction: 'Geoffrey was not a religious when he wrote this play' (Ward, Hist. Drama, p. 5, note), and 'one more unfortunate' (Hood).

many words, such as *like*, *better*, etc.,[1] which, if felt as
adjectives, would demand other constructions. Cf. *He
was your better, sir* (Sheridan Knowles, Hunchback,
III. ii.) ; *To consult his superiors* (Cooper, Spy, ch. i.) :
He is my senior.

There are many adjectives in all languages which
are completely transformed, such as *sir* (cf. supra) ;
priest (a shortened form of what in French appears
as *prêtre*, older form *prestre* (cf. Dutch *priester*), all
from Greek *presbuteros*, 'older,' the comparative of
presbus, 'old') ; *fiend*, M.E. *fend*, A.S. *féond*, 'an
enemy,' originally the present participle of the verb
féon, 'to hate ;' *friend*, M.E. *frend*, A.S. *freónd*,
originally present participle of *fréon*, ' to love ;' etc.

The transformation of a substantive into an adjective is less familiar, and perhaps more interesting. In
the process, we disregard some parts of the meaning
of the substantive, excluding from that meaning first
and foremost the meaning of substance, so that only
the qualities attaching to the substance remain in
view. This transformation virtually occurs as an
occasional use whenever a substantive is employed as
predicate or attribute : *a king's cloak* (for *a royal cloak*);
He is an ass, etc. A substantive in apposition approaches the nature of an adjective, especially when it
is used to denote a class ; and, again, more especially
when the combination is abnormal and metaphorical :
cf. *a virgin fortress ; a maiden over ; boy-competitors ;
turkey-cock, hen-sparrow ; a house-maid ;*[2] *music-vows*
(Hamlet, III. i.) Sometimes an adverb which can

---

[1] Mätzner, iii. p. 222.

[2] It will be noted that in these examples, the more they are usual
the more they appear as compounds, and the less clearly and definitely
we feel the force of the first noun as adjectival ; cf. a *maiden over* with
a *maiden speech*.

strictly speaking be connected with an adjective only,
is joined to the substantive, and serves to mark its
adjectival nature. Thus we often hear such expressions as *He is ass enough, idiot enough* ; *More fool
you*, etc.

In other cases, again, such as *twenty thousand
troups were taken prisoner*, the word *prisoner* shows
by its absence of inflection that it is apprehended as an
adjective.

It might be thought practicable to draw another
distinction that would hold good as between substantive and adjective. The adjective, it might be alleged,
denotes a simple quality, the substantive connotes a
group of qualities. In such a word as *blue*, we have
the one broad idea of one colour fairly defined and
commonly understood within certain definite limits.
In the meaning of, e.g., *rose*, we embrace all the qualities which go to make up our conception of *flower* in
general, and the *special flower* which we call *rose* in
particular. And no doubt the definition may be considered in the main correct. But the distinction
cannot be consistently maintained throughout. For
instance, there are many adjectives which cannot be
said to indicate really one quality only. Such are
most adjectives in *like* or *ly* (*warlike, manly*, etc.) ; and,
on the other hand, substantives are again and again
used so as to denote one quality and only one. The
transition from the denotation of a simple quality to
that of a group of qualities is effected by the use *in a
special sense* of a substantival adjective; as, 'the blacks,'
for 'the negroes'='a radical,' 'a conservative.' When
once such usage has been started, there is no necessity for the train of thought, which led the first
employer to specialise the word, to be present in the
consciousness of other speakers. Directly the word

has come to be so specialised, and the train of thought which led to its specialisation has been forgotten, the word stands isolated as an independent substantive.

The converse process is not uncommon ; in which, out of a group of qualities, a single one is dwelt on and the rest are left out of consideration : such are, for instance, the names of colours ; as, *lilac, rose, mulberry*, etc., used adjectivally. From this use the adjectives with specialised meanings, derived from substantives, we may gather that *adjectives*, i.e. *terms for simple qualities, arose out of terms for groups of qualities*, i.e. *substantives*. The process must have been from the very beginning that the speaker singled out one notion from a group and dwelt on it, passing over the others bound up in the group. In fact, the speaker must, at a very early stage, have used words in a figurative sense. In such expressions as *That man is a bear, That woman is a vixen* (as, indeed, when we say *bearish* or *vixenish*), we are ascribing to him or her only some one particular characteristic of the whole number of characteristics of the thing which the substantive indicates when used in its usual sense. The distinction between noun and verb might seem, at first sight, to be well marked both by the diversity of forms which characterise these separate parts of speech, and by the diversity of functions which they severally fulfil. But in English, we are at once met by the fact that we have numerous verbs which are identical in form with nouns, and in many cases are actually nouns employed as verbs ; as, *to lord it, to walk, to dog, to run :* while we constantly see the process going on before our eyes, of the transference of a noun into the category of verbs ; as, *to chair a man, to table a motion.* How near they may approach in function may be seen from sentences like *I looked at the show*, and *I had a look at the show.* No doubt it may be said that verbs have certain formal characteristics, which distinguish the verb from the noun, such as personal terminations, distinctions between voices, and forms to denote mood and tense. But, in the first place, these forms have, to a great extent, disappeared in English, with its other inflections ; and, in the second place, even in the most highly inflected languages we find verbs defective in some of these characteristics, and thereby approaching in form to nouns : cf. the Italian *bisogna andare* (=' I need to go ') as against *Che bisogna andare* (' What need to go ? '). While, again in nouns, forms occur defective in case and gender-signs ; as, *cornu*, 'horn ;' *genu*, 'knee ;' etc. Further, in the Slavonic languages, we actually find the verb in the past tense agreeing in gender with its subject ; as, *Tui jelala*, ' Thou (feminine) didst wish,' etc. Lastly, the differentiation of the construction of the two parts of speech is anything but sharply marked, as we may see in cases where a substantive actually takes the case which would naturally be taken by the verb with which it is connected : *Seeing her is to love her ; Hearing him recite that poem is enough to draw tears from the eyes.*

Even in highly inflected languages, like Latin and Greek, the personal endings, commonly regarded as the special formal characteristic of the verb, have no place in the participles and infinitives.

Again, such an expression as *Rex es*, ' Thou art king,' is identical in meaning with *Regnas*, ' Thou rulest ;' so that the verbal termination, as such, need not serve to mark any distinction of meaning between the verb and the adjective or substantive used predicatively.

If we say that it is of the essence of the verb to describe a mere transient process limited by time, while the adjective or substantive denotes a permanent quality, we must observe that the adjective may describe a transient quality; as, *dirty, pale*: while verbs may be used to describe states; as, *to glow*, cf. *candere* = to be white.

The participle must be regarded as partaking of the nature of the verb as well as of that of the adjective. The peculiarity of the participle, as compared with the adjective, is that it enables us to express an occurrence or event attributively; as, *They, looking, saw*. We must look upon adjectives as the older formation of the two, and indeed we must suppose that adjectives had been completely developed before participles could take their rise at all.

The characteristic difference between the participle and the so-called verbal adjective is that the participle, unlike the adjective, is capable of denoting tense; as, τύψας (= 'having struck'). The participle, when standing as an attribute to a noun, partakes of the construction of a noun (*i.e.* substantive or adjective); as, *Vir captus est* ('The man is caught'). But it may depart from the character of a noun by departing from such nominal construction, and striking out a new path of its own.

Thus, in *He has taken her, He has slept*, we have a use of the participle quite unlike the use of the adjective. No doubt it is true that such a phrase as *He has taken her* signified originally *He has or holds her as one taken;* cf. *Cura intentos habebat Romanos*, (Liv., xxvi. 1), but we do not now apprehend the construction thus. In French, the transition from the general adjectival into the special participial construction is clearer: *J'ai vu les dames*, 'I have seen the ladies;' but *Je les ai vues*, 'I have seen (fem. plur.) them,' and *les dames que j'ai vues*, 'the ladies that I

have seen (fem. plur).' In Italian, we say *Ho vedute*
(fem. plur.) *le donne* = 'I have seen the ladies,' as
well as *Ho veduto le donne* (masc. or genderless sing.).
In Spanish, all inflection in the case of periphrases
formed with 'haber' is abolished; it is as correct to
write *la carta que he escrito* = 'the letter which I
have written,' as to say *He escrito una carta* = 'I
have written a letter.' On the other hand, in periphrases made with *tener* (*to hold*, used as auxiliary
like *to have*), a later introduction into the language, the
inflection is always retained ; in *tengo escrita una carta*,
= 'I have written (fem.) a letter (fem.),' it is as imperative to observe the concord of gender as in *Las
cartas que tengo escritas* = 'The letters which I have
written.'

Conversely: it is possible for the participle to
gradually recur to a purely nominal character. Bearing in mind our definition of the participle, we may
say that this recurrence has taken place as soon as the
present participle is used for the *lasting* activity; as
when we talk about *a knowing man:* and as soon as
the perfect participle comes to be used to express the
result of the activity; as, *a lost chance.* The more
such participle is employed in a specialised meaning
—as, for instance, metaphorically,—the more speedily
and thoroughly will the transformation become accomplished; as in such cases as *striking, charming,
elevated, drunken, agèd, learnèd, crabbèd, doggèd*, etc.
Nay, such words may even combine with another,
after the laws of verbal construction : as in the case of
*high-flying, well-wishing, flesh-eating, new-born, well-
educated.*

The participle, again, like other adjectives, may
become a substantive, e.g. *the anointed;* and the substantival participle, like the adjectival, may either

denote a momentary activity (or, rather, an activity limited as to time), *e.g.* the *patient*, *i.e.* the *suffering one*, or a state, *e.g.* the *regent* = the *ruling one* = the *ruler*. It may, indeed, entirely lose its verbal nature, as, *friend*, *fiend*, i.e. the *loving one*, the *hating one*, etc.

The nomen agentis, resembling in this respect the participle, may denote either a momentary or a lasting activity ; as, *the doer* = 'he who *does ;*' *the dancer* (if = 'he who is wont to dance,' *e.g.*, as his profession). In the former application it remains closely connected with the verb ; and there is no reason, except custom, why it should not, like the participle, take an object, just like the verb ; in fact, that it should not be correct to say *the teacher the boy* for 'he who teaches the boy,' just as it is possible to say *the school-teacher.* We actually do find in Latin, *dator divitias*, 'giver riches (acc. plur.) ' = 'he who gives riches ;' *justa orator* (Plautus, Amphyt., 34), 'the just things (acc. neut. plur.) orator or speaker' = 'he who speaks just things.'

In Shakespeare, we find *and all is semblative a woman's part* (Twelfth Night, I. iv.), where an adjective, *semblative*, is similarly construed with a verbal force ; the sentence being equivalent to 'and all resembles that which we might expect in a woman.' On the other hand, the nomen agentis, when denoting lasting activity, may separate more and more from the verb, and thus finally lose its special character, as noun in-dicating a 'doer,' e.g., *owner*, *actor*, *father* (lit. 'he who feeds or who protects;' from a root which means either *to nourish* or *to protect*).

The transition from verb to noun is again seen in nomina actionis, like *transportation*, *liberation*. These may also approximate to the verbal construction ; as, *My transportation from England to Ireland* ('I was transported from England to Ireland'); *pearl fishery* ('the fishing for pearls'). Here, again, the notion of a lasting activity inherent in the substantive tends to make the original idea of a nomen actionis grow faint ; and the connotation of a lasting condition sets in. And, again, the more that metaphorical and other unusual or special usages attach to the word, the more does such word become isolated as against its original use, cf. *position, transportation, conviction, goings-on.* It may, indeed, become so far isolated as to lose all connection with the verb, as in *reckoning*, in the sense of an account; cf. *addition*, in French, in the same meaning (cf. the French expression for 'Waiter! the bill, please,' *Garçon ! l'addition s'il vous plaît !*)

The infinitive is really a case of the noun of action, and must originally have been constructed in accordance with the usage in force at the time for the syntactical combination of the corresponding verb with other nouns. But, in order that it may be felt as a true infinitive, its mode of construction must no longer be felt as it originally must have been felt; it must, in fact, have become isolated in its employment, and such isolation became then the basis of further development. But the infinitive having thus developed, reverts in many cases to the character of a noun : its want of inflection, however, always has a tendency to prevent this ; and, accordingly, the most common cases in which it appears as a substantive are as subject or object. In sentences like ' not to have been dipped in Lethe's Lake Could save the son of Thetis from *to die* ' (Spenser, Faëry Queen) ; ' Have is have ' (Shakespeare King John, I. i.) ; ' I list not prophecy ' (Winter's Tale, IV. i. 26) ; ' I learn to ride,' etc., it seems certain that the infinitive is constructed after the analogy of a noun ; but in such constructions as *I let him speak, I hear him walk*, it is hardly apprehended as so constructed by the instinct of language of the present day.

Languages which possess declined articles possess exceptional facilities for thus approximating the infinitive to a noun, as the Greek τὸ φιλεῖν, τοῦ φιλεῖν, etc. (='the "to love"—of the *to-love*,' etc.): cf. such instances as the English *Have is have* (Shakespeare, King John, I. i.); *Mother, what does 'marry' mean?* (Longfellow); *Him booteth not resist* (Spenser, Faëry Queen, I. iii. 20.) And similarly the German *das lieben* ('the "to-love"'); French *mon pouvoir* ('my "to-be-able"'). In Latin, the same approximation is rendered possible by the demonstrative pronouns; as, *totum hoc philosophari* (Cicero), 'all this "to-philosophise;"' *Inhibere illud tuum* (ibid.), ('that "to-prohibit" of yours'). Modern High German and the Romance languages have gone so far as to employ the infinitive as the equivalent to a noun pure and simple, even in respect of inflection; as, *Meines sterbens* (='of my "to-die"'); *Mein hier-bleiben* (='my "here-remain,"' *i.e.*, 'my remaining here'). In the Romance languages, the process is rendered easier by the abolition of case-difference; cf. *mon savoir-faire* (='my "to know—to-do"'='my cleverness of management'). Old French and Provençal actually invest the infinitive with the *s* of the nominative case—*Li plorers ne t'i vaut rien:* 'The "to-weep" not to thee there avails anything' ='It avails thee nothing to weep' (cf. Mätzner, iii., pp. 1-2).

It is possible for the verbal construction to be maintained in many cases, even in spite of the use of the article. For instance, τὸ σκοπεῖν τὰ πράγματα (lit. = 'the "to-see" the matters.').

The oldest adverbs seem to be mainly in their

origin crystallised cases of nouns (adjectival or sub-stantival), in some cases of which they are the result of the combination of a preposition with its case. Thus, in English, we have the genitive suffix appearing in *else* (formerly *elles*, the genitive of a root *el* or *al*, meaning ‘other’), *once* (=‘ones’), *twice needs. Much* and *little* were datives, *miclum* and *lytlum*; cf. *whilom* (= hwílum.)

Thus, in Latin, many adverbs are derived from the accusative—as, *primum*, ‘first;’ *multum*, ‘much;’ *foras*, ‘abroad;’ *alias*, ‘at another time;’ *facile*, ‘easily;’ *recens*, ‘freshly:’ from the locative—as, *partim*, ‘partly;’ or the ablative, as *falso*, ‘falsely;’ *recta*, ‘by the right way;’ *sponte*, ‘voluntarily.’ The following are in-stances of the combination of a preposition with its regime: *amid* (= *on-middum*), *withal*, *together*, *anon*; French, *amont*, *aval* (= prep. *a* (‘at’) *mont*, ‘mountain,’ and *val*, ‘dale’ = *upwards*, and *downwards*).

This formation of adverbs leads us to suspect that the original method of forming them will also prob-ably have been from nouns; and that as some of them may have proceeded from nouns before the development of inflections, in such cases merely the stem form, pure and simple, was employed to express adverbs. Thus such expressions as *to speak true, to entreat evil*, will represent the oldest types of adverbs.

The adverb stands in close relationship to the adjective. It bears a relation to the verb and to the adjective as well, analogous to that borne by an attributive adjective to a substantive; thus *He stepped lightly* is analogous to *His steps were light*; and *That is absolutely true* to *The truth of that is absolute*. This analogy manifests itself, among other instances, in this — that an adverb may, generally speaking, be formed from any adjective at will.

The adverb differs formally from the adverb in this, that the adjective, commonly speaking, admits of inflection, and hence of agreement with the substantive. In English, where this test is absent, it is difficult for the instinct of language to draw a sharp line between the two, as in *to speak loud, to speak low.* It is difficult, in English, to maintain that there is any real difference between the use of *good* in *good-natured* and the same word in *he is good ;* or the use of *well* in *he is well dressed,* and in *he is well.*

Again, many adverbs in different languages resemble adjectives in this, that, when joined to another adverb, they take an adjectival inflection.   Thus, in French, it is correct to say ' *toute* pure,' ' *toutes* pures ' = ' entire, (fem. sing.) pure,' ' entire (fem. plur.) pure (fem. plur.) ; ' both = ' entirely pure,' ' quite pure : ' in Italian, *tutta livida* = ' all (fem. sing.) livid ' = ' quite livid : ' in Spanish, *todos desnudos* = ' all (masc. plur.) nude ' = ' quite naked.'

There are many cases in which an attributive adjective is employed convertibly with an adverb ; cf. *Hispania postrema perdomita est* = ' Spain LAST (fem. sing.) was conquered,' for ' AT LAST ' (Livy, xxviii. 12) ; *Il arrive toujours le dernier,* ' He always comes last ; ' *Il est mort content* = ' He died happy.'   Compare also these two usages—*De ces deux sœurs la cadette est celle qui est le plus aimée,* ' Of these two sisters the younger is the one who is the (neut.) more loved (fem. sing.) ; ' or *la plus aimée,* ' the (fem.) more loved (fem.) ' (Acad.) [1]

Adjectives used in connection with nouns signifying the agent or the action are used in a way hardly to be distinguished from an adverbial use ; as, *a good story, a good story-teller, an old bookseller.*   In English,

---

[1] Mätzner, Fr. Gr., 157, sqq.

owing to its lack of inflections, an ambiguity may arise in such cases as the last cited ; we might apply the word *old* to the man who sells the books, as well as to the books themselves. The common custom in English is to shun ambiguity by the use of the hyphen ; as, *an old-book seller.* But English attempts likewise to remove the ambiguity by maintaining the adverb for one case, after the analogy of the construction with the verb—as, *an early riser, a timely arrival,* etc.—though this distinction is not consistently carried out.

The resemblance of adjectives and adverbs produces uncertainty in the meaning to be attached to certain adjectives ; the adjective, when attached to a noun, may be conceived of as referring either to the person, or as referring to one of his qualities ; thus, *a bad coachman* may either mean 'a wicked coachman,' or 'a coachman looked upon as bad in the quality of his driving.'   In the latter case, the adjective is used in the special sense acquired by the adverb; as, *he drives badly.*

It is natural, then, as the adjective and the adverb so generally exist in pairs, that we should feel the need of possessing both parts of speech for all cases. There are, however, many adverbs which are derived from no adjective, and which thus have no adjective parallel to them.   In this case we are compelled to employ the adverb with the function of the adjective, as in ' He is *there,*' ' He is *up,*' ' The door is *to,*' ' Heaven is *above ;*' in which cases the instinct of language apprehends the construction as identical with that found in such phrases as *He is active, The door is open,* etc. Again, in such sentences as *the mountain yonder, the enemy there, the drive hither,* the adverb marks its difference from the adjective by its position in the sentence.   But this rule is not consistently observed ;

there are cases in English where the adverb is inserted between the article and its substantive ; as, *on the hither-side, the above discourse, the then monarch,* and more extensively in the vulgar *that there mountain, this here book,* where the adjectival adverbs are pleonastic.

Just as, *e.g.,* in Latin, we find the adverb used in *sic sum* ('so I am'), *Ego hunc esse aliter credidi,*[1] 'I him to be otherwise believed' = 'I thought he was a different kind of man ;' so we find in English *While this scene was passing in the cabin of the man, one quite otherwise* (i.e. *different*) *was passing in the halls of the master* (Mrs. Beecher Stowe, Uncle Tom's Cabin, i. 43), in which, and other similar constructions, the adverb again has all the functions of an adjective.

Prepositions and conjunctions as link-words or connecting elements took their origin from independent words through a displacement of the distribution. Prepositions were once adverbs, serving to denote more closely the direction of the verbal action ; as, 'to go *in,*' 'to carry *off,*' 'to throw *up,*' 'to fall *down.*' They then became displaced, *i.e.* detached from the verb, and came to belong to the noun, furthering the disappearance of its case-endings and assuming their office.

To stamp a word as 'connecting word,' this displacement must have become customary and general. For, in their occasional usage, the most various parts of speech may serve as connecting words. The functions of the adverb, as such, have been sufficiently illustrated. It is thus only where such adverbs are with a certain regularity, or preferably, used as link-words, that they begin to be felt as prepositions or conjunctions. But even then, notwithstanding such

[1] Quoted by Storm, Englische Philologie, p. 332.

syntactical development, the word can still be used independently in its former function, and it remains impossible to definitely range it in any particular class. This only becomes rational and feasible when the word has become obsolete in its original usage.

We may accordingly define a preposition as a link-word which may be followed by any substantive in some of its case-forms where this combination is no longer syntactically parallel to that between noun or verb and the word in its original independent sense. Accepting this definition, we shall not explain *considering*, in such a sentence as *considering everything he has done very well*, as a preposition, because its construction is that of the verb *to consider*. When we come to *instead of* it is different. *Stead*, A.S. *stede*, meant 'a place;' and *in the stead of the man* would have been a perfectly natural construction, the genitive case showing the independence of the noun : but whether the genitive is still felt as a genitive depends on the question whether we think of *instead* as a compound of the preposition *in* with the noun *stead*. As soon as we cease to feel it as such, we do not think of the genitive as regularly depending on the preceding substantive, and the preposition is created. No doubt the instance which we have given proves that the instinct of language is vacillating ; we still find *in his stead* looked upon as somewhat archaic indeed, but still current English. In some cases the isolation has become looser, and in others it has become absolute. The word *nigh* (A.S. *neáh*, M.E. *neigh*, as in 'neighbour') was originally an adverb, and identical in meaning with the word *near* (A.S. *néar*, the comparative degree of *néah*). But we do not think of *nigh* and *near* as connected. The word *till* is still more peculiar. It is, properly speaking, a case of A.S. *tíli*, a noun (cf. Germ. *Ziel*, Gothic *tils*) meaning 'aim' or 'goal, whence the idea of *towards* developed. *Off* and *of* are not thought of as connected, and yet they are the same word. In this case the relationship becomes obscured, owing to divergency in the development of signification. In other cases the isolation of the word is due to the disappearance of the old method of construction in which it was used. Thus *since*, M.E. *sithens*, is from *siðð̣en* = A.S. *siðð̣an*, which is itself a construction for *siðð̣an*, put for *siðð̣am*, 'after that.' Here the *ðam* is the dative case masculine of the demonstrative pronoun used as a relative ; it answers exactly to the N.H.G. *seit dem ;* cf. *ni ðanaseiðs* (Ulphilas, Mark ii. 14) + ' no more.' In the same way, the word *ere* is a comparative form derived from A.S. *ǽr*, ' soon.'

The origin and rise of the conjunctions may, like that of the prepositions, be followed historically. Many of them arise from adverbs or pronouns in their function as connective words, as we have discussed in the foregoing paragraphs. These words, then, are already connecting-words ere they become established as conjunctions pure and simple. All depends thus upon the linguistic consciousness of the speaker, whether he will consider them as still pronoun or adverb, or as real conjunction, and this consciousness, again, is largely dependent upon the degree to which the word in question has been etymologically obscured.

We have seen how the demonstrative *that* has become a conjunction, and can easily realise how to some extent in many others, such as *because, in case*, etc., though no demonstrative word proper has entered into their composition, the relation of the noun which forms their second part to what follows is of a demonstrative kind.

Prepositions and conjunctions are more clearly distinguishable in such languages, as, *e.g.*, German, where the flection of noun and adjective, or the absence of flection, shows whether the word is used as the one or the other. In English, this test has disappeared. But even in highly inflected tongues this test is not applicable in cases where a preposition is used before an indeclinable word or combination of words. And that such difference could not arise before the flection had arisen, is self-evident.

CHAPTER XXI.

WE have now to consider the question of the relation of writing to language; how far it has influenced it, and continues to influence it; and for what reasons it seems an inadequate representation of language. The first thing necessary for us to remember is that, though writing is the only means whereby the speech of the past has been preserved for us, yet it is equally true that, before we can consider writing at all, we have to convert it into spoken language, and to affix sounds to the symbols of language which have descended to us from the past. All such translation of symbols affixed to language in the past must necessarily be imperfect; we can only arrive approximately, for instance, at a satisfactory conjecture of the actual sounds of the English language as spoken by Shakespeare; and the data for determining such questions must always be more or less incomplete.

The written representation of language must, however, always be an interesting object of study to the philologist—partly because it has been the vehicle of the sounds of language, and partly because it is an important factor in the development of language itself.

Writing appeals, in the first place, to a much larger

community than speaking. A single page of written matter may appeal to thousands more easily than the most eloquent sermon or address. Nay, writing may in this way appeal to the whole of a linguistic community, causing those of the present time to exert their influence on generations yet unborn.

Writing which consistently and regularly represents the spoken language must be more effective in perpetuating that language than writing which does not so represent it. Theoretically, we assume that written languages fall into one or other of these classes, and we classify them as languages spelt phonetically and spelt non-phonetically, or, as some prefer to express it, historically.

But we must remember that no alphabet, however perfect, can assume to be a correct picture of language. Language consists of a continuous series of sounds, never broken, but consecutive. Just as no amount of drops of water separately considered could give the picture of a river, so no amount of symbols, however minute, could give the real picture of a sentence. A sentence, nay, a single word, is a continuous whole ; the symbols whereby we represent it can represent only the chief parts, and represent them as disconnected. The transitions, the links remain unindicated, and so do such important factors as quantity, accent, and tone.

Further, the alphabets in use are, even the best of them, imperfect. It is plain that, when the members of a particular linguistic community, like, *e.g.*, the Germans or the Portuguese, seek to make their alphabet a consistent picture of the sounds of speech, they aim merely at representing the sounds of their own language. A scientific alphabet should aim at representing all possible sounds, and not merely those needed in an alphabet of a particular linguistic community.

Even in the case of the best-spelt languages, *i.e.* the languages in which the principle of one sound standing for one sign, and one sign for one single sound obtains, we shall find that these aim only at satisfying the ordinary practical needs of the language. They make as few distinctions as is consistent with ordinary clearness and consistency. For instance, they deem it unnecessary to denote the difference of sounds arising from the position of a letter in a syllable, a word, or an accent, provided only that a similarity of position produces habitually similar results. A certain degree of consistency is thus attained without a superfluity of symbols. In Modern High German, for instance, the *hard* s sound in *lust, brust*, etc., has the same symbol to represent it as that which elsewhere represents the *soft* s sound : but no ambiguity arises from this, because s, when followed by t, unless the group *st* is initial, is always hard ; thus the s in *reist* is pronounced as in *lust*. Similarly, final s is habitually pronounced hard or unvoiced; as, *hass, glas, eis*.

In the same way, in English, it would have been superfluous, in an alphabet merely directed to satisfy practical needs, to adopt a special sign for the front nasal n in *sing ;* because n, followed by and combined with g, always has the same sound. Similarly, n, in such combinations as the Fr. *vigne*, Ital. *ogni*, has a consistent and regular pronunciation, and therefore there is no need for any special representation of it.

There are indeed languages, like Sanscrit, in which the principle of phonetic spelling is more or less carefully carried out. Generally, however, we find that the same sign of any particular alphabet has to serve for more than one sound, and it almost invariably happens that we augment the confusion by employing different signs for one and the same sound. The chief reason for these defects is because most nations, instead of creating symbols to represent the sounds in their own language, have been content to adopt an alphabet ready to hand, made to suit the requirements of the language of another nation. Thus the alphabet used by most civilised nations was that which the Phenicians elaborated from the Egyptian hieroglyphics; and the Russians adopted with modifications the Greek adaptation of this. Another reason for the inconsistency is that, as pronunciation changes, it is obvious that the denotation of symbols ought to change as well. These same causes may also produce an unnecessary superfluity of symbols. In English, for instance, the alphabet suffers alike from superfluity and defect. Several signs serve to denote the same sound, as *c, k, ch ; c, s ; oo, ou ; ou, ow ; a, ai ; e, i, ee, ea, ie, ei ; i, y ; cks, x ; oa, aw ;* and many others might be cited. Again, there are many cases in which the same symbols denote different sounds, such as *th* in *thin* and *then ; a* in *hat* and *fatal ; i* in *pin* and *pine.*[1]

It is not the place here to point out in detail the advantages of a well-spelt language over a less well-spelt one.[2] Practically, however, the consideration cannot be disregarded that, if English orthography represented English pronunciation as closely as Italian does Italian, at least half the time and expense of teaching to read and to spell would be saved. This

---

[1] Modern English spelling has been ably treated of by Skeat, Principles of English Etymology, p. 294, sqq. Clarendon Press.

[2] Cf. Spelling Reform, by J. H. Gladstone, F.R.S. (Macmillan); Pitman's Plea for Spelling Reform; and Max Müller's Essay on Spelling (Selected Essays, vol. i., pp. 252–299. Longmans, 1881).

is assumed by Dr. Gladstone[1] to be twelve hundred
hours in a lifetime, and as more than half a million of
money per annum for England and Wales alone. A
few instances, taken mainly from Pitman's work, may
serve to show how all-pervading the irregularity is.

The same symbol serves to denote different vowel
sounds (1) even in words etymologically connected; as,
*sane, sanity; nation, national; navy, navigate; metre,
metrical; final, finish; floral, florid; student, study;
punitive, punish:* (2) in words etymologically unconnected, as in *fare, have, save; were, mere; give, dive;
notice, entice; active, arrive; doctrine, divine; gone, bone;
dove, move, rove, hover.* Again, cf., *change, flange;
paste, caste; bind, wind; most, cost; rather, bather;
there, here; fasting, wasting.*

By collecting examples in this way, Mr. Pitman
has arrived at the conclusion that, in English, we endeavour to express fourteen distinct sounds by using
five signs in twenty-three different ways, without any
real means of discriminating when one sound and when
another is intended, or what sign should be used to
denote a particular sound. But besides these separate
vowel signs, digraphs and trigraphs to the number of
twenty-two are used to express the same fourteen
sounds which the five vowel signs have already attempted to represent; though they, in addition, attempt
to represent two more diphthongal sounds, making
sixteen distinct sounds in all. For instance, *pail, said,
plaid; pay, says; heat, sweat, great, heart; receive,
vein, height; key, prey, eye; sour, pour, would; town,
sown.*[2]

Of the consonants, we may remark, in the first
place, that many are silent, as in *debt, limb, indict,
condemn:* in some cases, silent consonants have been

[1] Page 27, u.s.   [2] Pitman, u.s., p. 8.

interpolated to suggest a mistaken derivation, as in *sovereign, foreign, island;* in others, again, they have been capriciously retained to mark the derivation of a word (as in *receipt*), and yet omitted in the case of other words derived from the same source. Then, for instances of the inconsistent use of consonants, we may take the following table from Pitman; (a few examples have been added) :—

　ch.—church, chaise, ache; yacht, drachm.
　ck.—pick (*k* or *c* superfluous).
　gh.—ghost, cough, hough ; dough, night, inveigh.
　ng.—singer, linger, infringer.
　ph.—physic, nephew ; phthisical.
　rh.—rhetoric ; myrrh, catarrh.
　sc.—science, conscience, discern, score.
　sch.—schism, schedule, scheme.
　th.—thistle, this, thyme.
　wh.—whet, whole.

If, in addition to these obvious defects in alphabets, we bear in mind the fact that the accentuation commonly remains for the most part undenoted, we must admit that our alphabets present us with a very imperfect picture of spoken language. For an attempt to realise a scientifically correct alphabet, we must refer to Sweet's ' Handbook of Phonetics,' and Melville Bell's 'Visible Speech,' ' Sounds and their Relations,' A. J. Ellis, etc., not to mention the works in other languages, such as those by Techmer, Vietor, Trautmann, Sievers, etc.

We have to bear in mind that writing is to living language nothing more than what a rough sketch is to a finished picture. The sketch is, commonly speaking, sufficient to enable one familiar with the figures which are meant to be represented, to recognise them. But should several painters attempt to reproduce a finished sketch from such rough outline, they would produce a set of pictures differing very much in details. For instance, each painter, if he did not recognise certain objects in the sketch, would be tempted to substitute in their place others with which he might be familiar. Just so, those who seek to reproduce the sounds of a language from written symbols, will be tempted to substitute similar sounds with which they are familiar for the sounds of the sketch, as, for our purpose, we may call the alphabet. Even in the case of a foreign language possessing an alphabet in some respects identical with our own, like the French, it is considered necessary to prefix to the alphabet a description of the sound intended to be conveyed by the symbol; and even this cannot obviate the necessity of hearing the sound, especially when the alphabet is not based upon scientific principles. It is equally true that the same remarks are applicable to the case of a dialect belonging to the same group of languages as our own.

In any linguistic area where the same language is spoken, there exist different dialects, *i.e.* variations from the standard language possessing a quantity of divergencies from the sounds of the standard language. The common alphabet has to stand as the representative of all these dialects alike, and the same symbol has to present, for instance, the *u* sound as uttered by a west countryman and as uttered by a Scotchman. *R*, again, is pronounced by a Londoner quite differently from the way in which it is pronounced by a Scotchman. *F* is pronounced like *v* in Devonshire and Cornwall; and the *h* is in many words notoriously written but not pronounced in the greater part of England proper. Besides such obvious differences, which might be multiplied indefinitely,[1] we have to

[1] See Storm, Die lebende Sprache, p. 259, sqq.

remember that the quantity, the pitch, and the accent remain undenoted by the standard alphabet in the different dialects ; and we shall easily see that a large quantity of dialectic differences is taken no account of in writing. The obvious result of this want of adequate representation of the sounds of the separate dialects must be that the speakers in the separate dialects must each consider that the sound with which he is himself familiar is the one intended to be represented by the symbol which he sees.

The result of our present system of representing sounds is that we are unable to give an idea of other dialects than our own, except in cases where the discrepancy between these and our own is very strongly marked. Even in such cases merely a rough indication of the pronunciation can be given ; but the delicate and manifold differences occurring between the speech of individuals of different communities and different generations must pass unmarked. It is needless to add that the present system of representation of sounds is useless as a register of the actual state of pronunciation, and of the changes which are gradually occurring. How interesting would it be to Englishmen had a scientific alphabet been employed to record the different stages of pronunciation of their language, so that the nineteenth century might know with approximate exactitude how Chaucer, Shakespeare, and Milton spoke !

But in any changes which we may see fit to make in orthography, we must beware of supposing that, in a perfect alphabet, we should possess an absolutely controlling influence over pronunciation and sound changes. No doubt if sounds were accurately registered by a scientific alphabet, the more educated classes of the community who were familiar with this alphabet and its denotation would be led to attempt to maintain their pronunciation in accordance with the standard afforded them by this. But, even assuming that such an alphabet were generally adopted, it is plain that it could only represent one particular dialect of any linguistic area, which dialect would, as a rule, be that of the best-educated classes in the community. Then, as now, dialects would remain unrepresented, or, at the best, would be registered for scientific purposes or for a limited use. Then, as now, absolutely different sounds occurring in different dialects would be denoted by the same letters. Then, as now, different sound images would be associated with different letters, which are, of course, merely connected with sounds by an association of ideas. Then, as now, the written language would be unable to record the changes that had passed upon the language of an entire community, confining itself to those that had passed over the normal or standard dialect, which, as we have seen, would be in England the dialect of the educated classes. But it must be held that language is not consciously altered to suit orthography; any such alteration would be contrary to the common development of language. The orthography may, however, be altered to suit the language; but, as it is obvious that the language must change more quickly than the orthography, it follows that the orthography must remain, at the best, an imperfect record of written sounds.

The defects of written speech which have been already indicated are not as great as those which set in when the orthography of a language has been long settled. The original spellers tried to commit the sounds of each word to writing; they broke up the word into its elements, and compounded the letters

corresponding to these elements to the best of their
ability.　But there is no doubt that practice in reading
and writing makes this process continually shorter.
The consciousness that the symbol is bound up with
the sound grows gradually fainter.　A group of
symbols represents a group of sounds ; and the sounds
are apprehended in groups, and not singly.　The
sentence, and not the word, becomes the basis of
reading.　Indeed, fluent reading and writing would
be impossible if this were not the case.　Poets, like
Burns, who write in their own dialect, however much
they may try to reproduce accurately the sounds of
that dialect, and however well they may succeed, still
are fain to content themselves with a certain conventional approximation to accurate representation ;
in fact they are very much influenced by the conventional orthography of the literary language.　They
are also constrained to attempt to produce an
approximate amount of accuracy with the smallest
amount of labour ; and their labour is considerably
lessened by their acceptance of conventional symbols.
Our forefathers really tried to indicate consistently
their pronunciation of their words.　They tried to
spell phonetically, and the result may be seen in the
different spellings of the manuscripts of Langland,
Chaucer, Shakespeare, etc.

The advantages of a fixed orthography are mainly
that the reader connects a definite orthographic image
with a definite signification.　We can understand this
if we take two words which are pronounced identically
but differently spelt, such as *bough*, and the verb to *bow*.
Were these words written identically, the written picture common to the two would associate itself with the
sound common to the two words, whereas, at present,
each meaning has its own distinct symbol.　Each

divergence in spelling, though from a phonetic point
of view it may be an improvement, increases the
difficulty of understanding what is written. Divergencies or want of fixity in spelling may arise from
the awkwardness of writers, who may have employed
several signs to denote the same sound, or a single
sign for more than one; or, again, it may arise from
the want of some controlling body, like an academy,
whose business it is to regulate orthography. On the
other hand, it may be due to the very perfection and
consistency of the characteristics of the language
which has to be reproduced. If, for instance, as in
Sanscrit, or in Welsh, the spelling of the same word
varies with its pronunciation according to its position
in the sentence, a single meaning must be expressed
by different symbols, and it is impossible for one
definite written picture to connect itself with the first
form. The more fixed the orthography, the more is
the process in reading and writing facilitated.

On the whole, it is true that the natural tendency
of the orthography is towards greater fixity, though
it is also true that retrogressive movements sometimes occur, as when marked phonetic changes set in.
There are three principal methods whereby it is
commonly sought to produce a fixed and uniform
orthography: (1) by the abolition of variations between
several different methods of spelling; (2) by regarding
etymology and taking it as a guide to orthography;
and (3) by holding to traditional spelling and dis-
regarding sound. The first of these methods is,
generally speaking, in accordance with the aims of
phonetic reformers; the two latter are in direct
contravention of their aims. But against these efforts
to produce fixity in orthography there remains always
the counter tendency to bring language and its written

expression into harmony; and this tendency exhibits itself partly in the effort to correct original deficiencies in spelling, and partly in a reaction against the discrepancies constantly produced in written language by sound-change. As these two tendencies are constantly operative, the history of orthography is a description of the temporary triumph of one or other of these two forces.

If we should institute a comparison between the development of writing and that of language, we shall find certain points of resemblance, and others of marked divergence. With reference to the latter; in the first place, changes in orthography are brought about more consciously, and with more purpose on the part of the writer, than changes of language on the part of the speaker. In the second place, whereas in language a whole linguistic community is exposed to a change, in the case of writing, only that portion of the community who write or print or publish are directly interested. And thus it is that the authority of single individuals is able to carry weight to a much larger extent than in language. Again, orthographical changes do not depend upon personal contact, but appeal to the eye, and therefore are capable of affecting a wider, if a less numerous, public than linguistic changes. A good instance of the effect of changed orthography is seen in the Welsh language as contrasted with the Gaelic. The Welsh has changed its old cumbrous orthography for a simpler and more phonetic system; and, in consequence, the Welsh language has become more easy to acquire, and, generally speaking, a handier instrument of literary intercourse. No reformer has arisen for Gaelic, which consequently is little read and little written in comparison with its Cymric sister.

One of the most obvious difficulties that meets the orthographical reformer at the outset is the presence in the alphabet of one or more signs to represent the same sound, a case which has been already referred to in this chapter. This superfluity of sound-signs may be an inheritance from the language whence the alphabet in use is borrowed; thus, in our alphabet, we have received *c* and *k* and *q*, all denoting the same sound. Or, again, it may happen that, in the language from which the alphabet was borrowed, two signs had a different value, but that the language which borrows them is unable to employ these signs to make such a distinction, which, indeed, does not exist in it. Thus, the Greek alphabet employed χ to represent the aspirated guttural; but, as we do not employ that sound at all, the symbol *ch*, as seen in *cholera*, is superfluous. Again, both symbols of the borrowed language easily pass into use in the language which borrows them, if the sound which the borrowing language means to represent lies between the two sounds represented by the symbols borrowed. Thus, for instance, in the Upper German dialect, at the time of the introduction of the Latin alphabet, there was no distinction answering to that between the Latin *g* and *k*, *b* and *p*, *f* and *v*, consequently, one of these symbols was, for that particular German dialect, superfluous.

In English there is one cause of vacillation which should be noticed as of interest, viz., the attempt of certain writers to omit certain letters which seem to them superfluous, as when *honor, color*, etc. are written instead of *honour, colour*, etc. As far as this spelling expresses supposed philological accuracy, it is, of course, erroneous.

Superfluities in spelling are disposed of in much the same way as superfluities in words and forms.

The simplest way is by the disuse of one of the two signs. The other way is by differentiating the signs which were originally used indifferently. This differentiation may serve to supply a want in the language ; as when, in Modern German, *i*, *u*, and *j*, *v* were gradually parted into vowel and consonant. Thirdly, it happens that one manner of spelling becomes usual in one word, and a different manner in another, the differences depending upon mere caprice. Thus we spell *precede*, but *proceed; proceeding*, but *procedure; stream* (from A.S. *stréam*) with *ea*, but *steep* (A.S. *stéap*) with *ee*. A.S. *bréad* is now written *bread*, but A.S. *réad* has become *red;* A.S. *nu* we write *now*, but *ðu* is at present *thou;* etc. Some of these and similar inconsistencies owe at least their preservation, if not their origin, to the desire of differentiating in the spelling such words as have the same sound but different meanings ; e.g., *to* and *too*, *steel* and *steal*, *red* and *read*, etc.

Etymology, or, more correctly, etymological grouping, and analogy have great influence upon spelling, as well as on the spoken language. Again and again an older phonetical spelling has been replaced by a real or fanciful etymological one. Thus, for instance, it is owing to the influence of etymological grouping when certain alternations of sound, due to flection or other change of position, are left without indication by any corresponding changes of spelling. Thus, in Anglo-Saxon, the word *dæg* had its plural *dagas*. Final *g* was dropped, and the vowel before it changed into the sound now represented by *ay* in *day*. A *g* between two vowels, however, generally became *w*, and, accordingly, *dagas* became *dawes*, a form frequently found in Middle English. In this case, *analogy* interfered, and a new 'regular' plural, formed directly from the singular

day, replaced the older historically correct form.   It is,
however, possible to imagine that this had not happened
in the spoken language, and that, whilst people SAID
day, *dawes*, they had WRITTEN *day*, *dayes*.   Or rather,
if the declined cases in the singular had remained in
use—in which cases, also, the *g* stood between two
vowels—that the *w* written in the declined cases of the
singular, and in all cases of the plural, had begun in
time to be *written* also in the nominative singular,
where the *y* was the 'regular' form.   This supposititious
case is only an instance of what has happened in many
languages, *e.g.*, in German.   German 'unvoices' all
final consonants ; *i.e.*, a *d* or *t*, when final, is pronounced
t, a *p* or *b* is pronounced *p*, etc.   Before terminations
of inflection, however, *d* and *b* remained 'voiced,' and
we find accordingly in Middle High German such
pairs as nom. *tac*, gen. *tages*.   The *g* of the declined
cases has, however, supplanted the *c* of the nominative
singular, and the word is now written throughout with
g, though no one pronounces the same sound in the
nominative singular, as in, say, *tages*, or nom. plur.
tage, etc.

Again, etymological considerations first caused and
now preserve the insertion of *b* in *debt*, *g* in *reign*.
That, in many cases, these etymological considerations
arose from sheer ignorance does not alter the fact that
it was their influence which, after causing the insertion
of, *e.g.*, the *g* in *sovereign*, the *h* in *rhythm*, the *l* in
could, the *w* in *whole*, the *p* in *receipt*, saved these
absurdities from desirable extinction.

It must, however, be admitted that, owing to these
very irregularities and inconsistencies of spelling, as
far as it is to be regarded as representing the spoken
language, we owe sometimes a greater uniformity and
regularity in the grammar of the *written* language than

could obtain if spelling followed pronunciation more closely than it does.

Thus, for instance, in most weak verbs the past tense is expressed in writing by the addition of *ed*, though sometimes, in the spoken word, nothing but the sound of *d* (*I roll, I rolled*), or even *t* (*I express, I expressed*), is added. The *ed*, in these cases, may be considered to be preserved partly from habit, partly from a feeling, to some extent etymological, that such and such a meaning (or change of meaning) is indicated by such and such a spelling or letter-group.

CHAPTER XXII.

ON MIXTURE IN LANGUAGE.

THERE are two senses in which we may speak of
mixture in language—the broader sense in which
every speaker must influence those who hear him, and
be influenced by them in turn, and the narrower sense
in which one language or one dialect is influenced by
another with which it is but distantly connected.

In order to understand the process of such mixture
as this, we ought to observe, in the first place, what
passes in the case of individuals. The circumstances
leading to such mixture may be best observed in the
case of persons who speak more than one language.
Bi-lingualism on a large scale, of course, is best seen
where a community resides upon the confines of two
linguistic areas, as on the borders of England and
Wales. It may, again, be due to the sojourn of a
person in a foreign country: it becomes more marked
still when persons pass from one country and settle in
another; and still more when large masses of people
are permanently transferred under foreign domination
by conquests and by colonisation, as in the case of the
inhabitants of British India or the French population
of Lower Canada.

The knowledge of a foreign tongue may also be
imparted by writing, as when we learn classical Latin

and Greek; but in this case, the influence exerted by the foreign tongue is felt only by the better educated classes of society.

In all cases where nations have been brought into contact, and have been mixed on a large scale, bilingualism is common. It is natural to expect that, of the two languages employed, that of the more prominent nation will gain a preponderance over the other, whether its prominence be due to its power, or industrial or intellectual capacity. There will be a change, in fact, from bilingualism to unilingualism; and the process will leave traces more or less marked on the superior language.

An instance of this process on a large scale was afforded by the Roman Conquest of Gaul, the consequence of which was a struggle between the tongue of the Latin conquerors and that of the Celtic conquered race. The result was that the Latin ousted the Celtic, but not without leaving traces of the Celtic idiom in certain words, in the pronunciation, and the construction of the language.

But it will be found that the mixture will not easily affect single individuals, so as to transform their diction into a language made up of elements equally, or nearly equally, taken from either of the two conflicting languages. Even assuming that a person is perfectly master of both languages, and that he may pass from one to another with perfect ease, he will yet adhere to one language for the expression of a clause or a sentence. Each tongue may, however, exercise a modifying influence upon the other in the way of affecting its idioms, its accent, its intonations, etc. It may happen that the influence of one tongue may be predominant in particular areas of language, as we see that the English is in Lower Canada in matters of commerce.

This leads to such expressions as *jobbeur, cheurtine* (shirting), *sligne* (sling), *charger le jury, forger, cuisiner les comptes*, etc. : see American Journal of Philology, vol. x., 2.[1]   Of course, where one of two or more languages has been learnt as the mother tongue, this will always have more influence over foreign languages, however perfectly acquired, than the latter will have over the mother tongue ; but we must not under-rate the influence which a foreign language may have upon the mother tongue, especially when it is looked upon as fashionable, or as the key to an important literature. The influence of the foreign tongue may obviously spread to persons who are wholly unacquainted with it, by the contact of these with persons who have adopted or assimilated the foreign elements.

The two principal ways in which a foreign idiom may influence the mother tongue are these.   In the first place, foreign words may be adopted into the mother tongue and retained, commonly speaking, in a more or less altered form.   The English language has borrowed words of this kind from numerous languages.   Thus, from Dutch, we get the word *sloop* (*sloep*, itself a loan-word from Fr. *shaloupe ;* whence we, again, have borrowed *shallop*), yacht: *yam*, from some African language, through the Portuguese: from Spanish—*flotilla, cigar* (Sp. *cigarro*), *mosquito :* from Italian—*domino, casino, opera, stucco :* from Persian —*chess* (Persian *sháh*, a king, through O. Fr. *eschac*), *orange, shawl, rice, sugar*.   India gives us *sepoy ;* Germany, *meerschaum ;* Russia, *a steppe ;* China, *tea ;* etc.[2]

In the second place, the method of connecting and arranging the sentences, and the idioms used by

---

[1] Cf. Dilke's Problems of Greater Britain, ch. ii., p. 53, where ' Je n'ai pas de change ' is cited as usual.

[2] See Skeat's Principles of English Etymology, p. 14 ; also Peile's Primer of Philology, p. 80.

the mother tongue may be taken from the foreign language, and this, even though the material of the language be maintained intact.

The chief cause for the adoption of foreign words into the mother tongue is, of course, the need felt for them in the mother tongue. Words are constantly adopted for ideas which have as yet no words to express them. The names of places and persons are the most common among such adopted words, to which may, of course, be added the names of foreign products, such as *tea, sago, chocolate*. The names of such products may be taken from the language of communities in a very low state of civilisation. On the other hand, when a language finds it necessary to introduce technical, scientific, religious, or political terms, it is fair to suppose that the language which lends the words must be that of a nation in a higher state of culture than the language of the nation which borrows them. There are many words relating to social subjects imported into English from French which may serve to give a good idea of the weak point of the nation which borrows, and of the strong point of the nation which supplies them. Such are numerous works having reference to ease in conversation, such as *bon-mot, esprit,* 'wit;' *verve,* 'liveliness;' *élan,* 'spring;' etc.; and it will be correspondingly found that the language whence such supplies are drawn is very rich in the qualities for which it possesses such abundance of names.

But languages may be tempted to borrow beyond their actual needs when the foreign language and culture is higher prized than the native, and when, accordingly, the usage of such words is considered fashionable or tasteful. Instances in point are the numerous Greek words introduced into classical Latin, such as *techinæ* (Plautus, Most., II. i. 23), and the numerous French words borrowed by German and English, such as *étiquette, chaperon, à outrance*.

If a speaker has an imperfect mastery of a foreign tongue, he will be apt to employ, when endeavouring to speak it, numerous loan-words from his mother tongue. He will, in fact, insert into the foreign tongue any number of words which may serve the purpose of expressing the idea which he feels necessary. Such loan-words, of course, take time before they become usual. They cannot become usual unless they are often repeated, and, as a rule, unless they proceed spontaneously from several individuals as the expression of a general need. Even then they may only become current in particular circles : as when, for instance, such technical terms as those applicable to music are borrowed. Such words, when fairly accepted by the language, are treated like other words in the language, and are regarded by the speakers of it as native, and inflected as such. Foreign words, when borrowed, are commonly treated thus. There are no two languages in which the two stocks of sounds are precisely identical. Consequently, the speaker will, as a rule, replace the foreign sounds by those which he conceives most nearly to represent them in his own language ; and, in cases where the foreign language possesses sounds not known in his own, he will fail to pronounce these correctly, at least till after much practice. It is well known how very seldom any one masters a foreign tongue so as to speak it without some incorrect accent. Thus it happens that in the cases where a conquering language spreads over a nation speaking a different language, the original language of the conquered people must leave some traces in the production of sounds, and changes will occur in other ways as in accentuation, etc. Numerous instances might be cited of where such invasion of a conquering tongue has occurred on a large scale, as in the case of the Moorish invasion of Spain, the Latin invasion of Gaul, the Norman-French invasion of Saxon England.

In cases where one people merely comes into contact with another in the course of travel or of literary intercourse, the number of those who acquire the language of the foreign people will be necessarily small. The word will, therefore, from the outset, be pronounced imperfectly; the persons who first introduced the word or those who immediately accepted it will insert sounds with which they are familiar among the foreign ones. It thus happens that when a foreign word has once made its way into a language, it commonly exchanges its proper sounds for those native to the language which borrows it. Even those who know the foreign language most perfectly, and are aware of the proper pronunciation of the loan-word, have to conform to the pronunciation of the majority, at the risk of passing for affected or pedantic. For instance, in English, in spite of all the numerous loan-words which occur in the written language, very few new sounds have been introduced, such as the nasal *m* in *employé;* and even these sounds are dispensed with among the uneducated, and imperfectly reproduced by many of the better educated. One common result of the adoption of a foreign word into another language is that popular etymology begins to operate, causing the word to appear less strange to those who have borrowed it, as in the familiar instance *rose des quatre saisons,* 'rose of the four seasons,' transformed by English gardeners into *quarter sessions rose.*[1]

[1] Cf. Peile, p. 41.

The changes which naturally affect foreign words upon their reception into the language, must of course be kept distinct from those which affect them after they have become an integral part of the language, when they change according to the laws of sound-change of the language into which they are adopted. In fact, it is often possible to tell the epoch at which a word has passed from one language into another, by noting whether it has or has not participated in certain laws of sound-change. Thus, where in Old High German the Latin *t* is represented sometimes by *t*, and sometimes by *z* (as *tempal* = *templum*), 'temple' as against *ziagil* (= *tegula* = ' till '), the form with *z* represents an older stage of borrowing than the form in *t;* and, again, words in which the Old High German represents the Latin *p* by *ph* or *f*, must be held to represent an older stage of borrowing than those in which it is found as *p* or *b:* cf. *pfeffer*, 'pepper ;' *Pfingsten*, 'Pentecoste,' as against *pîna*, (Lat. 'pæna ') : *priester* (Gk. 'presbuteros ').

Similarly, such a word as *chamber*, or *chant*, must plainly have been borrowed before the period of sound-change when the sound of *ch* regularly took the place of the Latin *c ;* and this we know to have been the history of the *c* sound in the dialect of the Ile de France, whence those and other similar forms come to us.

But foreign words are exposed, after their adoption, to the same assimilating forces as when they are first adopted : and one of the transforming forces which should be mentioned is the transference of the native system of accentuation to foreign words. In English, a study of Chaucer or Langland will show us how French words originally adopted and pronounced according to the French method of accentuation, by degrees, and not till after a period of vacillation, passed over to the system common in Teutonic languages : thus Chaucer has *lánguage* and *langáge ;* *fórtune* and *fortúne ; báttaile* and *battáile ; láboure* and *labóur :* thus Pope accentuates *gallánt.* Of course, words may be so far phonetically modified as to become unrecognisable even by persons who know the language whence they are borrowed. Who, for instance, would recognise in the word *pastans*[1] the French *passe-temps,* our *pastime;* or in the common Scotch word *ashet,* the French *assiette.* Thus, in the same author, Gavin Douglas, we find *veilys* (calves), representing the old French word, *véel* (vitellus). The strangeness may be increased still more by changes which have occurred in the language from which the word is borrowed. Thus our word *veal* represents an older form of the French language than *veau ;* and the German pronunciation of many French words is that of an older period of French pronunciation ; as *París, concért, offizíer.* German words adopted by Romance languages have been even more violently transformed : who, in the French words *tape, taper,* would recognise the German *zapfen ;* in the Italian *toppo,* the German *zopf;* in the French *touaille,* the South German *zwehle;* in the Italian *drudo,* the German *traut ?* In the same way, the signification of the word in the parent speech may change ; as in the case of the French *emphase,* ' bombast,' as against *emphasis ; biche* (' hind '), etc. Finally, it may disappear in the parent language and survive as a loan-word in the language which has borrowed it ; as, for instance, the French word *guerre,* ' war,' in which survives the Old High German *werra,* ' quarrel,' the same word as our *war.*

[1] Quoted by Peile, Primer of Philology, p. ii., from Gavin Douglas's translation of the Æneid.

The word may be borrowed several times at different periods. It appears in different forms, of which the more recent bears the stamp of the parent language, while the older has been exposed to phonetic changes which have more or less violently acted upon its form. It will generally be found that the meaning attaching to the word when it is borrowed a second time will differ from that which it bears on the first occasion. These words which are more than once borrowed are commonly called doublets; they are very numerous both in French and English, and have been treated of at length by Bréal and Skeat.   Instances of such are *priest, presbyter; champagne, campaign; preach, predict; prove, probe.*   Proper names constantly afford instances of repeated forms of borrowing processes; cf. *Evans, Jones, Johns; Thomasson, Thomson; Zachary, Zachariah.*   It sometimes happens that a loan-word long since naturalised in a language receives a partial assimilation to its form in the language whence it originally came; a good instance of this is seen in such forms as *honor, color,* etc., which, especially in America, are often so written, instead of *honour, colour,* etc. Sometimes words are adopted into a language from two kindred languages; the signification will then be similar, and the sound will differ but little—the sense, as well as the form, contributing to keep the two words together.   German has several of such loan-words borrowed from the French and Latin; as, *ideal* and *ideell; real* and *reell;* which at a former period had an actually identical meaning, but now are differentiated. In English, *spiritual* and *spirituel* differ like *spiritus* and *esprit.*   Some words, again, are borrowed from a language in which they already occur as loan-words. Thus the French have borrowed from English the word *square,* O.Fr. *esquarré.*   Thus, again, Greek words come to us through the medium of the Latin : whence it is usual to write such forms as *Æschylus*, *Hercules*, instead of *Aischulos*, *Heracles*. Thus, again, Latin words borrowed from Greek have come into English through the medium of French—cf. such words as *music*, *protestant*, *religion*, etc.; and also such proper names as *Horace*, *Virgil*, *Ovid*, and *Livy*. Persons conversant with the original naturally refer such words to the language through which they came; and thus, in adopting Greek words, they employ the Latin accent and the regular English termination which represents that French termination whence the English one came. Such words are *alopecy*, *academy*, etc.

Derivatives formed with unusual suffixes often receive in addition the regular normal suffix. This is specially the case when a native synonymous suffix is added to the foreign one: as in Waldensian, Roumanian, sometimes the native suffix is substituted for the original suffix of the foreign language ; as, *Sultana*, for *Sultaneh*. Words are borrowed in their entirety ; but not suffixes, whether derivative or inflectional. When, however, a large number of words is borrowed containing the same suffix, these range themselves into a group, and fresh formations are formed upon the analogy of these. Thus, in English, after the analogy of such words as *abbey*, *rectory*, etc., we have such words formed as *bakery*, *tannery*, *brewery:* and, again, we find Romance words like French *mouchard*, 'a spy,' Italian *falsardo*, 'impostor,' with the Teutonic suffix: and very many English words with a French suffix ; as, *oddity*, *eatable*, *drinkable*, *murderous:* and, again, *poisonous*, as against *vénéneux* in French. In English, again, we find such suffixes as *-ist* in *jurist* forming fresh additions to their group by analogy, mostly, however, in educated circles; as, *Elohist* and *Jahvist*, though such words spread eventually to the whole nation, as in the case of *protectionist*. -*Ism* is another of these, as in *somnambulism;* and -*ian*, as in *Hartingtonian*.

Inflectional terminations are also thus adopted, but more rarely, and only between nations that have been in close contact. In German it is common to use *Christi* as the genitive of *Christus*, and often the French plural in *s* is applied to German words, as in *Frauleins*. In English, we speak of *phenomena*, etc., and we employ *indices* in a mathematical sense. The English genitive ending has found its way into Indo-Portuguese, as in *Hombres casa*, 'the man's house.' The gypsy dialects have adopted the inflectional terminations of each country where they are spoken.

Words are sometimes affected in their meaning by other languages ; and further, the idioms peculiar to one language are affected by those current in another.   This influence is called the influence upon *linguistic form*.   The most common instance of the effect of one language upon another in this case, is where, when two words partially coincide in meaning, they are assumed to exactly tally in the whole extent of their meaning.   This is, of course, one of the most common faults in translation.   Thus an English child, learning French, will often be heard to use expressions like 'Cela n'est pas le *chemin,*' for ' That is not the *way* ;' a German will say ' *brought* a leading article,' for *wrote ;* a Frenchman, ' Can you *conduct ?* ' for ' Can you *drive ?* ' Sir Charles Dilke, in his Problems of Greater Britain,[1] gives an interesting account of the French Language as spoken by the French settlers in lower Canada.   It appears that the more educated of these speak a somewhat archaic and very pure French, but that the peasant or

[1] Vol. i., p. 53.

shopkeeper will say *Je n'ai pas de change*, for ' I have no change.'   He will describe dry goods on his sign-board as *marchandises sèches*, and will call out when busy ' J'ai un *job* à ramplir.'   In public meetings we hear of 'les minutes,' and the seconder of a resolu-tion is called officially 'le secondeur.'   The 'speaker' is *l'orateur*, and 'Hear! Hear!' is rendered by *Ecoutez*.

Sometimes a word is coined in one language after the model of one existing in another language, to supply a want felt by the language which borrows. This is especially the case with technical terms, as when accusative, ablative, etc., are introduced into English from the Latin model ; and such words as these are liable to be misunderstood, as they may only tally with one portion of the meaning of the original word, or, indeed, in some cases be a mistranslation, as where, *genetivus*, 'the begetting case,' was taken as the Latin equivalent of γενικός, 'the general case,' and *accusativus*, 'the accusing case,' of αἰτιατική, 'the con-ditional case.'   'Another instance is the word *solidarity*, which we have coined to express the French *solidarité*.

Again : entire groups of words, or idioms, are lite-rally translated from one language into another.   Thus we hear, in the mouths of Irishmen, such expressions as *I am after going*, this being the literal translation of the Irish idiom for the rendering of the future tense.   Thus the Austrians say *Es steht nicht dafür*, for 'it is not worth the trouble,' because the Bohemians express this phrase by *nestojé za to*.   The following idioms are current in Alsace ;[1] it will be seen that they are literal French renderings of German phrases.   *Est-ce que cela vous goûte ?* 'Does that please your taste ?'   *Il a frappé dix heures*, 'It has struck ten ;'   *Il brûle chez M. Meyer*,

---

[1] Schuchardt Romanisches und Keltisches, p. 280, sqq.

'There is a fire at M. Meyer's;' *Ce qui est léger, vous l'apprendrez facilement,* 'That which is easy, you will learn it easily;' *Cher ami, ne prends pas pour mauvais,* 'Dear friend, do not take it amiss;' *Pas si beaucoup,* 'Not so much;' *Attendez; j'apporterai une citadine,* 'Wait; I will bring a citadin (drink).' On the other hand, the South-West Germans employ phrases after the French model; as, *Es macht gut wetter,* 'It is fine weather.'

Finally; the syntax of one language may exercise an influence over that of another language. An instance of this has been already given. The form of the French language, which is a Romance language grafted on to a Celtic stock, has been much influenced by Celtic syntax (cf. the mode of expressing numerals, *soixante-dix* = 60+10, parallel to Celtic 3 *scores*+10; *quatre-vingts* = 4×20 = Celtic 4 *scores*, etc.).

Again: as the Slavonic languages can employ one form for all genders and numbers of the relative, we find in Slavo-German the word *was* (what) correspondingly employed; cf. *ein mann, was hat geheissen Jacob: der knecht, was ich mit ihm gefahren bin.*

Of course authors may consciously imitate a foreign idiom with the view of producing a particular effect, as when Milton wrote 'and knew not eating death;' 'Fairest of all her daughters Eve.'

In the case of dialects, almost the same remarks hold good as in the case of different languages. Word-borrowing is the most common process. Such words are most readily borrowed as are needed by the borrowing dialect for its own purposes; such as the Scotch words *dour, douce, feckless,* etc. Sounds, on the other hand, are not easily influenced by kindred dialects. The nearest native sounds are commonly substituted for those of the alien dialect. Of course the case may occur where two dialects have, in the course of their development, so far parted that words etymologically connected have lost all connection in sound. In this case, the sound of the alien dialect will as a rule be maintained. An instance of this is the Scotch *unco'* in the phrase *unco' guid*, which is really the same as *uncouth ;* but the accent has shifted, and this tends to disguise the origin of the word.

CHAPTER XXIII.

THE STANDARD LANGUAGE.

In all modern civilised countries, we find, side by side
with numerous dialects, a standard language, professing
to stand aloof from all dialects, and to represent what
may be called the classical form of the language. This
standard language is in fact an abstraction, an ideal, a
supreme court of language prescribing rules to be
followed in the case of each language. It bears the
same kind of relationship to the actual processes active
in language, as a particular code of laws to the
aggregate of all the cases in any district in which that
code is applied; or of a definite dogmatic text-book to
the religious practices and faiths of all the individuals
of a community confessing the particular faith embodied
in that book.

Such a standard language as we have described,—
as it does not result from the various processes natural
to the life of language,—necessarily differs from
language in general by its fixity; wherever a change
takes place in a standard language, the element of consciousness is more clearly present than in the ordinary
changes of language. Not that a standard is absolutely
all-foreseeing in its provisions, or can claim to decide
on the entirety of the cases for which its gives the
example. A code of law, in the same way, or a con-

fession of faith, may be liable to several interpretations, and may not cover some of the cases which come under its purview. Besides this, we must always take into account the possible lack of intelligence on the part of those who ought to act up to its provisions; and, again, the feeling which must set in from time to time, that many of the provisions of the code are obsolete, owing to fresh moral or economical views which may have become current since it was drawn up. When such a feeling has set in strongly, the code is commonly altered to suit the demands of the day. Just so the standard language may, and indeed must, alter from time to time; but its alterations are, like those of the code, adoptedly designedly, or at all events with much more consciousness than those which set into the ordinary course of language.

This standard language is, speaking generally, the language of a certain restricted circle in an entire community — most commonly, as in England, the language of the best-educated classes. The standard language may be settled in two different ways: (1) by spoken language; (2) by written authorities. Supposing that a standard language is to result from a spoken language, it is necessary that the persons who are regarded as authorities should be in continuous and full communication with each other, in order to keep the standard as consistent as possible. Sometimes we find a particular town or district cited as speaking the language which is quoted as the standard. Thus it is common to quote Hanover, in Germany, and Tours in France, as places where the purest German and French are heard. But it is clear that, even assuming the correctness of such model towns or districts, none but the better-educated classes even of those districts can be looked upon as likely to maintain the standard

language in its purity. In England, the standard language can be defined in no other way than as the
language of the well-educated classes, who make it
their object to speak alike, and to exclude abnormal or
dialectic variations from the standard language. In
France, besides the appeal to the usage of the educated,
there is the further tribunal of the Academy, whose
verdict is final upon all questions of literary taste and
diction. In Germany, the language which must be
taken as the standard language is not that of any town
or district, but the purely artificial language employed
on the German stage in serious drama. This language
forms a very interesting and remarkable example of a
standard language which is consciously maintained as
the most effective medium of communication for a
nation which is more divided into dialects than most
other European nations. The stage language of
Germany is maintained by a continuous and careful
training, based on a knowledge of the science of
phonetics. The objects aimed at by the actors have
been twofold : in the first place, it was necessary to
practise an eclecticism in the choice of their language,
which should succeed in making it intelligible to the
largest number of German speakers : in the next place,
beauty and grace could not be left out of consideration.
Hence a fixed norm had to be settled on and maintained, as it is plain that a consistent pronunciation
maintained unchanged is a main factor in promoting
intelligibility. Again, inconsistency in pronunciation
is practically the admission of dialectical peculiarities :
and such peculiarities at once suggest characterisation
where none would be in place. Those points, then, in
the varying dialects, were alone selected for this normal
language which seemed more conducive to clearness.
Sounds and intonations peculiar to any dialect were

admitted into the standard language if they contributed
to this result.   Syllables which had come, in the course
of time, to be slurred over on account of their light
stress were reinstated in the integrity of their original
sounds.   The orthography was made to aid in the
reconstruction of the pronunciation.   Such studied
straining after clearness must necessarily prevent the
stage language from passing into a colloquial language.
Its very clearness would savour of a stilted affectation.
But, with all its rigidness and precision, the stage
language still exercises some influence upon the sounds
of the colloquial language—considerably more than
that exercised by any particular dialect.   But its form
is to a large extent poetical; indeed, it receives much
of its language ready made from the poets.

As we stated above, in the case of our own language the only normal standard that we are able to
point to as the purest English is that commonly spoken
among educated people.   In this case it is obvious that
the agreement between the different classes who aim
at maintaining the norm can be at best but an imperfect one.   Each class of educated men will have a
tendency to fall into certain peculiarities of speech
which will mark them off in some degree from all
others.   The language of the bar is not quite that of
the army.   The language of the Church differs from
that of both.   The language of the educated in England, however,—in other words, the language of those
who aim at following the *norm*,—agrees in one respect,
that in all an emancipation from *dialect* is aimed at, and,
to a large extent, attained. This result is largely owing
to the fact that in England the better-educated classes
are in the habit of sending their sons to be educated
out of their own dialectical district, and the result is
that they come into contact, at an early period of their

lives, with companions whose language is characterised
either by different dialectical peculiarities from their
own, or by an absence of any.   But even so it must
always be remembered that those who speak their
language in its greatest purity, *i.e.* with the greatest
absence of dialectical peculiarities, are subject to the
changes which mark all language and are an inseparable
concomitant of its existence.

But there is another means whereby a standard or
common language may become fixed, and may come to
serve as the normal or ideal language of the speakers of
any given language.   This means is the reduction
of such normal language to writing.   The reduction
of the standard language to writing renders it independent of those who speak it, and enables it to be
transmitted unchanged to the following generations.
It further permits the standard language to spread
without direct intercourse.   Of course, the influence of
a written language upon dialects is much more powerful
upon the material than upon the phonetic side.   A
Scotch peasant may read a page of the *Times* every
day, and, if he reads it aloud to his family, the absence
of Scotticisms will act powerfully upon the younger
generation, and to a certain extent upon himself.   But
he will probably continue to pronounce the standard
language in much the same way as his native dialect.

It is possible to make strict rules for the mainten-
ance of a written language, by adhering to the usage
of definite grammars and dictionaries, or of particular
authors, and admitting no other authorities.   This happens when, for instance, modern Latinists aim at reproducing the style of Cicero, like Mr. Keble in his
celebrated Prælectiones.   But if so-called purity of style
and expression be gained by this process, surely far
more is lost.   The author writing under such restrictions

must necessarily lose much of his power of original expression, and must find himself very much cramped in his vocabulary. In fact, writing at a period when the whole character of the civilisation has changed from that of his model's epoch, he will find himself at a loss for words to express his most common conceptions.

The fact is that a written language, in order to live and be effectual, must change with the changing times, and admit into itself words and methods of expression which have become usual among those for whom it is to serve as the model. It may maintain a conservative influence by refusing to admit such words and expressions too hastily; but it must allow of no absolute barriers to their ingress. Modern Latin, in the shape of the Romance languages, has survived, and has proved adequate to the expression of modern thought; but in its ancient form, it has died out as a living language; and the fair dream of the Humanists that the tongue of Cicero might serve as the medium of communication to all civilised Europe was destined to pass away unrealised, from the simple fact that they insisted too strongly that this tongue should be exclusively modelled upon that of Cicero himself.

A literary language which has emancipated itself from its models must, of course, become less regular as time goes on, and each individual who employs it introduces into it some of his own peculiarities of idiom. But it need not split up into varieties geographically situated, as must needs be the case under similar circumstances with spoken language. For instance, the English written in America is much more like the English written in England than is the dialect spoken in Cornwall like that spoken in Yorkshire. Sound-change, of course, under our present alphabetic system remains wholly undenoted. Inflections, word-significations, and syntax are of course exposed to change, but to a less extent than in the spoken language. Such a word as *bug* may have retained its older significance of insect in America, and have been specialised in England; but the word is written in the same way in the two countries alike. Similarly, *will* and *shall* may be exchanged, or one of these used to the exclusion of the other; but they will remain spelt in the same way. Besides this, it must be remembered that the so-called classical models in any language will always continue to exert a large influence upon those who write in it; and this will always be an influence antagonistic to change.

The method whereby a standard language may best secure the greatest possible agreement over the largest possible area, and may join to this agreement the necessary adaptation to the changed circumstances of civilisation, is by keeping to the ancient models in syntax and accidence, and by allowing, at the same time, a certain freedom in the creation of new words, and in the application of new significations to old ones.

Our great national languages are at once literary and colloquial, and hence they possess a standard literary language and a standard colloquial pronunciation and vocabulary. The problem is how to keep those two languages in harmony. The colloquial language is, of the two, as we have seen, liable to change in its phonetic conditions—a change to which the written language is not so much exposed. It is therefore obvious that the more a language changes phonetically, the less will it be represented by the written language; and it is also plain that in a language like English, whose spelling is so very far from phonetic, the discrepancy between the written and spoken language may go so

far that the former may cease to exert much, if any,
influence upon the latter. To remedy this state of
things, phonetic alphabets have been drawn up, and
various reforms in spelling have been recommended
from time to time, in order to bring the written into
harmony with the spoken language.

The more that the natural language of each individual departs from the standard language, the more
will he naturally regard the standard language as
something foreign ; the effect of this will often be that,
as the discrepancies between his natural dialect and
the standard language are more clearly felt, he will
make a more conscious effort to seize and get over
those differences. Thus, in the border counties of
Wales, or of the Highlands, a more correct *literary*
English is spoken than in many English counties.

The different individual dialects of any country, *i.e.*
the forms of · language used by each individual, are
constantly changing their position in respect to the
norm, or standard written language. On the one
hand, the natural changes incident to all language are
always tending to alienate these from the norm ; on
the other, the conscious and artificial efforts made to
approximate the individual language to the norm are
constantly in play side by side with the other tendency.
The main method whereby this conscious approximation is effected is, in the first place, the instruction
given in civilised countries at school ; and, in this case,
the standard language, or an approximation to it, is
learnt at the same time as the language of the
district. But the dialect of each individual's home
cannot fail to influence largely his acquisition of the
standard language. England, as before remarked,
forms an exception to most other countries in this
respect, that many children are brought up com-

paratively free from the dialect spoken in their geographical area.

But, when all is said, there remains to be taken into account the difference in each individual's pronunciation, and his greater or less capacity for assimilating the difference between the artificial dialect and his own. These considerations will always operate as powerful solvents of the integrity of a standard language.

It must further be noticed that the stock of words and their meanings, as well as inflections and syntax of the artificial or standard language, are constantly being recruited from the natural language. Instances in point would be the different Scotch words, such as *ne'er-do-weel*, adopted into standard English. Where the same word occurs both in the natural and the artificial language, it sometimes happens that both words are preserved in the latter ; sometimes with a differentiation of meaning and sometimes without ; instances are *birch, church, shred*, as distinct from the Northern *birk, kirk, screed*. It will thus be seen that the colloquial language which serves as the model of each individual is itself a compromise between the strict normal language and the home dialect.

In the second place, the artificial language affects the natural language by supplying it with words and inflections in which it is deficient. Such terms would naturally be such as the artificial language is more fitted to supply. No dialect throughout Britain is free from such influence as that described.

In the third place, it should be observed that when persons speak an artificial and a natural language side by side, the use of the former spreads at the expense of the latter. The artificial language was originally confined to writing, and was employed as a means of

communication with persons speaking a strange dialect.
Once established as an official channel of communication, it has a tendency to spread to all literature,
and gradually to private correspondence. And this is
easy to understand, seeing that the young generation
generally learns to read and write from written records,
and that it is obviously easier to accept a form of
orthography made ready to our hand than to invent a
system of orthography which shall be applicable to
other dialects besides one's own.

When the artificial language has once become the
fashion, then, and not till then, will the employment of
dialect seem a mark of want of culture. There are
many countries still in which the most educated persons
are not ashamed to speak in their natural dialect. This
is the case, for instance, in Switzerland and in Greece
at the present day, and, to a less extent perhaps, in
Scotland. It is therefore a mistake to suppose that
the natural language must necessarily be deemed
inferior or more vulgar than the artificial. It is, in
fact, the necessity for the employment of the artificial
language which causes it to be universally adopted.

We have now briefly to consider under what circumstances a common language becomes established.
It seems to be certain that no common language would
have arisen without some necessity for its appearance ;
and that necessity arose from the fact of the different
dialects into which any linguistic area must naturally
be split up becoming so far alienated from each other
as to be reciprocally unintelligible, and, of course, the
difficulty of comprehension would be greater in the
case of dialects, geographically more widely separated,
than in the case of those spoken by neighbouring
people. Indeed, the wider the area over which a
common language spreads, and the more numerous

the dialects which it embraces, the more successful does it commonly turn out. Good instances of this truth are afforded by the Greek κοινή, and in that of the Latin language in its spread over the Romance-speaking areas.

We assume, then, in the first instance, the necessity felt for a common language, before such is called into existence. It is further an indispensable preliminary that a certain degree of intercourse, whether literary, commercial, or otherwise, should exist between the areas, however distant they may be, which are to partake of the common language. It might seem natural to suppose that as soon as, and whenever any certain given number of dialects had reached a certain degree of difference from each other, there would naturally be evolved a common language which would suffice for their needs. But, as a matter of fact, we do not find this to be the case. The common language sometimes develops between two or more areas possessing dialects less nearly related to each other, more readily than between similar areas linguistically nearer related, supposing that there are special circumstances to favour the development. In some cases political circumstances may effect this, as where a common dialect for Germany was called into being on the basis of a common German nationality. As a contrast to this, we may take the case of Polish and Czechish, which are, linguistically speaking, more nearly related than High and Low German, and which yet, as in the main belonging to different political areas, have no necessity for a common language, and have therefore never created one.

If a common language has once established itself in a large area, it is rare for another common language to arise for a portion only of that area. Thus a

Provençal common language would be an impossibility in the face of the powerful French which has spread over the greater part of France. Again, a common language can hardly arise for any large area whose single parts have already some common language which suffices for their needs. This may be seen in the failure of the Panslavists to create a common language in an area already occupied by Polish, Servian, etc. No example of this fact can be drawn from England.

The introduction of printing is a powerful aid to the extension of a common language. Thanks to the invention of printing, a written record can quickly be communicated to a large linguistic area in the shape given to it by the author, and an impulse is likewise given to studying what is presented to readers in such an attractive and commodious guise. But it is necessary that the alphabet employed should be identical for all the people in the linguistic area in question ; and, of course, the language expressed by that alphabet must be widely understood over that area.

It should further be noticed that a common language must, generally speaking, be based upon an existing dialect, and that this dialect then modifies itself to suit the demands of the different dialectic areas which demand the common language. Thus, Luther expressly tells us that he based his translation of the Bible upon the dialect of the Saxon Chancellery : Modern French is based upon the dialect of the Ile de France : Chaucer chose the London dialect as the most appropriate for his purpose. Such cases as the modern attempts to form a common language in the instance of Volapük, etc., have been but partially successful ; there was no strong existing basis upon which to found them.

It must be assumed as a necessity to the success of any common language, that there are a number of persons compelled by circumstances to make themselves acquainted with one or more foreign dialects. This may be brought about by the demands of commerce, or from the fact that the persons in question are compelled to live in the foreign linguistic area, and to employ its tongue. We can see the operation of these causes in such cases as the creation of such a *lingua franca* as Pigeon English, which arises not merely from the fact that the English and Chinese who use it as a vehicle of communication are ignorant of each other's language, but further from the fact that the Chinese who employ it speak dialects so different as to be partially or wholly unintelligible to each other. Similar remarks hold good of the Spanish in South America,—which is learned by Italian immigrants speaking different dialects, and serves as a *lingua franca* to them. But even when such *lingua franca*, or common language, has been formed, it is liable in its turn to further development. It may be influenced, for example, by the more perfect acquisition of the standard language on the part of those who use the dialect based upon it as a common language ; as is probably the case with the Pigeon English spoken by the Japanese : or, by the adoption into the common language of an increasing number of words from the vocabulary of those who are gradually allowing their own dialects to be superseded by the common language.

Supposing, however, that a special dialect has been selected as the model for a standard language, even in civilised countries, we must not assume that it is possible to adopt it as the actual and pure model. The model dialects cannot fail to be influenced by the dialect of the special speaker or writer, and in many cases this mixture may make itself very prominent. This is especially seen, perhaps, in the case of literature which, like journals and periodicals, is intended mainly to circulate in the special dialectic area. Thus, for instance, Americanisms, Scotticisms, and Hibernicisms, are more common in the newspaper press of America, Scotland, and Ireland than in the standard literature published in those countries. Again, the dialect, on which the model or normal language was based, will, from the very nature of language, change more rapidly than the normal language itself, which must from its nature be more conservative; so that here, again, a discrepancy cannot fail to set in between the dialect and the model language. The truth of this may be well seen in the changes which have passed over the London dialect in comparatively recent times. The habit of omitting the aspirate, or, as we say, dropping the *h*, seems to be quite a recent development in English,[1] and to have spread probably at the end of the last century. Dickens' Londoners frequently drop their aspirates: and he seems to be the first writer who makes his characters do this on a large scale. On the other hand, the *ven* and *vy* of his characters are hardly now heard in London.

And thus the artificial language, if it extend over a large area, becomes differentiated into dialects more or less strongly marked, in much the same way as the natural language within a particular district. Probably English is the language in which this fact can be

---

[1] A good instance of this is seen in the 'Somersetshire Man's Complaint,' dating from the seventeenth century, as against the 'Exmoor Scolding,' published at Exeter, in 1778 : both are published by Elworthy in the 'Specimens of English Dialects' (1879). In the former of these the aspirate is fairly maintained; in the latter, it is frequently dropped.

noticed more easily and on a wider scale than in the case of any other language, from the fact that the areas of English-speaking races are so widely separated in many cases ; and all isolation must tend to strengthen the power of the dialect as against the artificial language.   So-called Americanisms, for instance, may be older forms of the English language retained by the American dialect and lost by the English.   On the other hand, they may be new importations into the standard or model language from the colloquial language, or from some dialect.   These Americanisms, again, spread to such English-speaking countries as Australia, Canada, and New Zealand more readily and quickly than they do to England.   Consequently, the artificial language, in spite of its tendency to conservatism, is manifestly changing in the different English-speaking areas, although the change is not, of course, as great or as quick in its fulfilment as that which comes to pass in the development of dialects in the area of a definite territory.

It is, of course, possible to arrest to some extent the change in an artificial language by the influence of academies, who shall authoritatively decide upon the permissibility or otherwise of the use of a certain word or phrase ; but under normal circumstances the involuntary development which we have spoken of is characteristic of a standard language as well as of language in general.

A single linguistic area may, under the proper conditions, develop a duality or even a plurality of standards, though instances of the entire co-ordination of two different standards are, in the history of language, very rare.   The classical example for the duality of standard is offered by the linguistic conditions in Greece during the period between 250 and

50 B.C. Two types of normalised or standard language, neither of them corresponding exactly to any one folk-dialect, and each of them almost entirely uninfluenced by the other, asserted their pre-eminence over the folk-dialects in two distinct districts. The one, which we may call 'Eastern Greek' or the Attic κοινή, was based upon the Attic dialect; the other, which we may call 'Western Greek,' was based upon the Laconian. The former was the language of those political and commercial interests that centred about the Ægean; the latter, of those that centred about the Gulf of Corinth. The former represented the new cosmopolitan spirit of Hellenism, the latter the conservative and provincial spirit that had its political expression in the Achæan and Ætolian leagues.

Here, as elsewhere, the levelling of the peculiarities of provincial speech in the interest of a standard language represents and corresponds to a levelling of provincial barriers in the interest of a unitary civilisation, and under the impulse of great common movements of commercial intercourse, political organisation, or religious thought, and the appearance of two areas of levelling in language betrays the existence of two areas of common commercial, political, literary, or religious interest. The division of German Protestantism into the Lutheran and Swiss wings, coupled with political distinctions, availed to maintain for a long time, even in the printed form, a Swiss standard of German, as distinguished from the so-called Modern High German.

To be distinguished from the cases of duality or plurality of standard are those of *complexity* of standard. A portion of a linguistic area, which recognises in general outlines, or in the most essential characteristics, the common standard of the whole,

may develop inside these limits a secondary standard
of its own, which, in its turn, asserts itself as a unifying
influence above the disparities of the popular dialects.
Such is the status of the American-English, if indeed
it be admitted that there be any American standard
at all.   The wide disagreement upon this latter much-
mooted question arises largely from a failure to recognise what the true nature of a standard in language is.
In the light of the preceding discussion, and by the
help of the abundant available material, it cannot be
difficult to reach some consistent solution of this
question.

The attitude of the extremists on the one side is
well represented by the dictum of Richard Grant
White:[1] 'In language whatever is peculiarly American
is bad.'   In other words, the absolute test of correctness is the English standard, which is notably the
usage of the educated classes in the great centre of
English life.   It must, however, be remarked, at the
beginning of any discussion of this sort, that the
question concerns not what ought to be or might best
be, but what is the fact.   If it be actually the fact that
any considerable body of men, whose usage, be it
through respect for their culture, their intelligence, or
their position, or for any other reason, commands the
deference of the great mass of American speakers
and writers, follows so loyally the English standard as
to regard as bad in language all that is peculiarly
American, then it is the *fact* that there is no such
thing as an American standard in language.   There
is, then, only one standard English speech, and that
the standard of London.

There exists, however, in America no educated or
cultured class in the English sense.   The educated

---

[1] *Atlantic Monthly*, vol. xli., 495.

stand nearer the people than in England. The children of the better classes are, furthermore, not so easily
isolated from the influence of the dialect of their
locality as in England. Certainly there exists in
general no class with which the popular mind associates the idea of authority in matters of speech, nor
whose speech is respected or admired as correct. The
class of men most likely to be imitated and most likely
to exercise an unconscious influence upon the usages
of society is the intelligent mercantile class, but this
is not a permanent or well-defined body. Certainly it
is not a body likely to follow puristically a foreign
standard of speech.

It is in part this absence of a homogeneous usage
among the more intelligent and influential classes, such
as undoubtedly exists in England, that occasions the
apparently immoderate use of dictionaries in America
as standards of orthoëpy. So various is the usage in
the pronunciation even of many common words, like
quinine, courteous, envelope, tribune, route, suite, wound,
that the ear in its confusion of impressions fails to
decide definitely, and recourse must be had to the
dictionaries. It is most frequently in cases of doubt
like these that appeal is made to the greater certainty
of the English standard. It plays the part of a convenient arbiter. This differs entirely in principle from
an attempt, for example, to introduce the totally non-
American pronunciation of *trait* with silent *t* final, or
of *bureau* with accent on the second syllable.

No single district or city in America ever has been
or can be generally recognised as furnishing a standard of speech. Washington is in no such sense the
capital of the United States as Paris is of France;
New York is not a metropolis in the sense that London
is. Eastern Massachusetts, with its chief city Boston,

enjoys a certain preëminence in the superior education
and intelligence of its people; but its local idiom, like
the general spirit of its population, is too strongly provincial to attract any imitation.   In fact, nowhere in
the United States have the schools and all their
adjuncts made more vigorous efforts to root out the
popular dialect, and nowhere does the English standard receive so full recognition.   The situation furnishes
a tolerably exact parallel to the rigidity of Hanoverian
German, an imported standard on Low German soil,
and constitutes a further illustration of the well-known
orthodoxy of recent converts.   The schools of Boston
teach the ultra-English pronunciation of *been* as *bīn,*
while the native dialect has *bĕn,* and the American
κοινή has extended to general use the secondary form
bĭn.[1]

The stage is not yet in a position to exercise any
marked influence upon the language, to say nothing of
furnishing a standard.   The influence of the pulpit is
probably greater.

But though neither the stage, an educated class, nor
any given locality has availed to vindicate for itself the
right of establishing a standard, it is an incontrover-
tible fact that, within certain limits and to a certain
extent, an American standard of English does exist.
There is a great number of words, of word usages, of
pronunciations, of phrases, and of syntactical constructions, which have, though not recognised in English
usage, a universal and well-accepted currency among
the best writers and speakers of America, and rise
entirely above all suspicion of provincialism.   To
avoid or rebuke them, or to attempt the substitution
of pure English words or expressions would be only
an ostentatious purism unsupported by the facts of

---

[1] See Sweet, Elementarbuch des gesprochenen Englisch, p. xxxi.

society and the necessities of language, and would expose the would-be corrector even to ridicule and to the reproach of alienism. As has already been remarked, we are not concerned in a case like this with the ideally desirable, but solely with the existing fact. On no other basis can the existence of a standard be determined. If, for example, any one should, in deference to English usage, assume to correct an established and universally accepted American expression like *railroad car*, which a well-known poet[1] has thought worthy a place in serious verse, into its foreign equivalent *railway carriage*, it would be generally regarded as an odious affectation. The relatively few Americans who, without any sufficient reason, but in a spirit of undisguised and helpless imitation, affect to adopt English manners, usages, and dress, are as a class notably unpopular with the mass of Americans, and, as unpopular, are uninfluential. What is true of their other usages, would be in like degree of their language.

To illustrate from the vocabulary alone, there is a large and constantly increasing body of non-English words, which are used in all sections of the country, which are shunned by no class of writers or speakers, but which are universally used and esteemed as sound and normal expressions. Such are *lengthy, to donate, to loan, to gerrymander, dutiable, gubernatorial, senatorial, bogus, shoddy, mailable*; these are slowly penetrating into the English of England, and the path of such words is rendered plainer by their previous adoption in the British Colonies, whose linguistic history is so akin to that of America. Many words of this kind are of French, Spanish, Dutch, or Indian origin, but have been so thoroughly assimilated into

[1] John G. Whittier, in a poem entitled The Landmarks, *Atlantic Monthly*, vol. xliii., p. 378.

the language by usage as to rank entirely with the purest English element; thus *levee, crevasse, prairie, canyon, ranch, stampede, to stampede, lasso, corral, boss, stoop, squaw, wigwam, hickory, racoon, moccasin, hammock, canoe, toboggan, hominy, opossom, terrapin.*

In determining the existence of a standard and what may belong to that standard, we are in no wise concerned with the *origin* of words or expressions. It is not a question of origin, but a question of usage and of 'good form.' The observation that *to guess*, in its sense of 'opinari,' is found in Chaucer and Gower, contributes nothing to either side of the discussion whether there is or is not an American standard. The only question is whether *guess*, 'opinari,' is in universal and accepted American use. The fact is, that, though in widely extended use, it still remains dialectic, and is not a feature of the standard. The word *fall* for *autumn* may in isolated instances be found in English writers, and is undoubtedly with some meaning or other a good old English word, but the fact is, that, as a substitute for *autumn*, it is not 'good form' in England, and is in America. *Spry*, 'active, nimble,' is an 'Americanism,' because, though found in the English dialects, it is a standard word only in America. The American use of *sick*, in retaining the old English value now expressed by the modern English *ill*, vindicates rather than controverts the existence of a separate standard. Differences in the uses of words common to the two types are illustrated by the following: *lumber*, in English, 'cumbersome material;' in American, equivalent also to English *timber: tiresome*, in English, 'dull, annoying;' in American, 'fatiguing,' as 'a tiresome day:' *to fix*, in English (and sometimes also in American), 'to fasten;' in American, 'to repair,' 'to arrange:' *corn*, in English, 'grain;' in American, 'maize:' *transpire*, in English, 'to exhale,' 'to become public;' in American, 'to occur:' *bright*, in English, (of persons) 'cheerful;' in American, 'quick of intellect.' Cases in which the two standards use different words for the same idea or object are, Amer. *piazza*, Eng. *verandah;* Amer. *bureau*, Eng. *dressing-table;* Amer. *elevator*, Eng. *lift;* Amer. *sleigh*, Eng. *sledge;* Amer. *trunk*, Eng. *box;* Amer. *store*, Eng. *shop;* Amer. *public schools*, Eng. *national schools;* Amer. *academies*, Eng. *public schools;* Amer. *to graduate*, Eng. *to take a degree;* Amer. *student*, Eng. *undergraduate;* Amer. *druggist*, Eng. *chemist*. Amer. *mush*, Eng. *porridge;* Amer. *biscuit*, Eng. *roll;* Amer. *cracker*, Eng. *biscuit;* Amer. *candy*, or *confectionery*, Eng. *sweets;* Amer. *pitcher*, Eng. *jug;* Amer. *tidy*, Eng. *antimacassar;* Amer. *postal*, or *postal-card*, Eng. *post-card;* Amer. *city*, Eng. *town;* Amer. *fall*, Eng. *autumn;* Amer. *sick*, Eng. *ill;* Amer. *rare* (of meat), Eng. *underdone;* Amer. *smart*, Eng. *clever*. Many articles of clothing, especially men's clothing, have different names. Thus, Amer. *vest*, Eng. *waistcoat;* Amer. *sack-coat*, Eng. *jacket;* Amer. *pants*, Eng. *trousers;* Amer. *drawers*, Eng. *pants;* Amer. *underwear*, Eng. *underclothing;* Amer. *waist*, Eng. *body*, *bodice;* etc., etc.

Especially instructive it is to note how special activities, particularly those of more modern development, have found themselves in England and America separate vocabularies. Let us take for illustration the language of railways and railway travel: compare Amer. *locomotive*, Eng. *engine* (also American); Amer. *engineer*, Eng. *driver;* Amer. *fireman*, Eng. *stoker* (limited in America to steamships); Amer. *conductor*, Eng. *guard;* Amer. *baggage-car*, Eng. *van;* Amer. *railroad*, Eng. *railway;* Amer. *car*, Eng. *carriage;* Amer. *cars* (as 'to get off the cars'), Eng. *train* (also

American) ; Amer. *track*, Eng. *line;* Amer. *to switch*,
Eng. *to shunt;* Amer. *switch*, Eng. *point;* Amer. *to
buy one's ticket* (not unknown in England), Eng. *to
book;* Amer. *freight-train*, Eng. *goods-train ;* Amer.
depot (pronounced deēpo), Eng. *station* (gaining ground
in America); Amer. *baggage*, Eng. *luggage;* Amer.
trunk, Eng. *box;* Amer. *to check*, Eng. *to register;*
Amer. *horse-car*, Eng. *tram* or *tram-car ;* Amer. *horse-
car track*, Eng. *tramway*. The Americans adhere to a
nautical figure, and speak of ' getting *aboard* the cars.'

American political life has developed also a vocabulary of its own. Some of these words have gained a
limited currency in England, but are mostly felt still
to be importations. Such political Americanisms are
*caucus, stump, to stump, filibuster, federalist, senatorial,
gubernatorial, copperheads, knownothings, carpetbaggers,
mass-meeting, buncombe, to gerrymander, to lobby, mile-
age* (as a money-allowance for travelling), *wire-puller*,
etc.

Many words have received derived or special
meanings which have become established in general
and unquestioned usage: thus, *locality*, 'a place;' *notions*,
' small wares ;' *clearing*, a cleared place in the forest;'
squatter, ' one who settles on another's land ; ' whereas
in Australia the latter word has developed into the
special meaning of one who rents a large area of
government land on which to depasture sheep.

Vastly more important for our purpose than these
mere differences of vocabulary are those differences in
phrases and turns of expression, which, as subtler and
less noticeable to the ordinary hearer and reader, are
less open to superficial imitation. Compare American
quarter of five with English *quarter to five* (also
American, but less common than the former) ; Amer.
lives on West Street, Eng. *lives in West Street ;* Amer.

2 E

sick abed, Eng. *ill in bed;* Amer. *that's entirely too,*
Eng. *that's much too;* Amer. *back and forth,* Eng. *to
and fro;* Amer. *there's nothing to him,* Eng. *there's
nothing in him;* Amer. *named after,* Eng. *named for*
(also American); Amer. *it don't amount to anything,*
Eng. *come to;* Amer. *fill teeth,* Eng. *stop teeth;* Amer.
walking, lying around, Eng. *walking about;* Amer. *are
you through?* Eng. *have you finished?* Amer. *that's too
bad,* Eng. *what a pity* (also American); Amer. *as soon
as* (also Eng.), Eng. *directly* ('directly he arrives'),
Amer. *right away,* Eng. *directly, straight away;* Amer.
once in a while, Eng. *now and then;* Amer. *quite a
while,* Eng. *some time;* Amer. *go to town,* or *go into
the city,* Eng. *go up;* Amer. *takes much pleasure in
accepting,* Eng. *has much pleasure;* Amer. *have a good
time,* Eng. *to enjoy one's self* (also American).

It is not totally without significance that American
usage has established and confirmed a standard of
orthography that is in some few points divergent from
the English: thus *honor, honour; wagon, waggon;
check, cheque; traveler, traveller; center, centre; by-law,
bye-law; jewelry, jewellery,* etc.

Much that in English usage is approved and standard sounds to American ears strange and outlandish.
The English use of *nasty,* for example, is to the
American, with whom it implies the quintessence of
dirtiness, distinctly abhorrent and all· but disgusting:
even more may be said of the semi-colloquialisms
knocked up, 'tired,' and *screwed,* 'intoxicated;' while,
e.g., *haberdasher* and *purveyor* are as good as foreign
words.

The possession of a common literature holds the
two languages strongly together, and assures a narrow
limit to the possibilities of divergence. It is only
within this limit that the American standard exists.

Freedom of trade and intercourse, that has come with the building of railways and especially since the close of the civil war, is rapidly replacing the local idioms with a normal type of speech, and it is upon the common usage in the chief centres and along the chief avenues of commercial activity and national life that this normal type is based.   It corresponds to no one of the local dialects, but stands above them all ; it corresponds in the main with the English standard, but maintains a limited independence within the scope of certain modern and special activities of American life.

INDEX.